SPAIN AND PORTUGAL IN THE EUROPEAN UNION

Books of Related Interest

SPAIN AND PORTUGAL IN THE EUROPEAN UNION

The First Fifteen Years

Editors

SEBASTIÁN ROYO
PAUL CHRISTOPHER MANUEL

FRANK CASS
LONDON • PORTLAND, OR

First published in 2003 in Great Britain by
FRANK CASS AND COMPANY LIMITED
Crown House, 47 Chase Side, Southgate, London N14 5BP

and in the United States of America by
FRANK CASS
c/o ISBS, 920 NE 58th Avenue, Suite 300, Portland, OR 97213-3786

Website www.frankcass.com

British Library Cataloguing in Publication Data

Spain and Portugal in the European Union: the first
fifteen years
1. European Union – Spain 2. European Union – Portugal
3. Spain – Politics and government – 1975– 4. Portugal –
Politics and government – 1974– 5. Spain – Social conditions
– 1975– 6. Portugal – Social conditions – 20th century
7. Spain – Economic conditions –1975– 8. Portugal – Economic
conditions – 1974–
I. Royo, Sebastian, 1966– II. Manuel, Paul Christopher
III. South European society and politics
320.9'46

ISBN 0 7146 5518 X (cloth)
ISBN 0 7146 8416 3 (paper)

Library of Congress Cataloging-in-Publication Data

Spain and Portugal in the European Union : the first fifteen years /
editors Sebastian Royo, Paul Christopher Manuel.
p. cm.
ISBN 0-7146-5518-X (Cloth) – ISBN 0-7146-8416-3 (Pbk.)
1. European Union–Spain. 2. Spain–Economic conditions–1975– 3.
European Union–Portugal. 4. Portugal–Economic conditions–1974– 5.
Democracy–European Union Countries. I. Royo, Sebastián, 1966– II.
Manuel, Paul Christopher. III. Title.
HC241.25.S6S695 2003
341.242'2'0946–dc22

2003016391

This group of studies first appeared in a Special Issue of *South European Society & Politics*
(ISSN 1360-8746) 8/1–2 (Summer–Autumn 2003)
[Spain and Portugal in the European Union: The First Fifteen Years].

Printed in Great Britain by Antony Rowe Ltd., Chippenham, Wilts.

Contents

Preface

The purpose of this volume is to use the fifteenth anniversary of the accession of Portugal and Spain to the European Union as an opportunity to reflect on what has happened to both countries since 1986. Have these changes been particular or global in nature? Have these changes led us to re-conceptualize economic relations and political citizenship in the new Iberian peninsular of the new Europe? If so, how? What are some of the lessons from the fifteenth anniversary of the accession of Portugal and Spain to the European Union?

We have assembled a group of leading scholars, policy-makers and researchers to write about these phenomena. The essays in this volume examine how the integration process has affected political, economic and social developments in Portugal and Spain over the last 15 years. We have divided the volume into two parts: the first part examines political and sociological aspects of the integration process; the second section looks at economic and social aspects. The essays compare and contrast the integration experiences of both countries, analyse the domestic impact of European Union membership and examine the role that both countries have played in the European Union.

This book is a result of the 'From Isolation to Integration: 15 Years of Spanish and Portuguese Membership in Europe' conference, which took place 2–3 November 2001 at the Minda de Gunzburg Center for European Studies, Harvard University. We would like to extend our thanks to the people and institutions that made this conference possible. Most important, we would like to express our gratitude to the conference participants who travelled at a difficult time to be there with us at Harvard University. In light of the events of 11 September 2001, we felt very fortunate that all the participants were willing to overcome fear and difficulties to attend the proceedings. Our profound gratitude goes to Robert Fishman, Kerstin Hamann, Andrés Ortega, Luís Salgado de Matos, Joaquín Roy, Jorge Braga de Macedo, Luís Campos e Cunha, Miguel Sebastián, Alvaro Espina, José Da Silva Lopes, Ana M. Guillén, Pepper D. Culpepper, Andrew Moravcsik, Antonio Goucha Soares, Charles Powell, Ramón de Miguel, Francisco Seixas da Costa, George Ross, Susan Alberts, António Costa Pinto, Juan Díez-Nicolás, Grover C.

Jones III, Nuno Monteiro, Jesús M. de Miguel, Ruth V. Aguilera, Jeffrey S. Kopstein, Kalypso Nicolaidis, Enrique Barón Crespo and Rui Machete for sharing their knowledge and experiences about the issues that were addressed in the conference.

This conference would not have been possible without the dedication, patience and support of the administrative staff from the Minda de Gunzburg Center for European Studies, particularly Lisa Eschenbach and Gevelyn McCaskill – the heart and soul of the organization process. The leaders of the Minda de Gunzburg Center for European Studies were all instrumental and offered strong support and guidance. Peter Hall, Director of the Center, Charles Maier, former Director, and Abby Collins, former Associate Director, were involved in the organizational efforts from Day 1. They enthusiastically embraced the proposal to organize this conference and worked hard to make it a reality. We would also like to thank the audience for their comments, questions and debates during the conference. They enriched the conference and helped strengthen the papers that have been included in this volume. Thanks are also due to our colleagues at the Center for European Studies, Sofía Pérez and Michael Baum, who co-chair the Iberian and Portuguese Study Groups with us, for their support in the organization of the conference.

We are grateful to the institutions that sponsored this conference with their generous contributions: the Tinker Foundation, the New Hampshire Institute of Politics at Saint Anselm College, the Real Colegio Complutense, the Embassy of Spain in Washington DC, the Calouste Gulbenkian Foundation, the Camões Institute, Suffolk University, the Spanish Consulate in Boston, the Portuguese Consulate in Boston, the European Union Center at Harvard University and the Minda de Gunzburg Center for European Studies at Harvard University.

The editors of *South European Society & Politics*, Susannah Verney, Nancy Bermeo and Paul Heywood, have been instrumental in putting this book together and we are deeply indebted to them. We would also like to thank Bobbie Goetler, who helped to edit the final version of the manuscript.

Paul Christopher Manuel would like to express his appreciation to Nancy Bermeo, João Espada, Carlos Gaspar, Walter Opello, António Costa Pinto and António Vitorino for the continuing benefit of their insights on his research on Portugal. He also would like to thank his colleagues and students at the New Hampshire Institute of Politics at Saint Anselm College for their support and assistance with this project. Paul was in residence at the Minda de Gunzburg Center for European

Studies at Harvard University as a visiting scholar during 2001–2, and would like to thank Peter Hall, Abby Collins and Patricia Craig for providing a wonderful environment for the research and editing of this volume.

Sebastián Royo owes a great debt to António Barreto, Agnes Bain, Nancy Bermeo, David Cameron, António Dornelas, Omar Encarnación, Robert Fishman, Miguel Glatzer, Peter Hall, Diego Hidalgo, Andy Martin, Andrew Moravcsik, Emilio Ontiveros, Charles Powell, Marino Regini, Michael Ronayne, Joaquín Roy, Philippe Schmitter and Susannah Verney for their guidance, support and encouragement during this project. He also wants to thank his colleagues and students in the Government Department at Suffolk University for providing a cordial and receptive research environment. This project would not have been possible without their motivation and assistance.

Last but not least, we would like to thank our families who have been eager champions of our work. Sebastian's family includes wife Cristina del Sol and daughters Andrea and Monica; Paul's family includes wife Anne Marie Cammisa and daughter Maria Teresa. None of this would have been possible without their support, love, commitment and encouragement. We dedicate this book to them.

S.R. and P.C.M.
Summer 2003

Foreword

NANCY BERMEO

This collection of essays emerged from a Harvard University conference marking the 15-year anniversary of the accession of Portugal and Spain to the European Union. Its insights will be of great interest to scholars and policy-makers of the EU and to the rapidly growing community of scholars and policy-analysts studying Spain and Portugal.

The rewards for studying Spain and Portugal have always been especially rich because Iberia has always been a place of consequential beginnings. Centuries ago, it was the birthplace of the age of discoveries and thus, the colonial world. In the 1920s and 1930s, Iberia was the birthplace of a new form of authoritarianism, a form of dictatorship emphasizing demobilization and corporatism, that would be copied in lands very distant from the peninsula itself. In the 1970s, these same Iberian dictatorships broke down and in so doing marked (along with Greece) the beginning of the Third Wave of democracy. At each of these beginning moments, an understanding of domestic politics in Portugal and Spain yielded a deeper understanding of phenomena that would have profound effects on politics in other parts of the world.

Some three decades ago, Portugal and Spain initiated another consequential beginning by petitioning for entrance into the European Community. Their eventual admission marked the first time that political systems emerging from long-standing dictatorships gained access to the club of market-based democracies. The actions of the newly democratized Iberian states presaged what a broad range of post-dictatorial regimes would do in Eastern Europe in the 1990s. How did entrance into the community of Europe change the countries of Portugal and Spain? What are the lessons that might be transferred to the countries of the East that are entering today? What are the limits of the cross-regional parallels? This collection addresses each of these crucial questions in essays that are rich in both ideas and empirical detail. The answers the essays provide are not always coincident. They point out important differences between the experience of Spain, with its large economy and its reformist transition to democracy, and the experience of

Portugal, with its small economy and its revolutionary transition. They also highlight the differences between the Iberian countries and the countries of Europe's east and southeast. The depth and quality of the empirical research presented here enables us to see cross-national and cross-regional comparisons with the nuance that good comparison requires.

This said, the volume as a whole also provides the reader with a clear and singular message regarding the general consequences of accession. As Philippe Schmitter points out in his conclusion, the essays' answers to the question concerning the effects of joining the EC/EU are surprisingly uniform – European integration has had deep and positive effects on the democracies and the citizens of both states. Though no author argues that the positive effects are universally felt or that opportunities for positive pay-offs have been fully exploited, the essays lead the reader to the conclusion that Portugal and Spain are decidedly better-off inside the European Union than they might have been outside it. Whether this positive picture will be duplicated 15 years after enlargement to the East remains an open question. On this score, both the implications and the explicit content of this collection are decidedly more ambiguous. The authors do not pretend that the trajectories of the South are the certain pathways for the very different states of the East, but they do give us the optics to view the relationships that will likely prove most consequential across the continent. The relationships that seem to have mattered most in the Southern enlargement were political ones, between politicians across borders, between parties and their followers within borders, between informal discourse communities of a global nature and between citizens' visions of Europe and their expectations of what a citizen of Europe rightly deserves. These relationships will be difficult to trace in the East, but these essays show conclusively that the endeavour will be worthwhile.

Some Lessons from the Fifteenth Anniversary of the Accession of Portugal and Spain to the European Union

SEBASTIÁN ROYO and
PAUL CHRISTOPHER MANUEL

INTRODUCTION

In the not-too-distant past, an apocryphal adage claimed that Europe ended at the Pyrenees Mountain Range, at the south-west corner of France. This saying suggested that the nations of the Iberian peninsular existed somewhere outside of the European consciousness. As is the case with such adages, it was based on certain truths: for many years Portugal and Spain were undeniably more focused on the politics of their respective colonial empires than they were on relations with their European neighbours. Further, Portuguese dictator Antonio de Salazar and Spanish dictator Francisco Franco were not interested in developing relationships with democratic Europe in the post-war period. As a consequence of this pattern of historical development, these two Iberian nations were indeed isolated from Europe for a long period of time. This political reality started to change with the democratic transitions in both countries in the 1970s. These new Iberian democratic governments were anxious to emulate the political stability and economic prosperity of their European neighbours. After years of difficult negotiations, Portugal and Spain both joined the European Union on 1 January 1986, starting a new phase of Iberian, and European, history.

This introductory analysis will examine the integration process of Spain and Portugal in detail. Among other concerns, it asks how 15 years of membership in the European Union has impacted economic relations and political citizenship in Spain and Portugal. What is the relationship between economic growth and political citizenship? Are these separate entities, or connected in fundamental ways? Is loyalty to a political unit driven by economic success, or by a sense of cultural identity? Does 'Iberian citizenship' exist? Does 'European citizenship exist'? If so, how would either of these differ from Portuguese or Spanish citizenship?

The issue of Iberian membership in Europe raises at least four important issues. First, it is important to keep in mind that the post-war construction of the European Union was first an economic reality (in the 1950s and 1960s) then a political one (in the 1970s and 1980s), and only now perhaps is becoming a cultural one (since the 1990s). Second, Portuguese and Spaniards are only slowly identifying themselves as 'European'. It is far more common for them to identify with their nation-state of origin. Third, although the Maastricht Treaty does contain certain statutes related to the rights of European citizens, no treaty spells out European citizenship and economic rights and guarantees. Finally, the construction of European Citizenship, arguably, faces some of the very same challenges inherent in Spanish citizenship relating to linguistic and ethnic cleavages.

THE OVERALL PATTERN OF HISTORICAL DEVELOPMENT IN SPAIN AND PORTUGAL

Portugal and Spain are two of the oldest nation-states in Europe, and each has a strong sense of national unity and mission that dates back to their battle of *reconquista* against the North African Moors. It should also be noted at the outset that there have been significant tensions between Spain and Portugal over the centuries. The 'Spanish question' has always been a pressing issue in Portuguese foreign policy. As many historians and observers have noted, these nations have shared a historic relationship based on fear and mistrust. This hostile relationship has been characterized by Spanish disdain for the Portuguese, and Portuguese defiance of perceived Spanish arrogance. And yet, since democratization there have been signs that some changes might be under way – both in the relations between Spain and Portugal, and their respective relationship with Europe.

The overall pattern of Spanish and Portuguese histories has been described, crudely, as a graph shaped like an upside-down version of the letter 'V'. That is, the graph rises – bumpily at times, through 600 years under the Romans, 700 years under or partly under the Moors, and a century of empire-building – to the peak of Spanish and Portuguese power in the sixteenth century. After that the history of each nation goes downhill until the 1970s. A vast empire was gradually lost, leaving

Portugal and Spain poor and powerless. And there was much political instability: Spain suffered 43 *coup d'états* between 1814 and 1923, a horrendous civil war between 1936 and 1939, followed by 36 years of dictatorship under *Generalísimo* Franco.[1] For its part, Portugal suffered great governmental instability during the First Republic (1910–26) and then 48 years of authoritarian rule under Salazar and Caetano.

After the 1974 'Revolution of the Carnations' in Portugal and Franco's death in 1975, the graph turned upward again. In Spain King Juan Carlos, Franco's heir, oversaw the return of democracy to the country. A negotiated transition period, which has been labelled as a model for other countries, paved the way for the elaboration of a new Constitution, followed by the first free elections in almost 40 years. In Portugal the democratic transition was more turbulent and included a revolutionary period (1974–76), but it culminated, as in Spain, in the establishment of a parliamentary democracy. These developments were followed by the progressive return of both Iberian countries to the international arena – where they have been relatively isolated during the dictatorship. The following decade also witnessed the Socialist party being elected to actual power in both countries (1976 in Portugal and 1982 in Spain), bringing a new aura of modernity to the country. The 1980s also witnessed Spain's integration into NATO (1982).

AN OVERVIEW: IBERIAN DEMOCRATIC REGIMES AND EEC INTEGRATION

From the strict bilateralism that characterized the relations among the European powers in the years after the Second World War, until the adoption in 1962 of a common agricultural policy, the six countries that were members of the European Economic Community (EEC) went through a long process of integration. For most of this period, Spain and Portugal were separated from this process. Spain only joined the Organization of European Economic Cooperation (OEEC) in 1959. When the dilemma about the European Community–European Free Trade Agreement (EFTA) was resolved, Spain decided to open negotiations to seek an economic arrangement in 1962. Portugal followed a different path. A traditional ally of Britain, it decided to join Britain when this country went ahead with the formation of a European Free Trade Association in 1959.

Spain and Portugal were marginalized from the European integration process for political reasons. Neither Spain nor Portugal officially participated in the Second World War, but leaned toward the Axis side.

The Axis powers had helped Franco win the civil war in Spain and had supported Salazar's regime in Portugal in the 1930s. This association between the Iberian dictators and the Axis regimes contributed to the French and British suspicions about the character of the Iberian authoritarian regimes.[2]

As such, a condition imposed by the EEC was that only democratic states could be members. Although each nation was interested in enjoying the economic benefits of EC membership, that requirement had the effect of banning Spain and Portugal from the European Union until the 1980s. After the democratic transitions in the 1970s, both Portuguese and Spanish democratic governments pursued feverishly the integration. Several deadlines were missed, but after years of long and strained negotiations, Portugal and Spain were each accepted to the EEC on 1 January 1986. After decades of relative isolation under authoritarian regimes, the success of processes of democratic transition in both countries finally permitted full membership in the European Community.

For Spain, Portugal, and their EEC partners, this momentous and long-awaited development had profound consequences. Spanish and Portuguese policy-makers expected that accession would help consolidate the newly established democratic institutions, modernize their outdated economic structures and, finally, normalize relations with their European neighbours. They also understood membership in the EEC as a form of political maturation. It would also help align the politics of both countries with their European counterparts, and accelerate the Europeanization and democratization of their antediluvian political structures. The urgent need for these reforms was highlighted by the stark environment in which it took place – the 1980s. Spain and Portugal experienced one of the worst economic recessions in their histories, in a political context deeply marked (particularly in the case of Portugal) by the instability of the institutions that had been established during the democratic transition.

Costs and Benefits of Integration

Clearly, accession set in motion a complex and multifaceted process of adjustment. Entry to the EC – renamed the European Union (EU) in the 1990s – has also brought many economic advantages to both countries. Portugal and Spain have benefited extensively from the EU's 'structural funds', which have been used to improve the physical infrastructure and capital stock of both countries. At the same time, Portuguese and Spanish trade with the Community has expanded dramatically over the past 15 years, and foreign investment has flooded into both countries.

One of the beneficial consequences of these developments has been a reduction in the economic differentials that separated each country from the European average. For instance, since 1986 Portugal's average per capita income has grown from 56 per cent of the EU average to about 74 per cent, and Spain's has grown to 83 per cent. The culmination of this process was the (largely unexpected) participation of both countries as original founders of the European Monetary Union in 1999.

The process of integration, however, has also brought significant costs in terms of economic adjustment, loss of sovereignty, and cultural homogenization. European integration has had, and will continue to have for the foreseeable future, a profound effect on Spanish and Portuguese society. It has had an impact on issues such as national identity, the sustainability of welfare institutions, and the adjustment of political and economic structures. Under the terms of the accession agreements signed in 1985, both countries had to undertake significant steps to align their legislation on industrial, agriculture, economic, and financial polices to that of the European Community. These accession agreements also established significant transition periods to cushion the negative effects of integration. This process meant that both countries had to phase in tariffs and prices, and approve tax changes (including the establishment of a value added tax) that the rest of the Community had already put in place. It also involved, in a second phase, the removal of technical barriers to trade. These requirements brought significant adjustment costs to both economies.

Overcoming Historical Tensions between Spain and Portugal?

In some ways European integration has also helped bring Spain and Portugal closer together. Improved relations between these two countries – reminiscent of improved Franco-German ties in the 1950s – have been a significant outcome of the EU integration process. For centuries both countries have shared a peninsula, but little else. The roots of the Portuguese–Spanish animosity date to 1385, when Portuguese forces successfully resisted Castellan hegemony through their defeat of the Spanish-led invading forces at the battle of Aljubarrota. Over the past 600 years, Portugal has steadfastly defended its independence. The one period of exception occurred between 1580 and 1640 when the Portuguese and Spanish crowns were joined in Madrid under the Hapsburg monarchy. Portuguese nationalists eventually rejected Spanish rule and restored national independence in 1640. Furthermore, at the height of their colonial power, both countries stepped heavily on each other's toes in Latin America. These historical antagonisms drove the people from both countries apart. Consequently, the two peoples have lived with their backs turned on each other. The one notable exception took place in 1939, when Spain and Portugal, under the rule of Franco and Salazar, signed a friendship agreement known as the 'Iberian Pact'.

This hostile climate between Spain and Portugal changed for the better in the 1980s. More importantly, since the transitions to democracy in the two countries, relations between them have steadily improved within the framework of the EEC (EU). Both Spain and Portugal joined the EEC on 1 January 1986, and both are now members of the North Atlantic Treaty Organization (NATO). For instance, one of the biggest immediate effects of membership in the EEC in 1986 was vastly increased trade between Spain and Portugal. In only two years, Spain emerged as one of Portugal's biggest suppliers, second only to West Germany. At the same time, Spain's imports from Portugal rose faster than those from any other country. In addition, direct Spanish investment in Portugal and Portuguese investment in Spain soared. These developments demonstrate the increasing economic integration of both countries. It is therefore worth exploring the impact of European integration on both countries simultaneously.

Finally, both countries have played a significant role in the European integration process. They participated actively in the establishment of the Single European Market, and in the enactment of the Maastricht and Amsterdam treaties. Portugal and Spain are strong supporters of the integration process and have intervened actively in this endeavour. At a time when Latin American and Eastern European countries are on the threshold of major changes, with an ambitious plan to integrate the economies of the Western hemisphere, the lessons derived from analysis of the Spanish and Portuguese experiences should be instructive to scholars, students, and policy-makers from Latin America and Eastern Europe working on expansion and integration issues. Moreover, the examination of these two cases sheds new light on the challenges (and opportunities) that less developed countries face when trying to integrate regionally or into the global economy.

From a cultural standpoint, the effects of integration are also significant. As part of their democratic transitions, both countries embarked on new processes of self-discovery. They have attempted to come to terms with their own identities, while addressing issues such as culture, nationality, citizenship, ethnicity, and politics. The process of integration into Europe has greatly influenced these developments. And what of the new European citizenship? In this regard, Juan M. Delgado-Moreira recently observed that

During the past five years, the European Union has been trying to sponsor a coming of age of European Identity awareness across national borders. In doing so, EU administration intends to square the circle of European Union as the super nation-state of the nation states of Europe. However prompted or justified by the political or economic context, it is noteworthy to what extent the texts of European statutes and policies lack theoretical alternatives to the territorial and relatively homogeneous state. In order for it not to become a threat perceived by the population in identity terms, the apparently forthcoming idea of European citizenship needs to address the concerns of both traditional and new ethno-national minorities at the state level and underneath. In the light of a global context, the tide of Europeanization is but a particular case of the worldwide extended tension between the two increasing and opposing processes of globalization and particularization.[3]

Delgado-Moreira's apt observation regarding the opposing processes of globalization and particularization centres our considerations. At the dawn of the new millennium, it would not be an exaggeration to say that the Spaniards and the Portuguese are in the process of becoming 'mainstream Europeans', and that many of the cultural differences that separated these two countries from their European counterparts have dwindled as a consequence of the integration process.

Spain, Portugal and the European Community: The Integration Process

Due to American distrust of Franco, Spain was not included in the Marshall Plan. During the 1940s and 1950s, Spain was mostly left aside and it only developed some bilateral arrangements with other countries. For its part, Portugal enjoyed better relations with the United States. During the Second World War, Salazar permitted the United States to build the Lajes Base in the Azores (Terceira Island). The United States provided military assistance to Portugal in exchange for the use of this base, and also included Portugal in the Marshall Plan. And yet, when the Schuman Plan was issued in 1950, both Portugal and Spain were left out. The Schuman Plan was restricted to the democratic regimes in Europe. Later on, the UK and Portugal formed EFTA along with Austria, Denmark, Norway, Sweden, and Switzerland. EFTA has emerged as a result of the abortive free trade negotiations, part of the so-called 'Grand-Design' initiated by Britain to create a broad free trade area. The termination by France of these negotiations in December of 1958 led

Britain to go ahead with the formation of a European Free Trade Association. Plans were approved in July of 1959, leading to the signing of the Stockholm Convention by the seven countries. The main aim of the Convention was to eliminate trade tariffs among its seven members, and to develop an industrial free trade area by 1970. It did not include a common external tariff. Portugal, a traditional ally of Britain, became a member of the EFTA in 1960.

Integration and the case of Spain. The Spanish government followed these developments very closely, and a commission was created in the Foreign Ministry especially devoted to them. In these years it seemed clear to the government that the country could not be left out of these integrationist movements, but due to the precarious economic situation of the country, the rapprochement was very slow. During the late 1950s, there was a controversy in Spain surrounding the convenience for the country of joining the Europe of the Six (EC) or the Seven (EFTA). This meant that Spain had to make a decision about which of those two alternatives to follow as the most appropriate framework for the country.

It soon became clear that the Treaty of Rome was better suited for Spain's interests. Since Spanish's agricultural exports were critical for the country's economy, the fact that the EC had set the creation of a common agricultural policy as one of its main objectives, whereas EFTA left agriculture aside, convinced Spanish authorities about the benefits of the EC. Furthermore, the commercial volume of Spain with the EC was 50 per cent higher than the one with EFTA countries. Finally, at the beginning of the 1960s, Spanish external trade was characterized by a chronic imbalance between a rigid export supply and an increasing import demand. A preferential trade agreement with the EC would offer the country the incentive of enlarging some markets that were very important for Spanish's exports, while at the same time contributing toward the acceleration of a series of structural reforms needed at that time.[4]

On 14 February 1962 the Spanish Foreign minister sent a letter to Walter Hallstein, President of the Commission of the European Community, asking for the opening of negotiations with the objective of examining the possible accession of Spain to the Community.[5] The request, however, received a cool reception from the Commission, which only acknowledged receipt of the letter. From the outside, several organizations pressured the Community to reject the Spanish request. In 1962 the Confederation of European Unions sent a letter to Hallstein pressuring for a rebuff. Several European newspapers joined in the campaign against Spain's request. 'The EC has to say no to Spain', stated the Netherlands's newspaper *Nieuwe Rotterdamsche Cournat*, 'until the spirit of democracy and liberty are present in the country'. The Congress of the European Federalist Movement meeting in Lyon at that time approved a resolution in which it rejected the possibility of any agreement between Spain and the EC. The Socialist Group on the European Parliament also said no to the Spanish request. Finally, the Congress of the European movement, meeting in Munich on June 1962, with the participation of a Spanish delegation, approved another resolution in which it was stated that only democratic countries could join the European Community – the Spanish representatives in this Congress were later punished with jail for their participation.[6]

During the following two years, there was no communication between Spain and the EC. This was the same period during which the UK received the De Gaulle veto. After these two years the Spanish government decided to try again and sent a new letter. On 6 June 1964 the Council authorized the Commission to open conversations to 'examine the economic problems that the EC causes to Spain, and to look for the appropriate solutions'. Three exploratory meetings took place between 1964 and 1966. As a result of these meetings, the EC Commission developed a report about the content of the meetings and about the possible formulas that could define the future relations between Spain and the Community. The Commission developed three proposals – association, a commercial agreement, and a preferential agreement. After several evaluations the Council picked the third option.

After eight years of negotiations, on 29 June 1970 the Spanish government reached an agreement with the EC. This agreement established a preferential system with the objective of eliminating the barriers to the commercial exchanges between Spain and the Community. The agreement lasted only six years.[7] Following Franco's death, on 22 July 1977 the first democratic Parliament was born after the 15 June general election. A few days later, on 28 July, Spain presented a formal membership request to the European Economic Community.

Integration and the case of Portugal. In Portugal, from 1933 to 1974, the government maintained an isolationist foreign policy, refusing close ties with other nations, and limiting its relations to its colonies.[8] After the anti-Portuguese wars of liberation broke out in the early 1960s in Angola, Mozambique and the other Portuguese colonies, the international environment declared itself against continued Portuguese colonialism.

Several international organizations organized economic boycotts of Portugal, and the continued colonial policies prevented any chance of Portugal's membership in the EEC. It became clear that Portugal would remain a pariah nation as long as it kept its colonies.

Three years after Salazar's death in 1970, junior officers, who were bearing the brunt of the war, demanded that Salazar's successor, Marcelo Caetano, reach a negotiated settlement to the conflict. Frustrated by his failure to do so, these rebel officers, calling themselves the 'Armed Forces Movement' (MFA), overthrew the 48-year-old Salazar/Caetano dictatorship on 25 April 1974. This military coup plunged Portuguese politics and foreign policy into a period of uncertainty. As Walter Opello has correctly observed, 'During the Estado Novo (New State), Portuguese foreign policy had one fundamental objective: the maintenance of Portugal's colonial empire ... All of this suddenly changed on 25 April 1974.'

Although the MFA rejected the colonialism of the previous regime, key members of the new military elite did not find agreement on any one idea regarding Portugal's place in the world. One group was led by the Communist Vasco Gonçalves, and it favoured close relations with the Warsaw Pact countries. A socialist faction, led by Melo Antunes, sought to adopt an independent-minded, French-style foreign policy. A radical alliance of officers, led by Otelo de Saraiva Carvalho, argued that Portugal should follow the revolutionary Cuban model. A more conservative approach was advocated by General Spínola, who was not part of the MFA. He suggested that Portugal should establish a 'commonwealth' with its soon-to-be former colonies.

This lack of agreement resulted in an extended period of ideological and political conflict. From 1974–76 there were six provisional governments, a failed right-wing coup attempt in March of 1975 (which discredited General Spínola), and a failed left-wing coup attempt in November of that year (which discredited both Otelo and Gonçalves). After this complex political and military domestic game, Melo Antunes and some political players, including Socialist party head Mário Soares, managed to prevail.[9] This military and ideological modality of the democratic transition simplified the question of foreign policy after 1976 in that it had swept both the pro-Salazar right-wing and pro-Warsaw Pact left-wing elements away from the political equation.

The main area of broad-based elite agreement since the adoption of the democratic Constitution of 1976 has been in the domain of foreign politics. This elite, which includes the centre-left *Partido Socialista* (PS), the centre right *Partido Social Democrata* (PSD), and the right-wing *Centro Democrático Social* (CDS), understand Portugal to be both an Atlantic and a European nation. The new Portuguese administration supports the long-standing American foreign policy that favours the development of democracy in the world. Both NATO and the EEC are committed to democratic forms of government, and have encouraged democratic development in Portugal since 1976.

At least since 1986 Portuguese foreign policy has functioned within a European framework. Indeed, the idea of Europe has played a central role in the development and consolidation of Portuguese democracy. In the ideological battles of 1974–76, the PS slogan of 'a Europa conosco' (Europe is with us) significantly improved the party's appeal to the people.[10] Or, as António Barreto has astutely noted,

> the democratic ideal ... was symbolized in the greater part by Europe. This gave a concrete, visible, rooted, palpable sense to the aspirations for freedom that, by themselves, demand risk. It gave territorial and geographical significance to the uncertain horizons of democracy. It was the real substitute for past glories. It was a home, where there was room for one more. Besides proximity, sympathy and affinity, Europe was security.[11]

Portugal has been a strong supporter of the 1986 Single Act and the 1992 Maastricht Treaty. These revisions to the original Treaty of Rome have expanded the EU's authority in economic and monetary matters, establishing an extensive internal European market. Lisbon decision-makers perceive these moves to better enable Europe to assist them with their plans for development. By the same token, Portuguese decision-makers have not been inclined to support an expansion of the EU. They fear that economic resources Portugal still needs will be diverted eastward.[12]

The Enlargement Process for Portugal and Spain

After a long and winding negotiation process that lasted for almost eight years, on 1 January 1986 Spain and Portugal joined the EU.

The accession process. Portugal applied for EEC membership in March 1977, Spain in July of the same year. Formal negotiations to enlarge the EC began with Portugal in October 1978 and Spain in February 1979. Spain and Portugal were poor countries and as in the case of the Central and Eastern European countries a decade later, these negotiations, which were viewed by many EC member states with apprehension, tested their commitment to help consolidate the political and economic reforms of the Iberian countries. Portugal, fully aware that EC countries feared the economic and social consequences of Spanish membership, sought to have its application considered separately. Consequently, the EC negotiated separately with each country. In reality, however, both applications were interrelated.[13]

Enlargement negotiations proved to be slow and protracted. For Portugal the most controversial bargaining issues affected agriculture and textiles, which represented over 40 per cent of the country's industrial output. During the negotiations Portugal and the EC signed a pre-accession agreement that revised pre-existing agreements and provided for assistance to Portugal. This agreement, which came into force on 1 January 1981, sought to modernize the Portuguese economy to facilitate the country's eventual integration into the EC (Dinan 1999: 104–5). By that time, however, the enlargement process was the subject of political controversy all over Europe with opposition led by the French government, which was immersed in a close presidential campaign, and thus viewed with dread the prospect of enlargement to the South.

The EC, particularly the French, had misgivings about southern enlargement that were focused more on Spain than on Portugal. Agriculture, textiles, fisheries, and the free movement of labour proved to be the most contentious issues throughout the negotiations. Agricultural policy within the EC has been the subject of historic disputes and clashes on interests. The proposed Spanish membership in the EC was framed within the debate of its presumed impact on the EC agricultural policy as well as the ongoing budgetary crisis and attempted reform of the Common Agriculture Policy. In this regard, it was estimated that Spain's accession would increase the EC agricultural area by 30 per cent. At the same time, France and Spain would compete directly in the production of fruits, olive oil and vegetables – hence, French misgivings. While the French and Italian governments wanted to protect domestic growers, the German, British, and Dutch governments supported the Spanish accession. Germany, however, placed the ongoing negotiations within the discussion about Common Agricultural Policy (CAP) reform and the settlement of budgetary issues.

Fisheries were also a very controversial issue. Since Spain's fishing fleet was larger than the entire EC fleet combined, there was also strong interest in limiting the access of the Spanish fleet to the Common Fisheries Policy. This dispute intensified throughout 1984 when French and Spanish fisherman attacked each other. At the same time, the French government, with presidential elections less than a year away, pandered to French farmers, a powerful constituency. For instance, in a 1980 speech to French farmer leaders in Paris, the French president, Valéry Giscard d'Estaing, declared that in view of the ongoing disputes over the British budgetary contribution, the EC should resolve that issue before undertaking another enlargement. This declaration provoked an outrage in both Spain and Portugal. France's opposition, however, failed to receive strong support from the other EC members. Britain, a historical ally of Portugal, supported Portuguese accession and the British Prime Minister, Margaret Thatcher, went as far as to declare in 1981 that Portugal and Spain did not need to join at the same time and that Portugal could become a member by January 1984 (Dinan 1999: 105). Despite repeated attempts on the part of Portugal to decouple the accession negotiations, the fate of Spanish and Portuguese negotiations became increasingly linked. Negotiations between the Iberian countries and the EC progressed throughout 1981 and 1982 over a wide range of less controversial issues including capital movement, regional policy, transport, and services.

François Mitterrand's victory in the 1981 French presidential election did not change France's opposition to enlargement. The new French government sought an acceptable arrangement for Mediterranean agriculture. Despite French opposition and Iberian rhetoric, however, the fault for the lack of progress in the enlargement negotiations did not lie entirely with the EC. For instance, the Spanish government was reluctant to introduce a value added tax, as well as to curtail subsidies and end protectionism. This recalcitrance prompted the European Council in 1981 to stress the need of the applicant countries to introduce the necessary reforms and prepare their countries for accession (Dinan 1999: 106–7).

The Iberian countries' application was strengthened in the early 1980s by the formation of stable administrations in both countries. The overwhelming victory of the Spanish Socialist party, led by its young and charismatic leader Felipe González, in the October 1982 general election, and the subsequent election in June 1983 of Mario Soares, leader of the Portuguese Socialist party, as Prime Minister, gave new impetus to the enlargement process. Both leaders were passionate Europhiles, and one of their primary political objectives was to bring their countries into the EC. They embarked on a series of visits to EC capitals to make the case for Iberian accession. In the domestic front both new leaders implemented ambitious economic agendas to modernize the outdated economic and social structures of their countries. In Portugal the new Socialist government reached an agreement with the International Monetary Fund to restructure its economy and reduce the country's foreign debt. In Spain the new Socialist government left aside demand-oriented policies and embarked on a supply-oriented restructuring stride that sought to address the imbalances of the Spanish economic structure. These reformist agendas illustrated both countries' determination to become model member states (Dinan 1999: 106–7). The new leaders also used their personal contacts and ideological affinity with their European counterparts to make the case for their countries' accession.

Despite progress in the negotiations, the European Council and the EC Commission concurred on the need for the Community to get its house in order before any Iberian expansion could occur. At the 1983 Council of Ministers' summit in Stuttgart, the heads of state of the ten member countries outlined the general conditions for southern enlargement. This summit stressed the need to solve the EC budgetary problems and reform the CAP before Spain and Portugal could join the Community. In addition, it linked French demands over Community policy on fruits and vegetables to the expansion. The budgetary crisis of the Community dated back to the 1970s and became a serious obstacle when Margaret Thatcher became British Prime Minister and began exasperating her EC colleagues by aggressively pursuing Britain's budgetary claims (see Dinan 1999: 88–93). In order to mollify British concerns, the European Commission issued in 1983 a Green paper on EC finances that proposed mechanisms to raise additional funds. The subsequent European Council summit that took place in Athens in December of 1983 failed to resolve the financial issues. This summit, however, brought into the open the issues that required resolution. This debate led to the development of a normative framework that became a new agenda of cohesion. German leadership in budgetary matters, and the country's decision to act as 'paymaster' for the enlargement, paved the way for the resolution of standing conflicts. During the 1984 winter summit of the Council of Ministers at Dublin, the EC Ten reached an agreement on Mediterranean agricultural production.

The Fountainbleu summit of June 1984 resolved the standing EC budgetary issues, set 1 January 1986 as the agreed date for Spain and Portugal entry into the EC, and called for an end to negotiations by 30 September 1984. This date proved too ambitious. In December 1984 the European Council reached an agreement on fruits, fish, wine, and vegetables that was accepted by the Spanish government. The formation of a new European Commission in Brussels led by the energetic and influential Jacques Delors in January 1985 gave a final impetus to the negotiations. Delors threw himself into the negotiations and assumed personal responsibility over the last roadblock, namely, the Integrated Mediterranean Programme (IMP), a Greek demand that sought to provide EC financial assistance to Greece to compensate for enlargement. In the first half of 1985, the EC foreign ministers agreed on a five-year enlargement-linked programme of structural aid to farmers, and resolved the remaining problems over fisheries, the applicants' budgetary contributions, and the free movement of labour in the EC. Finally, based on a new Commission proposal, the European Council of Brussels approved a seven-year programme of 6.6 billion ECUs for grants and loans to assist the existing EC Mediterranean regions. These agreements resolved the final obstacles for Southern enlargement. Spain and Portugal joined the EC on 1 January 1986.

LESSONS

Let us suggest some lessons based on information from the preceding sections.

Lesson 1: The Accession of Portugal and Spain to the European Union Contains both Global and Particular Elements

The process for Portugal and Spain to join the EU was influenced by the traditional European nation-state rivalries, typical of international relations since the 1648 Peace of Westphalia. The eventual decision to allow Portugal and Spain to join the EU was replete with the opposing processes of particularization and globalization. It was *particular* in that the focus was on the nation-state, and *global* in that EU decision-makers were concerned with harmonizing the economies of all of the member states to the world-wide process of capital development. Within the framework of the European Community, Spain and Portugal are now better prepared to compete in the global market against colossi such as Japan and the United States. Furthermore, European integration allows them to co-operate on their research and technological programmes. This process may represent a watershed in Iberian and European relations, and may provide us with a unique opportunity to reconceptualize economic relations and political citizenship in Europe and Iberia in new ways.

Lesson 2: Political Considerations were the Main Motivation behind Portugal and Spain's Application to Join the European Community

On the one hand, Portugal and Spain both wanted to strengthen their new democratic regimes, and they both held the desire to end the relative isolation they had experienced during the authoritarian years. These were critical political factors behind their decision to join the European Community. On the other hand, the economic implications of European integration were also very profound and played an important role in their applications for membership. The expected static effects of the integration were mixed. Spain, for instance, was expected to gain in some sectors, namely, agriculture. The asymmetry of trade barriers before integration, however – with Spanish barriers five times higher than those of the European Community – indicated a strong possibility of trade creation. This was translated into a risk of difficult adjustment problems for many Spanish manufacturing and agricultural sectors that were not ready for competition. Integration would allow them to confront the international economic recession from a stronger position. Without EC integration both countries would have never attracted as much investment as they did after 1986, and there was the real possibility, given the intensity of the economic crisis, that they would have fallen into third world economic levels.

Lesson 3: Economic Success Can Improve Political Ties – EU Integration Has Brought Portugal and Spain Together

European integration has also brought Spain and Portugal together as a region. The Spanish and Portuguese have finally realized that joining together will make their integration into the international system more beneficial, and they will be more likely to have their regional interests addressed, as they really do have many common characteristics, needs, and goals. This has been an important outcome of the European integration process. Indeed, there have been significant tensions between Spain and Portugal over the centuries.

As we have seen, the so-called 'Spanish question' has always been a pressing issue in Portuguese foreign policy. The two countries separated when Alfonso VI of León and Castile (the Cid's king) gave the country of Portugal to his son-in-law Henry of Burgundy in 1093. These nations have shared a historic relationship based on fear and mistrust. This hostility has been characterized by Spanish disdain for the Portuguese, and Portuguese defiance of perceived Spanish arrogance. Spain often tried (and once managed) to absorb its neighbour. Portugal defeated

Castille at Aljubarrota in 1385 and expelled the Spanish garrisons for good in 1640. Furthermore, at the height of their colonial power, both countries stepped heavily on each other's toes in Latin America. These historical antagonisms drove the people from both countries apart from each other.[14]

As many historians and observers have noted, while Spain historically developed what José Saramago, the Portuguese Nobel laureate, has defined as an 'amputation complex', the Portuguese people tend to blame Spain for all the bad things that have happened to their country. In fact, there is a popular Portuguese adage that enshrines these feelings: '*De Espanha, nem bom vento, nem bom casamento*' ('neither good winds nor good marriages come from Spain').[15] In Spain Salvador de Madariaga, a Spanish liberal historian, defined the Portuguese as 'a Spaniard with his back turned to Castille and his eyes on the Atlantic'. Consequently, these two cultures for centuries have shared a peninsula but little else, and the two peoples have lived with their backs turned away from each other. Yet, in recent years, there have been signs that some changes might be underway – both in the relations between Spain and Portugal, as well as their respective relationship with Europe.

This hostile climate changed for the better in the mid-1980s. While theirs is still a challenging relationship, it is unquestionable that Spain and Portugal are drawing closer together through European integration. Portuguese and Spaniards appreciate each other more. There is increasing awareness of a shared history, including the legacies of empire, the manipulation of the great powers after their imperial decline, the incompetence of kings and military strongmen of the nineteenth century, and finally, the frustration with fascist authoritarian rulers in the twentieth century.

Several developments demonstrate the increasing economic integration between both countries. For instance, one of the biggest immediate effects of membership in the European Community in 1986 was vastly increased trade between Spain and Portugal. By 1990 Spain traded more with Portugal than with all of its Latin American trading partners, and Spanish imports from Portugal are rising faster than those from any other country. Direct Spanish investment in Portugal and Portuguese investment in Spain has soared, and Spain has emerged as the largest investor in Portugal. By 2000 there were more than 3,000 Spanish firms in Portugal, compared with fewer than 400 in 1989, and the Portuguese own more than 400 firms in Spain. It is also true, however, that these economic asymmetries lie at the root of some of the tensions that have arisen as the two countries have drawn closer. These developments demonstrate the increasing integration of the Iberian economies.

Following the example of the French and Germans, relations between Portugal and Spain have also dramatically improved over the last 15 years. The increased economic co-operation fostered by membership in the European Union has also resulted in greater cultural exchanges and political harmony. Large numbers of Spaniards visited the 1998 World Expo in Lisbon, and Portuguese dailies have taken to printing some part of their editions during Easter Week in Spanish for the convenience of the many Spanish who visit the country during this time. In addition, the success of the year 2000 initiative to promote a new and more modern image of Portugal in Spain, with the joint organization of a programme of cultural, political, and economic activities (including the installation of a Portuguese pavilion to host most of these events in the heart of Madrid) under the title: '*Portugal: A Bet for the Future*' illustrates the dramatic transformation in the relationship between the countries. These developments demonstrate their increasing integration.

Lesson 4: Economic Success Drives Public Opinion

The decision to join the European Union in both Portugal and Spain was supported by most of the political parties in each country. Furthermore, according to a recent Eurobarometer study (see Table 1), the overwhelming majority of the population understood the importance and significance of this step and supported the decision. EC membership would increase economic growth, thus increasing the standards of living of the Iberian people.

The polls conducted by European and Iberian institutions show that the opinions and attitudes of Iberian citizens towards the process of European integration are in general favourable. It is important to stress, however, that there is a large portion of Iberian citizens that does not have an opinion about this issue. In addition, the *Centro de*

TABLE 1

SUPPORT FOR EU MEMBERSHIP AND EMU

	It is a Good Thing	It is a Bad Thing
Portugal	56	45
Spain	53	61

Source: *Eurobarometer*, No.48, Oct.–Nov. 1998.

Investigaciones Sociológicas (CIS) and Eurobarometer data show that one of the key factors to account for the attitude of Portuguese and Spaniards towards European integration has been the perception about the personal and collective benefits derived from membership. In this regard the CIS data show that Iberian citizens have a very utilitarian concept of the European Union – that is, they evaluate the consequences of membership over issues such as living costs, infrastructures, job opportunities, wages, and so on, and in function of this cost/benefit analysis, they adopt a position in favour of or against European integration. Finally, when comparing the attitudes of Spanish and Portuguese citizens *vis-à-vis* other European citizens, the former support the European Union more, and express more positive opinions about the benefits derived from membership. They also stress further the need to build a social Europe that should emerge from below with the support from the people, and not only an economic Europe advanced by the bureaucracy and the elites.[16]

Lesson 5: EU Membership Has Altered the Iberian Role in the World

EC membership put an end to the relative isolationism of both countries, which had been a key cause of the economic, cultural, and social backwardness of both Portugal and Spain. After years of backwardness and isolation, Spain and Portugal have become players in Europe again. Iberia's place throughout history has been at the centre of Europe. After years of isolationism it was time to reclaim their place there. The alternative was between the past and the future, between hope and fear, and both countries chose the right path, as time has proven.

Lesson 6: EU Membership Has Given Spain and Portugal a Better Competitive Position

Portugal and Spain took part in the process of European integration, a development that would have significant economic consequences for both countries. Spain and Portugal had traditionally been countries of emigrants. In 1986 there were more than 1 million Portuguese and Spanish emigrants throughout Europe, and the entry of Portugal and Spain into the European Community made Spanish and Portuguese citizens European citizens, thus ending some of the discrimination that those emigrants had suffered in the past. The Spanish and Portuguese fishers, who could not fish from the Community waters, would now have access to them. It would be a way to avoid surpluses of Spanish agricultural goods – which reached one-third of total output during some years. Some of these products would be sold more easily on the European markets. Spain and Portugal had to speed up the reform of their productive and economic structures in order to increase the productivity of their labour force, which at the time was half of the average of the European Community. Integration would facilitate this process and improve the competitive position of the country. In fact, Spain was a highly protected country by European standards. This was translated into a non-competitive industrial sector.

The Oil Crisis hit Spain hard. The unemployment level was 22 per cent in 1986. Spain was also facing increasing competition for its main exports – clothing, textiles, and leather. Countries from the Far East were starting to produce all of these goods at cheaper costs by exploiting their low wages. These countries were attracting foreign investment in sectors in which Spain and Portugal had been favoured traditionally. This situation convinced the Spanish and Portuguese leaders that their countries had to shift toward more capital-intensive industries requiring greater skills in the labour force but relying on standard technology (for example, chemicals, vehicles, steel and metal manufacturers). Portugal and Spain's entry into the European Community would facilitate this shift. They would have access to the EC market, thus attracting investment that would create these new industries. Furthermore, Spain and Portugal would also receive financial assistance from the EC: structural funds, the European Regional Development Fund, the Social Fund, the Agriculture Guidance and Guarantee Fund, and the newly created IMP for agriculture. The interdependence of the markets and economies offered no other alternative if Portugal and Spain wanted to become competitive in the world market. That is, Spanish and Portuguese producers would have access not only to their respective national markets, but also to the European one. This fact offered incentives for investment and for the development of economies of scale, which in turn has resulted in more competitive products in the European market. Finally, no matter how impressive the economic results might seem, Spain and Portugal still have a long way to go in reaching the EC average in wealth.

Lesson 7: Real Economic Convergence is a Slow Process

More than four years ago, on 1 January 1999, Spain and Portugal became founding members of the European Monetary Union. At the end both countries, which as late as 1997 were considered outside candidates for joining the Euro-zone, fulfilled the inflation, interest rate, debt, exchange rate, and public deficit requirements established in the Maastricht Treaty. This development confirmed the nominal convergence of both countries with the rest of the European Union. Nominal economic convergence *vis-à-vis* the European average, however, has advanced at a faster pace than real convergence.

For the Iberian countries to increase their living standards to the EU average, it is necessary that their economies grow faster than the other countries. This will require further liberalization of their labour and service markets and better utilization of their productive resources. In addition, convergence will also demand institutional reforms in Research and Development (R&D) policies, in education, and in civil infrastructures, as well as further innovation, an increase in business capabilities, more investment in information technology, and better and more efficient training systems. Finally, a successful convergence policy will also demand a debate about the role of public investment and welfare programmes in both countries. In the Iberian countries increases in public expenditures to develop their welfare state have caused imbalances in their national accounts. Both countries still spend significantly less in this area than their European neighbours (for example, Spain spends 6.3 points less on welfare policies than the European Monetary Union [EMU] average). Effective real convergence would demand not only effective strategies and policies, but also a strong commitment on the part of Spanish and Portuguese citizens to this objective.

The Iberian integration in the European Union has allowed these economies to become integrated internationally and to modernize, thus securing convergence in nominal terms with Europe. In spite of this progress, however, Iberian economies still have to achieve convergence in real terms, reconciling convergence in productivity with the creation of employment. In terms of convergence and growth in the long run, while contributing to important progress, 15 years have not been long enough.

Lesson 8: European Integration Has Not Led to Convergence in Social Expenditures

While social expenditures have increased in both countries over the last two decades, the gap in social expenditures between the Iberian countries (particularly Spain) and the European Union has not narrowed (see Figure 1).

At the same time, it is worth noting that European Funds have helped develop social policies and the construction of infrastructures related to them. They have also enhanced new undertakings in social policy.

FIGURE 1

EVOLUTION OF SOCIAL PROTECTION EXPENDITURE, % OF GDP, 1980–97

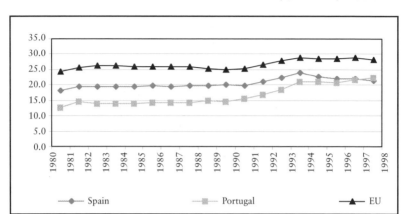

Source: Guillén *et al.* (2001: 4). Data from Eurostat 1997 and Eurostat 2000.

Without these funds the increase in social expenditures would not have been sustainable. The absence of such funds for other countries (that is, Latin America) will significantly hinder efforts to develop and expand their welfare states.

Lesson 9: EU Membership has both Benefits and Costs

As we indicated in the introduction, entry into the European Union has so far brought many advantages to both countries. Portugal and Spain have benefited extensively from the European Union's cohesion policies, which have contributed to improving the physical infrastructure and capital stock of both countries. At the same time Portugal and Spain's trade with the Community has expanded dramatically over the past 15 years, and foreign investment has greatly increased. One of the main consequences of these developments has been a reduction in the economic differentials that separated both countries from the European average. For instance, since 1986 Portugal's average per capita income has grown from 56 per cent of the EU average to about 74 per cent, while Spain's has grown to 83 per cent. The culmination of this process was the (largely unexpected) participation of both countries as original founders of the EMU in 1999.

From a social and cultural standpoint, the effects of integration are also significant. As part of their democratic transitions, both countries embarked on new processes of self-discovery. They have begun to come to terms with their own identities, while addressing issues such as culture, nationality, citizenship, ethnicity, and politics. The process of integration into Europe has greatly influenced these developments. At the dawn of the new millennium, it would not be an exaggeration to say that the Spaniards and the Portuguese have become 'mainstream Europeans', and that many of the cultural differences that separated these two countries from their European counterparts have faded as a consequence of the integration process.

The process of integration, however, has also brought significant costs in terms of economic adjustment, loss of sovereignty, and cultural homogenization. European integration has had, and will continue to have for the foreseeable future, a profound effect on both countries' societies. It has had an impact on issues such as national identity, the sustainability of welfare institutions, and the adjustment of political and economic structures. As discussed earlier, under the terms of the accession agreements signed in 1985, both countries had to undertake significant steps to align their legislation on industrial, agriculture, economic, and financial polices to that of the European Community. These accession agreements also established significant transition periods to cushion the negative effects of integration. This meant that both countries had to phase in tariffs and prices, and approve tax changes (including the establishment of a value added tax) that the rest of the Community had already put in place. This process also involved, in a second phase, the removal of technical barriers to trade. These requirements brought significant adjustment costs to both economies.

The Iberian enlargement illustrates that EU integration required a set of measures including increased competition, privatization of public enterprises, industrial restructuring, and deregulation. These measures have translated into efficiency gains, which have been reinforced by a more stable macroeconomic framework. At the same time, lower inflation and fiscal consolidation have led to lower real (and nominal) interest rates which, in turn, have resulted in a higher sustainable growth. There have also been short-term costs, however, associated with monetary integration. Indeed, the losses of the exchange rate and of monetary sovereignty require a process of nominal convergence and fiscal consolidation, as well as higher cyclical correlation, for euro membership to be successful. This should be taken into account by other countries. The Iberian enlargement shows that prior to monetary integration, candidates must carry out a process of modernization and nominal convergence without fixing their exchange rates.

Lesson 10: Structural and Cohesion Funds Play a Key Role

As we previously indicated, the role of Structural Funds has also been crucial. These allow for the construction of public infrastructure vital for private sector productivity and real convergence. The structural funds and cohesion funds are the instruments designed by the European Union to develop social and cohesion policies within the European Union (see Table 2). The cohesion funds were established in the Maastricht Treaty in order to compensate for the efforts countries with the lowest per capita income (Ireland, Greece, Portugal and Spain) relative to the European Union would need to make to comply with the nominal convergence criteria. These funds, which amount to just over one-third of the EU budget, have contributed significantly to reducing regional disparities and fostering convergence within the European Union. At the same time, they have played a prominent role in developing the factors that improve the competitiveness and determine the potential growth of the least developed regions.[17]

During 1994–99, EU aid accounted for 1.5 per cent of gross domestic product (GDP) in Spain and 3.3 per cent in Portugal.[18] EU funding has allowed rates of public investment to remain relatively stable since the mid-1980s. The percentage of public investment financed by EU funds has been rising since 1985, to reach average values of 42 per cent for Portugal and 15 per cent for Spain. It has been estimated that the impact of these funds on the ratio of public investment in the Spanish economy in the past few years has been 0.5 per cent higher as a consequence of EU funding, which in turn had a

TABLE 2

STRUCTURAL AND COHESION FUNDS

	Greece	Ireland	Spain	Portugal
GDP %				
1989–93	2.6	2.5	0.7	3.0
1994–99	3.0	1.9	1.5	3.3
2000–6	2.8	0.6	1.3	2.9
% on Gross Fixed Capital Formation				
1989–93	11.8	15.0	2.9	12.4
1994–99	14.6	9.6	6.7	14.2
2000–6	12.3	2.6	5.5	11.4

Source: Sebastian (2001: 25). Data from European Commission. Estimates based on *Eurostat* data and forecast for 2000–6.

positive effect on private investment and per capita income in the long run.[19] Moreover, the European Commission has estimated that the impact of EU structural funds on GDP growth and employment has been significant: relative to the GDP forecasted in the absence of this aid, GDP rose in 1999 by 9.9 per cent in Portugal and 3.1 per cent in Spain. In the absence of these funds, economic integration in the Americas is bound to be far slower and unbalanced.

Lesson 11: Financial Institutional Reform Will Not Produce the Necessary Institutional Reforms in Other Areas

Financial institutional reform has not forced institutional changes in other areas (that is, the labour market or fiscal policies). The virtual collapse of the European Monetary System in 1982, caused in part by successive devaluations of the Iberian currencies, showed the limits of financial and monetary instruments to impose institutional reforms in other areas and the difficulties trying to balance domestic and external economic objectives. This is a potential danger. Institutional reforms require action on the part of the governments that are willing to pay the short-term political price for unpopular policies.

Lesson 12: The Democratic Pre-Requirement for Membership is a Powerful Incentive for Democratization

As we have seen, long-standing authoritarian regimes prevented Spain and Portugal from joining European organizations and kept both countries on the fringe of the integration process that began in Europe after the Second World War. The emergence of democratic regimes in both Spain and Portugal in the second half of the 1970s paved the way for the successful consideration of these countries' applications for membership in the European Community. This was a prerequisite. As long as the political setting of these countries remained authoritarian, membership was not feasible. This was a powerful incentive for democratization and also for the consolidation of democratic institutions (that is, the failure of the 1981 *coup d'etat* in Spain and the revolutionary attempt in Portugal). Whereas other agreements (that is, the North American Free Trade Agreement – NAFTA) have left aside such a precondition, including it would provide a powerful incentive for Eastern European and Latin American countries to consolidate their democratic processes and avoid authoritarian temptations.

CONCLUSION

When Portugal and Spain applied to the European Community, most of the political parties in each country supported this decision. The overwhelming majority of the population understood the importance and significance of this step. After years of backwardness and isolation, Spain and Portugal wanted to become players in Europe again. Iberia's place throughout history has been at the centre of Europe. After years of isolationism, it was time to reclaim its place there. The alternative was between the past and the future, between hope and fear, and both countries chose the right path, as time has proven. The interdependence of the markets and the economies offered no other alternative if Portugal and Spain wanted to become competitive in the world market.

Throughout this introductory contribution, we have analysed the main political and economic factors that motivated the accession to the European Community. We have showed that political considerations were the main motivation behind Portugal and Spain's application to join the European Community. Their wish to strengthen the new democratic regimes, coupled with their desire to put an end to the relative isolation that both countries had suffered during the authoritarian years, were critical factors behind their desire to join the European Community.

The economic implications of European integration were also very profound, however, and played an important role in Spain and Portugal's application for membership. The expected static effects of the integration were mixed. In addition, the asymmetry of trade barriers before integration – with Spanish barriers five times higher than those of the European Community – indicated a strong possibility of trade creation. This asymmetry was translated into a risk of difficult adjustment problems for many Iberian manufacturing and agricultural sectors that were not ready for competition.

The advantages and benefits that the Iberian countries expected from their integration into the European Community clearly offset the disadvantages:[20]

(1) EC membership contributed to the termination of secular isolationism of both countries, which had been one of the roots of both countries' economic, cultural, and social backwardness.

(2) Membership has allowed them to confront the international economic recessions of the 1980s–1990s from a stronger position.

Without EC/EU integration both countries would have never attracted as much investment as they did after 1986, and there was the real possibility, given the intensity of the economic crises, that they would have fallen into third-world economic levels.

(3) Portugal and Spain have taken part in the process of European integration. They have become significant players and have been able to influence important decisions (such as the establishment of the cohesion funds) that have had significant consequences for both countries.

(4) The EU framework has better prepared Spain and Portugal to compete in the global market against colossi such as Japan and the United States. European integration has allowed both countries to co-operate and benefit from European education, research, and technological programmes.

(5) Spain and Portugal had traditionally been countries of emigrants. In 1986 there were more than 600,000 Spanish emigrants throughout Europe. EU membership has contributed to better economic performance, which has provided better opportunities for Iberian citizens, and this helped to reverse this historical pattern. In addition, EC/EU membership has made Spanish and Portuguese citizens European citizens, thus ending some of the discrimination that those emigrants had suffered in the past.

(6) EU membership has given the Spanish and Portuguese fish, agricultural, industrial products, and services access to European markets.

(7) EU membership has forced Spain and Portugal to speed up the reform of their productive and economic structures in order to increase the productivity of their labour force.

(8) EU accession helped consolidate new democratic institutions.

(9) Finally, EU membership has increased economic growth, thus improving the standard of living of the Iberian people. As we have seen, after Portugal and Spain joined the Community, GDP rose faster, investment soared, unemployment decreased, inflation was kept under control, and the deficit in the current accounts' balance was sharply reduced. The Iberian governments' actions to liberalize these economies and open their countries to the European Community contributed to this remarkable turnaround. As expected, much of the

expansion was financed from abroad. The flow of foreign direct investment into Spain doubled over the first two years of membership and reached $80 billion in 1986–91.[21] Between 1970 and 1998 foreign investment in Spain grew from one per cent of GDP to more than six per cent.

No matter how impressive these results might seem, Spain and Portugal still have a long way to go to reach the EC average wealth. For instance, as we have mentioned before, since 1986 Portugal's average per capita income has grown from 56 per cent of the EU average to about 74 per cent, while Spain's has grown to 83 per cent. In Spain, unemployment currently stands at 12.5 per cent of the labour force, and is the highest in the Union. Imports have been growing faster than exports and the trade deficit has tripled. The competitive position of both countries is also worrisome. Spending on R&D is still below one per cent of GDP – low compared with the richer EU countries. Spending on training and education of workers is insufficient, too. Low wages – which were one of the most attractive factors for investors – have risen over the last decade. Unit labour costs have therefore been increasing faster than those of these countries' main EU competitors. Indeed, wages are still lower than in Germany, but they are roughly equivalent to those in Britain. Finally, labour flexibility is still hampered by rigid labour laws.

This is not to say, however, that Spain and Portugal are worse off after the integration – as some claim. Economic adjustment was unavoidable and should have taken place anyway – within the European Union or out of it – if both countries wanted to become competitive. EC entry accelerated some tough economic measures, and has aggravated some of the already existing imbalances. Portugal and Spain's entry into the EC/EU, however, attracted billions of dollars in foreign investment that helped to alleviate adjustment problems.

The path towards 'convergence' has been (and will be in the foreseeable future) long and winding. Over the last two decades, Iberian governments have been forced to reform their pension and welfare systems, namely by freezing health spending, cutting subsidies, and setting restrictions on the entitlement to unemployment pay. They have also had to privatize most public companies to more efficiently enforce the laws to stop unemployment fraud – which is still rampant – and to cut excessive bureaucracy. All of these measures led to social problems because the unions did not accept these reforms easily. Some of these processes remain unfinished.

In our view, and on balance, Spain and Portugal have benefited from accession. Since the last century the obsession of Spanish and Portuguese reformists has been to make up the lost ground with modernized Europe. EU membership has been a critical step in this direction. The record of the past 15 years is that this dream is becoming an economic reality. The question of Iberian and/or European citizenship, and its impact on the Portuguese and Spanish, remains open.

NOTES

1. 'After the Fiesta', *The Economist*, 25 April–1 May 1992, p.60.
2. See Tamames (1986: 167).
3. J. Delgado-Moreira, 'European Politics of Citizenship', *The Qualitative Report*, Vol.3, No.3, Sept. 1997 (http://www.nova.edu/ssss/QR/QR3-3/delgado.html).
4. See Guerrero, González and Burguet (1989: 145).
5. See Tamames (1989: 170).
6. See Pou Serradell (1973: 112–15).
7. See Tamames (1986: 168).
8. The Portuguese dictator, António Salazar, approached international relations with a unique world-view called 'lusotropicalism'. In his view a higher power had assigned Portugal the special duty of civilizing non-European populations around the world. As such, Portuguese colonialism was supposedly different from the other European powers. Whereas France and England had used their colonial empires to exploit native peoples, Salazar contended that Portugal had improved life in its colonies by forming new, multiracial nations around the world, and cited the case of Brazil as evidence for this theory. See Manuel (1996b).
9. See Manuel (1995) and Manuel (1996a).
10. A. Barreto, 'Portugal, Europe and Democracy', paper delivered at the conference Portugal and the European Community: Adaptation and Evolution, Department of Portuguese and Brazilian Studies, Brown University, Providence, Rhode Island, 3 Nov.
11. See Barreto, p.24.
12. See discussion by J. Medeiros Ferreira, 'Contemporary Portuguese Foreign Policy', paper delivered at the conference Portugal and the European Community: Adaptation and Evolution, Department of Portuguese and Brazilian Studies, Brown University, Providence, Rhode Island, 3 Nov. 1994, pp.1–4.
13. This section draws from Dinan (1999: 104–9) and Nicholson and East (1987). For a detailed analysis of the impact of integration, see Silva Lopes (1994) and Almarcha Barbado and Schweitzer (1993).
14. See 'Not Quite Kissing Cousins', *The Economist*, 5 May 1990, Vol.315, No.7653, p.21; 'Ever Closer, Inside Europe Union: Spain and Portugal', *The Economist*, 14 Feb. 1998, Vol.346, No.8055, p.53; 'Joining the Club', *The Economist*, 28 May 1988, Vol.307, No.7552, p.14; 'El "Modulo de Portugal" abre en Madrid un espacio para la nueva cultura lusa' [The 'Module Portugal' opens in Madrid a new space for Portuguese culture], *El País*, 18 Oct. 2000.
15. 'Neither good winds' refers to the sandy winds that blow from Spain onto the wine country in the North of Portugal hurting the crops; 'nor good marriages' refers to the union between the Spanish and Portuguese Crowns by marriage. The last King of the Aviz dynasty in Portugal, Henry I, who was also a Cardinal of the Roman Catholic Church, succeeded his nephew, the young King Sebastian (who had been killed in the battle of Alcazar). When Cardinal King Henry died in 1580, the throne was taken by force by Philip II of Spain, who claimed royal legitimacy because his Portuguese mother was the elder sister of Cardinal King Henry. From 1580 to 1640 the Spanish greatly profited from the wealth

generated by Portugal's colonies. This chapter of Iberian unity was a disaster for Portugal. It lasted until 1640 when Portugal reclaimed her independence.

16. See CIS: *Opiniones y actitudes de los españoles ante el proceso de integración europea*, Madrid: 1999, pp.131–2.
17. See Miguel Sebastián (2001: 25–6).
18. As Sebastián (2001: 25–6) indicates, 'this is set to fall slightly in the period 2000–2006, to 1.3% of GDP. The decline reflects, on the one hand, a reduction in structural funds over the new programming horizon (structural funds will represent around 0.3% of EU GDP in 2006, compared with 0.45% in 1999) and, on the other hand, the impact of enlargement (accession aid). This fall-off in funding will clearly affect the long-term growth of the Iberian economies.'
19. See Sebastián (2001: 26).
20. See Gomez Fuentes (1986: 47–8).
21. See 'After the Fiesta', p.3, and Hine (1989: 23).

REFERENCES

Almarcha Barbado, A. and C.-C. Schweitzer (eds.) (1993): *Spain and EC Membership Evaluated*, New York: St. Martin's Press.

Dinan, D. (1999): *Ever Closer Union: An Introduction to European Integration*, Boulder, CO: Lynne Rienner.

Fernández Guerrero, I., A. González and C. Suarez Burguet (1989): 'Spanish External Trade and EEC Preferences', in G.N. Yannopoulos, *European Integration and the Iberian Economies*, New York: St. Martin's Press.

Gómez Fuentes, A. (1986): *Asi Cambiara España: La Batalla del Mercado Común* [How Spain will Change: The Common Market Battle], Madrid: Plaza & Janes Editores.

Guillén, A., S. Álvarez and P. Adao e Silva (2001): 'Redesigning the Spanish and Portuguese Welfare States: The Impact of Accession into the European Union', Paper presented at the conference 'From Isolation to Europe: 15 Years of Spanish and Portuguese Membership in the European Union', Minda de Gunzburg Center for European Studies, Harvard University, 2–3 Nov.

Hine, R.C. (1989): 'Customs Union Enlargement and Adjustment: Spain's Accession to the European Community', *Journal of Common Market Studies*, Vol.XXVIII, No.1.

Manuel, P.C. (1995): *Uncertain Outcome: The Politics of the Portuguese Transition to Democracy*, Lanham, MD: University Press of America.

Manuel, P.C. (1996a): *The Challenges of Democratic Consolidation in Portugal: Political, Economic and Military Issues, 1976–1991*, Westport, CO: Praeger.

Manuel, P.C. (1996b): 'Foreign Policy and Regime Change in Portugal, 1960–1991', *Perspectives on Political Science*, Vol.25, No.2 (Spring).

Nicholson, F. and R. East (1987): *From the Six to the Twelve: The Enlargement of the European Community*, Chicago, IL: St. James Press.

Pou Serradell, V. (1973): *España y la Europe Comunitaria* [Spain and the European Community], Navarra: EUNSA.

Royo, Sebastián (2002): '*A New Century of Corporatism?' Corporatism in Southern Europe: Spain and Portugal in Comparative Perspective*, Westport, CT: Praeger.

Sebastián, Miguel (2001): 'Spain in the EU: Fifteen Years May not be Enough', Paper presented at the conference 'From Isolation to Europe: 15 Years of Spanish and Portuguese Membership in the European Union', Minda de Gunzburg Center for European Studies, Harvard University, 2–3 Nov.

Silva Lopes, Jose da (ed.) (1994): *Portugal and EC Membership Evaluated*, New York: St Martin's Press.

Tamames, R. (1986): *Guía del Mercado Común Europeo: España en la Europe de los Doce* [Guide of the European Common Market: Spain in the Europe of the Twelve], Madrid: Alianza Editorial.

Shaping, not Making, Democracy: The European Union and the Post-Authoritarian Political Transformations of Spain and Portugal

ROBERT M. FISHMAN

In the long quarter of a century elapsed since the transitions to democracy in Spain and Portugal, the two Iberian neighbours have undergone fundamentally important political transformations that have thoroughly redefined the countries' *regimes* and the structure of their *states*.[1] The democratic regimes installed in the 1970s have lasted far longer and attained a vastly greater degree of stability than earlier democratic episodes in those countries, but the implications of this success extend well beyond the national borders and histories of the two Iberian cases. In the post-authoritarian period, both Iberian states have experienced thorough *external* transformations: for Spain, its full incorporation into the major international structures of Europe and the West – not only the European Union but also the North Atlantic Treaty Organization (NATO) – thus breaking with the country's prior relative autonomy from such structures as reflected in its neutrality in both world wars; and for Portugal, the rapid – if historically late – end of its colonial empire and its full incorporation into Europe. The Spanish state has also experienced a massive *internal* transformation: the thoroughgoing, if asymmetric, process of devolution that has turned a highly centralized political and administrative system into the multilingual and (for a minority) multinational State of Autonomies. In Portugal the most fundamental internal transformation of the state occurred quickly after the demise of authoritarianism with the rather wide-ranging purge of the state apparatus,[2] an experience with no parallel in the larger Iberian case. Similarly, the Spanish experience of thoroughgoing devolution holds no equivalent in Portugal, where regionalization was defeated in referendum (Gallagher 1999; Rodrigues Lopes 2001). The democratic regimes that have emerged in both countries are substantially different as well.

The two Iberian transitions were thoroughly dissimilar despite the shared experience of incorporation into Europe once democracy had been consolidated.[3] The linkages among the processes of internal and external transformation are far more than a mere chronological accident, but that is not to say that a rigorously causal ordering of this interrelationship is easily ascertained. In this essay I focus on one aspect of that interrelationship, the connections between the two Iberian countries' successful democratic transitions and their incorporation into Europe. To what extent can Spain and Portugal's evident success in inaugurating and consolidating democratic regimes be attributed in one fashion or another to their roughly simultaneous – and also successful – effort to achieve membership in the European Community? As we shall see, the argument has been made that the two processes – European integration and democratization – are thoroughly intertwined; indeed, some analysts have seen the attraction of EC membership as the more deep-seated of the two phenomena, motivating and underpinning the turn to democracy.

In this essay I argue, instead, that the forces and attitudes shaping the politics of transition in the two Iberian cases should be understood as prior to and deeper than those underpinning the ultimate form taken by the politics of European integration (although clearly EC membership had been pursued by some actors prior to democratization). The Spanish and Portuguese democracies have been shaped, but not made, by the successful effort of both countries to achieve full EC membership (Schmitter 1996).[4] The process of European integration has interacted with a wide variety of domestic political and economic factors, thus shaping the new democracies. European integration has not eliminated major differences between the cases, however, and above all it cannot explain the broader pattern of political transformation with its clearly identifiable (yet remarkably dissimilar) underpinnings in the two cases.

The understandable temptation to causally link the Iberian democratic transitions to internationally rooted and domestically supported pressures for European integration has long been evident in scholarly work. Poulantzas' stimulating, but empirically insubstantial, claims in *The Crisis of the Dictatorships* (1976) stand as an early example of such work. Many accomplished authors – including Laurence Whitehead (1991, 1996), Geoffrey Pridham (1991, 1996), and Charles Powell (1996), to name but a few – have since taken up the challenge of providing greater empirical substance and rigor to the search for interconnections between Iberian democratization and international processes, such as the countries' external redefinition via the process of European integration. For quite evident reasons, the literature on the international and external dimensions of Portuguese democratization has tended to emphasize decolonization and the global strategic implications of socialist revolution in a country belonging to NATO, rather than the push for membership in the European Community as such (Opello 1998; Costa Pinto 1998). Discussions of the international components of Spain's democratic transition, in contrast, have tended to focus either on the diffuse importance of Europe as a model of democratic political and social arrangements (Pérez Díaz 1993) or, more directly, on the interconnection between regime transition and the attraction of EC membership. For this reason, we will focus here somewhat more heavily on the Spanish case.

A growing body of scholarly work among students of the Spanish case focuses precisely on the interconnections between regime transition and European integration. Perhaps the most audacious claim in this literature is that of Jonathan Story and Benny Pollack (1991) who conceive of democratization and European integration as essentially two sides of the same coin: For these authors, 'The struggle for the shape of Spain's domestic future thus merged into a struggle for Spain's external orientation'.[5] This attempt to argue for a seamless interconnection between democratic transition and European integration leads Story and Pollack to their rather startling assertion redefining the last decade and a half of Franco's authoritarian rule: 'Spain's transition, at its outer limits, lasted from 1959 to 1986, if we include here the "pre-transition" phase as well as early democratic consolidation.'[6] Perhaps no other single claim in the literature can so effectively underscore the danger of scholarly efforts to inextricably entangle the process of regime change with the long evolution in Spain's relationship to the European Community.

The historical antecedents of Spain's ultimate incorporation into the EC are indeed to be found in the Franco period but that is not to say that the approach towards Europe signified that the regime was anything other than authoritarian during the long – and for many, highly repressive – 16 years between 1959 and Franco's death in November 1975. Indeed, the most important conceptual and theoretical works in the comparative and international literature on authoritarian regimes were written by a Spanish political scientist during the 1960s and 1970s[7] – when Story and Pollack place the Franco system in its 'pre-transition' phase. It is worth noting that when Juan Linz proposed that authoritarian rule could assume the form of a relatively un-institutionalized 'situation' as opposed to a more predictable and regularized 'regime', he did so on the basis of the Brazilian (Linz 1973) and not the Spanish case. For most political actors in Spain during the 1960s and early 1970s, the attraction offered by Europe unfortunately provided no guarantee that the country's political trajectory was headed inexorably toward a prompt return to democracy. Numerous challenges of democratic transition – many of them unconnected or at best loosely connected to European integration – remained to be confronted by pro-democracy actors, not the least of which was the need to de-legitimize authoritarian rule for many of its core supporters.

In criticizing the claim of a seamless interconnection between democratization and European integration, a thorough merging of one process into the other, I do not mean to question the undeniable importance of exploring genuine linkages between the two phenomena. In order to do so, however, it is essential to distinguish analytically between the two processes and to advance only those empirical claims that can be supported by evidence. Clearly, regime transitions to democracy do not in principle require European integration – or any other external transformation of the states in which they take place. Of course, the goal of full Spanish membership in the European Community did come to be explicitly linked by the EC to the European requirement for democratic rule, but that is not to say that Spain's political regime was the only significant issue in the country's long approach towards full membership. It is worth remembering that both Portugal and Greece attained more favourable arrangements with the EC than Spain during the period of authoritarian rule in those three Southern European countries.

Perhaps the most systematically reasoned analysis of the interconnections between these two processes is the carefully researched and elegantly argued comparative study of Berta Álvarez-Miranda Navarro (1995). Álvarez-Miranda takes as the starting point of her analysis the clear contrast between Spain and Southern Europe's other two late democratizers, Portugal and Greece, both in the nature of their regime transitions and in their political handling of European integration after the return of democratic rule. As she stresses, Spain's new democracy enjoyed a pro-European consensus among all relevant political forces, whereas both Portugal and Greece experienced division and debate among relevant political parties over the issue of EC membership. The three countries had experienced fundamentally different regime transitions – in part as a result of disparities in the way democratic forces were able to approach the challenge of delegitimizing authoritarian rule for many of its core supporters. In both Portugal and Greece, clear military failures of the incumbent regimes generated what I have called a crisis of failure, whereas in the Spanish case, absent any military humiliation or equivalent calamity, democratic forces contributed instead to solidifying the regime's crisis of historical obsolescence (Fishman 1990). In the Portuguese case, the crisis of failure was especially strong, thus engendering a Skocpolian state crisis[8] that opened a period of social revolutionary mobilizations.[9]

In Spain, lacking such a crisis of external failure, opposition actors and democratic reformers within the regime engaged in tireless efforts to build consensus and guarantee moderation, thus thoroughly undercutting Francoism's founding legitimization formula: its claim that only authoritarian repression could guarantee peace and order in a society that had been divided into two bitterly opposed camps in the 1930s. Nearly four years after the regime-initiating democratic elections of June 1977, the serious military coup attempt of 23 February 1981 reminded all Spaniards how crucial it had been (and remained) to undercut the legitimacy of the authoritarian formula in terms compelling not only to principled supporters of democracy, but also to potential defenders of the Francoist past within the armed forces and elsewhere in the Spanish state. As Álvarez-Miranda argues, the exigencies of transition confronted by Spanish political actors led to a broadly inclusive consensus in favour of EC membership. In Portugal (and Greece) the fundamental contours of regime transition were thoroughly different, the political pressures for consensus were far weaker, and major political forces, especially on the Left, opposed EC membership. Much more could be said on differences among the three transitions – and on the enormous disparity among the cases in the form taken by popular protest during the transition years – but for Álvarez-Miranda it is Francoism's crisis of obsolescence that assumes special importance in accounting for Spain's pro-EC consensus.

Álvarez-Miranda argues for an explanatory connection between the Spanish regime transition and the country's pro-European consensus, but she inverts the causal ordering assumed by others. She presents democratic, and other political commitments, rather than socially or economically based interests as the fundamental explanation for Spain's broad embrace of European integration. She elaborates this interpretation in introducing her comparative examination of abundant evidence:

> The definition of interests by the relevant economic actors, expressed by the interest groups that supposedly represent them, do

not seem to respond to their (expected) position in the EC economy. The dominant influence of political parties over interest groups which explains this reality inverts the direction of the causal nexus, thus it would not be social pressures that determine the attitudes of parties toward [European] integration, but rather the parties which influence the opinion of economic groups [Álvarez-Miranda 1995: 26].

In the view of Álvarez-Miranda, European integration was an especially appealing objective for Spanish advocates of democracy because it simultaneously (1) underscored the moderation and consensual behaviour of the country's principal political actors, (2) introduced disincentives protecting against a return to dictatorship that would have frozen or reversed the plans for EC membership, and (3) highlighted a clear symbolic break with the Francoist past in a newly democratic political system otherwise in search of differentiating markers clearly separating it from the Francoist past. Thus Álvarez-Miranda finds Spain's broad embrace of European integration to be largely motivated by the prior features and distinctive challenges of its democratic regime transition. By the same logic, she ties the lack of consensus in Portugal (and Greece) to prior political agendas rooted in the nationally distinctive processes of regime transition.

Much additional empirical work supports at least the rough outlines of the Álvarez-Miranda argument. One of the least known but most important sources of relevant evidence is the careful study by Robert Martínez of business elites (Martínez 1993). Martínez surveyed a broad sample of employers and business association leaders in the early years of Spain's new democracy, asking them a wide range of questions concerning political transition, European integration, and associational politics. His findings introduce substantial doubts over the degree to which an allegedly strong underlying business commitment to EC membership might help explain democratic transition and consolidation, as some have assumed. Martínez finds majority, but by no means unanimous, business support for European integration. This relatively broad support is not based, in most instances, however, on specific calculations of the expected consequences of EC membership on employers' firms or sectors: only 35.8 per cent of the employers and 33.9 per cent of the business association leaders expected direct positive effects as a result of full European membership. How, then, does one explain the broader business support for integration? A combination of expected indirect and long-term effects, as well as a tendency to accept and adjust to trends seen as inevitable, probably explains the survey findings. On the issue of regime change, Martínez finds that a majority of employers in 1981 continued to look back on the Franco regime somewhat favourably, but a larger majority also supported the reform-oriented transition to democracy, viewing it as 'the only game in town'.[10]

The implications of the Martínez study are clear: Business support for European integration was not strong enough to motivate employers to enthusiastically adopt the democratic banner as a way of attaining EC membership. Moreover, employer support for democratization was too weak and passive to account for the broad consensus in favour of Spain's democratic transition. The search for an explanation accounting for democratic transition and consolidation does not lead us to employers and their economically based attitudes toward European integration. The available empirical findings on business attitudes strongly support the Álvarez-Miranda thesis that political attitudes toward democracy explain – rather than follow – Spain's broadly shared embrace of EC membership.

Further empirical evidence confirms the interpretation offered by Matinez. A major study on attitudes toward the European Community carried out by the *Centro de Investigaciones Sociológicas* (CIS) in 1988 showed a degree of Euroscepticism within the ranks of Spanish business: among the employers and executives interviewed, just 54 per cent indicated that EC membership had produced positive consequences, whereas in the overall sample 61 per cent of those interviewed saw membership as positive. In the occupational breakdown provided by the CIS, only agricultural workers proved less pro-European than employers and executives (CIS 1989). The economic pull of EC membership was less universally felt within the business sector than many have assumed. The weak basis for arguing that economic forces generated the political consensus in favour of European integration leaves us with the obvious need to examine more carefully political attitudes toward democracy – and Europe.

Important work on the legitimacy of Spain's democratic regime underscores the strong attitudinal support for democracy. The richly comparative analysis of Maravall (1997) and complementary systematic work of Morlino and Montero (1995) as well as Linz and colleagues (1981) all point in the same direction. Spain's new democracy quickly attained a remarkably high level of support. Over 70 per cent of the Spanish public consistently viewed democracy as the best political system for their country. Moreover, this commitment to democracy tended to grow, if only a bit, over time, and it proved to stand increasingly independent from the often critical assessments of democratic performance. Spaniards were broadly committed to democracy even if they did not always think it proved effective at addressing the country's problems. Spanish support for democracy has been somewhat more widespread than the embrace of EC membership. The 1988 CIS study reports than in the period from November 1986 through November 1988, the percentage of Spaniards expressing the view that membership had been a good thing ranged from a low of 46 per cent in February 1987 to a high of 60 per cent in November 1986. This is not to say that Spaniards were opposed to EC membership; most of them favoured it. Yet that support was somewhat less broadly shared, and almost certainly, somewhat less deeply felt, than the embrace of democracy itself.

Especially suggestive is the historical pattern of oscillation in stated support for democracy. In the wake of the menacing coup attempt of 23 February 1981, the legitimacy of Spain's then-endangered democracy actually increased, attaining the level of 81 per cent in the finding of Juan Linz and his collaborators at DATA, the Spanish survey research firm (Linz *et al.* 1981). When push came to shove, Spaniards overwhelmingly placed themselves on the side of democracy thus underscoring their strong commitment to such a regime. No equivalent reaffirmation (and increase) of democratic principles appears evident at crucial moments in the country's process of European integration. Spaniards did not require the achievement of EC membership status in order to solidify their commitment to democracy. The country's commitment to a democratic regime appears somewhat deeper than, slightly broader than, and – for most – also prior to, the also important support for EC membership. Moreover, the underlying forces already leading Spain in the direction of democracy in the 1975–77 period were in many respects stronger, and the added inducements afforded by the promise of EC membership were substantially weaker, than is often assumed.

One related point merits consideration: Available evidence quite directly suggests that the appeal of Europe was strongly rooted in prior political concerns or calculations. The (generally favourable) image Spaniards held of Europe in 1988 emphasized culture and democracy as fundamental European traits. The Spanish public was far more likely to link development, wealth, and technology to Japan and the United States (CIS 1989). Support for Europe was strongly rooted in cultural and democratic values or assumptions. Important recent cross-national work on the underpinnings of public support for the European Union yields findings highly relevant to this discussion. Through rigorous quantitative analysis, Ignacio Sanchez-Cuenca (2000) shows that pro-European sentiments are built on an implicit comparative assessment, weighing the relative value or performance of national versus EU political institutions. Attitudes toward Europe, in the logic formulated by Sanchez-Cuenca, are constructed by each member state's citizenry, on the basis of prior judgements concerning their national political arena and institutions. The thrust of Sanchez-Cuenca's important contribution offers broad support to the argument developed here: For Spaniards – and Portuguese – the political motivations guiding their assessment of Europe during the crucial years leading up to EC membership were strongly shaped by their deeply held attitudes toward democracy and regime transition, attitudes formed within the context of the distinctive political experience of each case.

The external redefinition of the Spanish state cannot explain the pattern taken by that country's political transition, but this is not to say that Spain's process of regime transition would be unaffected by issues of state transformation. The inward redefinition of the Spanish state, leading to the asymmetric State of the Autonomies, was without question an absolute requirement for the consolidation of the new post-Franco political system. This is not the place to review the issue in depth, but a highly cursory mention does seem appropriate given the extraordinary importance of this dimension of state redefinition for democracy's stability in the larger of the two Iberian countries (Linz and Stepan 1996: 98–115).[11] Successful negotiations between moderate Catalan nationalists and nationwide political forces leading to a broadly acceptable Catalan Statute of Autonomy helped to guarantee the enduring peace of Catalan society and the dual 'national' identity – both Catalan and Spanish – of many Catalans. The problematic and less consensual process leading to a Basque Statute of Autonomy has helped to contain, but not eliminate, the serious terrorist movement rooted in the drive for Basque independence.

The general adoption of (less extensive) autonomy provisions for other regions throughout Spain has thoroughly redesigned the political and administrative contours of a formerly centralized state. For Francoist loyalists this process represented perhaps the gravest threat of democratic rule, as they consistently argued in their opinion-shaping mouthpieces such as the then-daily *El Alcazar* in the period immediately prior to the 1981 coup. The effort to resist state decentralization represented a central battle cry for die-hard anti-democrats in the early years of Spain's post-Franco political regime. At the same time, opposition veterans in

Catalonia and the Basque Country would clearly have rejected the new regime had it failed to accommodate their autonomy aspirations. This helps explain why Linz and Stepan date the end of the democratic regime transition with the approval of the Catalan and Basque autonomy statutes, whereas they place the achievement of full democratic consolidation at the moment of successful government prosecution of the 1981 coup leaders. European integration, despite its pervasive importance for Spanish politics and society, cannot so easily be bound up in the process of democratic transition and consolidation.

If one accepts this analysis, does that leave the European Community – or the broader European context – as largely irrelevant factors in the post-authoritarian transformations of Spain and Portugal? In examining the evidence thus far, we have focused primarily on the larger of the two Iberian cases since the strongest scholarly claims linking European integration to democratic transition are found in the literature on Spain. In examining the ways in which Europe has shaped democracy, however, there is no reason to privilege one Iberian case over the other and thus we shall address both national experiences.

The strong relevance of Europe for the direction taken by democracy in both national cases is unmistakable – despite continuing large differences between Spain and Portugal. Moreover, as many analysts have noted, the broader European context has been strongly supportive of both countries' democratic transformations in numerous ways not directly linked to the European Union as such. Whereas the European context of the interwar years proved highly detrimental to the survival of Iberian democracy, the post-war climate of Europe represented an enormously favourable environment. Europe as a political example was probably far more important for both Spain and Portugal than the European Union as a set of material incentives favouring the post-Franco regime transition (Pérez Diaz 1993; Powell 1996).

Wherein, then, lies the importance of formal European integration for Spain and Portugal's post-authoritarian democracies? The answer is found throughout their political systems, societies, and economies (da Silva Lopes 1993; Barbado 1993). The external redefinition of both states generated by European Union membership has created a pervasive set of influences reshaping, but not making, Iberian democracies. Paradoxically, Portugal may have been more broadly reshaped by this external transformation than Spain, even though the pro-European consensus was historically wider in the larger Iberian country. The economy of Portugal has significantly outperformed that of Spain in the years elapsed since the democratic transitions, especially on the crucial point of unemployment, and EC membership has been part of the larger configuration of factors generating that favourable Portuguese outcome.[12] The European structural funds have clearly benefited Portugal more than Spain, although the larger issue concerning economic consequences of membership is a highly complex one – especially for the agricultural sector (Marques-Mendes 1993; Avillez 1993). One crucial additional point deserves emphasis: EC regulations and the models afforded by member states concerning the potentially important role of public enterprises in a modern market-oriented economy have likely been more important in the Portuguese than the Spanish case given the history of state ownership in the two countries. Although the early revolutionary wave of nationalizations was largely reversed,[13] public enterprises have played a larger role in post-transition Portugal than in Spain, and for that reason EC regulations on state involvement in the economy have been especially important in the smaller of the two Iberian cases.

In a more general vein, Spanish and Portuguese bureaucracies, courts, and policy-makers are all constantly engaged with EU institutions, counterparts, regulations, and expectations. In crucial instances legally guaranteed social rights afforded by European Union law have decisively expanded more limited provisions found in Spanish law (López 2001). In other institutional terrains, extending well beyond the most obvious examples such as regional development funds, the positive effects of EU membership on both countries have been pervasive. It remains to be seen how thoroughly Iberian state structures will be remade by the institutional engagement with Europe, but many residents of the peninsula hope that the recasting will prove both deep and broad.

One important cautionary note deserves emphasis: Europe does not offer one unique set of models and solutions for countries such as Spain and Portugal attempting to 'catch up' with their most developed EU counterparts. Portuguese and Spaniards constantly face the question of which Europe they wish to draw lessons or examples from. The overall set of EU member countries is characterized by large differences in policies, institutions, and performance on a wide range of questions including employment, welfare state and family provisions, and demographic trends. The goal of European integration cannot eclipse the need to critically assess the array of models or configurations presented by more economically advanced member states.[14] Although Spain is the more 'advanced' of the Iberian countries by most conventional economic indicators, on several important measures or phenomena, such as female participation in the labour force and the matching of positive employment growth with an improvement in demographic trends, Portugal is closer than Spain to the most 'advanced' northern European models. Differences between the two cases in their highly dissimilar transitions to democracy may well help to explain why on some crucial indicators Portugal has come closer than Spain to 'leap-frogging' into the group of Europe's most successful countries.

Both countries have, on occasion, received reprimands of one form or another for practices held to violate European Union policy. The pattern manifested by such cases is highly instructive. In the most recent publicized instances of Iberian run-ins with EU regulations, both Portugal and Spain have received formal notification of such violations during the summer of 2002. With the support of the current centre-right *Partido Social Democrata* (PSD) government in Lisbon, Brussels has cited Portugal for an unacceptably high budget deficit, thus increasing the incentives in favour of budgetary policies already favoured by that government.[15] The Spanish government has been the subject of a vote of condemnation in the European Parliament during the summer of 2002 as a result of a border incident that was heavily covered by the Portuguese press while receiving scant attention within Spain. Left-wing Portuguese activists, bound for a demonstration in Seville being held during an EU summit there in late June, were stopped at the border by Spanish police and denied access to the country – in apparent violation of the Schengen provisions. A deputy in the Portuguese Parliament, himself a participant in the group denied access, protested to the Spanish authorities involved that his rights as a European citizen were being violated. In a scene captured by video cameras and shown repeatedly on Portuguese television, the deputy was then beaten by Spanish police. The incident at the border quickly became a theme of public debate in Portugal but in Spain it went virtually unnoticed, even after the vote in the European Parliament had taken place.

The contrast between these two encounters with Europe may well create an exaggerated sense of the differences between the two Iberian cases. Both Spain and Portugal are consolidated democracies with a broad array of legal guarantees, and typically they have been in good standing as EU members. Nonetheless, the unmistakable conclusion one must draw is that the pattern of contrast between the two Iberian neighbours manifested in these two (exceptional) incidents could be more easily 'predicted' by a retrospective review of their dissimilar transitions than by a thorough-going analysis of the intrinsic logics of European integration. Portuguese and Spaniards have addressed the challenges of European integration through the lens provided by their two rather different sets of post-authoritarian political experiences.

Following this line of reasoning, I wish to briefly suggest one way in which EU membership could potentially produce quite unexpected negative consequences for Spanish or Portuguese society. The often voiced goal of 'modernization', that Spanish elites and many in the broader public have advocated with great energy and conviction, is conventionally seen in contemporary Spain to be best pursued by the full pursuit of European integration. There is a great deal to be said for this strategy, including the fact that no compelling alternative seems to exist. Nonetheless, it is quite unclear that the sincere pursuit of 'modernization' via EU membership has encouraged Spanish elites to effectively focus on all of the society's most pressing problems and failures. The extraordinarily low Spanish birth rate and the accompanying spectre of drastic demographic decline, the relative unaffordability of housing for young workers (and the unemployed), the low investment in research and development by Spanish (and Portuguese) firms, the extraordinarily inadequate public investment in the university system – to name but a few of the society's most pressing problems – have not been adequately addressed.

Successful 'modernization' addressing these and related problems requires not only an external but also an internal reordering of much state behaviour and policy. Portugal, as well, faces its distinctive problems, including inadequate investment in research and development, but arguably Portuguese elites – perhaps in part as an indirect result of their distinctive transition[16] – may have done a better job than their Spanish counterparts at focusing on their own society's specific challenges in the broader context of European integration. The extraordinary vitality of small business in the Portuguese case and the significant public investment in the country's university system stand as but two illustrations of this broader record of notable successes. The ability of Iberian elites to simultaneously look outward to the multiple Europes and inward to their societies' distinctive problems will ultimately help to determine whether EU membership can in the future positively reshape the politics and societies of Portugal and Spain. Europe as a generalized, diffuse, and undifferentiated image of 'modernization' cannot provide Iberian policy-makers with a sufficiently concrete set of guidelines to orient efforts at addressing nationally specific problems.

NOTES

1. I take as a given the usefulness of distinguishing analytically between regime – which is to say the rules governing access to political power – and state – which is to say the typically enduring administrative, coercive, and judicial structures through which power holders exercise (or encounter institutional restraints on) their rule. I elaborate the relevance of this longstanding (yet often forgotten) social science distinction for the study of Southern Europe's democratic transitions in 'Rethinking State and Regime: Southern Europe's Transition to Democracy' (April 1990). For a conceptually innovative and empirically wide-ranging analysis of democratic transition and consolidation that incorporates both regime and state dimensions, see Linz and Stepan (1996). The analytical distinction between state and regime has assumed growing importance in comparative studies of political development and change. See the important works by Ertman (1997) and Goodwin (2001).

2. For an excellent discussion of the purge process, see Costa Pinto (2001). For a parallel discussion of the Spanish case strongly emphasizing the impact of collective memories of the civil war, see Aguilar (2001). See also Costa Pinto (1998).

3. I emphasize these differences in 'Rethinking State and Regime'.

4. See especially p.33.

5. Ibid., p.125.

6. Ibid., p.151.

7. For extensive analysis and a wealth of bibliographic references, see Linz (1975).

8. The discussion of Theda Skocpol on state crisis and revolution in her now classic *States and Social Revolutions* (1979) remains required reading for understanding the Portuguese transition.

9. See the excellent study on urban workers by Durán Muñoz (2000). On social revolution in the Portuguese agricultural sector, see the outstanding work of Bermeo (1996).

10. See pp.160–61.

11. For a stimulating argument attempting to identify economic explanations for the contrasts between Basque and Catalan nationalism, see Medrano (1995). For a recent analysis of the implications of decentralization for the identities of Spaniards, see Martínez-Herrera (2002). For an important analysis of how Spaniards maintain their multiple identities – national, regional, and European – see Medrano and Gutiérrez (2001).

12. Limitations of space and time make it impossible to address this question in appropriate depth in this context.

13. On the handling of public enterprise privatizations in the two cases, see Menchero (2001).

14. For excellent studies on the wide range of variation among European states on these questions, see Esping-Andersen and Regini (eds.) (2000) Esping-Andersen (1999).

15. The public debate over the exact amount of the deficit recorded by Portugal in the 2001 budget has been a theme of much importance in Portuguese politics during 2002.

16. I am currently working on several components of this theme, well aware that many will see this assertion as rather controversial.

REFERENCES

Aguilar, P. (2001): 'Justice, Politics and Memory in the Spanish Transition', in A. Barahona de Brito *et al.* (eds.), *The Politics of Memory: Transitional Justice in Democratizing Societies*, Oxford: Oxford University Press, pp.92–118.

Álvarez-Miranda Navarro, B. (1995): *Los partidos políticos en Grecia, Portugal y España ante la Comunidad Europea: explicación comparada del consenso europeísta español*

[Political Parties in Greece, Portugal and Spain before the European Community: A Comparative Explanation of the Spanish Consensus on Europe], Madrid: Instituto Juan March.

Avillez, F. (1993): 'Portuguese Agriculture and the Common Agricultural Policy', in J. da Silva Lopes (ed.), *Portugal and EC Membership Evaluated*, London: Pinter.

Barbado, A.A. (ed.) (1993): *Spain and EC Membership Evaluated*, London: Pinter.

Bermeo, N. (1996): *The Revolution within the Revolution: Workers' Control in Rural Portugal*, Princeton, NJ: Princeton University Press.

Centro de Investigaciones Sociológicas [CIS] (1989): *La opinión pública española ante Europa y los europeos* [Spanish Public Opinion Before Europe and the Europeans]: Madrid: CIS, 1989.

Costa Pinto, A. (1998): 'Saneamentos Políticos e Movimentos Radicais de Direta na Transicão para a Democracia, 1974–1976' [Political Purges and Radical Right-wing Movements in the Democratic Transition, 1974–1976], in F. Rosas (ed.), *Portugal e a Transicão para a Democracia (1974–1976)* [Portugal and the Transition to Democracy], Lisbon: Edicoes Colibri, pp.29–48.

Costa Pinto, A. (ed.) (1998): *Modern Portugal*, Palo Alto, CA: Society for the Promotion of Science and Scholarship.

Costa Pinto, A. (2001): 'Settling Accounts with the Past in a Troubled Transition to Democracy: The Portuguese Case', in A. Barahona de Brito *et al.* (eds.), *The Politics of Memory: Transitional Justice in Democratizing Societies*, Oxford: Oxford University Press, pp.65–91.

Durán Muñoz, R. (2000): *Contención y Transgressión: las movilizaciones sociales y el estado en las transiciones española y portuguesa* [Contention and Transgression: Social Mobilization and the State in the Spanish and Portuguese Transitions], Madrid: Centro de Estudios Politicos y Constitucionales.

Ertman, T. (1997): *Birth of the Leviathan: Building States and Regimes in Medieval and Early Modern Europe*, Cambridge: Cambridge University Press.

Esping-Andersen, G. (1999): *Social Foundations of Postindustrial Economies*, Oxford: Oxford University Press.

Esping-Andersen, G. and M. Regini (eds.) (2000): *Why Deregulate Labour Markets?* Oxford: Oxford University Press.

Fishman, R.M. (1990): 'Rethinking State and Regime: Southern Europe's Transition to Democracy', *World Politics* 42/3, pp.422–40.

Gallagher, T. (1999): 'Unconvinced by Europe of the Regions: The 1998 Regionalization Referendum in Portugal', *South European Society and Politics* 4/1, pp.132–48.

Goodwin, J. (2001): *No Way Out: States and Revolutionary Movements, 1945–1991*, Cambridge: Cambridge University Press.

Linz, J. (1973): 'The Future of an Authoritarian Situation or the Institutionalization of an Authoritarian Regime: The Case of Brazil', in A. Stepan, *Authoritarian Brazil: Origins, Policies and Future*, New Haven, CT: Yale University Press.

Linz, J. (1975): 'Totalitarian and Authoritarian Regimes', in F. Greenstein and N. Polsby (eds.), *Handbook of Political Science Vol.3 Macropolitical Theory*, Reading, MA: Addison-Wesley, pp.175–411.

Linz, J. *et al.* (1981): *Informe sociológico sobre el cambio político en España 1975/1981 (Informe FOESSA)* [Sociological Information on Political Change in Spain 1975/1981], Madrid: Euramerica.

Linz, J. and A. Stepan (1996): *Problems of Democratic Transition and Consolidation*, Baltimore, MD: Johns Hopkins University Press.

López, J. (2001): 'Famiglia e condivisione dei ruoli in Spagna' [Family and the Subdivision of the Roles in Spain], in *Lavoro e Diritto* [Work and Law] XV/1, Bologna: il Mulino, pp.163–85.

Maravall, J.M. (1997): 'Democracies and Democrats', in Maravall (ed.), *Regimes, Politics* and Markets: Democratization and Economic Change in Southern Europe and Eastern Europe, Oxford: Oxford University Press, pp.200–44.

Marques-Mendes, A.J. (1993): 'The Development of the Portuguese Economy in the Context of the EC', in J. da Silva Lopes (ed.), Portugal and EC Membership Evaluated, London: Pinter, pp.7–29.

Martínez, R.E. (1993): Business and Democracy in Spain, Westport, CT: Praeger.

Martínez-Herrera, E. (2002): 'From Nation-building to Building Identification with Political Communities: Consequences of Political Decentralization in Spain, the Basque Country, Catalonia and Galicia, 1978–2001', European Journal of Political Research 41/4, pp.421–53.

Medrano, J.D. (1995): Divided Nations: Class, Politics and Nationalism in the Basque Country and Catalonia, Ithaca, NY: Cornell University Press.

Medrano, J.D. and P. Gutiérrez (2001): 'Nested Identities: National and European Identity in Spain', Ethnic and Racial Studies 24/5, pp.753–78.

Menchero, M.A. (2001): El Proceso de Reforma del Sector Público en el Sur de Europa: Estudio Comparativo de España y Portugal [The Reform Process of the Public Sector in Southern Europe: A Comparative Study of Spain and Portugal], Madrid: Instituto Juan March.

Morlino, L. and J.R. Montero (1995), 'Legitimacy and Democracy in Southern Europe', in R. Gunther, P.N. Diamandouros and H.-J. Puhle (eds.), The Politics of Democratic Consolidation: Southern Europe in Comparative Perspective, Baltimore, MD: Johns Hopkins University Press, pp.231–60.

Opello, W. (1998): 'Portugal: A Case Study of International Determinants of Regime Transition', in Pridham (1991), pp.84–102.

Pérez Díaz, V. (1993): The Return of Civil Society, Cambridge, MA: Harvard University Press.

Poulantzas (1976): The Crisis of the Dictatorships, London: New Left Books.

Powell, C. (1996): 'International aspects of Democratization: The Case of Spain', in The International Dimensions of Democratization: Europe and the Americas, Oxford: Oxford University Press, pp.285–314.

Pridham, G. (1991): Encouraging Democracy: The International Context of Regime Transition in Southern Europe, Leicester: Leicester University Press.

Pridham, G. (1995): 'The International Context of Democratic Consolidation: Southern Europe in Comparative Perspective', in R. Gunther, P.N. Diamandouros and H.-J. Puhle (eds.), The Politics of Democratic Consolidation: Southern Europe in Comparative Perspective, Baltimore, MD: Johns Hopkins University Press, pp.166–203.

Rodrigues Lopes, E. (ed.) (2001): Una Experiencia Única, 1998, MPU: Um Movimento Cívico contra a Regionalizacao [A Unique Experience, 1998, MPU: A Civic Movement Against Regionalization], Porto: Porto Editora.

Sanchez-Cuenca, I. (2000): 'The Political Basis of Support for European Integration', European Union Politics 1/2, pp.147–71.

Schmitter, P. (1996): 'The Influence of the International Context upon the Choice of National Institutions and Policies', in L. Whitehead (ed.), The International Dimensions of Democratization: Europe and the Americas, Oxford: Oxford University Press, pp.26–54.

da Silva Lopes, J. (ed.) (1993): Portugal and EC Membership Evaluated, London: Pinter.

Skocpol, T. (1979): States and Social Revolutions, Cambridge: Cambridge University Press.

Story, J. and B. Pollack (1991): 'Spain's Transition: Domestic and External Linkages', in G. Pridham (ed.), Encouraging Democracy: The International Context of Regime Transition in Southern Europe, New York: St. Martin's Press, pp.125–58.

Whitehead, L. (1991): 'Democracy by Convergence and Southern Europe: A Comparative Politics Perspective', in G. Pridham (ed.), Encouraging Democracy: The International Context of Regime Transition in Southern Europe, New York: St. Martin's Press, pp.45–61.

Whitehead, L. (ed.) (1996): The International Dimensions of Democratization: Europe and the Americas, Oxford: Oxford University Press.

European Integration and Civil Society in Spain

KERSTIN HAMANN

INTRODUCTION

Spain joined the European Community in 1986,[1] about a decade after the beginning of the country's transition to democracy. Many observers had by then concluded that Spanish democracy was consolidated and that the prospect of becoming a member of the European Community had contributed to this consolidation process. At the same time, however, Spanish civil society was, and still is, notoriously weak. This is a somewhat curious phenomenon given that the process of democratic consolidation has been discussed in conjunction with concepts such as the internalization of democratic values and procedures at large and the 'mobilization of civil society into political forms of expression' (Maravall and Santamaría 1986: 73; also Diamond 1999). How was it possible for Spanish democracy to consolidate when civil society was so weak? How did the EU influence civil society and its relationship to the state once Spain had gained membership? I argue that, implicitly or explicitly, the promise of EU membership helped the country's democratization and consolidation process, partially overcoming Spain's notorious dearth of voluntary associations. In addition, the EU also exerted significant influence on prominent segments of civil society, most notably organized labour, which helped shape the context for state–society relations.

The concept of civil society contains several dimensions, such as the density of civil society (the number of organizations pertaining to civil society and their membership levels), the level of activity of these organizations, or the degree to which civil society influences the formulation or implementation of policies. Instead of providing a map

The author thanks the participants and discussant at the 'From Isolation to Integration' conference, especially Paul Manuel and Sebastián Royo, for their comments and suggestions, and John Kelly and Bruce M. Wilson for helpful comments on the earlier draft.

outlining these different dimensions of Spanish civil society, I will present a brief overview and then analyse a case study of one of the most important associations of Spanish civil society – organized labour. This case study allows us to look in more detail at the dynamics that condition the role of civil society. It will also help distinguish the effect EU membership has had both on organizations belonging to civil society and the consolidation of democracy.

CIVIL SOCIETY AND EUROPEAN INTEGRATION

The Concept of Civil Society

Civil society can be defined either from a political or sociological perspective. A political conceptualization emphasizes a specific type of 'political society based on the principles of citizenship, rights, democratic representation and the rule of law' (Manor 1999: 3), whereas a conceptualization grounded in a sociological perspective centres on the role of intermediate associations. In this essay I define civil society as the 'intermediate realm situated between the state and the household, populated by organized groups or associations which are separate from the state, enjoy some autonomy in relations with the state, and are formed voluntarily by members of society to protect or extend their interests, values, or identities' (Manor 1999: 3; also Pérez-Díaz 1993: 76–86).[2]

Civil society has been credited with having vital functions in democratic transitions and consolidation.[3] It is important because intermediary organizations play a part in 'limiting authoritarian government, strengthening popular empowerment, reducing the socially atomizing and unsettling effects of market forces, enforcing political accountability, and improving the quality and inclusiveness of governance' (Manor 1999: 1). From the standpoint of efficient government, civil society matters in that interest organizations can also help in the provision and sometimes administration of social services and public goods (Manor 1999: 1). Furthermore, as intermediate organizations provide linkages between elites and masses, they are in a position to contribute to effective policy implementation, provide important input in the process of formulating policies, and exercise both control and representative functions, thus helping to legitimize the political system (Hamann and Manuel 1999). In existing democracies civil society has been ascribed with supplying the social capital necessary to support a political and economic environment that flourishes best if supported by the social trust supplied by civil society (Putnam 1993). In sum, it is commonly assumed that the 'presence of a civil society ... contributes positively to the consolidation' of democracy, without, however, being the sole cause of the success or failure of democratic consolidation (Schmitter 1997: 240).

These qualities presuppose, though, that civil society is democratically oriented and furthermore,[4] that its power is limited. For example, excessive pressures 'from below' are sometimes considered potentially threatening to an emerging democratic order. Consequently, it has been argued that labour mobilization needs to be contained so as not to endanger democratic transitions (Bermeo 1997: 305–7).

On occasion, political parties are considered part of civil society; at other times, they are categorized as part of political society and therefore excluded from analyses of civil society. This essay will refer primarily to other actors of civil society and their relationship to political parties, whose autonomy from the state is not always clear, especially when in government. Therefore, I exclude political parties from my definition of civil society.[5]

Civil Society, European Integration, and Democratic Consolidation

Spanish civil society is notoriously weak and has been characterized as 'underorganized' (for example, McDonough, Barnes and López Pina 1984, 1998: Ch.6). Possible reasons are many, including Spain's history, in particular Franco's ban on independent organization coupled with the mandate to join other associations, such as the mandatory *Organización Sindical* (OSE) (Hamann 2001). Spain did experience an initial surge in registered interest organizations, mostly political parties, when legal restrictions on associations were lifted. For example, over 200 national and regional parties competed in the 1977 elections. Spaniards joined the rapidly rising numbers of associations during the transition to democracy, and especially union affiliation increased drastically in the late 1970s. Although estimates of membership vary and are likely to be somewhat inflated, affiliation rates have been reported as high as 40 per cent during the transition period (Jordana 1996).

After the brief period of associative activity during the transition and early consolidation periods, however, membership in intermediate organizations, including unions, fell again in the early 1980s. Spaniards relied primarily on electoral politics and the state administration to represent their interests (ISEB, n.d., 'Evolución del asocianismo en España'). It has been argued that the democratic state, especially through the establishment of a welfare state, assumed many of the representative but also of the service-oriented functions that had previously been occupied by social movements and organizations. The expansion of the state has thus been linked to the weakening of civil society (ISEB, n.d., 'Evolución del asocianismo en España'). Whatever the precise reasons, by the time Spain joined the EU, associative life was thin. In a 1987 Eurobarometer survey, Spain ranked second to last with just over one-quarter (25.2 per cent) of the population affiliated in any kind of association; only Italy had lower levels of associative life (ISEB, n.d., 'La participación ciudadana'). According to later estimates, however, membership in associations increased throughout the late 1980s and early 1990s to include about one-third of the population over 18 (ISEB, n.d., 'La participación ciudadana'). Among those affiliated, unions had a large share of the members, and union affiliation followed a pattern that paralleled that of other associations with a decrease in the first half of the 1980s and a slow and gradual recovery since the mid-1980s to about 16 per cent (Miguélez 1999).[6]

Although Spanish civil society was thin during the transition to and consolidation of democracy, the most visible organizations supported the democratic project and therefore helped stabilize democracy. Many associations expected to be able to organize and voice their interests more effectively in a democratic order. This was true for neighbourhood associations as well as employers' and workers' organizations (Martínez 1993; Fishman 1990; Hipsher 1996).

Of particular interest and importance are labour unions, which were rapidly resurrected after their legalization in 1977. The General Workers Union (UGT), closely tied to the *Partido Socialista Obrero Español* (PSOE), had retained pockets of resistance during the dictatorship and held its first national congress in 1976, while unions were still officially outlawed. The Workers Commissions (CCOO) had emerged out of factory-level committees and maintained a semi-clandestine existence for much of the 1960s and early 1970s. CCOO co-operated closely with *Partido Comunista de Espana* (PCE) leaders and emerged with relatively strong ties to the workforce during the transition period (Fishman 1990). Despite a surge in mobilizations from the mid-1970s until about 1980, the newly legalized unions were careful to avoid endangering the nascent democratic institutions. Unions were willing to make short-term sacrifices to stabilize democracy. The then CCOO general secretary, Marcelino Camacho, summarized the rationale for the unions' restraint regarding economic demands by explaining that 'If the economy is not saved, democracy is neither' (*Cambio* 16 #301, 18 Sept. 1977: 11). Maravall (1993: 84) points out that unions were instrumental in bringing about a successful democratic transition because, despite their restraint, they exerted considerable pressure 'from below' to add to the 'reforms from above' (also Bermeo 1997). Similarly, Morlino (1998: 242) argues that in spite of their low affiliation rates, unions were 'influential or very influential with regard to their social groups'. Thus, the support of the unions for the new democracy was of considerable import. Consequently, the prominent civil society organizations were supportive of a democratic political order and had a crucial role in stabilizing the nascent democracy that was primarily negotiated by political elites.

While civil society, then, was one of the factors that contributed to the consolidation of Spanish democracy despite its organizational weakness, European integration was another potent factor that helped stabilize Spain's new democracy. European integration, a concept that Spaniards often used concurrently with 'modernization', had been one of Spain's aspirations even prior to the transition to democracy. Western European countries, however, refused to grant Spain access to the European Community as long as Spain lacked a democratic political system. To the extent, then, that integration into Western Europe was considered a desirable and necessary goal to achieve economic and political 'modernization', the prospect of EU membership presented a strong incentive to work toward consolidating democracy. Participating in European institutions appeared as the 'antithesis to the authoritarian institutions of the Franco regime' (Marks 1997: 77). Leaders of the Socialist party, as part of the anti-Franco opposition, believed that political integration of Spain into Europe would lead to 'democracy, political openness, and social freedoms' (Marks 1997: 78). According to Eurobarometer surveys, between 1981 and 1984 about half of all Spaniards thought that EU membership would be a 'good thing'; from 1984 to 1986 this increased to about 60 per cent, which was around the average of the EU member states (European Commission 2002). As the EU was considered a positive force in the future of Spain, and democracy was a necessary precondition to achieve entry, the vision of Europe played a supportive role for democratic consolidation in Spain implicitly and explicitly.

This commitment to EU goals meant, however, that the economic policy course of the democratic governments, including the PSOE governments under Felipe González, was influenced by the guidelines posed by the European Common Market. The discussion focused on the anticipated benefits of EC membership rather than the potential costs of economic adjustment. As Youngs (1999: 49) concludes, the PSOE government understood Spain's membership in the EC 'in largely political and symbolic terms, and in particular as a guarantor of political freedoms'. This allowed the PSOE to advocate publicly a traditionally leftist economic policy path in the early 1980s. However, even when the failed French and Greek leftist economic policies illustrated to PSOE leaders that European integration was also about market adjustment and not always reconcilable with traditionally redistributive economic policies, the prospect of democratic stability and long-term economic benefits weighed heavier than the potential economic and political costs. Consequently, the choice of economic policies was constrained (though not predetermined; see Royo 2000) and eventually reflected a considerable modification from the economic policies the PSOE had advocated prior to taking office.[7] This also meant that the current and future member countries had to adopt the EC's preoccupation with solving its financial crisis as one of their predominant concerns (Marks 1997: 85–7). These policies, in turn, had important ramifications for civil society.

The most visible effect of European integration on civil society has probably been with respect to economic interest groups, especially organized labour, and their relationship to political parties. As Morlino (1998: 242) posits, during the transition and consolidation period, the main interest groups (which include organized labour) 'were able to build linkages with their reference groups and establish either an influence on or even control over them'. The role of labour in Spanish society and politics has undergone fundamental modifications since the inception of democracy. I will thus examine how EU membership has influenced organized labour as a case study that is not necessarily paradigmatic for other actors in civil society, but serves as an illustrative example.

THE EFFECTS OF EUROPEAN INTEGRATION ON CIVIL SOCIETY: THE EXAMPLE OF LABOUR UNIONS

EU Integration and Economic Policies

When the PSOE took office in 1982 with a parliamentary majority, many Spaniards considered democracy to be consolidated, and unions hoped for social and economic policies that clearly benefited workers, particularly given the UGT's close ties to the PSOE. As detailed elsewhere (for example, Hamann 2000; Smith 1998), however, unions were quickly disappointed with the government's policies of industrial restructuring, which led to massive job losses in targeted industries, and with the economic and social policies Prime Minister González implemented.

Spain's economic policies were tightly linked to the country's aspirations to join the EU in 1986. The economic crisis in the 1970s hit Spain extremely hard due to the country's inefficient production processes and dependence on oil imports. Prime Minister Suárez had plans for economic adjustment policies, which were, however, put on the backburner during this period while the democratic political institutions were being defined. By the time the PSOE was elected, many Spaniards were holding the politics of consensus (prevalent during the transition period) responsible for the lack of decisive new policies to reinvigorate Spain's economy. Thus, although González had campaigned on a platform of moderate social democratic reforms, he was in a position to implement economic austerity measures that contradicted his campaign promises, concentrated on structural adjustment, and eventually led to hostile relationships with the unions (Hamann 2000). González's economic policies were at least in part driven by the idea that EU membership would provide the solution to Spain's economic problems (Marks 1997). As EU accession drew closer, PSOE leaders had to accept that their originally expounded leftist economic policy programme was unrealistic and not coherent with EU membership. Yet, the prospect of political stability and long-term economic benefits insured that EU membership remained a top priority of the government.

It could be argued that EU membership decreased the policy autonomy of the Spanish government and was thus responsible for much of the government's economic policy agenda. By supporting EU goals the Spanish government had implicitly accepted policy priorities – especially deficit reduction – that ranked the EU criteria over unemployment, one of the most pressing problems in the Spanish economy. The Spanish peseta entered the European Monetary System (EMS) in 1989, although there was some questioning about the timing of tying the peseta into the EMS. As it turned out, the peseta had to be devalued three times in 1993 for a total of 19 per cent, a consequence of the government's policy mix coupled with a lack of flexibility in moving exchange rates that resulted from the peseta being tied to the Deutschmark (Pérez 1999; Marks 1997). Spain attempted from the beginning, then, to support the health of the EU as an organization and aimed at being a full member of the EU, which implied a choice of economic policies that appeared supportive of this goal.

When Spain became a full member of the EU in 1986, González was running for re-election (which he won, again with an absolute majority of seats in the lower house of parliament), and the unions had begun to voice open opposition to the government's policies. The PSOE had campaigned on a moderate social-democratic platform, emphasizing the need to create new jobs, expansionary economic policies, and extensive social welfare reforms. The González government continued, however, to pursue an economic adjustment programme centered around a reduction of the public deficit and inflation with a selective expansion of the welfare state. These policies continued in an effort to meet the EU convergence criteria set out in the Maastricht Treaty and to join the first round of countries adopting the euro. The government was less successful, however, at battling the high unemployment rates and the high rate of temporary contracts (about one-third of all contracts). Spanish policy-makers were aware of the potential political cost of economic dislocation, which was evident at least in the short run (Marks 1997: 115–16). The political costs included a fundamental change in the relationship between the governing PSOE and the labour unions, in particular the UGT, as detailed below.

Throughout the 1980s, then, leading government elites supported the idea of Europe and Spanish integration into Western Europe. This look toward Europe was mirrored by a general consensus among Spanish citizens. Given the inflow of money Spain received after joining the EC, and the fact that Structural Funds provided a visible and obvious net benefit to Spain, popular support for the EU is hardly surprising. For example, over 60 per cent of the EU Cohesion Fund (established in 1993) was directed toward Spanish regions, and Spain received over 20 per cent of all Structural Fund spending between 1994 and 1999 (Cooke, Christensen and Schienstock 1997: 197). EU assistance amounted to an average of 0.7 per cent of the gross domestic product (GDP) annually between 1989 and 1993, which increased to 1.7 per cent per annum on average for 1994–99. Together with the national public counterparts and private sector financing linked to these funds, on average about 1.5 per cent of the annual GDP was mobilized in the context of EU structural assistance during the first period, and about 3.4 per cent during the second period (European Commission 1997: 45). These obvious benefits appeared to hide or compensate for some of the economic costs of adjustment and sheltered the EU from widespread criticism (Newton 1997: 306).

The Role of Organized Labour Prior to EU Membership

The government's economic policies, on some level driven by the goal of EU membership, had considerable effects on labour unions. Unions' functions in the policy-making process as well as their relationship to political parties and the state were shaped by the government's economic priorities.

During the democratic transition unions acted as a mediator between political parties and workers. Given the governing UCD's (*Unión de Centro Democrático*) minority position and the consequently strong role of the PSOE as the largest opposition party, unions had an important part in helping stabilize the new political order and legitimize democracy by extending the compromises concluded by the leading political party elites to sectors of the masses. Especially the UGT was also able to influence policies through its strong ties with the PSOE, the largest opposition party in parliament. Unions were not directly included in the policy-making process, however. For example, unions did not participate in the negotiations of the 1977 Moncloa Pacts, which were negotiated by the parliamentary parties. The Moncloa Pacts set wage ceilings around inflation rates in return for a set of economic policies and reforms in the welfare state, such as an extension of unemployment insurance, many of which were never implemented. Important issues regarding labour policies were postponed until after the immediate transition period; the Workers Statute, for example, was not passed until 1980; many of the social and economic reforms promised to the unions were either never implemented or postponed, such as the distribution of the patrimonio sindical (Balfour 1989: 237); and the constitutionally mandated advisory Social and Economic Council (CES) was not established until 1993. While fulfilling an important political and social function, then, union interests were often of secondary importance to the political elites.

Furthermore, Spain's severe economic recession weakened the union movement in addition to prompting their exclusion from direct input into the policy-making process. Other factors that debilitated the unions included the ideological differences among the unions, the competitive nature of their relationship given the importance of union elections (workplace elections for workplace representatives that workers can participate in regardless of whether they are affiliated), and their divergent conceptions about the preferred nature of the future union system. Instead of building a co-operative relationship between the main confederations, they relied heavily on proximate political parties to represent their interests in parliament during this period, supplemented by a high level of mobilization.

Once the democratic constitution had been ratified, unions began to be included in framing policies through their participation in national social pacts. From 1979 until 1986 five major national pacts were concluded between one or both of the major unions, the government and/or the employers' organization *Confederación Española de Organizaciones Empresariales* (CEOE). The UGT and the CEOE signed the first agreement, the Basic Interconfederal Agreement (ABI), in 1979. Parliament subsequently incorporated most of the agreement into the 1980 Workers' Statute. The PSOE was instrumental in securing the adoption of the agreement into law with very little modification. The ABI was followed by the Interconfederal Framework Agreement (AMI) between the UGT and the CEOE in 1980/81; the National Employment Agreement (ANE) between the government, the CEOE, and both major union confederations in 1982; and the Interconfederal Agreement (AI) between the employers organization, the UGT, and the CCOO in 1983 (see Table 1). Unions had thus some policy-making influence during this period: on the one hand, they were included in a series of socio-economic pacts; on the other, they were able to use their ties to leftist political parties to represent their interests in parliament.

This relatively high profile of the unions can be explained with a variety of factors: the UCD minority government was weak, both within the party and in parliament; therefore, there existed a perceived need to build a consensus inside and outside of parliament; the economic crisis had the potential to polarize the population; the government needed to build legitimacy for itself as well as for the democratic system as a whole; and unions had significant and potentially destabilizing mobilization potential. In addition, Spanish union strength is less dependent on affiliation rates since bargaining coverage is broad (70–75 per cent in the 1990s; Miguélez and Rebollo 1999: 331) and coverage is unrelated to membership; union bargaining rights are not determined by membership rates, but by the outcomes to the elections to works committees that are open to non-unionized workers also; and unions' mobilization power has been among the highest in Western Europe despite low affiliation rates. The significance of unions went thus beyond what mere affiliation rates would suggest. Unions' democratic support and the inclusion of civil society during the transition period constituted a weighty counterpart to potentially destabilizing forces and unresolved questions, such as regional autonomy. Unions had thus a substantial role in stabilizing the new democracy.

While the substance of the PSOE's economic policies contrasted quite drastically with the lack of alternative economic programmes during the

TABLE 1

SOCIAL PACTS IN SPAIN

Year	Pact	Signatories	Major Issues
1977	Moncloa Pacts	parliamentary parties	wages, inflation, political reform
1979	ABI	UGT, CEOE	industrial relations system
1980–81	AMI	UGT, CEOE, USO	wages, workweek, collective contracts, union presence in firms
1982	ANE	government, CEOE, UGT, CCOO	wages, union rights, job creation, pensions
1983	AI	CEOE, CEPYME, UGT, CCOO	wages, workweek, job creation
1985–86	AES	government, CEOE, CEPYME, UGT	wages, job creation, pensions

Sources: Comisiones Obreras (1989: especially 150–51); García Delgado y Serrano Sanz (1992: 294–5); Gutiérrez (1990: 124).

UCD governments, the policy-making patterns during the early PSOE period kept some resemblance to that of its conservative predecessor, especially regarding the formation of consensus. In addition to policies ratified in parliament, the PSOE government initially continued to include unions in social and economic pacts at the national level. The AES (Social and Economic Agreement) was concluded in 1985 and extended to 1986 (see Table 1). Unions were thus involved in determining economic policies by defining wage bands and so on, but they were also instrumental in defining the industrial relations framework, a major issue addressed in the pacts.

During the years immediately preceding EU membership, then, the relationship between the unions and the government was not fundamentally changed although the PSOE had already adopted an economic adjustment programme that conflicted with much of the unions' interests. Unions, as part of civil society, had considerable impact in shaping the new democracy, or at least some of its subsystems during the early 1980s, although this role was never institutionalized. Furthermore, they added legitimacy to the new democracy and its policies, and established themselves as influential actors of civil society in the policy-making process. The pacts thus had not only an immediate impact on politics and the economy, but also recognized the role of organized labour as part of Spanish society and politics (Fishman 1990).

The EU, Economic Adjustment and Trade Unions

The influence unions were able to exert during the early democratic years, however, was considerably reduced once Spain had joined the EU. Unions were marginalized relatively easily during the PSOE years as their earlier access to policy-making had never been institutionalized and instead had been contingent on several factors, such as a weak government, a potentially volatile situation in a young democracy, and an economic crisis that demanded consensus solutions to minimize social dislocation and legitimized both the government and its policies. When these factors changed, so did the role of the unions. The UGT initially supported the PSOE's economic policies, whereas the CCOO voiced clear opposition early on. Even the unions' strike capacity did not threaten Spanish democracy, nor did it threaten the government's success in winning re-election. This became particularly evident after the 1988 general strike. Despite the popularity of the strike that directly attacked the PSOE government's economic and social policies, Felipe González was re-elected in 1989. The PSOE was thus in a position to follow an economic policy course that was opposed by the unions, one of the most visible and strongest associations of civil society.

Given the government's majority position in parliament,[8] González had considerable political leeway to implement policies that alienated his former allies, the labour unions, especially the UGT. In response to the government's policies, UGT leaders resigned from their parliamentary seats that they had obtained on PSOE lists, and the UGT did not endorse the PSOE during the 1989 election campaign. The PSOE, for its part, changed its party statutes and no longer required PSOE members to also join the UGT, which meant the end of the official ties between the two socialist organizations.

The government's economic policy choices, closely tied to EU membership, affected more than just the relationship between the PSOE and the unions (especially the UGT), however. Another implication was the changing patterns of policy-making after the mid-1980s. Whereas before, the main union confederations had participated in a series of social and economic pacts on the national level, no new pacts were signed after the mid-1980s. The unions' role in setting economic policies thus decreased considerably. On the one hand, they had less influence on policies formulated by the governing party as the relationship between the unions and the PSOE deteriorated and the official ties between the Socialist union and party were cut. On the other hand, they also lost effective influence in the policy-making process outside of parliament as no national-level agreements were concluded.

Unions, however, devised new strategies to maintain or improve their position. Recruitment efforts led to a slow increase in membership starting in the mid-1980s, and the two major union confederations downplayed their ideological differences and emphasized co-operation and joint programmes instead ('unity of action'). As part of this new cross-union co-operation, they also engaged in an effort to change some of the institutions that had emphasized competition between the unions, such as the rules guiding the elections to works committee representatives ('union elections').

Despite these new strategies, unions' effective influence in defining economic and social policies remained weak compared to the earlier period. Given the government's policy priorities of meeting EU criteria and standards, union preferences were not viewed as instrumental to the fulfilment of these goals. When González and the PSOE returned to the government in a minority position in 1993, new attempts at negotiating national-level agreements with the unions were undertaken, but failed. As a consequence, the government unilaterally passed a series of labour market reforms and against the vociferous opposition of the unions, who were once more on the defensive. The government claimed that stringent labour market regulations kept the labour market unnecessarily rigid and provided a disincentive for new hires, especially for permanent contracts, which inflated the unemployment problem.

After the election of José María Aznar's conservative *Partido Popular* (PP) in 1996, however, negotiations between the government and the unions resumed once again, and some new national-level agreements were concluded. These agreements, however, are somewhat different in nature from the earlier pacts. Instead of broad social pacts, the new national-level agreements address more narrowly defined issues. They included an agreement on Social Protection and Pensions, Professional Training Plans, an agreement on Worker Safety and Health, as well as agreements regulating the resolution of Labour Conflicts, and finally, an agreement on a new reform of the labour market (Baylos 1999: 250–51; Espina 1999: 388). In addition, the scope of centrally negotiated bargaining issues has been broadened, which affords unions a larger role in collective bargaining although the bargaining process itself remains relatively fragmented (Hamann and Martínez Lucio 2003).

It has been cogently argued that one of the reasons the government showed renewed interest in national-level bargaining has been the government's failure to pursue EMU goals by relying on a tight monetary policy in a context of undisciplined and fragmented bargaining. With the prospect of the European Monetary Union (EMU) governments thus began to seek centralized framework bargaining in an attempt to control inflation (Pérez 2000). This has resulted in a renewed strengthening of the political role of the unions.

At the same time, unions have become considerably more autonomous from political parties. Instead of relying on ideologically proximate parties to represent their interests, unions now use their independence from leftist parties to engage in pragmatic bargaining with José María Aznar's conservative PP government. This increased autonomy can be interpreted as a strengthening of the unions themselves (Royo 2002) and thereby of civil society. At the same time, however, they have also become more tightly involved with state institutions and regulatory functions. For instance, unions take part in the CES, a consultative tripartite body established in 1993. They have also adopted regulatory functions, such as the monitoring of new contracts, which was previously within the exclusive remit of the state. Although the effectiveness of those state institutions and functions has been debated (Hamann and Martínez Lucio 2003), there has nonetheless been a tendency to replace the formerly close ties to political parties with more state involvement, thus imposing new limits on the autonomy the unions had gained after they had increased their independence from political parties.

CONCLUSION: EU MEMBERSHIP AND CIVIL SOCIETY IN SPAIN

Spain's membership in the EU has not only exerted a considerable impact on the consolidation of Spanish democracy, but also on civil society. This is not to argue that other factors – such as political learning on the part of both the elites and the general population or the media – did not also play an integral part in strengthening elite and popular commitment to democratization (Aguilar 1999; Edles 1998). The vision of European integration provided an incentive to democratize, a goal that was supported by political elites, the masses, and labour, as well as other actors in civil society. Once the decision to join the European Community had been made, the political and economic choices of Spanish leaders, including the PSOE governments, were constrained. EU membership promised political and economic modernization, even when the implications – economic adjustment – went against the PSOE's traditional programme. The government's economic policy choices, in turn, affected one of the most important and prominent actors of civil society, labour unions. In response to the Socialist government's economic and social policies, unions opposed governmental policies after the mid-1980s. When the formerly close relationship turned distant, if not hostile, the unions increased their autonomy from political parties, in particular the governing PSOE. Instead, the two major unions, UGT and CCOO, followed a strategy of mutual co-operation or 'unity of action'. They also became less involved in policy-making. In addition to losing direct access to parliamentary policy-making procedures (previously provided primarily through close ties to the PSOE), the unions also lost their influence on policy-making that the social pacts of the first part of the 1980s had provided.

The consequences of economic integration thus had political and social ramifications and profoundly affected civil society. Unions, whose role some observers (Bermeo 1997) have judged as instrumental in ensuring a successful transition to democracy, became politically marginalized during the successive PSOE governments. Their capacity to influence policies in the early years of the democracy was contingent and was never institutionalized. It has also been argued, however, that it was indeed the exigencies of the EMU that led to renewed national-level bargaining after the mid-1990s, which included the unions. This was so because a decentralized and fragmented bargaining structure in an underorganized economy made it difficult, if not impossible, for the government to fulfil the economic targets necessary for full participation in the EMU (Pérez 2000).

If the EU provided a major incentive for the consecutive governments to pursue their chosen economic policies, the political and social consequences of those policy choices cannot be ignored. Unions were one of the most prominent actors of civil society, and their increased autonomy from political parties since the late 1980s signalled perhaps a strengthening of civil society. This functional, organizational, and political separation came with a price, however, namely, a considerable loss in policy-making influence. Nonetheless, unions have begun to recover some of that lost ground and, it could be argued, are now in a stronger position as they are less dependent on specific parties. Instead, they are slowly assuming a larger and more important institutionalized role, either through a gradual expansion of their collective bargaining function (inclusion of new issues) after labour market reforms ended the Francoist labour ordinances, or through assuming functions previously in the exclusive remit of the state, such as oversight of new contracts. It is this new involvement as a state actor, however, that takes away from the autonomy of the unions as an actor of civil society.

The prospect of European integration was a crucial factor that helped consolidate Spanish democracy. Membership in the EU also had substantial consequences for the relationship between actors of civil society and the state. Thus, while the prospect of and the membership in the EU may have contributed to a weakening of major actors of civil society, it may simultaneously also have helped the consolidation of Spanish democracy by providing an image and hope of a better future. While Spanish civil society remained relatively weak, the prospect of being a member of modern, democratic, progressive Europe helped smooth out the cost of economic adjustment and the lack of a strong civil society. Support for the EU is still relatively high among Spanish citizens – in 2001, 72 per cent felt 'very' and 'fairly proud' to be European (compared to an EU average of 60 per cent), and 55 per cent were 'very' or 'fairly satisfied' with democracy in the EU – compared to 44 per cent EU-wide (European Commission 2002: 17). Similarly, 60 per cent stated that Spain had benefited from EU membership (European Commission 2002: 22).

The changes in Spanish civil society bear important lessons for the transition to and consolidation of democracies. Conventional wisdom posits that strong civil societies are necessary for democracies to consolidate. In the Spanish case, however, civil society was – and still is – overall weak. Prominent actors of civil society, however, such as unions, were committed to strengthen the nascent democracy and were included in the policy-making process, though in an unsystematic and non-institutionalized fashion, during consequential time periods. In the absence of a strong civil society, the prospect of a better future as part of Europe may have absorbed much of the function with which civil society is credited – such as reinforcing a commitment to democracy. European integration, however, has not played a deterministic role for defining the relationship between actors of civil society and the state. As the changing policy-making patterns and role of the unions illustrates, the EU specifies targets that governments choose to follow, but how they go about achieving these goals is not prescribed or determined by the EU. Instead, both governing parties and civil society actors have considerable leeway in configuring their relationship as the changing role of organized labour in the Spanish policy-making process illustrates.

Finally, the curious coincidence of a weak civil society with a simultaneous successful transition to democracy questions the assumed importance of civil society. Spaniards may not be bowling in organized bowling leagues, but they are also not 'Bowling Alone' (Putnam 1995); instead, they bowl with family, friends, and neighbours, which may well provide some of the social fabric that holds democracy together.

The Portuguese case lends further support to the argument that a strong civil society may not be instrumental to successful democratization. Much like Spain, Portuguese civil society was 'extremely weak and almost nonexistent' (Magone 2001: 120) when the military staged a coup against the dictatorship in 1974, and labour unions were also among the most prominent actors of civil society. Two major unions dominated the union movement, and affiliation grew rapidly in the late 1970s. However, ideological splits and fragmentation and wildcat strikes and workers' committees that were not controlled by an organized union during times of high worker mobilization debilitated the union movement. Neighbourhood associations and social movements emerged rapidly, but for the most part did not last much past the first elections (Schmitter 1995: 287–8). In fact, Diamandouros (1997: 15) concludes for the Portuguese case that 'central and direct involvement of mass actors in the transition can ... derail democratization and reduce the chances of consolidation'. Although trade union membership is significantly higher in Portugal than in Spain, during the immediate transition period, civil society was overall weak, and was not a crucial actor in a process that was dominated by the military and political party elites (Hamann and Manuel 1999). Yet, Portugal has also managed to establish a stable democratic system.

It could be argued that the EU had a positive effect on democratic consolidation in Portugal. The prospect of joining the EU increased support for democracy among businesspeople (Manuel 1996: 75), and EU economic support has helped improve Portugal's economic performance. When Portugal joined the EU in 1986, almost 70 per cent thought that membership would be a 'good thing', and Portuguese citizens have consistently scored way above average when assessing the benefits of EU membership for their country (European Commission 2002: 34). In 2001, 73 per cent of Portuguese agreed that their country has benefited from EU membership (European Commission 2002: 22). The EU's anticipated benefits and rewards may well have functioned as an incentive for democratization (Whitehead 1986: 23; Linz and Stepan 1996: 140–41).

European integration also had profound effects on the system of interest mediation in Portugal and, by extension, on trade unions and civil society, emphasizing self-regulation and social dialogue (Magone 2001: 116). During the second half of the 1980s, social pacts included trade unions, and social pacts were revived after the mid-1990s. In contrast to Spain, Portuguese trade unions have retained relatively close ties to ideologically proximate political parties, and they also have a more solid membership base. Despite existing differences in the industrial relations system between the two countries, however, the overall similarities are striking: both countries emerged from their authoritarian periods with weak civil societies; in both countries support for EU membership was – and still is – consistently high; and both countries have been able to consolidate their democracies despite the differences with respect to the ending of the authoritarian regime, the role of the military, or the state of the economy, among others.

Again, the argument is not that the EU was necessarily the causal determinant for a successful transition to democracy. However, both cases lead us to rethink the assumptions about strong civil societies. First, civil society can be stronger than mere membership numbers suggest. For example, Spanish unions may be numerically weak, but their extensive bargaining rights and coverage are not based on affiliation. Affiliation itself thus measures only part of the strength of Spanish unions. Second, if crucial (though maybe numerically weak) actors of civil society support democracy, they can still have an integral role in leading to a successful democratic transition. And third, it should not be surprising that civil societies are often weak during democratic transitions. After all, civil societies are assumed to be part of democratic culture, which is exactly what many authoritarian regimes are trying to suppress. Instead of expecting civil societies to be strong during transitions to democracy, we should perhaps scrutinize whether and how they develop once democracy has been established. Both Spain and Portugal are examples of civil societies beginning to grow once democracy was introduced (Schmitter 1995: 290–92). Finally, the promise of EU membership (and EU membership itself) may have provided an incentive for citizens to support democratization when a vibrant civil society was absent.

NOTES

1. When Spain joined the organization in 1986, it was called the European Community (EC), which was later renamed the European Union (EU). I use these terms interchangeably throughout my discussion.

2. An alternative, yet similar definition has been proposed by Schmitter (1997: 240), emphasizing dual autonomy (from firms and families), collective action, non-usurpation, and civility.

3. For some studies that focus on the role of civil society in Southern Europe, see Bermeo (1997); Drake (1996); Morlino (1998); Hamann (1998); Hamann and Manuel (1999). Schmitter (1997) details the potential positive, but also negative, contributions civil society can make to democratization processes. See also Diamond (1999: especially Ch.6) for an extensive discussion of civil society in developing democracies.

4. Obviously, the assumption here is that these associations and organizations support democracy in some fashion, such as through their internal organization or their purpose. If associations or organizations are explicitly nondemocratic in nature, the argument that they would be beneficial to democratic government would not hold.

5. This does not mean, however, that parties could never be considered parts of civil society (Manor 1999; Elshtain 1997; Stepan 1988). However, here I look at governing parties more as 'gatekeepers' that regulate access and influence to governmental policy-making (Morlino 1998). This approach positions governing parties closer to state institutions instead of treating them as independent and autonomous organizations, and therefore justifies an analytical distinction between political parties and other actors of civil society.

6. McDonough, Barnes and López Pina (1998: 16) present data, however, that contradict this trend toward increasing membership in associations. According to their data, 69 per cent of Spaniards did not belong to any association in 1990, compared to 60 per cent in 1984, while 22 per cent belonged to one association (25 per cent in 1980) and eight per cent were a member in two or more associations (15 per cent in 1984). Either way, Spanish civil society was – and still is – weak.

7. It has been argued that factors other than EU integration were responsible for the PSOE's chosen economic policies, or at least for specific components of their economic liberalization package. Pérez (1999), for example, argues cogently that those policies were formulated as a result of the preferences of parts of PSOE elites that were not necessarily tied to EU goals, but in fact preceded them. Nonetheless, even if some or all of the PSOE's economic policy ideas reflected endogenous policy choices made by party elites, it is also true that in any event, the EU provided a justification for the PSOE's economic policies to the public. Otherwise, the implementation of neoliberal policies would have been considerably harder, if not politically and electorally impossible. Whether the EU in effect provided the reason or more of an excuse for the reorientation of the PSOE's economic policies is thus less important for the argument of this essay than the fact that it gave the PSOE leadership the justification for a redefinition of its economic policies (on the PSOE's Project Europe, see also Holman 1996).

8. After 1989 the PSOE obtained exactly half of the 350 seats in the lower house of parliament. However, they formed effectively a majority government since some Basque deputies refused to take their seats.

REFERENCES

Aguilar, P. (1999): 'The Memory of the Civil War in the Transition to Democracy: The Peculiarity of the Basque Case', in Paul Heywood (ed.), *Politics and Policy in Democratic Spain: No Longer Different?* London and Portland, OR: Frank Cass, pp.5–25.

Balfour, S. (1989): *Dictatorship, Workers, and the City*, Oxford: Clarendon.

Baylos, A. (1999): 'La intervención normativa del estado en las relaciones laborales colectivas' [Normative Intervention by the State in Collective Labor Relations], in Miguélez and Prieto (1999: 239–58).

Bermeo, N. (1997): 'Myths of Moderation: Confrontation and Conflict during Democratic Transitions', *Comparative Politics* 29/3, pp.305–22.

Cambio 16, #30, 18 Sept. 1977.

Cooke, P., T. Christiansen and G. Schienstock (1997): 'Regional Economic Policy and a Europe of the Regions', in M. Rhodes, P. Heywood and V. Wright, *Developments in West European Politics*, New York: St. Martin's Press, pp.190–206.

Comisiones Obreras (1989): *De los Pactos de la Moncloa al AES* [From the Moncloa Pact to AES], Madrid: Confederación Sindical de CCOO.

Diamond, L. (1999): *Developing Democracy: Toward Consolidation*, Baltimore, MD and London: Johns Hopkins University Press.

Diamandouros, P.N. (1997): 'Southern Europe: A Third Wave Success Story', in L. Diamond *et al.*, *Consolidating the Third Wave Democracies: Regional Challenges*, Baltimore, MD: Johns Hopkins University Press, pp.3–25.

Drake, P.W. (1996): *Labor Movements and Dictatorship: The Southern Cone in Comparative Perspective*, Baltimore, MD: Johns Hopkins University Press.

Edles, L. Desfor (1998): *Symbol and Ritual in the New Spain: The Transition to Democracy under Franco*, New York: Cambridge University Press.

Elshtain, J.B. (1997): 'Civil Society Creates Citizens: It Does Not Solve Problems', *Brookings Review*, 15/4, pp.13–15.

Espina, A. (1999): 'El "Guadiana" de la concertación neocorporatista en España: De la huelga general de 1988 a los acuerdos de 1997' [The 'Guadiana' of the Neocorporatist Concertation in Spain: From the General Strike of 1988 to the Accords of 1997], in Miguélez and Prieto (1999).

European Commission (1997): *The Impact of Structural Policies on Economic and Social Cohesion in the Union 1989–99*, Luxembourg: Office for Official Publications of the European Communities.

European Commission (2002): *Eurobarometer*: Report No.56, Brussels: Directorate-General Press and Communication.

Fishman, R. (1990): *Working-Class Organization and the Return to Democracy in Spain*, Ithaca, NY and London: Cornell University Press.

García Delgado, J.L. and J.M. Serrano Sanz (1992): 'Economía', in M. Tuñon de Lara (dir.), *Historia de España*, Barcelona: Labor, pp.189–311.

Gutiérrez, A. (1990): 'Concertación social y coyuntura política en España' [Social Concertation and Political Situation in Spain], in A. Zaragoza (ed.), *Pactos sociales, sindicatos y patronal en España* [Social Pacts, Unions and Employers' Associations in Spain], Madrid: Siglo XXI, pp.107–43.

Hamann, K. (2000): 'Linking Policies and Economic Voting: Explaining Reelection in the Case of the Spanish Socialist Party', *Comparative Political Studies* 33/8 (Oct.), pp.1018–48.

Hamann, K. (2001): 'Spain: Changing Party–Group Relations in a New Democracy', in C.S. Thomas (ed.), *Political Parties and Interest Groups: Shaping Democratic Governance*, Boulder, CO: Lynne Rienner, pp.175–92.

Hamann, K. (1998): 'Civil Society and the Democratic Transition in Spain', *Perspectives on Political Science* 2/3, pp.135–41.

Hamann, K. and P.C. Manuel (1999): 'Political Change and Civil Society in Twentieth-Century Portugal', *South European Society & Politics* 4/1 (Summer), pp.71–96.

Hamann, K. and M. Martínez Lucio (2003): 'Spanish Unions: Dynamics of Revitalization', *European Journal of Industrial Relations* 9/1, pp.61–78.

Hipsher, P. (1996): 'Democratization and the Decline of Urban Social Movements in Chile and Spain', *Comparative Politics* 28/3 (April), pp.273–98.

Holman, O. (1996): *Integrating Southern Europe: EC Expansion and the Transnationalization of Spain*, New York: Routledge.

Iniciativa Social y Estado de Bienestar (ISEB) (n.d.): 'Evolución del asociacionismo en España' [Evolution of Associanism in Spain].

ISEB (n.d.): 'La participación ciudadana' [Civic Participation].

Jordana, J. (1996): 'Reconsidering Union Membership in Spain, 1977–1994', *Industrial Relations Journal* 27/3, pp.211–24.

Linz, J.J. and A. Stepan (1996): *Problems of Democratic Transition and Consolidation*, Baltimore, MD: Johns Hopkins University Press.

McDonough, P., S.H. Barnes and A. López Pina (1984): 'Authority and Association: Spanish Democracy in Comparative Perspective', *Journal of Politics* 46/3, pp.652–88.

McDonough, P., S.H. Barnes and A. López Pina (1998): *The Cultural Dynamics of Democratization in Spain*, Ithaca, NY and London: Cornell University Press.

Magone, J.M. (2001): *Iberian Trade Unionism: Democratization Under the Impact of the European Union*, New Brunswick, NJ: Transaction.

Manor, J. (1999): 'Civil Society and Governance: A Concept Paper', Institute of Development Studies, University of Sussex, England.

Manuel, P.C. (1996): *The Challenges of Democratic Consolidation in Portugal: Political, Economic and Military Issues, 1976–1991*, Westport, CT: Praeger.

Maravall, J.M. (1993): 'Politics and Policy: Economic Reforms in Southern Europe', in L.C. Bresser Pereira, J.M. Maravall and A. Przeworski, *Economic Reforms: A Social-Democratic Approach*, New York: Cambridge University Press, pp.77–131.

Maravall, J.M. and J. Santamaría (1986): 'Political Change in Spain and the Prospects for Democracy', in O'Donnell, Schmitter and Whitehead (1986).

Marks, M.P. (1997): *The Formation of European Policy in Post-Franco Spain: The Role of Ideas, Interests and Knowledge*, Brookfield, VT: Avebury.

Martínez, R.E. (1993): *Business and Democracy in Spain*, Westport, CT: Praeger.

Miguélez, F. (1999): 'Presente y futuro del sindicalismo en España' [The Present and Future of Unionism in Spain], in Miguélez and Prieto (1991).

Miguélez, F. and O. Rebollo (1999): 'Negociación colectiva en los noventa' [Collective Bargaining in the 1990s], in Miguélez and Prieto (1999).

Miguélez, F. and C. Prieto (eds.) (1999): *Las relaciones de empleo en España* (Employment Relations in Spain], Madrid: Siglo XXI.

Morlino, L. (1998): *Democracy Between Consolidation and Crisis: Parties, Groups, and Citizens in Southern Europe*, New York: Oxford University Press.

Newton, M.T. (with P.J. Donaghy) (1997): *Institutions of Modern Spain: A Political and Economic Guide*, New York: Cambridge University Press.

O'Donnell, G., P.C. Schmitter and L. Whitehead (eds.) (1986): *Transitions from Authoritarian Rule: Southern Europe*, Baltimore, MD: Johns Hopkins University Press.

Pérez, S. (1999): 'From Labour to Finance: Understanding the Failure of Socialist Economic Policies in Spain', *Comparative Political Studies* 32/6, pp.659–89.

Pérez, S. (2000): 'From Decentralization to Reorganization: Explaining the Return to National Bargaining in Italy and Spain', *Comparative Politics* 32/4, pp.437–58.

Pérez-Díaz, V. (1993): *La primacia de la sociedad civil* [The Return of Civil Society], Madrid: Alianza.

Putnam, R. (1993): *Making Democracy Work: Civic Traditions in Modern Italy*, Princeton, NJ: Princeton University Press.

Putnam, R. (1995): 'Bowling Alone: America's Declining Social Capital', *Journal of Democracy* 6/1, pp.65–78.

Royo, S. (2000): *From Social Democracy to Neoliberalism: The Consequences of Party Hegemony in Spain, 1982–1996*, New York: St. Martin's Press.

Royo, S. (2002): *A New Century of Corporatism: Corporatism in Southern Europe*, Westport, CT: Praeger.

Schmitter, P.C. (1995): 'Organized Interests and Democratic Consolidation in Southern Europe', in R. Gunther, P.N. Diamandouros and H.-J. Puhle (eds.), *The Politics of Democratic Consolidation: Southern Europe in Comparative Perspective*, pp.231–60.

Schmitter, P.C. (1997): 'Civil Society East and West', in Diamond *et al.* (eds.), *Consolidating the Third Wave Democracies: Themes and Perspectives*, Baltimore, MD and London: Johns Hopkins University Press, pp.239–62.

Smith, W.R. (1998): *The Left's Dirty Job: The Politics of Industrial Restructuring in France and Spain*, Pittsburgh, PA: University of Pittsburgh Press.

Stepan, A. (1988): *Rethinking Military Politics: Brazil and the Southern Cone*, Princeton, NJ: Princeton University Press.

Whitehead, L. (1986): 'International Aspects of Democratization', in O'Donnell, Schmitter and Whitehead (1986).

Youngs, R. (1999): 'The Domestic Politics of Spanish European Economic Policy, 1986–1994', *South European Society & Politics* 4/1, pp.48–70.

Portugal and Eastern Europe: After the Revolution, Democratic Europe

LUÍS SALGADO DE MATOS

INTRODUCTION

European integration was as much a magnet for Portugal a quarter of a century ago as it is for eastern European countries today. Portugal went from having an authoritarian regime to democratic, European capitalism, avoiding a Communist takeover because it was a strong nation-state, had a cohesive society with a competitive elite, and a level of development about half that of the EU (European Union) average.[1] Eastern European new democracies are weak on these basic features and will, therefore, face wider difficulties than Portugal did in the institutionalization of democracy and European integration.

In Portugal, as in eastern European countries, the fall of non-democratic political regimes was followed by the institutionalization of democracy and negotiations for integration in the EU.[2] This study will not analyse the transition processes.[3] Instead, the path of comparative statistics will be followed. This essay will confront Portugal and the Eastern European candidates at two moments: revolution (Portugal: 1974–75; Eastern Europe: fall of Berlin wall) and the date of accession to EU (Portugal: 1985; Eastern Europe: 1995, or latest year for which relevant, comparable statistics are available). This second moment has a close connection with the institutionalization of liberal democracy.

When appropriate, Portugal and the eastern European candidates will be compared with the EU. I will not consider the EU situation after possible enlargement.[4] As a rule, I will not take the pre-revolution situation into consideration. The word 'revolution' is used to mean deep social and political change. 'Coup' is used for decisive acts in the revolutionary process. My underlying assumption is that there is a crucial triangle for speedy European integration and the institutionalization of

The author wishes to thank José da Silva Lopes and Magalhães Mota for advice and information.

representative democracy: a strong state-nation, strong elites and a reasonable level of economic development. We will study Portugal's triangle in more detail than the EU Eastern candidates.

This essay will privilege political (state-nation) independent variables. Social sciences often disregard the role of the state-nation; one should consider 'the sovereign state as a prerequisite to democracy'.[5] The following independent variables will be taken into account: strength of the state-nation, strength of the country's elite, average economic development, presence of the welfare state, and society cohesiveness. I consider the strength of the state-nation as a condition for the other independent variables, but also allow it some autonomy. The dependent variable is the ability of each country to transform revolution into representative democracy and implement European integration.[6]

This essay will begin by identifying the European influence and will then analyse the independent variables in the above-mentioned order. Two historical aspects will be considered both for Portugal and the eastern European countries: international environment (world economic growth and character of international conflict) and the domestic political agendas at the moments of revolution and EU accession. The conclusion will propose an explanation for the behaviour of the dependent variable: national ability to cope with revolution and European integration.

THE EUROPEAN MAGNET

European integration worked as a magnet for Portuguese society in the years before the revolution of 25 April. European society was richer and freer than the Portuguese. This was so from a broad, social viewpoint. About 1.5 million Portuguese had immigrated to western European countries, in particular to France.[7] Tourism had been a growth industry and most of the tourists came from Western Europe.[8] These factors became evident to all that the Portuguese, as individuals, could integrate into a modern, liberal democracy.

Tourism and emigration were also important from an economic viewpoint. Portuguese trade balance was traditionally in deficit, and the 'Estado Novo' did not solve the problem.[9] Portuguese trade was primarily with Western Europe.[10] The equilibrium of foreign payments was achieved through emigrant workers' remittances[11] and foreign tourist spending in Portugal.[12] Thus the European character of these new phenomena was obvious.

Foreign direct investment was also important for the economy: it created jobs, contributed directly to the reserves of foreign currency, and indirectly through the exports it created (textiles, garments). Most foreign capital came from European countries.[13]

All Portuguese society shared the attraction of European integration. Portugal had been a founding member of the Organization for European Economic Co-operation – OEEC, established under the Marshall Plan (1948), but even in the Salazar government, at the end of 1959, some ministers wanted immediate entry into the EU.[14] In 1960 the central bank, *Banco de Portugal*, stated publicly that it took for granted the future integration of the country into the EU, but it said this *en passant*.[15] However, the exact position of financial and industrial capital concerning European integration is not known. Most likely, banking and insurance would not accept not following the United Kingdom, and most industrialists needed access to trans-Pyrenees markets.

At the beginning of the 1960s, a new factor changed perspectives towards Portuguese integration into the EU: the African colonial war in Angola and, later, Guinea-Bissau and Mozambique. Then, Europe meant integration into the EU-Six and EU-Nine. European integration required some degree of economic development and democratic institutions. Although Portugal was underdeveloped, it might acquire an 'association agreement' from the EU, such as Greece did in 1962. Portugal was not only underdeveloped: it conducted a colonial war that was unpopular and required a dictatorship. A colonial dictatorship, however, would never be accepted as a full member of the EU, and the elite knew this.

At the end of the 1960s and beginning of 1970s, a large and open debate took place in Portuguese society – 'Europe or Africa'. The last *Estado Novo* government, headed by Marcello Caetano, had to recognize publicly that its supporters were divided over the EU,[16] but that the EU attracted the Portuguese. The trade agreement he signed with the EU (1972) was presented as a 'dynamic' agreement, implying that the regime would be able to apply for full membership.[17]

A larger portion of *Estado Novo* looked then towards trans-Pyrenees Europe as a political model. This was obviously the case of the liberal wing (*al a liberal*), which the *Estado Novo* had allowed since 1969. Portuguese traditional and democratic opposition looked in the same direction.[18]

The United States served as a weaker model. Portuguese immigration into the United States was limited and from the Azores islands. Trade,[19] tourism,[20] and foreign direct investment relations were weaker than with

Europe.[21] America's role was restricted to military and defence affairs. Portugal had been a founding member of the North Atlantic Treaty Organization (NATO – 1949), and the collaboration between the US armed services and the Portuguese Navy and Air Force remained strong, despite the Portuguese African wars.

Apparently, western European integration today works as a magnet for eastern European countries as well. America's economic role is smaller in eastern Europe than it was for Portugal at the time of the latter's entry into the EU.[22] Nevertheless, the US example is politically stronger in eastern European countries for three main reasons: America led the cold war against the USSR, the Communist empire that oppressed these countries; several of them have strong immigrant communities in the United States; Washington promoted the eastward enlargement of NATO, the first westward integration of candidate countries after the fall of Russian communism. It should be noted that Russian trade is still important for Eastern candidates, although it is diminishing.[23]

Before the revolution Portugal was politically isolated because of the colonial war but, as we have seen, it was isolated neither in defence nor in economic affairs. Prior to their revolution Eastern candidates were integrated into the Soviet bloc and could not belong to international economic institutions outside this bloc.

STRENGTH OF THE NATION-STATE

I consider the state-nation a sovereign entity with a permanent territorial basis and an organized people.[24] It is a classification based on Continental constitutional law,[25] *Allgemeine Staatslehre*,[26] and international politics.[27]

'Nation' is best viewed as a word and not a concept tinted by disguised or unacknowledged racialism. 'Nation' is inevitably connected with race, culture – a specific culture – and '*Volk*', and has romantic, ethnocentric and biological connotations. Its connection to 'state' was born between the Vienna Congress and the First World War and presupposes that the people of the state are a constant, homogeneous stock of human beings. This presupposition is not proven. The metaphor of the old axe can help us view the people of a state: the owner has changed both the head and the handle, but it is still the same axe. The owner is the state-nation; the people are the axe. The state-nation is able to change the head and handle with its emigration policy and nationality law. Thus the liaison between state and nation also takes for granted that a state is more efficient when it is a 'nation' – when it is ethnically/

culturally homogeneous. This idea lacks proof. Writers have tried to discover the alchemy through which a 'nation' concocts a 'state', but they have failed: they cannot separate it from *Volk*, mix *Volk* (a '*Gemeinschaft*') with nationalism (a '*Gesellschaft*'), or, last but not least, do not identify the way a *Volk* or culture creates a state legitimacy.[28] It is a truism that perceived non-homogeneity in cultural/ethnic matters may affect a state-nation.[29] However, because it is clear that the same 'nations' have different state effects, the explanation must be found elsewhere. I will therefore use the concepts of social integration and social cohesion.[30] I still use the word 'nation', however, because it is traditional. It qualifies the state as neither an empire nor a federation.

The state-nation is important in the EU, which is a specific kind of association of state-nations. Its federal element is weak, for there is no directly elected president or executive; the Parliament is directly elected but has few (although growing) powers and fails to attract citizens' attention and respect; and the EU budget is less than 1.27 per cent of EU-15 gross domestic product (GDP).[31]

Without being a strong state-nation, a country cannot successfully integrate into the EU.[32] I will try to measure the strength of state-nation on political grounds.

The first criterion is how long a country has been independent.[33] Every state-nation wants to persevere in its independence. The fact that it has not failed in its bid for independence is the best indicator of strength.[34] The older the country, the stronger it is: political age shows a capacity for reproduction and is an indirect measure of institutionalization.[35]

Age is not enough, however, for this might mean senility. I take, as the second criterion of state-nation strength then, the state's ability to persevere in independence. Independence requires appropriate means, which will be the indicator of this variable. Sheer size, as we shall see below, is an ambivalent means indicator. The best is GDP per capita at purchasing power parity (PPP).[36] Military criteria could be used, but these are less certain. If the above-mentioned criteria had been used in 1914 (prior to the First World War), the US victory in both world wars could not have been anticipated. As a matter of fact, '*l'argent est le nerf de la guerre*' (Rabelais). In practical terms, moral factors count. I will measure these factors indirectly through the behaviour of the elite.

The third criterion is the number of land frontiers with other state-nations. *Rebus sic stantibus* – the more frontiers, the more difficult the task of keeping independence. The number of potential alliances – either friendly or adversarial – increases quickly with the number of state frontiers and so increases the uncertainty of the policy of a given country. Uncertainty decreases security, and security is the raw material of independence.[37]

The number of inhabitants and area are traditionally seen as sources of state power. Area includes the land and the maritime surface – although the latter is less strongly protected in international law than the former. Maritime area increases the freedom of communications of a given state and has economic value.[38]

The role of population and area in creating state strength is ambivalent. They may be a liability for state-nations who have powerful neighbours and lack stable, strong allies. In any case, inside EU-15 population is an asset because it carries voting power. Let us apply these criteria to Portugal and Eastern European candidates, at the time of accession.

Age of independence is favourable to Portugal.[39] Portuguese independence (twelfth century) is older than Eastern candidates: only one of the Eastern countries was independent before the First World War; these countries are typical products of the nineteenth-century 'nationality principle'.[40] Several newborn states have strong national cultures (Baltic states, Poland, Hungary), but these cultures failed to have a translation in the state-nation.[41] By this criterion EU-14 member states are not stronger than Portugal and are stronger than Eastern candidates.[42]

If we take into account the population deflated by GDP per capita at PPP, Portugal has an advantage. Portuguese population is 2.5 times smaller than EU-15 member states and eastern European candidates' population is 2.4 times smaller. If we deflate population with GDP per capita, Portugal at the time of accession (1985) was 4.4 times smaller and eastern Europeans' candidates were 7.5 times smaller than the EU-15 average. Portuguese and eastern European state populations are small by this criterion.

The criterion of the number of land frontiers is quite advantageous to Portugal, which has only one land frontier. In the EU-15 the average of land frontiers per state is 3.2; among Eastern candidates this figure rises to 4.5. Hungary, Poland, Romania and Slovakia, by this order, are the countries most afflicted by the land frontier problem.[43]

The conclusions from the population viewpoint are more encouraging to Eastern candidates. The average population of EU-15 member states is 25 million. Portugal and eastern European candidates have sizes similar to one another: a little more than 10 million each, with the Portuguese slightly smaller than the eastern European candidates. There is a wide dispersion of population among eastern European candidates, however: Poland and Romania are above the EU-15 average; the others are under it and have a population equal to (Hungary) or less than the Portuguese.

Portugal may derive some advantage from area criteria as well, if we take into account maritime surface. The average land area of EU-15 countries is 80,911 square miles — almost double that of the eastern European candidates' average (41,558 square miles) and more than double that of Portugal's (35,552 square miles). There is a large variation in the land area of Eastern candidates, with Poland and Romania above the EU-15 average, the other candidates below this average but higher than (Bulgaria), equal to (Hungary), or smaller than (the others) Portugal.

The situation is reversed if we take into account land and sea areas: the EU-15 average is 190,298 square miles; the Eastern candidates' is 41,558 square miles, while Portugal has 639,531 square miles.[44] All in all, according to the state-nation criteria, Portugal is stronger than the eastern European candidates. The date of independence is a big advantage, as is the number of land frontiers; population deflated by riches and by area is also relevant. The findings on the former criteria are summarized in Figure 1 and Table 1.

FIGURE 1

POLITICAL STRENGTH OF EUROPEAN NATION-STATES

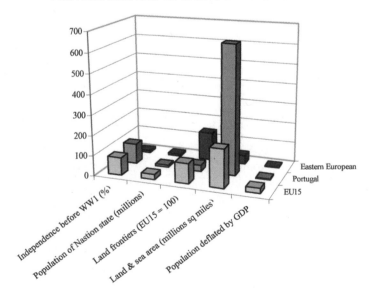

TABLE 1

POLITICAL STRENGTH OF EUROPEAN STATE-NATIONS

	Date of independence	Population taking into account PPP	Number of land frontier countries	Population, millions	Land area (square miles)	Sea area (square miles)	Land and sea area (square miles)
Austria	Before Westphalia	9.05	3	8.082	32,377	0	32,377
Belgium	Vienna Congress	11.44	1	10.213	11,780	800	12,580
Denmark	Before Westphalia	6.16	9	5.313	16,629	31,042	47,671
Finland	First World War	4.95	3	5.16	130,127	21,300	151,427
France	Before Westphalia	63.09	2	58.966	176,460	272,739	449,199
Germany	Vienna Congress	90.24	6	82.038	137,803	14,440	152,243
Greece	Vienna Congress	6.95	1	10.533	50,942	44,400	95,342
Ireland	First World War	3.48	4	3.744	27,135	138,600	165,735
Italy	Vienna Congress	59.34	3	57.612	116,305	60,100	176,405
Luxemburg	Vienna Congress	0.73	2	0.429	998	0	998
Netherlands	Before Westphalia	16.86	7	15.76	14,413	19,400	33,813
Portugal	Before Westphalia	6.69	1	9.98	35,552	639,531	675,083
Spain	Before Westphalia	30.33	3	39.394	194,884	79,200	274,084
Sweden	Before Westphalia	8.94	2	8.854	173,731	28,262	201,993
United Kingdom	Before Westphalia	5.33	1	59.247	94,525	291,000	385,525
EU-15		375.33	48	375.325	1,213,661	1,640,814	2,854,475
Bulgaria	First World War	1.98	4	8.23	42,822	9,923	52,745
Czech Republic	First World War	5.66	4	10.29	30,387	0	30,387
Estonia	First World War	0.33	2	1.446	17,413	4,479	21,892
Hungary	First World War	3.73	7	10.092	35,919	0	35,919
Latvia	First World War	0.44	3	2.439	24,749	6,023	30,772
Lithuania	First World War	0.89	4	3.701	25,174	1,390	26,564
Poland	First World War	11.99	7	38.667	120,726	7,490	128,216
Romania	Vienna Congress	5.17	5	22.489	91,699	6,950	98,649
Slovakia	After the fall of Russian communism	2.21	5	5.393	18,859	0	18,859

TABLE 1 (cont.)

	Date of independence	Population taking into account PPP	Number of land frontier countries	Population, millions	Land area (square miles)	Sea area (square miles)	Land and sea area (square miles)
Slovenia	After the fall of Russian communism	1.17	4	1.978	7,836	0	7,836
Eastern Candidates		33.51	45	104.725	415,584	36,254	451,838
Total		408.84	93	480.050	1,629,245	1,677,069	3,306,314
X		5.65	1	10.014	35,552	639,531	675,083
Average 15		25.0	3.2	25.000	80,911	109,388	190,298
Average Eastern		3.4	4.5	10.500	41,558	13,998	41,558

Notes and sources: *Date of independence* – The New York Times Almanac 2001; Interruptions of independence caused by the First World War and the Second World War were not taken into account; the First World War data include countries whose date of independence is shortly before 1914.

Population, millions – COM (2000) 34; The New York Times Almanac 2001.

Land area (square miles) – The New York Times Almanac 2001 (2.590024 square km = 1 square mile).

Sea area (square miles) – http://www.wri.org/wr-00-01/pdf/cmi3n_2000.pdf; state-nations claims. Exclusive economic zone: France, Portugal; exclusive fishing zone: Belgium, Greece, Ireland, Netherlands, Spain, United Kingdom.

Number of land frontier countries – Andorra, Liechtenstein, Monaco, and Vatican were not taken into account.

Population taking into account PPP – Measured in millions.

Sources: Agenda 2000. 2 Le défi de l'élargissement, p.69; basis for EU-15 average: GNP PPP, 1995; Portugal 1985: Barreto (1996): p.369; 56.4 per cent of the European average in 1981–90.

STRENGTH OF THE NATION-STATE ELITE

A state-nation needs a ruling elite; without it, it will not survive. I will measure the strength of the ruling elite by three indicators: duration of national independence, survival of pre-revolution ruling elite, and degree of political fragmentation.

Let us begin with the question of the duration of the independent state-nations: because they all want to be independent, the longer they are, the stronger the elite – *rebus sic stantibus*. By this criterion, Portugal comes out ahead of the Eastern European candidates. In this case, *rebus sic stantibus* seems a heavy clause. Stronger neighbours and foreign alliances may conceivably defeat a strong state-nation elite.

The issue can be put the other way round, however: regardless of the strength of the country, a strong elite in a small country with a big neighbour can build permanent alliances that safeguard its independence against the potential enemy. If we compare two pairs of neighbours – Poland–Germany and Portugal–Spain – we see that the demographical factor is more favourable towards Poland than towards Portugal: there were fewer than 2.3 Germans for one Pole and more than 3.5 Spaniards for one Portuguese.[45] The Portuguese elite ruled a strong state-nation that could find permanent allies, while the Polish elite was unable to rule a strong state and was uncertain towards its allies: after the Second World War the Communist takeover was preceded by a brief civil war between Westernophile and Russianophile sectors of the Polish elite.[46]

The second indicator is the presence in post-revolution government of political parties of the pre-revolution ruling elite. This presence indicates a weak elite, unable to assure the rotation of leading personnel. Portugal was able to replace the former elite in the immediate aftermath of the military coup and during the first phases of the Revolution. However, it is difficult to quantify the replacement because we lack case studies and have to work with broad statistics. The replacement rate was likely to be close to 75 per cent. There was an element of compulsion in the replacement of leading personnel but it was comparatively minor: few people were arrested;[47] the law forbade a large number of former regime dignitaries to exercise political rights.[48] I shall examine briefly the elite replacement in government; civil service, local government; armed services; schools and universities; media; private enterprise and parliament. No post-revolution minister belonged to the previous regime. Later, however, a few former political leaders were accepted as individuals because they had been critical members of the *Estado Novo*.

The purge of the civil service started immediately after the coup. The *Junta de Salvação Nacional* (JSN – the supreme revolutionary organ) approved legislation to reintegrate civil servants dismissed for political reasons and to purge civil servants who did not accept the new democratic regime.[49] Purge commissions, one in the ministerial department, were created on 19 August 1974; their jobs were designated to end on 28 February 1975.[50] After the abortive coup of 11 March 1975, new '*saneamento*' (purge) laws were approved.[51] These were retroactive: civil servants could be purged because they had been fascists before the Revolution, and many *saneamentos* did not follow the legal procedure ('*saneamentos selvagens*', 'wild purges', in a literal translation).

At the end of 1975, more than 20,000 civil servants had been '*saneados*', by legal and illegal means, including every kind of sanction, from dismissal to mild reprehension.[52] The number of *saneados* was about eight per cent of the total number of civil servants.[53] Purges were stronger at higher echelons, and top echelons, in a generous definition, amounted to approximately 10,630 persons.[54] The total number of 'purged' therefore was more than double that of high-ranking civil servants. The extent of the purges varied with departments. It was particularly mild in the foreign service, but in several others, most or all of the mandarins were purged.

During the first weeks after the coup, the JSN maintained local government organs of the former regime and nominated military representatives for the biggest 'concelhos'.[55] *Movimento Democrático Português* (MDP), an electoral opposition alliance, that was becoming a front organization for the Portuguese Communist party, promoted meetings of citizens that elected a new town hall and occupied its premises. There were such movements in every one of the 18 'distritos' but they were stronger in Coimbra, Aveiro, Leiria e Braga, and in littoral areas where traditional Democratic opposition had a stronger machine. In some cases, the town hall was occupied without formalities.[56] There were movements for the replacement of the previous mayors and town councillors in more than one-third of the '*municípios*'[57] of the Portuguese mainland.[58] Not all of them were successful. The movement was stopped because *municípios* did not have sufficient funds and the central government declared it would not provide financial support for illegal town halls. When the first free local elections took place, there was an almost universal replacement of the ruling local elite. All generals and admirals were replaced shortly after 25 April. The winners of the coup wanted to make a deep and quick military *saneamento*, but failed. The purge was broadened during the social revolution of 1975.

The military Junta dismissed the chancellors of all public universities who had been nominated by the *Estado Novo* and, in many cases, faced student rebellions. In most faculties students and professors elected governing boards. In May 1974 a large portion of secondary school teachers dismissed their headmasters, nominated by the *Estado Novo*, and elected governing bodies. The first provisional government recognized the 'right to democratic management of schools'. The change in faculty and secondary school management was almost total in the period of just a year.

In many faculties professors were dubbed '*saneados*' at student meetings or by elected revolutionary committees. The *saneamentos* were particularly harsh at the Lisbon Law Faculty, the Lisbon Engineering School (IST), and Lisbon Architecture School.[59] Nevertheless, only a small number of professors were purged.

All leaders of national television, radio and press were replaced immediately after the coup. State monopoly television changed hands. Radio Renascença, a Roman Catholic Church radio station, was given to its revolutionary employees. Other national radio stations were controlled by a mix of military and workers rule. Almost all editors of national dailies and weeklies were replaced; journalists elected councils at each newspaper ('*conselhos de redacção*'). These councils had the power of veto over nominations. Only the local press did not change hands.

In the business sector there was also a widespread call for *saneamento*. Three main political factors provoked mobility of the entrepreneurial elite: labour fights, '*intervenções*' of the state in the management of enterprises (intervention in Allende's Chile style), and nationalizations. The results are even harder to quantify.

One of the objectives of workers' struggles after 25 April was the *saneamento*, either of the owner or of the management (or both). In May 1974 more than one-third of workers' movements aimed at *saneamento* of the bosses.[60] Between May 1974 and February 1976, *saneamento* was present in 18 per cent of labour conflicts.[61] *Intervenções* was a temporary replacement of owners and management. It respected property rights, but the state nominated the new management. It started in 1974 and accelerated after the coup of 11 March. The replacements were often determined by financial problems of the enterprise. Workers often requested '*intervenção*'.

Nationalizations took place on a large scale after the 11 March coup. Banking, insurance, copper mining, cement, glass mining, breweries, steel making, oil refining, fertilizers, paper manufacturing, naval shipyards, power utilities, road transport, air transport, railroads and shipping were all nationalized. The CUF group (*Companhia União Fabril*), the biggest, was nationalized. The owners were displaced by the state. The new management came usually from top layers of the former private enterprise, but political criteria were not forgotten. The political climate was anti-business. Some businessmen were arrested, while many fled to Brazil. Almost one-fifth of the industrialists left Portugal and at least two per cent were purged, mostly in the big enterprises of Lisbon and Setúbal.[62] After the 11 March coup, authorities allowed the occupation of land, south of the Tagus River, by land wage earners. Such occupation implied the transfer of ownership and management of most of the land.

Most eastern European candidates had a different elite replacement. The majority of them had post-revolution governments made of the former ruling (Communist) party. That was the case with Bulgaria, Hungary, Lithuania, Poland, Romania, Slovakia and Slovenia. Only Estonia, Latvia, and the Czech Republic escaped. Apparently the replacement of the elite was slower and less complete than in Portugal. The former communist elite became the new economic elite.[63]

This pluralistic, competitive character of the Portuguese elite was also evident in the first free elections with universal vote (25 April 1975). The law forbade leaders of the former regime to vote and to be elected.[64] Some small parties were also forbidden, both on the right and on the left, but no front party for the deposed regime tried to compete in the elections. The absence of political fragmentation is also a distinctive feature between Portugal and eastern European candidates. Fourteen parties competed for the first free elections (25 April 1975) but only six elected representatives. Since then, the two biggest parties have had more than 64 per cent of the vote.

The eastern European countries have more fragmented assemblies than the EU-15 or Portugal: the sum of parliamentary mandates of the two biggest parties, a rough indicator of non-fragmentation, is 60 per cent against 85 per cent in Portugal and 70 per cent in EU-15. Their party systems do not seem to follow the constituent principles of EU-15 party systems: conservative and liberal; Socialist and non-Socialist; Communist and non-Communist; and ecological. There are no ecological parties. There are political relics, such as the agrarian parties; the strength of ethnic parties does not look much greater than in some western countries, but it is more widespread. Some party systems do not appear to be stabilized. Results of political fragmentation for the time of accession are summarized in Figure 2 and Table 2.

FIGURE 2

% OF MP OF THE TWO BIGGEST POLITICAL PARTIES IN THE ELECTED ASSEMBLY

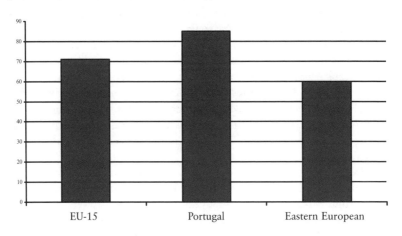

TABLE 2

POLITICAL STRENGTH OF STATE-NATIONS

	Former ruling party returning to power	Sum of seats of two biggest parties as a % of total seats		Former ruling party returning to power	Sum of seats of two biggest parties as a % of total seats
Austria	X	64	Bulgaria	Yes	77
Belgium	X	30	Czech Republic	No	69
Denmark	X	67	Estonia	No	48
Finland	X	63	Hungary	Yes	57
France	X	67	Latvia	No	45
Germany	X	81	Lithuania	Yes	60
Greece	X	94	Poland	Yes	75
Ireland	X	85	Romania	Yes	62
Italy	X	84	Slovakia	Yes	57
Luxemburg	X	57	Slovenia	Yes	49
Netherlands	X	55	Eastern Europe candidates	X	60
Portugal	No	85			
Spain	No	88			
Sweden	X	61			
United Kingdom	X	88			
SUBTOTAL		71			

Source: CIA, The World Fact Book 2001; year of the election: the last one (generally between 1995 and 1999).

Criteria of choice of Assemblies: elected by direct vote; the lower chamber, bar Belgium (Senate).

To summarize the situation, I must underline that the Portuguese revolution was endogenous; it was started by a military coup that was planned and executed without foreign consent or knowledge. The eastern Europe revolutions were exogenous: they were the result of the fall of Russian communism. Several Eastern European countries had staged anti-Russian uprisings (Hungary, 1956; Czechoslovakia, 1968), which were smashed by Russian troops, and Communist regimes of Hungary, Poland, and Romania tried to resist Moscow rule in 1980s. They all failed, however.

AVERAGE ECONOMIC DEVELOPMENT

Average economic development is important: the less developed a country, the more difficult it becomes to attain average EU-15 development. To assess average economic development, I take three variables: individual income, openness of the economy, and degree of development of the 'welfare-state'. The choice of these sub-variables is almost self-evident. If too poor a country is integrated with a rich one, the former's economy will be damaged. The openness of the economy is a sign of competitive capacity.[65] The welfare dimension of the state is indispensable as a cushion for social and economic shocks. The indicators for these variables will be: GDP per capita at PPP, for individual income; imports plus exports, as a percentage of GDP for the openness of the economy; infant mortality rate, for the degree of development of the 'welfare-state'. (I use an output, synthetic indicator for economic data for social security; other welfare payments are not available or not reliable.)

FIGURE 3

STRENGTH OF ECONOMY AND WELFARE STATE

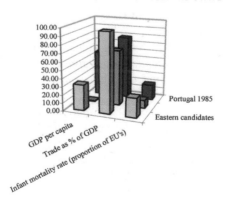

The Portuguese economy at the time of accession to the EU (1985) had a GDP per capital that was more than half that of the EU-15 average.[66] The Eastern candidates' in the mid-1990s were less than one-third of the EU average. Slovenia and the Czech Republic (both together a small portion of the candidate population) were the only countries whose personal income was better than or equal to the Portuguese.[67] The openness of eastern European economies is remarkable, probably because they are smaller. The openness is bigger than Portugal's and the EU-15's average in 1985. Actually they look too open but, nevertheless, they pass the test.

The dimension of the welfare state is weak. The Portuguese infant mortality rate was nearly double that of the EU-15 average of 1985; the eastern candidates' was 2.4 times bigger. Portugal and the eastern European candidates seem to spend too large a proportion of their GDP on welfare, and it is doubtful whether they can sustain this effort. They do not pass this test.

One could also use a technology variable. Portugal and Eastern Europe candidates are at the same level: they are both adapters.[68] A summary of the results is in Figure 3 and Table 3.

SOCIETY COHESIVENESS

Society cohesiveness is a strong variable during a process of social transformation. If different social conflicts interact, the transformation process is more difficult. I will consider four sub-variables of social cohesiveness: strength of the family, strength of the individual, strength of voluntary associations, and political character of ethnic/cultural minorities. These sub-variables are almost self-justified: if the family is not strong, social problems will increase. If every individual has too many difficulties, social problems will arise. If voluntary associations are weak, social disintegration will follow.[69] The indicators are: rate of divorce, for the strength of the family;[70] rate of suicide, for the absence of personal difficulties; proportion of atheists, for the strength of voluntary associations;[71] and proportion of immigrant population, as an indirect indicator for potential social trouble.[72]

The rate of divorce in Portugal at the moment of accession was rather more than one-third of the EU-15 average and almost 2.5 times smaller than that of the Eastern candidates. The Eastern candidates' divorce rate is almost equal to the EU-15's. In accordance with secularization theory, this rate is higher than expected. The rate of suicide in Eastern candidates

TABLE 3

GDP, FOREIGN TRADE, AND WELFARE STATE

	GDP per capita divided by EU-15	Trade as % of GDP, 1995	Infant mortality rate 1998, per thousand newborn
Austria	1.12	77	5
Belgium	1.12	143	6
Denmark	1.16	64	5
Finland	0.96	68	4
France	1.07	43	5
Germany	1.10	46	5
Greece	0.66	57	6
Ireland	0.93	136	6
Italy	1.03	49	6
Luxemburg	1.69	x	5
Netherlands	1.07	99	5
Portugal	0.67	66	8
Spain	0.77	47	6
Sweden	1.01	77	4
United Kingdom	0.09	57	6
SUBTOTAL	1.00	68.6	5.5
Bulgaria	0.24	94	14
Czech Republic	0.55	108	5
Estonia	0.23	160	18
Hungary	0.37	67	10
Latvia	0.18	91	18
Lithuania	0.24	108	19
Poland	0.31	53	10
Romania	0.23	60	21
Slovakia	0.41	124	9
Slovenia	0.59	113	5
Eastern Europe candidates	0.32	97.8	2.4
Portugal 1985	56.4	78.1	1.9

Notes and sources: *GDP per capita*

Sources – In so far as I know, EU gives no figure for average GDP per capita PPP of Eastern candidates. To calculate the average I took the scale of GDP per capita at PPP for 1995 given by EU, Agenda 2000. 2 Le défi de l'élargissement, p.69; I deflated with these PPP figures the gross national product per capita given by the World Bank for 1995 (values of the above table); Portugal 1985: Barreto (2000): p.369 (quoting EU sources).

Trade as a % of GDP – Export + imports.
Sources – World Development Report 1997; subtotals: means; Portugal 1985: Economic Indicators, Banco de Portugal, July 1987.

Infant mortality rate – Per thousand newborn in the rows until Slovenia; last two rows of first and third column: (Eastern candidates and Portugal 1985): values for infant mortality rate (mean for Eastern European candidates) divided EU-15 average in 1998 and 1985, respectively.
Sources – Human Development Report 2000; Portugal 1985: Barreto (2000): p.85; ibid., EU-15, p.258.

is three times greater than the EU-15 average and five times greater than the Portuguese rate at the moment of accession.

The proportion of atheists in Eastern Europe's candidates (17 per cent) almost doubles the Portuguese one (nine per cent),[73] and is nearly 50 per cent higher than the EU-15's (12 per cent).[74] Only Poland has a low atheistic proportion. Without Poland the figures would be higher for Eastern candidates (24 per cent of atheists, double the EU-15 average).[75] According to secularization theory, this rate is also higher than expected since average economic development in these countries is inferior to the EU-15's.

The percentage of immigrants in Eastern European candidates is more than double that of the EU-15 (13 per cent and six per cent). Portugal, at the time of accession, had almost no immigrant population. Poland is the only Eastern candidate without a significant immigrant population. The word 'immigrants' hides a deep difference between EC-15 and eastern European candidates. Immigrants in EU-15 came in recently (a generation ago) for economic reasons. In the Eastern countries they include ethnic minorities who live in the given country for a considerable time. These latter minorities have a claim to political rights – as opposed to EU-15 immigrants – and as a rule they belong culturally (or ethnically) to a neighbour country. This fact increases the likelihood of conflict, of the Balkans type – a product of the 'nationality principle'.[76]

Some EU-15 countries (for example, UK, Belgium, and Spain) have the second type of minority. As a rule, however, their claims are pacific and are not supported by neighbour countries. Potentially they are less dangerous. On every count of social cohesion, the Eastern European candidates are in a weak situation. The case is summarized in Figure 4 and Table 4.

THE INTERNATIONAL ENVIRONMENT

The economic and the overall international pictures were the opposite at the time of Portuguese revolution (1974) and EU accession (1985) and at the time of Eastern Europe revolution (1990) and demand for EU accession (end of the nineteenth century). In 1974–75 the world economy was slowing down to a recession due to the oil crisis. In the 1980s there was a slow growth.[77] On the other hand, the Eastern revolutions took place in a climate of economic expansion of the 1990s. The economic environment was more favourable for the eastern European revolution than for the Portuguese one.[78] The same was true

FIGURE 4
SOCIAL COHESION OF EUROPEAN NATION-STATES

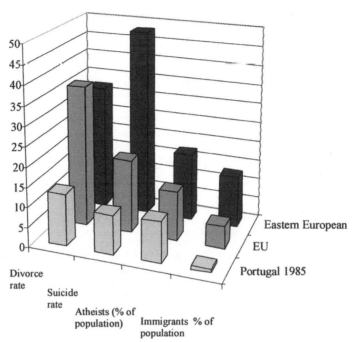

TABLE 4
SOCIAL COHESION OF EUROPEAN STATE-NATIONS

	Divorce rate	Suicide rate	Atheists (% of population)	Immigrants (% of population)
Austria	38	30	10.0	9
Belgium	56	26.7	10.0	9
Denmark	35	24.3	18.0	3
Finland	56	38.7	14.0	1
France	43	30.4	19.0	7
Germany	41	22.1	23.0	9
Greece	18	5.7	2.0	1
Ireland	0	17.9	4.0	2
Italy	12	12.7	7.0	1
Luxemburg	39	29	n.a.	31
Netherlands	41	13.1	11.4	9
Portugal	21	10.3	9.4	3
Spain	17	12.5	3.0	4
Sweden	64	20	12.0	12
United Kingdom	53	11	6.3	4

TABLE 4 (cont.)

	Divorce rate	Suicide rate	Atheists (% of population)	Immigrants (% of population)
EU-15	36	18.5	12.4	5.6
Bulgaria	28	25.3	24.0	20
Czech Republic	61	24	57.0	19
Estonia	102	64.3	38.0	31
Hungary	46	49.2	20.0	10
Latvia	63	59.5	11.0	48
Lithuania	55	73.7	12.0	17
Poland	19	24.1	6.0	3
Romania	24	21.1	14.0	20
Slovakia	34	n.a.	16.0	20
Slovenia	26	48	27.2	7
Eastern European candidates	32	48	17.2	13
Portugal 1985	13	9.8	n.a.	1

Notes and sources: Divorce rate – Divorces as a % of marriages per year: I applied this rate to 0.07 per cent of total population (0.07% is second best for yearly number of marriages as a proportion of total population).
Sources – Human Development Report 2000; Portugal 1985: 13.1 per cent (Barreto 2000:86: divorces as a % of marriages).

Suicide rate – Male suicide per 100,000, 1993–98.
Sources – Human Development Report 2000; Portugal 1985: Barreto (2000): p.98.

Atheists (% of population) – I tried to pinpoint the 'hard core' atheists, those who are firmly convinced that God does not exist and firmly reject the possibility of life after death (see Jagodzinski and Greeley, 'The Demand for Religion: Hard Core Atheism and "Supply Side" Theory', http://courses.smsu.edu/mdg421f/resources/Religious%20 Studies.htm. Sources are not homogeneous.
Sources – Austria, Belgium, Denmark, Finland, France, Germany, Ireland, Italy, Spain, Sweden, Bulgaria, Estonia, Hungary, Latvia, Lithuania, Czech (Census), Romania (Census), Slovakia: Carles Vilar, Estadísticas Internacionales de Religión Reales, http://home.talkcity. com/spiritst/yebisannu/norelesp.htm; The New York Times Almanac 2001; see also International Social Sciences Survey, several surveys, quoted in 'The Demand for Religion: Hard Core Atheism and "Supply Side" Theory' by Jagodzinski and Greeley.

Immigrants as % of population – Includes first generation of foreign-born children. Sources are not homogeneous.
Sources – Austria, Belgium, Denmark, Germany, Greece, Ireland, Italy, Luxemburg, Finland, United Kingdom: 'Workers of the World', The Economist, 30 Oct. 1997 (source: OCDE; numbers out of chart); Netherlands, Sweden: The New York Almanac 2001; France: http:// fr.encyclopedia.yahoo.com/articles/cl/cl_778_p1.html#cl_778.54; Spain: press reports on the legalization of immigrants plus 0.6 million gypsies ('Europe's Spectral Nation', The Economist, 10 May 2001); Portugal: 'Ucranianos Já São a Terceira Maior Comunidade de Imigrantes', por Ricardo Dias Felner, Público, 23 June 2001 (figures of legal immigrants 2001); Eastern candidates: The New York Times Almanac 2001; Portugal 1985: rough estimate.

for the institutionalization of democracy, but no one can tell in what economic environment the membership of the Eastern postulants will take place.

The international political situation was also less favourable for the Portuguese case. The Revolution took place during the cold war, when negotiations for the Organization for Security and Co-operation in Europe were taking place. It was the time of strong Euro-Communist parties in France and Italy. Italy was crucial for the NATO military arsenal against USSR. Franco's regime in Spain was in agony after the brutal assassination of the heir-designated, admiral Carrero Blanco. There were widespread fears of a Communist takeover in Western Europe.

During the Portuguese Revolution, Henry Kissinger, then US Secretary of State, 'never doubted that Portugal would fall definitively in the communist orbit'.[79] 'La politique du pire' did not win in Portugal because Mário Soares, European Socialists, and the US ambassador in Lisbon, Frank Carluci, fought it, but it was a hindrance for the institutionalization of democracy. Portuguese accession to the EU took place in a climate dominated by the intensification of the cold war. On the other hand, Eastern revolutions and democratic institutionalization took place during a period of international détente and generalization of representative democracy. Both economic and international political factors played against Portugal's transition and for eastern Europe's.

DOMESTIC POLITICAL AGENDA OF THE REVOLUTION

After the overthrow of the former regime, the political agendas of Portugal and eastern European revolutions were essentially different. In Portugal there was a conflict between representative democracy and a coalition between far left groups, soviet communism, and council aspirations. In eastern Europe there is a single-minded effort to establish representative democracy; the only conflicting set of goals is the nationalist paradigm. In Portugal the fight was between revolution and democratic capitalism; in Eastern Europe the question is how to implement democratic capitalism. The only eastern European alternative is nationalism. The candidates have not followed this road. Portugal, despite a hostile economic environment, was able to deliver a continuous growth of GDP per capita (only interrupted shortly in the mid-1980s) and Eastern European candidates had to face temporary declines in their standard of living.[80]

CONCLUSION

Portugal was able to accomplish a democratic revolution and accession to the EU because it had a strong state-nation, competitive elites, and a cohesive society. Accession was a big risk.[81] Portugal has not yet reached a stable outcome in the European arena.

Eastern Europeans candidates are weaker on these variables. They all have weak state-nation. They are also weaker on economic development and social cohesion. Being weaker, they will be unable to negotiate good conditions with the EU-15. The averages are misleading. Some eastern European candidates have better muscle than others. An Eastern candidates' union would be bad for all of them. The laggards should ask (and receive) help for adaptation, improving the free-trade agreements they have already signed.

Eastern European candidates should rebuild their elites and increase social cohesiveness before becoming full EU state-members. If they come in too quickly, they will be unable to cope with the challenges they will have to meet later on. *Mutatis mutandis*: this is also good advice for Portugal.

NOTES

1. The official name (or names) of the association(s) of European States, generally known as Common Market, changed in the time-span covered in the present study, but I refer to it as the 'European Union', adding the number of member-states when appropriate (EU-15, for instance for the membership at the time of writing; EU-14 is EU-15 without Portugal, for statistical reasons).
2. Bulgaria; Czech Republic; Estonia; Hungary; Latvia; Lithuania; Poland; Romania; Slovakia; Slovenia.
3. This job was done brilliantly in Linz and Stepan (1996).
4. That's the reason why in the following figures and tables, I will not print the sum for the EU-15+10.
5. Linz (1996). In the same direction, according to Schmitter (1999: 355): 'It is preferable, if not indispensable, that national identity and territorial limits be established before introducing reforms in political (or economic) institutions.'
6. Justification of the variables and indicators will be given at the beginning of each section. The reader is asked to accept strong simplifications and rough indicators. Number crunchers are asked to read the table notes where the statistical methodology is stated.
7. 1,409,222, 1996–73, in Barreto (1996).
8. In 1973 Portugal was visited by 4 million tourists; 3.4 million were Europeans (annual report of Banco de Portugal 1973. Vol.I: 111).
9. The trade deficit was 4.5 per cent of GDP in 1960 and 7.8 per cent in 1973 (Lopes 1996: 136).
10. In 1985, 52 per cent of Portuguese imports and 72 per cent of exports came from EU-12 + the remaining of EFTA (Lopes da Silva, in Barreto 1996).
11. Emigrant remittances were four per cent of GDP and covered 85 per cent of the trade deficit, in 1964; they were ten per cent of GDP and 120 per cent of the trade deficit in 1973 (Lopes 1996: 136).

12. Net receipts of tourism were 2.3 per cent of GDP in 1964 and around three per cent at the beginning of the 1970s (Lopes 1996: 136). Later, emigrant receipts decreased and tourism increased.

13. In 1986, 76 per cent of all incoming FDI came to Portugal from the EU (Lopes da Silva, in Barreto 1996: 298). In 1969–71 the proportion was smaller: 68 per cent (Matos 1972: 206).

14. Others wanted integration with the African colonies. Salazar sided with UK, and Portugal joined EFTA (Nogueira 1984: 105–7; unfortunately, no names are given for pro-EU ministers).

15. 'In fact, if accession of Portugal to GATT will imply a number of considerable modifications in the definition and implementation of our trade policy, in the direction of a progressive liberalization of trade, the effects of adhesion to the Common Market will be deeper and larger. It is not conceivable that Portugal may not follow the movement of approximation between EFTA and the European Economic Community' (report of *Banco de Portugal* 1961: Vol.I: 15, 37). 'Adhesion' to EU was conditional on British entry and meant that Portugal could not be economically isolated from the UK.

16. He said, after the negotiations with EU for a trade agreement: 'A division was outlined between defenders of approximation with Europe and defenders of integration with Overseas' (television speech made 14 Nov. 1972, in Caetano: 32). Until the end of the 'Estado Novo' (25 April 1974), the far-right, led by the President of the Republic, admiral Américo Thomaz, gave priority to 'Portuguese unity' with the colonies.

17. Speaking to the Luso-British Chamber of Commerce in Lisbon, 28 July 1971, during the negotiations with Brussels, the then-Minister of Finances, João Dias Rosas, insisted on the idea of a 'dynamic agreement' with the EU 'so that a progressive harmonization of economic policies takes place, enabling the effective integration of the Portuguese economy in the economy of Western Europe' (Lisbon daily press, 29 July 1971).

18. Schmitter (1999: 343) wrote that the 'prospect for entry into the European Community played a key role' in the consolidation of democracy.

19. In 1985, ten per cent of Portuguese imports came from the United States (Lopes da Silva, in Barreto 1996: 294).

20. In 1973, around ten per cent of foreign tourists in Portugal came from the United States and Canada (annual report of *Banco de Portugal* 1973, Vol.I, p.111).

21. In 1986, nine per cent of all incoming FDI came to Portugal from the United States (Lopes da Silva, in Barreto 1996: 298). In 1969–71 the proportion of US FDI was higher: 24 per cent (Matos 1972: 206).

22. Eastern European candidates' imports from the United States at the end of the 1990s were less than five per cent of their total imports: Bulgaria four per cent; Estonia 4.7 per cent; Poland 3.8 per cent; Romania 4.2 per cent (CIA, *The World Fact Book 2000*).

23. It is particularly relevant to the Baltic States, Bulgaria, Hungary, and Slovakia.

24. 'State-nation' is used instead of the more usual 'nation-state' to signify that the nation element is a subordinated one. Inspiration for the formula comes from Linz and Stepan (1996: 34).

25. Burdeau (1962: 14) defines the 'conditions for the existence of the state' as 'territory', the 'national community', and 'power and consent' pp.14ff.).

26. Zippelius (1974: 11); Kriele (1994: 20–22).

27. See Duchacek (1975: 7).

28. Among recent efforts: Hobsbawn (1994); Smith (1997).

29. Portugal is strong on the supposed 'cultural' dimension: it is 'the oldest state-nation in Europe and one with a population among the continent's most religious, linguistically and culturally homogeneous' (Schmitter 1999: 356–7). The same cannot be said about Eastern European candidates, although German Nazi action during the Second World War increased 'nation' homogeneity in the area. The case will not be studied.

30. Durkheim 1893, in particular the conclusions.

31. US federal budget is 20 per cent of US GDP (*The New York Times Almanac 2001*, pp.137, 314).
32. The death certificate of the 'state-nation' has been written (Habermans 2000). The case cannot be studied here. The report of this death, as of Mark Twain's, seems 'an exaggeration'.
33. Puppet states are not considered.
34. I deal with these criteria according to the importance I give them, starting with the most relevant, but I will not try to justify my scale thoroughly.
35. I follow the four basic criteria of institutionalisation: adaptability, complexity, autonomy, and coherence (Huntington 1973: 12).
36. PPP is the exchange rate between two currencies that buy the same basket of goods and services.
37. Maritime, non-coastal frontiers will not be considered because they are less vital, more flexible, and easier to defend.
38. I allow for considerable changes in the area of the state, provided it doesn't become a microstate.
39. I will classify the date of independence according to landmarks of the European state system: Westphalia peace (1648); Vienna Congress (1820); First World War (1918); Second World War; fall of Russian communism (1990).
40. Romania, 1878. Bulgaria and Hungary were semi-independent some time before the First World War.
41. The same is true of Germany.
42. Of the EU-14, eight were sovereign states prior to the Westphalia peace and only two (latecomers) were independent after the First World War (Finland, Ireland).
43. The situation would be less favourable to Portugal if maritime frontiers were taken into account.
44. Some of the candidates are landlocked countries. This topology subtracts roughly 0.7 percentage points from a country's annual growth (Sachs 1997).
45. Portugal–Spain: 1800–2000, average: 3.6; Germany–Poland: 1900–2000, average: 2.3 (more or less ten-year periods; Mitchell (1975). The comparison, of course, does not take into account ethnicity or cultural vicinity.
46. Poland had more land frontiers than Portugal but the case is not overruled with this argument: one can argue that Poland was unable to have a state.
47. The new regime made a point of not putting into jail too many former political leaders. Thomaz and Caetano, after a short stay in prison, were exiled to Brazil. The former Ministers of Interior, Colonies, and Army were also kept in jail for some time. Not more than a dozen other leaders were also imprisoned; as a rule they were *bêtes-noires* like admiral Tenreiro, Cazal-Ribeiro and captain Maltês. In 1975, after the abortive coup of 11 March, more arrests were made. Only the political police (PIDE-DGS) members were arrested *en masse*, around 900 of them; more than 1,000 agents were in the Colonies and escaped.
48. The Provisional Government authorized a meeting, however, of several hundred former members of ANP, the only party of *Estado Novo* [New State], on 13 Aug. 1974. It also allowed newspapers supporting the ancient regime. Repression increased after 11 March
49. Legal diplomas of 9 May and 25 June 1974.
50. Decree-Law no 544/74, 16 Oct.
51. Decree-Laws no 123/75 and no 124/75, 11 March. '*Saneamento*' is to make something or someone healthy. It is the usual euphemism for 'purge'.
52. Pinto (1993: 32). As Pinto remarks, the *saneamento* has not been thoroughly researched.
53. Total of civil servants (265,802) estimated from OECD data in Matos 2000.
54. Grades A to H or equivalent in terms of wages. This is a generous estimate of top echelons (cf. Matos 2000).

55. News in the Lisbon press, collected in *Maio '74 dia-a dia* [May 1974, day-to-day].
56. The movement of occupation of the town halls started in Coimbra and was everywhere presented as a popular demand; later, the Portuguese Communist party claimed for itself the initiative of that occupation (http://www.coimbra.pcp.pt/Historia/evocacao. htm).
57. The *'município'* (or *'concelho'*) [Districts] in the Portuguese Continent has an average of 127 square miles and 35,000 inhabitants. *Municípios* are weaker in Azores and Madeira Regions. *'Freguesias'* [Parishes] are around 4,000 and have considerably less power than *municípios*.
58. From press reports collected in *Maio'74*. The real figure was certainly higher.
59. For a description of the situation in IST, see the interview with Carlos Pimenta in *Diferencial*.
60. Patriarca (1999: 141). *Saneamento* came third, after wages and working time, for 156 labour conflicts.
61. Muñoz (1997: 128). *Saneamento* came fourth, after general claims, broken promises, and firing of personnel.
62. Data of H. Makler quoted in Pinto (1999: 37).
63. In Hungary, 81 per cent of the new economic elite had been employed in economic departments by the Communist state (Linz 1996: 309). Apparently, this was the rule for Eastern European candidates. The Czech model, based on the distribution of bonuses, 'provided perfect cover for an often unscrupulous game of insider dealing' ('Bohemia's Fading Rhapsody', *The Economist*, 29 May 1997). The EBRD's research has found that management-employee buy-outs (MEBOs) were the preferred method, at least in countries such as Bulgaria and Romania (*Dunn and Bradstreet Special Report Eastern Europe – June 2000 Politics and the reform process*). This method favours the *nomenklatura*. Common sense in Eastern European countries seems to be that 'the people who bossed us about before, the communist *nomenklatura*, are still on top. It was the clever *apparatchik*, the tough factory manager, who best made the switch to capitalism, benefiting from insiderish privatisation deals' ('Ten Years since the Wall Fell', *The Economist*, 4 Nov.).
64. Decree-Law 621-b/1974, 15 Nov.
65. And an indicator of growth potential: open economies grew 1.2 percentage points per year faster than closed economies, controlling for everything else (Sachs 1997).
66. A rough estimate was more pessimistic about Portuguese PPP GDP; it suggested that Portugal had almost 50 per cent of EU-15 GDP per capita at PPP in 1986: 57 per cent of the Spanish purchasing power, 46 per cent of the French, 48 per cent of the British, and 43 per cent of the (West) Germans' (Matos and Ferreira 1995: 165).
67. A study of the Austrian WIFO says that GDP per capita of the ten Eastern candidates was 40 per cent of the EU-15 average at the end of the 1990s (Lurdes Ferreira, 'Portugal É o País Que Mais Perde no Alargamento a Leste' [Portugal is the Country Which Has the Most to Lose by Eastern Enlargement], *Público*, 24 July 2001). These types of studies have a large measure of uncertainty but probably the economic situation of Eastern candidates has improved.
68. Sachs (2000).
69. The tradition of Durkheim (1897) is followed. Associations are also important for the type of political culture (Almond and Verba 1962). Putnam (2001) has recently highlighted the importance of associations.
70. Many divorcees live alone. Taking into account that the overheads of private living (housing, lightning, heating and so on) are costlier for singles, divorce is comparatively more expensive for poor countries.
71. Churches are the type of associations with more members. As a rule, believers belong to an association (their church) and atheists are – and have to be – isolated individuals.
72. Immigrants, like minority 'nations', may or may not cause trouble. The current European perception is that they may cause trouble.

73. There are no reliable figures for atheists in Portugal, 1985. Some data available suggest they were smaller than the 1990s figures with which I work.
74. This type of statistic is hazardous. I register 'hard core' atheists (don't believe in God, don't believe in life after death). The figures give only a rough indication.
75. This is probably the result of specific anti-religious policies of different communist regimes. According to Zulehner/Denz surveys of 1993, in former East (Russian-controlled) Germany, 49 per cent of the population were atheistic (quoted in Vilar).
76. Western European immigration generates problems of its own, but those problems have been less lethal.
77. EU GDP increased 1.4 per cent in 1974 and decreased 1.2 per cent in 1997 (*Historical Statistics 1960–1980*). In 1980–84, EU GDP grew less than two per cent every year (*Historical Statistics 1960–1989*).
78. Nevertheless, the EU was in a generous mood in the mid-1980s and started a vigorous policy of economic and social cohesion that helped quicken Portugal's economic growth. It is unsure whether eastern European candidates will receive a similar subvention.
79. Mário Soares in Avillez (1996: 354). On 14 September 1975, at a meeting of the Socialist International, Soares criticized US policy publicly: 'in the face of USA resignation, Portugal might become the Cuba of Europe.' Perhaps Kissinger wanted to apply a 'vaccine theory' against the danger of communism in Europe.
80. Between 1973 and 1992 Bulgaria, Czechoslovakia, Poland, Romania, but not Hungary, suffered a decrease of their GDP per capita (Madison 1995: 23). GDP started growing in the mid-1990s, except in Romania ('Ten Years since the Wall Fell', *The Economist*, 4 Nov. 1999).
81. Mostly for economic reasons.

REFERENCES

NB: Sources for the tables are given in the notes to tables.

Theory

Almond, G.A. and S. Verba (1962): *The Civic Culture Political Attitudes and Democracy in Five Nations*, Princeton, NJ: Princeton University Press.
Burdeau, G. (1962): *Droit constitutionnel et institutions politiques* [International Law and Political Institutions], Paris: Librairie Générale de Droit et Jurisprudence.
Duchacek, I.D. (1975): *Nations and Men: An Introduction to International Politics*, Third Edition, Chicago, IL: Dryden Press.
Durkheim, E. (1897): *Le Suicide* [Suicide]. Paris: Presses Universitaires de France.
Durkheim, E. (1996): *De la division du travail social* [On the Division of Labour] (1893), col. Quadrige, Paris: Presses Universitaires de France.
Habermas, J. (2000): *Après l'État-nation: Une nouvelle constellation politique* [After the Nation-State: A New Political Constellation], trans. Rainer Rochlitz, Paris: Fayard.
Hobsbawm, E. (1994): *Nations and Nationalism since 1780: Program, Myth, Reality*, col. Canto, Second Edition, Cambridge and Melbourne: Cambridge University Press.
Huntington, S.P. (1973): *Political Order in Changing Societies (1968)*, New Haven, CT: Yale University Press
Kriele, M. (1994): *Einführung in die Staatslehre Die geschichtlichen Legitimitätsgrundlagen des demokratischen Verfassungsstaates* [Introduction to the Historical and Legitimacy Foundations of the Democratic Nation-State], Wiesbaden: Westdeutscher Verlag.
Linz, J.L. and A. Stepan (1996): *Problems of Democratic Transition and Consolidation:*

Southern Europe, South America, and Post-Communist Europe, Baltimore, MD and London: The John Hopkins University Press.
Putnam, R. (2001): *Bowling Alone*, New York: Simon & Schuster.
Sachs, J. (2000): 'A New Map of the World', *The Economist*, 22 June.
Sachs, J. (1997): 'Nature, Nurture and Growth', *The Economist*, 12 June.
Schmitter, P.C. (1999): 'The Democratisation of Portugal in Its Comparative Prospective', in *Portugal e a transição para a democracia, 1974–76* [Portugal and Its Transition to Democracy, 1974–1976], *Edições Colibri – Fundação Mário Soares*, Lisbon: Instituto de História Contemporânea da Faculdade de Ciências Sociais e Humanas da Universidade Nova de Lisboa.
Smith, A.D. (1997): *A identidade nacional* [National Identity], Lisbon: Gradiva.
Zippelius, R. (1974): *Teoria geral do Estado* [General Theory of the State], trans. António Cabral de Moncada of the First German Edition (1969), with text from the Second and Third Editions (1969, 1971); preface by L. Cabral de Moncada, Fundação Calouste Gulbenkian.

Statistics

Banco de Portugal, annual reports.
Barreto, A. (org.) (1996): *A situação social em Portugal, 1960–1995* [The Social Situation in Portugal, 1960–1995], Lisbon: Instituto de Ciências Sociais da Universidade de Lisboa.
Barreto, A. (org.) (2000): *A situação social em Portugal 1960–1999, Volume II: Indicadores sociais em Portugal e na União Europeia (1995)* [The Social Situation in Portugal, 1960–1999, Volume II: Social Indicators in Portugal and in the European Union], Lisbon: Instituto de Ciências Sociais da Universidade de Lisboa.
CIA: *The World Fact Book 2000* at http://www.cia.gov/cia/publications/factbook/index. html.
Madison, A. (1995): *Monitoring the World Economy*, Paris: Development Centre Studies, OECD.
Mitchell, B.R. (1975): *European Historical Statistics 1750–1975*, New York: Facts on File Publications.
OECD (1982): Historical Statistics 1960–80, Paris.
OECD (1991): Historical Statistics 1960–89, Paris.
Wright, J.W. (ed.) (2000): *The New York Times Almanac 2001*, New York: Penguin Books.
Vilar, C.: Estadísticas Internacionales de Religión Reales, at http://home.talkcity.com/spirits/ yebisannu/norelesp.htm

Studies about Portugal 1974–75

Newspaper articles are quoted in notes.
Ferreira, J.M. (ed.) (1995): *Portugal em Transe, Vol.VIII* [Portugal in Transition, Vol.VIII], in José Mattoso, *História de Portugal* [History of Portugal].
Lopes, J. da Silva (1996): *A economia portuguesa desde 1960* [The Portuguese Economy since 1960], Lisbon: Gradiva (also printed in Barreto 1996).
Maio '74 dia-a dia [May 1974, Day-to-Day] (2001): Ed. Teorema-Abril em Maio.
Matos, L. Salgado de (1972): *Investimentos Estrangeiros em Portugal Alguns Aspectos* [Some Aspects of Foreign Investments in Portugal], Lisbon: Seara Nova.
Matos, L. Salgado de (2000): 'Um "Estado de Ordens" contemporâneo – a organização política portuguesa' [A Contemporary 'State of Order' – Political Organzation in Portugal], Ph.D. thesis, Instituto de Ciências Sociais da University of Lisbon, May 2000.

Matos, L. Salgado de and Ferreira, J.M. (1995): 'A evolução económico-social do 25 de Abril de 1974 à integração na CEE' [The Social and Economic Evolution from 25 April 1974 to Integration in the EEC], in José Medeiros Ferreira, *Portugal em Transe, Vol. VIII* [Portugal in Transition], in José Mattoso (ed.), *História de Portugal* [History of Portugal].

Muñoz, R.D. (1997): *Acciones colectivas y transiciones a la democracia, España y Portugal, 1974–1977* [Collective Actions and Democratic Transitions, Spain and Portugal, 1974–1977], Madrid: Centro de Estudios Avanzados en Ciencias Sociales.

Patriarca, F. (1999): 'A Revolução e a questão social' [The Revolution and the Social Question], in Colibri – Fundação Mário Soares, *Portugal e a transição para a democracia (1974–1976)* [Portugal and the Transition to Democracy (1974–1976)], Lisbon: Instituto de Histórica Contemporânea da Universidade Nova de Lisboa.

Pinto, A.C. (1999): 'Saneamentos políticos e movimentos radicais de direita na transição para a democracia' [Political Purges and Right-Wing Radical Movements in the Democratic Transition], in Colibri – Fundação Mário Soares, *Portugal e a transição para a democracia (1974–1976)* [Portugal and the Transition to Democracy], Lisbon: Instituto de História Contemporânea da Universidade Nova de Lisboa.

Documents

Avillez, M.J. (1996): *Soares Ditadura e Revolução*, Público.

Caetano, M.: *As grandes opções*, Verbo, Lisboa, s.d. http://www.coimbra.pcp.pt/Historia/evocacao.htm

Nogueira, F. (1984): *Salazar Estudo biográfico, vol. V: A resistência (1958–1964)*, Livraria Civilização (ed.), Porto.

Chronologies

http://www.fundacao-mario-soares.pt/webchcl/contexto/cronologia/cronologia9.html.
http://www.iscsp.utl.pt/~cepp/Cronologias/1974.htm.

Santos, B. de Sousa, Cruzeiro, M.M. and M. Natércia (1997): *O pulsar da Revolução. Cronologia da Revolução de 25 de Abril (1973–1976)* [The Beating of the Revolution. A Chronology of the Revolution of 25 April–1976)] *(1973*, s.l., Edições Afrontamento – Centro de Documentação 25 de Abril da Universidade de Coimbra.

Maio '74 dia-a-dia [May '74 day-to-day] (2001): Teorema and Abril em Maio, Lisbon.

Morais, J. and L. Violante (1986): *Contribuição para uma cronologia dos factos económicos e sociais em Portugal 1926–1985* [Contribution to a Chronology of Economic and Social Facts in Portugal 1926–1985], Col. Horizonte Económico, Livros Horizonte.

Portuguese Attitudes Towards EU Membership: Social and Political Perspectives

MARINA COSTA LOBO

INTRODUCTION

The deepening of integration has widened the importance of decisions taken in Brussels for all European citizens. A corollary of this is that public opinion increasingly also matters in the European Union. In fact, the Maastricht referendums in Denmark and France and the Amsterdam Treaty referendum in Ireland proved this point emphatically. In this contribution Portuguese citizens' attitudes towards Europe will be presented and discussed using Eurobarometer data from between 1985 and 1999. The attitudes of European citizens have been analysed extensively in a comparative manner. Social factors and political attitudes will be used to explain Portuguese views on membership in the next section, followed by an in-depth analysis of Portuguese parties positioning towards the EU integration in Portugal, as well as of the relationship between party positions and the electorate's attitudes. Thus, both social and political data will be used to understand Portuguese attitudes toward the EU.

Research on the nature of support toward the EU has been extensive. Short-term factors, such as economic indicators, as well as long-term social factors, namely gender, stratification and education, and age or generation, have been examined.[1] Studies concur that there is a persistent difference between social and demographic groups within countries in their awareness of the EU and their attitudes towards it. According to Wessels most approaches seeking to explain positive orientations toward the EU are based on a simple assumption: if people are better able to cope with a remote

The author would like to thank Stefano Bartolini for his comments and André Freire for his comments and guidance in the quantitative part of this essay.

entity such as the EU, after a while they will also come to know it better and support it; that is, a 'positive awareness' develops (Wessels 1996: 120). The linkage between a citizen's position *vis-à-vis* the EU can be conceptualized following three models. In the 'enlightment' model knowledge is seen as an indicator of sophistication: the more enlightened an individual, the more positive his or her attitude towards internationalized governance. Education would be the main indicator of an enlightened citizen. In the 'mainstream' model greater mainstream attachment develops from greater knowledge and involvement; that is, more participation and interest in politics would foster positive attitudes toward the EU. Given that mass media coverage and political discourse toward the EU is generally supportive of it, then a greater involvement in political affairs would lead to greater support for the EU. In the 'cognitive consistency model', endorsement of a specific policy position stems from general political attitudes and orientations. Here three types of orientations can be analysed: left–right, materialist–postmaterialist, and degree of religiosity.

Historically, the left-wing parties in Western Europe were more reticent about the EU project, and thus the hypothesis is that a left-wing individual will be less supportive of EU integration. Regarding the materialist–postmaterialist scale, the latter leads to greater support for Europeanization, understood as a cosmopolitan sense of identity, whereas material orientations are rather more concerned with the nation-state. Third, concerning religiosity, the more secular, and therefore more 'modern', the individual, the more positive an attitude toward integration is expected. Given these hypotheses it seems that certain bear out while others do not for all of the EU countries between 1970 and 1991. Thus, the findings support the enlightenment model, with groups with higher education levels tending to support the EU to a larger extent. Similarly, the 'mainstream model' is also confirmed, with those who are politically involved in political discussion being more supportive of European integration than those who are not. In the third model the results tend to confirm   the   hypotheses   on   the   left–right   and   the materialist–postmaterialist scales, although concerning the latter the effects are not very strong. The hypothesis on religiosity is not confirmed by the data. Therefore, although individuals form opinions according to their general political attitudes, these variables show less impact than education and occupation do. Thus, concerning the importance of social factors in determining attitudes toward the process of European integration, the main hypothesis of this study is to confirm the literature findings presented above, namely, that in Portugal those belonging to the groups just outlined will also be those who are more pro-EU integration for the period 1985–99.

The analysis then investigates the linkages between parties' and electors' views on European integration. Research on parties' attitudes toward European integration has concluded that their positioning on a left–right scale and on the pro- and anti-European dimension have become more independent (Bartolini 2001). Originally, among the six founding EC member-states, the right-wing parties – and especially the Christian Democratic parties – had been more enthusiastic towards the process of integration, whereas the Left had been more reticent toward it. More recently, the socialist and social-democratic embracing of the project of European Union, as well as the growing opposition by right-wing parties of the process of European integration, has made the two cleavages more independent from one another.

This growing independence between the left–right scale and the pro- and anti-integration dimension can derive from at least two factors. The first is whether the party belongs to the range of governing parties. Parties that are periodically in government will tend to be more pro-integration, in view of the roles they are called on to assume in community institutions. On the other hand, parties that are constantly excluded from government will tend to be anti-integration, if only for the effect that the process of integration has had on the *de facto* power of national parliaments, and more generally for the perception of loss of power of institutions where that party is represented (Miranda 2000). The second factor is the extent to which certain parties on each side of the left–right scale appeal to a less mobile electorate, with relatively less education and income. It would be expected that these parties would voice their constituents' opposition to the European project.

The literature has shown that an important source of political cues is partisanship, providing a useful guide to political behaviour. Indeed, partisanship is helpful for the individual in making sense of new political issues, and is viewed as the main link connecting the citizen and the political process. The hypothesis, therefore, is that those electors who identify with a given party will also share that party's views on attitudes toward Europe. This hypothesis has been confirmed in the literature, and also for Portugal (Wessels 1995: 132). The article in question, however, only analyses the relationship between parties and the electorate between 1985 and 1991. In Portugal fundamental changes in the parties' outlook on European integration have occurred since that date, and this essay will look at whether the party members followed the party's changes at the elite level.

In order to test this hypothesis, mean values of support for membership of the European Union for individuals who stated vote intention for a given party will be compared.[2] Next, these attitudes will be compared to the parties' stance on Europe presented above. This will show at a very basic level whether there is indeed a linkage between each party and the electors who intend to vote for that party on the issue of European integration. Second, it will show whether there is a pro- and anti-Europe cleavage in Portugal, and whether it bisects the existing left–right cleavage, both at the electorate and the party level.

The study is thus divided into three sections. The first presents data on the evolution of attitudes toward Europe among the Portuguese since membership. In the second section, using regression analysis, the importance of various social factors, as well as political attitudes, is used to explain these attitudes. The third explores the relationship between the parties' and electorate's views on Europe.

PORTUGUESE CITIZENS' ATTITUDES TOWARDS THE EU

Portuguese citizens' opinions on the European Union have been monitored since 1985. On that date Portugal was included in the Eurobarometer studies, annual surveys inquiring on a number of political attitudes, but also and systematically on attitudes toward the EU. Mário Bacalhau has analysed some of the Eurobarometer data on Portugal (Bacalhau 1993, 1993a). The first fact that stands out on all issues related to the European Union is the large number of non-responses in the Portuguese survey. Portugal is consistently one of the EU countries where the percentage of 'don't know/no answer' is highest. This absence of opinion is difficult to interpret. It can be derived from both positive and negative factors. A positive interpretation might see this absence of opinion in terms of 'permissive consensus' (Bacalhau 1993a: 182). On the other hand, it can be interpreted as apathy toward the political system as a whole, or even hostility towards realms that are perceived to function with and for elites, and that function with little input from electors. Looking at data until 1990, Bacalhau concludes that 'for those Portuguese who have an opinion, there exists an image and a fairly positive assessment and sense of identity, [which is] more positive than in the majority of Community countries' (1993a: 187). Still, that study only presents longitudinal data from between 1985 and 1990 on two questions, namely, the desirability of the unification of western Europe, and whether membership of the EU could be considered a good thing.

It is relevant to distinguish between types of attitudes towards the EU, which can be derived from Eurobarometer data. The set of questions periodically put to Europeans regarding European integration reflects the ambiguous nature of the European Community and how it has evolved over time. The EU is neither a state nor an international institution to which nation-states belong. It is also a political institution that enjoys a direct institutional relationship with EU citizens via the elections to the European Parliament, and indirectly via the great number of decisions made at the EU level that have repercussions on the everyday lives of EU citizens. Despite these linkages with the electors, however, most of EU dealings still occur at the elite level, between the member-states' governments and EU officials. The questions regularly put to the Europeans in the Eurobarometer surveys try to capture these two types of dimensions of the attitudes toward the EU: first, opinions concerning the relationship between the respondent's country and the EU, and second, opinions on the EU as a political institution.

FIGURE 1

ATTITUDES TOWARD THE EU, 1985–99

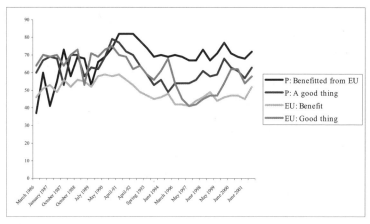

Source: Eurobarometers, various years

Figure 1 shows opinions on the EU as measured by two questions that have appeared almost uninterruptedly in Eurobarometers since 1985.[3] The question on whether Portugal has benefited from European integration begs a narrow retrospective analysis of the advantages and disadvantages of belonging to the EU. It is clear that, among those who replied to this question from 1987 onwards, there is an overwhelming consensus that Portugal has indeed benefited from European integration. After reaching a peak of 82 per cent in 1991, the question's positive response percentage decreased to 67 in 1997. Notwithstanding this overwhelming consensus, a trend can be discerned: between 1986 and 1991 the consensus on the benefits of European membership increased. Since then, and until 1998, there was a slight decrease. Still, the percentage of Portugese that consider Portugal has benefited from EU integration has not fallen below 67 per cent from 1991 to 2001.

Whereas the question on the benefits of European integration seems to imply a rather utilitarian perspective of integration, the question on whether Portuguese membership is a good thing begs a wider view of Portuguese membership in the EU. Apart from May 1995, the majority of the Portuguese concurs that membership in the EU is a good thing. This consensus is nonetheless smaller than the consensus on the 'benefits of membership since 1991'. The same trend is followed, however; namely, it reaches a peak in 1991 and its minimum value in 1995.

In the EU the index values for these indicators are also positive between 1970 and 1990. Moreover, the distributions suggest that the indicators are hierarchically ordered, with support being lowest when the survey asks for an instrumental evaluation on the EU (the benefits question), and largest when it asks for a diffuse evaluation. Interestingly, this is not the case in Portugal. Thus, the instrumental question on the benefits of the EU for Portugal elicits a much wider consensus than two of the three questions that seek to measure diffuse support. This may mean, therefore, that support in Portugal is rather more instrumental and dependent on 'benefits', and less so on a more affective diffuse support of the EU. Still, compared to the 1973 entrants to the EU (Ireland, the UK, and Denmark), Portugal and Spain, which joined in 1986, showed much higher levels of diffuse support for the EU until 1991.

There is less data to evaluate the second dimension on perceptions of the EU as a political institution. These can be assessed from Eurobarometer data summarized in Figure 2.[4] In this figure the responses to two questions put to the Portuguese at different times are presented: one concerns the level of information respondents feel they have on the EU; the other concerns their satisfaction with the way democracy functions in the EU.[5] In the 1990s there was a consensus that the Portuguese felt overwhelmingly poorly informed on the EU, a level before the EU average. In spring 1992 only 39 per cent felt 'quite or very well informed' about EU affairs. This percentage has been steadily decreasing, with only 19 per cent sharing the same opinion in 1999. Most importantly perhaps, the percentage of those who claim to be reasonably satisfied with the way in which democracy functions in the EU has been decreasing since 1998, with a slight increase in 2002, and has also been lower than the EU average since 2000.

From the dimensions summarized in Figures 1 and 2, the Portuguese seem to have very different stances on the process of European integration. When asked about the degree of support for the EU, either instrumentally or affectively, there is a wide consensus, albeit with fluctuations, on the merits of EU integration. On the other hand, when asked about the EU as a political institution, opinions are rather more negative: the majority of the Portuguese feel they lack information on the EU, and are increasingly dissatisfied with the way democracy works in it. To these indicators must be added those presented above on the level of non-response in Portugal, which also reaches comparatively high levels. To the extent that as the process of EU integration deepens the

FIGURE 2

INFORMATION ABOUT THE EU, INTEREST IN EU
AND SATISFACTION WITH DEMOCRACY IN THE EU

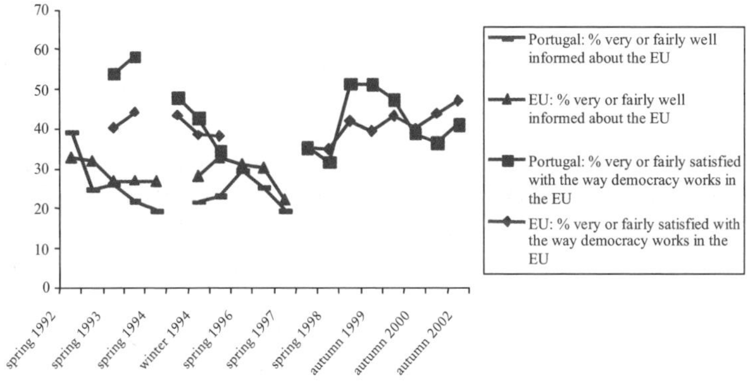

Source: Eurobarometers, various years.

importance of the direct links to European citizens increases, the EU's inability to alter these negative political attitudes may have dire consequences for the long-run changes in Portuguese citizens' overall attitudes toward the EU. This is especially true since the consensus surrounding the EU seems to be built on an instrumental assessment of the benefits accruing to Portugal rather than a diffuse support for it. Next we explore the social and political factors that may be determining these attitudes toward the EU.

SOCIAL FACTORS AND POLITICAL ATTITUDES: TOWARD AN EXPLANATION OF ATTITUDES TOWARDS EUROPEAN INTEGRATION IN PORTUGAL

This section will explore the attitudes presented above. Multiple regression analysis will be used to measure the strength of social and political factors in explaining attitudes towards European integration. In the multiple regression (see Table 1), the dependent variable chosen to represent a scale of 'European attitudes' was MEMBRSHP.[6]

The inclusion of the independent variables followed the three models presented above, namely the 'enlightenment', the 'mainstream', and the 'cognitive consistency' models. Given these models, correlation between the dependent variable, attitudes toward membership, and various socio-demographic and political variables were performed. Of these, a few were chosen that correlated significantly with the dependent variable chosen. As such, I included in the linear regression the variables income and years in education as well as age. Concerning political attitudes, satisfaction with democracy, frequency of political discussion, and vote intention were included in the linear regression, once again because they fulfil the criteria set above, namely, stronger correlation, availability of data, and being attributes of those who have greater mobility.[7]

The adjusted r^2 for this regression is 0.057, which is very low. The model is therefore a poor predictor of attitudes toward membership. This poor result may be due to the fact that traditional models of political attitudes are inadequate to understand the relationship between citizens and this new form of political organization, the EU.

Other results within the model are more encouraging, however. In the first place the relationships between the variables are those we expected to find, except in the case of age. Namely, the relationship is positive between the dependent variable and the following variables: income, education, satisfaction with democracy, and political interest. The relationship is negative with age.[8] Furthermore, all variables are significant for 1985–97. Looking at the regressions for each year, it is clear that the political variables are systematically significant, whereas that is not the case with the socio-demographic variables. This shows that in Portugal individuals' political attitudes are more important in determining their positioning *vis-à-vis* the EU than socio-demographic indicators. This has been shown elsewhere concerning voting behaviour, too.[9]

Therefore, comparatively, satisfaction with democracy is the most important variable in explaining support for the EU, followed by vote intention, as coded in this study. Indeed, democratization and Europeanization were linked by the political elite in Portugal, as will be seen in the next section. Education and frequency of political discussion also confirm the 'enlightenment' and the 'cognitive consistency' models presented above. Since political attitudes seem fundamental to Portuguese attitudes toward European integration, we turn now to an analysis of the party's positioning toward the EU in Portugal and how party followers react to those stances.

TABLE 1

LINEAR MULTIPLE REGRESSION:
DEPENDENT VARIABLE ATTITUDES TOWARD MEMBERSHIP IN THE EU

	All years	1985	1987	1989	1991	1993	1994	1997
Education	0.020*	0.080	0.046	-0.032	0.047	0.007	0.057	0.003
Income	0.024**	0.076	0.050	-.027	0.019	-0.009	0.013	0.052
Age	-0.033***	0.089	-0.066**	-.014	-0.049	0.023	-0.082	-0.121***
Satisfaction with Democracy	0.179***	0.049	0.082**	0.179***	0.193***	0.245***	0.095*	0.224***
Political Discussion	0.039***	0.076	0.061*	0.039	0.008	0.039	0.033	0.004
Vote intention (PCP/others)	0.117***	0.220***	0.132***	0.118***	0.111***	0.058*	0.091*	0.046
N Total	34,011	1,000	2,000	4,000	3,000	3,000	2,999	4,004
(N Valid)	(7,438)	(289)	(919)	(1,159)	(671)	(779)	(347)	(738)
Adjusted r^2	0.057	0.063	0.044	0.053	0.056	0.061	0.018	0.065

Notes: * $p < 0,1$.
     ** $p < 0,05$.
    *** $p < 0,01$.
Source: Eurobarometer trendfile, 1979–1999.

EXPLORING THE RELATIONSHIP BETWEEN PARTY POSITIONING AND
PARTY SUPPORTERS' VIEWS CONCERNING EUROPEAN INTEGRATION

This section analyses the relationship between electors' positions
towards the European Union and the parties' stance on Europe. As seen
above, western Europe saw a growing independence between the pro-
and anti-European cleavage, and the left–right cleavage. Among the
founding members of the EEC, the Christian-Democrats were at the
forefront of the support for the project, whereas the Socialists showed
misgivings concerning the aims of the EEC. Before we analyse the
attitudes of parties and electors in Portugal since 1985, it is necessary to
understand the positioning of Portuguese parties, because they were
fundamentally different from those of the founding members of the
EEC.[10]

In Portugal, and until 1985, the pro- and anti-Europe cleavage
overlapped completely with the pro- and anti-West European pluralist
democracy cleavage at the party level. This latter cleavage was
fundamental at the political level, and indeed bisected the left–right
cleavage, which severely conditioned party relationships on the Left. The
process of European integration was a tool for the pro-pluralism parties
in the turbulent transition period and thereafter. It served as an adequate
alternative model to the left-wing revolutionary society model presented
by the Communist party (PCP – *Partido Comunista Português*) and other
extreme-left wing parties, which in the process of transition even
threatened to become dominant in Portuguese society.[11]

Berta Alvarez Miranda carried out an important study on political
parties in Southern Europe countries before they entered the EU,
namely, Greece, Spain, and Portugal. In it she analysed the parties'
stances *vis-à-vis* the EU in three key areas: the economic impact of the
EU for the national economies, the limits European integration
imposed on the *contours* of the new economic and political regimes,
and the international status European membership imparted (Alvarez-
Miranda 1995: 4). All pro-pluralism parties made European
integration a cornerstone of their vision for Portugal. The socialist PS
(*Partido Socialista*) and the centre-right PSD (*Partido Social
Democrata*) evolved during the transition period to become, in 1976,
fully Europeanist (Barroso 1983). On the Right the small CDS (*Centro*

Democrático Social) embraced the cause of European integration, although it adopted an explicitly 'atlanticist' slant to its discourse (Alvarez-Miranda 1995: 8). Among pluralist parties the PS was perhaps the most ardent supporter of European integration (Lobo and Magalhães 2001: 28). Not only did it have the opportunity in the governments it formed to pursue that objective vigorously, but also its historic leader, Mário Soares, used his personal and party networks to pursue that goal.[12]

Only the Portuguese Communists, similarly to their Greek counterparts, were opposed to European integration in the three key areas mentioned above, namely the economy, the political institutions, and the international outlook of Portugal once it became a member of the European Community (Alvarez-Miranda 1995: 9; Bosco 2001: 337). Entry into the European Community was vehemently rejected on various grounds. The first reason was that economically Portugal was not considered ready to enter the EU: membership would imply 'the ruin of vast sectors of the economy, with particular incidence on small and medium enterprises and causing unemployment' (Alvarez-Miranda 1995: 14). Second, and fundamentally, membership would 'liquidate the conquests of the Revolution [Nationalizations, Agrarian Reform, Workers' Management Control, and other workers' rights], restore monopolistic capitalism, and end the democratic regime' (p.14) as understood by the Communists. Third, membership would diminish national sovereignty and turn Portugal into an instrument of imperialists' neo-colonial policies.

Thus, unlike the parties in the six EC founder members, the main Portuguese parties' stance on Europe bisected the left–right cleavage from the outset. The split occurred on the Left with Socialists' support for the European project conflicting with the Communists' rejection of it. Another difference from the EC founder members was the salience the issue of EC membership assumed in the pre-accession period in the political system. Because the issue was a component of the fundamental pro- and anti-West European cleavage, it constrained relationships between parties, especially on the Left. Indeed, the first decade of democracy and its chronic government instability can in part be explained by the Communists' exclusion as an anti-system party, which itself was in part a function of its stance on Europe (Lobo 2001: 649). Thus, on the eve of membership, the cleavage existed and divided the Communists from the rest of the main parties, namely, the CDS, the PS, and the PSD.

Membership did not change Communist opposition to the EU immediately. The turning point occurred in 1988. In that year the PCP acknowledged some of the inherent benefits of Portugal's accession to the EU, although it continued to criticize the way in which the governing parties, namely PS and PSD, approached the process of integration. Most likely, this change occurred in preparation for the first direct elections to the European Parliament. The PCP realized, pragmatically, that if it continued its outright rejection of the European Community, it might damage its electoral chances in this supranational body by placing itself outside all matters European. In that light a conference in 1988 entitled 'Portugal and the EC Today', with leading Communists, was a necessary starting point for the change. The concluding document started by acknowledging that although 'membership of the EU is not an irreversible phenomenon, Portugal's exit from it does not seem likely, at least in the short term' (PCP 1988: 91). Furthermore, 'much like the Portuguese membership of the EU, the permanence of Portugal in a capitalist system does not constitute the Communists' choice. And yet, that is the framework in which we live and fight' (p.91). Further on, the document states that the European Parliament's elections will have internal political consequences, and therefore the PCP wants to elect a number of competent representatives to that institution. The Communists underline that 'the elections of 1989 are not a referendum for or against the EU. It is not integration itself which will be voted on, but who, within the framework of integration has greater competence and dedication to represent the people's and Portugal's interests in the European Community' (p.123).

Thus, between 1986 and 1991, the date of the Maastricht Treaty, the main change concerning party stances on the EU is the PCP's pragmatism: faced with the evident support, as well as the benefits accruing to Portugal, it was illogical to maintain total rejection of the EU. Inclusion within the EP also served to approximate the Communists to the EU. They obviously understood there was every advantage in being able to defend their interests from that new political platform.

The next turning point concerning Portuguese attitudes toward the EU was the signing of the Maastricht Treaty. This time not only the PCP adjusted its position, but also the CDS-PP and even the PS. The most fundamental change toward the process of European integration occurred in the CDS-PP. In 1991 that party was fighting extinction, faced with ever-dwindling votes at successive elections. In those elections the CDS-PP adopted for the first time a critical stance toward the EU, making it an important part of their political ideology. Indeed, the PSD's successive absolute majorities affected the CDS-PP profoundly.[13] The electoral decline of the CDS had important repercussions within the party elite, and saw successive leadership changes (Frain 1997: 92).

The most fundamental change occurred in 1991 in the party's Xth Congress, with the election of Manuel Monteiro as President of the Party (Robinson 1996: 969). Monteiro's goal was to prevent the end of the party, which in 1991 seemed like a distinct possibility. The CDS took up the issue of European integration in order to distinguish itself from the PSD. The CDS thus hoped to capitalize on the rise in popular dissatisfaction with the direction and certain consequences of the process of European integration. The direction, according to the CDS, was clearly federal, as agreed in the Maastricht Treaty, and therefore would diminish Portuguese national sovereignty. The consequences of the Single Market and the introduction of the Maastricht criteria had negative consequences for certain vulnerable groups in Portuguese society, and the CDS hoped to gain votes by becoming critical of the PSD's adherence to those European objectives. Thus, adopting a critical stance toward the EU was a strategy to avoid decimation. In effect, the CDS voted against the ratification of the Maastricht Treaty in December 1992.[14]

This anti-European stance had important international repercussions for the party. In 1992 the CDS was suspended from the EPP (European People's Party), with the formal excuse being that it was not fulfilling its financial obligations to that party. More likely, however, it was a result of its anti-European stance (Robinson 1996: 969). Shortly after, the Konrad Adenauer Foundation stopped financing the homologous CDS foundation, the IDL (*Instituto Democracia e Liberdade- Amaro da Costa*) – a clear sign of the divorce between the CDS and the Christian Democratic ideological family. This was significant in that the CDS from the outset had important links to the German *Christlich Demokratische Union* (CDU) during the transition to democracy.[15] Since then it has assumed a clearly conservative-nationalist stance toward European integration.

As expected, the PCP also reacted negatively to the Maastricht Treaty. The Political Resolution published as a result of the XIV PCP Congress in 1992 provides an overview of the Communists' perspective on it. At the time, the PCP had campaigned vigorously for a referendum on Maastricht, but to no avail. The PCP presented five main criticisms to the Maastricht Treaty. First, it gave a juridical nature to the EU, and set it on a clearly federalizing path, in detriment of national sovereignty, with examples being the single currency project and increased QMV (Qualified Majority Voting), among others. Second, the single currency objective itself was rejected, since it would only serve international capital to the detriment of the peoples of Europe. Third, the Maastricht treaty laid the foundations of a political-military bloc, which is inherent in the Political Union set out by the Treaty. Fourth, and related to the previous point, the Treaty foresaw the creation of an integrated police system the PCP believed would endanger civil liberties and human rights. Finally, the Communists criticized the double democratic deficit, namely the lack of power both of national Parliaments and the European Parliament in community affairs (Robinson 1996: 38–9).

Concerning the two parties in the centre of the party spectrum, Maastricht inadvertently helped the Socialists return to power. Indeed, whereas the governing party, the PSD, committed itself to the Maastricht criteria, which created some economic difficulties in certain sections of society between 1992 and 1994–95,[16] the PS, lead by its new Secretary-general, António Guterres, was able to criticize the PSD's excessive attention to nominal convergence to the detriment of real economic convergence (Lobo and Magalhães 2001: 31). Thus, maintaining its European credentials intact, the PS was able to distance itself from the rigorous and unpopular measures undertaken by the PSD. More recently, the PSD used the same tactics in the 2002 election campaign. It accused the Socialists of disregarding the EU limits on deficit spending, trying to portray the Socialists as fiscally irresponsible in the face of EU constraints.

The fact that the two main parties who control two-thirds of the vote have chosen not to politicize a pro- or anti- integration cleavage has probably influenced the diffuse support that exists in Portugal for European integration. Unfortunately, it has probably also determined the small degree of information that Portuguese have on the process. Because it is not really discussed, the level of interest and information is also relatively reduced. A campaign study of the 2002 legislative elections analysed the themes most discussed by the party leaders during the campaign. 'Europe' does not even figure on the list of the 19 themes with which the campaign dealt.[17] The reasons for the CDS/PP and the PCP to adopt an anti-integration stance stem from ideological reasons, and from their strategic placement *vis-à-vis* the other parties for vote maximization. Indeed, the parties positioning described above is not independent of elector's attitudes toward the EU. The PCP's warming to the EU in 1988 and the CDS-PP's increase criticism of it were supposed to give voice to recent changes in public opinion concerning the EU, as mentioned above. Both elite and mass attitudes feed off each other. Here I distinguish between them for the sake of clarity, but their interdependence is acknowledged. Having established the parties' stance on Europe on the eve of membership, I turn now to the analysis of the party's electors' attitudes toward Europe from 1985 on.

Figure 3 shows the mean value of electors' views on membership of the European Union, according to vote intention.[18] The evolution of each party's electorate on the EU issue, between 1985 and 1999, presents some interesting facts. It confirms that on accession, the pro- and anti-European cleavage that existed in the political system, separating the Communist party from the PS, PSD, and CDS, was mirrored in the

FIGURE 3

ELECTORS' PERCEPTIONS OF MEMBERSHIP IN THE EU, ACCORDING TO VOTING INTENTION: AGGREGATE MEANS (1985–99) FOR EACH PARTY

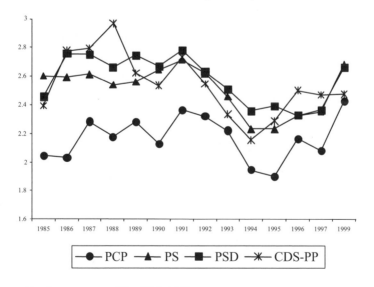

Source: Eurobarometer trendfile, 1979–1999.

electorate. Thus, the figure shows that the Communist electorate is systematically less enthusiastic about membership of the EU than all other parties' electors for the entire period. Effectively, there is a pro- and anti-European cleavage at the electorate level that bisects the left–right cleavage.

The graph's overall trend is for the *difference* in scores for each party to decrease; that is, polarization of attitudes toward the European Union decreases between 1985 and 1999. Whereas in 1985 the difference between the minimum and maximum scores was 0.6, in 1991 the difference was 0.4 and in 1999 it was 0.3. This decrease in polarization is a result of two tendencies: between 1985 and 1991 the Communist electorate warms considerably to the European project, with mean scores increasing from 2.0 to 2.4. This then shows that the change in the Communist party stance toward European integration, in order to prepare for the European elections, was also accompanied by greater support among its electorate. From 1992 to 1995 the PS, PSD, and CDS electors become relatively less supportive of membership, and thus come closer to the Communist score. This evidence partly coincides with the evidence found among the parties presented above. Between 1992 and 1995 the CDS-PP alters its stance on Europe, becoming critical of it. The PS, although still firmly Europeanist, chooses to criticize the way in which the PSD pursues the European objectives with which Portugal is faced. From 1995 on the tendency is for an improvement in all electorates' scores on support of membership.

Another point the graph illustrates is that the PSD electorate is slightly more pro-Europe than the PS electorate. This is slightly puzzling from a Portuguese perspective, since the PS was always at the forefront of support first for EU membership, and then for subsequent EU objectives. The PSD, in government between 1985 and 1995, however, was naturally also a staunch defender of European Union,[19] and this helps explain this support for integration. Interestingly, this situation is only inverted when the PS is in government. Thus, in 1985 and between 1996 and 1999, the Socialists mean value is above that of the PSD. This suggests that party followers tend to support EU integration to a greater extent when their party is in government. This is, of course, understandable in the Portuguese (and European) context since increasingly governmental action derives from interaction with the EU. Thus, supporters for the party in government will tend to have a more benevolent view of the European integration.

Linked to the previous point, the analysis of the support for European integration of CDS-PP followers shows the opposite side of the coin to this argument. Indeed, the CDS-PP electorate presents the most erratic support for EU membership. Between 1985 and 1991 the mean support was very similar to that of the PS and the PSD. In the aftermath of the Maastricht Treaty, the CDS supporters become considerably more Euro-sceptic. From 1995 on there has been an improvement in mean scores among the CDS electorate in favour of EU membership. Still, excluding 1996 and 1997, from 1991 on the CDS-PP's electorate is less supportive of the EU than the other party on the right, the PSD. It often approximates the opinions of the Communist on the other extreme of the party spectrum. This lends credence to the idea that what increasingly matters is whether a party is within the group of parties that regularly form government. The party followers of those within government will tend to have a more positive view of integration, whereas those regularly excluded from government will tend to have a more negative view of integration.

Finally, it is relevant to discuss what Figure 3 does not show, namely, the number of respondents who over the years have stated a voting intention in Eurobarometer surveys. The proportion of respondents who declare a voting intention has decreased substantially: whereas in 1985 43.5 per cent of respondents chose one of the four parties analysed above, in 1990 only 36.1 per cent did; in 1995, 37.2 per cent; and in 1999, only 29.7 per cent declared s/he would vote for one of the four parties shown above. This downward trend mirrors electoral participation in Portugal, where abstention in legislative elections has risen from 26 per cent to 39 per cent between 1985 and 1999 (Freire and Magalhães 2002: 49).

CONCLUSION

This study proposed to present and analyse Portuguese attitudes toward European integration. The first section presented the evolution of attitudes between 1985 and 1999. Because the EU is neither a full-fledged state nor a remote international organization, two types of Eurobarometer indicators were chosen. The first type relates to the individuals' perceptions of the relationship between Portugal and the EU, as well as feelings of affection toward the institution. The second type of attitudes tries to understand how citizens interact with the EU as a political organization. In this section it was seen that support for the relationship between Portugal and the EU is widespread despite fluctuations. Still, the greatest consensus elicited toward the EU is instrumental, with levels of diffuse affective support for the EU being lower, although high in comparative perspective. Concerning the second type of attitudes, it was found that there is great lack of information on the EU as an institution, and a decline in satisfaction with the way democracy works in the EU. Thus, the attitudes that elicit greatest consensus in Portugal concerning integration are instrumental, and could change if the economic situation deteriorates or structural funds end. The other indicators presented here, which presumably will matter more in the future as integration deepens, show negative developments.

The second section undertook an analysis of the determinants of attitudes toward the EU, using data between 1985 and 1997. The model was found to be a poor predictor of attitudes toward the EU. This conclusion leads to the question of whether traditional models of political attitudes may be inappropriate when applied to the EU because they were devised for studies of national political participation, and therefore cannot measure attitudes toward a supranational institution. Although the model was relatively poor in terms of prediction, it was found that all variables chosen had significant statistical relationships with the dependent variable. In particular, political variables, namely satisfaction with democracy and voting intention, have been systematically significant in determining attitudes toward the EU.

The third section explored the parties' stance on Europe, as well as their electorates', measured by expressed voting intention in the Eurobarometer surveys. The evidence showed that a pro- and anti-European cleavage exists, although it is not very salient, and has been decreasing over time. Indeed, it is shown that the *difference* in mean scores for each party decreases; that is, polarization of attitudes toward the European Union decreases between 1985 and 1999. The pro- and anti-EU cleavage bisects the left–right cleavage, and nowadays is not related to the originally pro- and anti-Western liberal democracy, as it first originated in the 1970s, given that it places the conservative CDS and the Communists together against the two large parties at the centre of the political spectrum, the PS and the PSD. It is possible to argue that it relates to those who feel excluded from the cartel parties' governing centre, which in Portugal consists of the PS and the PSD. The fact that this cleavage exists does not mean it carries an equal weight to the left–right cleavage. In fact, it does not. Between them the PS and the PSD have polled over 72 per cent of the vote since entry into the European Community.[20] Thus, it is only minor parties, which have been systematically excluded from government since 1982, that have adopted an anti-integration stance.

Thus, in Portugal in the 1990s the issue of European integration bisected the left–right axis, with the parties on the extreme of the party system, namely the Communists and the CDS/PP, being relatively anti-integration, and the two main governing parties, the PS and the PSD, being largely in favour of integration. These findings, however, have to be placed in the context of the decreasing links between the public and the parties. Indeed, the number of respondents ready to acknowledge a voting intention has decreased substantially over the years in Portugal.

Still, for those who do profess a voting intention, the evidence on the coincidence between the electorate's attitudes on European integration and the parties' stance on it is refreshing. Indeed, the essay shows that the Portuguese electorate continues to use parties in order to make sense of complex reality, adopting their chosen party's stance on European integration. This leads to another conclusion relating to the relationship between the EU and the public in general: the national parties seem to be the missing link for an improvement in the relationship between the EU as a political institution and the public in general.

NOTES

1. For an excellent review of the field's developments, see Wessels (1996).
2. In this essay 'vote intention' is used instead of 'party identification' as a measure of the political orientation of the elector, due to data availability. Thus, those who state they intend to vote for a certain party are considered followers of that party. The question of party identification does not exist for all the years included in this study.
3. The questions relating to the percentages shown above are the following: (1) 'Taking everything into consideration, would you say that [your country] has on balance benefited or not from being a member of the European Community?' (2) 'Generally speaking, do you think that [your country's] membership in the Common Market is a good thing, a bad thing, or neither good nor bad?' (this is later referred to as the membership question).
4. Initial studies believed that there was a relationship between attitudes toward Europe and the propensity to vote in European elections. More recent studies, however, have shown that this relationship is in fact spurious, the result of failing to control for other variables, namely, contextual variables such as timing of the election, whether voting is obligatory, and whether the election is the first for the member-state. For a review, see Franklin (1996).
5. The wording on the question relating to the level of information on the EU was the

following: 'All things considered, how well informed do you feel you are about the European Community, its policies, its institutions – very well, quite well, not very well, not well at all?'

6. The variable corresponds to the EB question, 'Do you consider Portugal's membership of the EU a good thing, neither good nor bad, or a bad thing?' Values were re-coded so that the highest value, '3', corresponded to good thing, '2' corresponded to neither good nor bad, and '1' corresponded to bad thing. There is an index of European attitudes that combines this question with a question on regret concerning the scrapping of the EU. The index has the advantage of having results on a 1–5 scale. This index was not used, however, since it only existed until 1995, whereas the MEMBRSHP variable covers the whole period.

7. The variable vote intention was coded in the following way: those who said they would vote for the Communist Party were coded '0'. Those who declared their voting intention for the PS, the PSD, or the CDS, the other main parties, who were traditionally in favour of European Integration were coded '1'.

8. Wessels (1996: 122) had found the same negative relationship between age and attitudes toward membership in Portugal between 1985 and 1991.

9. Cf. Gunther and Montero (2001) and Freire (2001).

10. For a presentation of European party families positioning on Europe, see Wessels (1996: 130–31).

11. The project of European integration also served to cushion Portugal's potentially difficult transition from a colonial power to a European state. It also helped to streamline all the relevant parties' programmatic outlook from very early on in the process of democratization. All these effects concur to the idea, widely espoused, that the EU functioned as a powerful international factor in the consolidation of democracy in Southern Europe. See Pridham (1995: 180).

12. On the external influences on the parties in the first decade of democracy, see Bruneau (1982) and Sablosky (1996).

13. In 1983, when the party contested elections after the end of the coalition with the PSD, the AD (*Aliança Democrática* – Democratic Alliance), the party had achieved 12.4 per cent of the vote and 30 parliamentary seats. In 1985 the CDS lost eight deputies, and won, for the first time, less than ten per cent of the vote. In the following legislative elections, in 1987, the CDS' parliamentary group was reduced to four parliamentary seats, and 4.3 per cent of the vote. In 1991, the party did only slightly better, obtaining 4.4 per cent of the vote and five deputies.

14. In the event Freitas do Amaral, founder of the CDS voted in favour of ratification of the Treaty, and as evidence of his disagreement with the CDS stance, left the party. See Amaral (1991).

15. The CDS' exclusion from the EPP opened the way for the PSD to be accepted within its ranks. The CDS then joined the EDA (European Democratic Alliance), which included the Gaullists and the Irish *Fianna Fail*. This Group was renamed UPE (Union for Europe) in 1995, when the Italian *Forza Italia* joined it, becoming the third largest force in the EP. *Forza Italia* left the UPE in 1998, joining the EPP instead. In 1999 the UPE was extinguished and the Union for Europe of the Nations was created, now including the Italian extreme right-wing party *Allianza Nazionale* (National Alliance) as well as the Charles Pasqua's *Mouvement Pour la France* (Movement for France), the Danish Popular Party, and the Irish *Fianna Fail*. Thus, it seems that without considering an extreme-right-wing group, it is possible to say its membership has been moving rightward since the mid-1990s. Information obtained from the CDS-PP representation at the European Parliament.

16. Cf. Silva Lopes (1996).

17. Study elaborated by Memorandum, a communications firm. See Lobo and Freire (2002).

18. The data used were the following: the attitudes toward membership of the European

Union were obtained from the variable MEMBRSHP, also used above, namely, 'Do you consider Portugal's membership of the European Union a good thing, a bad thing, or neither good nor bad?' The scale was inverted so that 1 = a bad thing; 2 = neither good nor bad; and 3 = a good thing. Then the respondents' scores were grouped by vote intention. The graph depicts the mean of these scores between 1985 and 1999 for those who declared their vote intention for the party in question.

19. See the various volumes by ex-Prime Minister Cavaco Silva (1995, 1989, and 1993) on the reforms enacted as a result of EU objectives the PSD aimed at fulfilling.
20. In 1987 the two main parties polled 72 per cent of the vote; in 1991, 79 per cent; in 1995, 77 per cent; in 1999, 78 per cent; and in 2002, 76 per cent of the national vote. For an analysis of the changes in the party system, see Bruneau et al. (2001) and Lobo (2001).

REFERENCES

Alvarez-Miranda, B. (1995): 'A las puertas de la comunidad: consenso y disenso en el sur de Europa' [To the Doors of the Community: Consensus and Dissention in Southern Europe], Working Paper, Juan March Institute.

Amaral, D.F. (1991): Um voto a favor de Maastricht – razões de uma attitude [A Yes Vote for Maastrich – reasons for an attitude], Lisbon: Inquérito.

Bacalhau, M. (1993): Atitudes, Opiniões e Comportamento Eleitoral dos Portugueses [Attitudes, Opinions and the Electoral Behavior of the Portuguese], Lisbon: FLAD.

Bacalhau, M. (1993a): 'The Image, Identity and Benefits of the EC', in J. Silva Lopes, Portugal and EC Membership Evaluated, London: Pinter, pp.182–8.

Barreto, A. and C.V. Preto (1996): A Situação Social em Portugal [The Social Situation in Portugal], Lisbon: ICS.

Barroso, J.M. (1983): Les Partis Politiques et l'integration Europeéne [Political Parties and European Integration], Lisbon: APRI.

Bartolini, S. (2001): 'A integração europeia provocará uma reestruturação do sistema de clivagens nacionais?' [Will European Integration Provoke a Restructuring of national cleavages?], Sociologia – Problemas e Práticas [Sociology – Problems and Practice] 37, p.97.

Bosco, A. (2001): 'Four Actors in Search of a Role', in Diamandorous and Gunther (2001), pp.329–88.

Bruneau, T. (1982): 'As dimensões internacionais da revolução portuguesa: apoios e constrangimentos no estabelecimento da democracia' [The International Dimensions of the Portuguese Revolution: Support and Obstacles in the Establishment of Democracy], Análise Social [Social Analysis] XVIII/72–74, pp.885–96.

Bruneau, T. et al. (2001): 'Democracy, Southern European Style', in Diamandorous and Gunther (2001).

Dalton, R. (2002): Citizen Politics, New York: Seven Bridges Press.

Diamandorous, N. and R. Gunther (2001): Parties, Politics and Democracy in the New Europe, Baltimore, MD: Johns Hopkins University Press.

Frain, M. (1997): 'The Right in Portugal', in T. Bruneau (1997), Political Parties and Democracy in Portugal: Organizations, Elections and Public Opinion, Boulder, CO: Westview.

Franklin, M. (1996): 'European Elections and the European Voter', in J. Richardson (1996), European Union Power and Policy-making, London: Routledge.

Freire, A. (2001): O Comportamento Eleitoral em Portugal, Oeiras: Celta.

Freire, A. and P. Magalhães (2002): A Abstenção Eleitoral em Portugal [Electoral Absention in Portugal], Lisbon: ICS.

Freire, A. and M.C. Lobo (2002): 'The Portuguese 2002 Legislative Elections', *West European Politics* 25/4, pp.221–8.

Gunther, R., P. Diamandorous and H.-J. Puhle (1995): *The Politics of Democratic Consolidation*, Baltimore, MD: Johns Hopkins University Press.

Gunther, R. and J.R. Montero (2001): 'The Anchors of Partisanship: A Comparative Analysis of Voting Behaviour in Four Southern European Democracies', in Diamandorous and Gunther (2001).

Lobo, M.C. (2001): 'The Role of Parties in the Consolidation of Democracy', *Party Politics* 7/5, pp.643–53.

Lobo, M.C. and P. Magalhães (2001): 'From Third Wave to Third Way: The Portuguese Socialists and European Integration', *Journal of Southern Europe and the Balkans* 3/1, pp.25–35.

Miranda, J. (2000): *O Parlamento e a União Europeia* [Parliament and the European Union], Coimbra: Coimbra Editora.

Niedermayer, O. (1996): 'Trends and Contrasts', in Niedermayer and Sinnott (1996), pp.56–68.

Niedermayer, O. and R. Sinnot (1996): *Public Opinion and Internationalized Governance*, Oxford: Oxford University Press.

PCP (1988): *Portugal e a CEE hoje, Contribuições para o XII Congresso do PCP* [Portugal and the EEC Today, Contributions to the XII Congress of the Portuguese Communist Party], Lisbon: Àvante.

Pridham, G. (1995): 'The International Context of Democratic Consolidation', in Gunther, Diamandorous and Puhle (1995), pp.170–90.

Robinson, R. (1996): 'Do CDS ao CDS-PP: o partido do Centro Democrático Social e o seu papel na política portuguesa' [From the CDS to the CDS-PP: The Social Democratic Party of the Center and its Role in Portuguese Politics], *Análise Social* [Social Analysis] XXXI/138, pp.951–73.

Sablosky, J. (1996): 'A actividade partidária transnacional e as relações de Portugal com a Comunidade *Europeia*' [Transnational Party Activity and the Relations Between Portugal and the European Community], *Análise Social* [Social Analysis] XXXI/138, pp.1007–20.

Silva, C. (1989): *Construir a modernidade* [Construct Modernity], Lisbon: INCM.

Silva, C. (1993): *Afirmar Portugal no Mundo* [Affirm Portugal in the World], Lisbon: INCM.

Silva, C. (1995): *As reformas da década* [The Reforms of the Decade], Lisbon: Bertrand.

Silva Lopes, J. (1996): 'A economia portuguesa desde 1960' [The Portuguese Economy since 1960], in Barreto and Preto (1996), pp.233–363.

Wessels, B. (1996): 'Development of Support: Diffusion or Demographic Replacement?' in Niedermayer and Sinnot (1996), pp.106–7.

Spaniards' Long March Towards Europe

JUAN DÍEZ-NICOLÁS

THE AIM TO BE EUROPEANS

Spaniards have long felt the need to be recognized as Europeans. After a period of more than a century of no participation in the most important European events, Spaniards needed to feel they were part of Europe and no longer different. Spain's neutrality in the First World War and Second World War, which were both mainly European wars, added to the fact that it had not participated in the previous war of 1870, and to the 40 years of greater or smaller isolation during the Franco regime, makes it necessary to go back to Napoleon's wars in order to find the last significant implication of Spain in European affairs.

Since the 1960s, and even more since the 1970s, Spaniards began to express more and more frequently and intensively their desire not to be different, and their aim to be, like other Europeans, fully integrated into Europe and, in general, the Western world. Certainly, Spain had already been admitted to the United Nations in November 1950, and therefore had become a member of all the international organizations that were part of the UN, such as UNESCO (United Nations Educational, Scientific and Cultural Organization), WLO (World Labour Organization) and others. It is also a fact that in 1953 Spain had signed a treaty with the United States for the joint use of some military bases in Spain, as well as a new treaty with the Holly See. Spain had even been a member, since the Organization for Economic Co-operation and Development's (OECD) inception in 1961, of this prestigious group of developed countries.

Even during the 1970s, however, Spain was banned from admission to other European 'clubs': the Council of Europe and the Common Market (as it was then named), as well as from the North Atlantic Treaty Organization (NATO). During the 1960s and 1970s supporters as well as opponents to the Franco regime agreed on their desire to see

Spain admitted to those three international bodies, though for very different reasons. Supporters of the Franco regime believed Spain's admission to the three exclusive 'clubs' would mean recognition and acceptance by the international (and particularly the European) community, of the regime born out of the Civil War (1936–39), as well as the definitive legitimization of a regime that exhibited a peculiar 'organic' democracy. Opponents of the Franco regime desired the incorporation of Spain to the three international organizations as an indirect way of achieving the political changes needed to abandon the old authoritarian structures and restore the basic civic rights and freedoms, especially the legalization of political parties and labour unions, as well as the calling of free democratic elections, thus restoring democracy in Spain.[1]

When Franco died in November 1975, and once civil rights and freedoms were restored during the transition to democracy, Spain was admitted to the three international (and mainly European) organizations. It was first admitted to the Council of Europe, immediately after the first democratic elections of June 1977. Admission to the Council of Europe was always considered a necessary, though not sufficient, condition to acceptance to the more restricted and exclusive Common Market (thereafter European Economic Community and at present European Union). When Spain was admitted to the Council of Europe in November 1977, the organization had 20 members, whereas the number of member countries in the EEC was only nine. In December 1981 Spain was admitted to NATO, and although Spanish leftist parties (particularly the *Partido Socialista Obrero Español* [PSOE] and the *Partido Comunista de Espana* [PCE]) questioned that decision at the time, the PSOE government of 1986 called for a referendum to maintain Spain within NATO, the result being a slight difference in favour of keeping Spain in (52 per cent voted 'yes', and 40 per cent voted 'no'; the rest were blank or invalid votes). The incorporation of Spain, years later, into the military structure of NATO produced little public controversy except among the *Izquierda Unida* (IU) party (the heir of the PCE). The admission of Spain to the European Economic Commission took place in 1986, 24 years after the first official petition by the Spanish Government (which was presented in 1962), and 16 years after the signature (in 1970) of a preferential treaty of the EEC with Spain that, contrary to European expectations, proved to be extremely favourable to the Spanish economy.

It is no surprise that, after such a long waiting period for full integration into Europe, Spaniards have developed a very pro-European orientation, probably the most European of all Europeans. Only recently have some signs of discontent begun to arise, although they are still far from any significant 'Euroscepticism' current of opinion. On the contrary, as will be shown below, a high consensus in favour of European integration is evident in all aspects that may be considered.

As early as 1966, only four years after Spain's first official petition for admission into the Common Market, a survey conducted by the – at that time – recently established *Instituto de la Opinión Pública* (Public Opinion Institute – IOP)[2] showed a relative majority in favour of Spain joining the European Common Market. In fact, 60 per cent of the population 21 years of age and over did not have an opinion. Thirty-three per cent, however, answered that the solution to Spain's economic problems was membership in the Common Market, whereas four per cent were in favour of economic autarchy and three per cent preferred an economic union with Latin America. In 1968 those not having an opinion had dropped to only 33 per cent, whereas the number in favour of joining the Common Market had grown to 58 per cent. That same year 41 per cent were in favour of Spain being integrated into the United States of Europe, even at the cost of 'losing some prerogatives as an independent state', and only 22 per cent opposed such integration. During the 1970s many different IOP surveys showed a persistent proportion of between 70–75 per cent in favour of Spain joining the Common Market. The number of those who expected benefits for the Spanish economy with respect to its industry, agriculture, or labour was usually between five and ten times as large as the number of those who expected negative consequences. That was also true with respect to politics, culture, trade, and tourism.

It may be interesting to note that a survey conducted by the CIS in 1983 asked respondents to mention what they considered the three most important issues in Spain's foreign policy.[3] The aggregate results were as follows: entrance into the European Common Market (50 per cent), relations with Latin America and recovery of Gibraltar (both 32 per cent), presence of Spain in international organizations (26 per cent), good neighbours policy toward France and Portugal (18 per cent), reinforcement of relations with the Third World (11 per cent), and good relations with Communist (European) countries, cordial relations with neighbours in North Africa, and relations with NATO (all under ten per cent).[4]

During the first few years after admission to the European Economic Community, however, Spaniards could not perceive any benefits for themselves, although they continued to expect them in the future, especially with respect to the national economy. Thus, in different surveys conducted by ASEP (*Análisis Sociológicos, Económicos y Políticos* – Political, Economic and Sociological Analysis) during the late 1980s,[5] 40 per cent of respondents agreed that entrance into the EEC had been negative for most Spaniards, 48 per cent did not agree that entrance had improved the standard of living of Spaniards, 57 per cent agreed that it would be very positive for most Spaniards, and 63 per cent agreed that the EEC would be a first step toward political unification in Europe.

In summary, Spaniards had long awaited integration into the European Economic Community because they wanted to lose the feeling of isolation that, to a greater or lesser degree, they had experienced for several decades during the Franco regime, and they were anxious to prove they were fully Europeans. That may be one of the main reasons for the pervasive pro-European attitude of Spaniards that is found in all surveys, as if the expression of strong wishes to join Europe and high expectations of benefits could make the dream come true. Although the high positive expectations did not seem to materialize during the first years of membership, however, Spaniards did not dismay, and continued to expect high benefits at the same time that they recognized their expectations had not yet become real. Optimism about the consequences of joining the ECC has been the main support for Spaniards' pro-European attitudes.

According to Díez-Medrano (2003) studies on European integration generally fail to differentiate between explanations for the behaviour of the countries' political elites and the attitudes of the population. The studies lack sufficient empirical support, and they fail to link historical and structural processes and elites' views to the general population's attitudes. In addition, he also points out the scarcity of studies on Spain's process of European integration.

The analysis that follows focuses only on Spain's public opinion with respect to the process of European integration, and contributes empirical findings, mainly based on time series data for a period of 12 years, that may be useful to test, at least partially, some of the main hypotheses that have been advanced to explain Spaniards' support for this process.

SPANIARDS' EUROPEAN IDENTITY

The project of a supranational identity community centred on the Spanish-speaking world, as promoted by the writer Ramiro de Maeztu (1931) among others, lost whatever meaning was left since the movements for independence in Latin America soon after the Spanish civil war (Díez Medrano, 2003). This has been reflected in surveys conducted since 1991, which show that a very small percentage of respondents agree with the statement that 'Spain is the Mother land of Ibero-America, and everything should be subordinated to her role as mother, even economic interests'. In short, Latin America was part of Spain's history, but Europe has not only been part of her history, it is also part of her present and future.

While identifying themselves as Europeans rather than as members of a *Hispanidad* community, however, Spaniards have maintained strong affective bonds with Latin America and Latin Americans that compete with those with Europe and the Europeans.[6] Because of Spain's long colonial presence in Latin America, the traumatic effects of the loss of Cuba and Puerto Rico in 1898, and huge migration flows from Spain to Latin America early in the twentieth century, it is easy to understand why Spaniards have been traditionally positively oriented toward Latin America. Although a common language, history, religion, and culture between Spain and Latin America have created very strong ties, however,

TABLE 1

INDEX* OF SENTIMENTS TOWARD GROUPS OF COUNTRIES

	I -91	I -92	I -93	I -94	I -95	IV -96	II -97	IV -98	IV -99	IV -00	IV -01	III -02
European Union	178	161	157	163	139	146	154	148	152	159	159	171
Latin America	161	142	145	150	143	144	148	143	147	155	156	156
East Europe	151	134	134	136	123	125	131	130	126	140	144	147
North America (US and Canada)	122	113	118	123	118	116	122	123	115	134	135	132
Arab countries of North Africa	112	104	122	118	108	108	110	107	111	119	117	107

Note: * The index has been constructed on the basis of the difference between the proportion of respondents that show favourable attitudes and the proportion that show unfavourable attitudes, adding 100 to make the index positive and varying between 0 and 200.

Source: ASEP Data Archive. (Data from 1991 to 1996 were collected for CIRES, a project sponsored by the BBV, Caja de Madrid and BBK Foundations.)

TABLE 2

EVALUATION* OF NATIONALS FROM DIFFERENT COUNTRIES

	I -91	I -92	I -93	I -94	I -95	IV -96	II -97	IV -98	IV -99	IV -00	IV -01	III -02
Argentineans	6.3	6.2	6.2	6.5	6.4	6.5	6.3	6.4	6.2	6.3	6.5	6.4
Italians	6.3	5.9	6.0	6.2	6.0	6.1	6.0	6.2	6.0	6.2	6.4	6.3
Portuguese	5.5	5.5	5.8	6.0	5.9	6.0	5.8	6.1	5.9	6.1	6.4	6.2
Germans	5.6	5.4	5.7	5.8	5.7	5.8	5.6	5.8	5.5	5.8	5.9	5.9
French	5.3	5.2	5.6	5.8	5.6	5.6	5.4	5.3	5.2	5.8	5.8	5.9
British	4.9	4.9	5.4	5.6	5.6	5.5	5.1	5.4	5.3	5.6	5.5	5.7
North Americans	5.2	5.1	5.3	5.6	5.6	5.5	5.3	5.4	5.1	5.5	5.5	5.3
Moroccans	4.1	4.1	4.6	4.9	4.9	4.9	4.8	5.0	5.0	5.0	5.1	4.7

Note: * The scale used varies from 0 (lowest) to 10 (highest).

Source: ASEP Data Archive. (Data from 1991 to 1996 were collected for CIRES, a project sponsored by the BBV, Caja de Madrid, and BBK Foundations.)

geography, a whole history of political, religious, and economic alliances and confrontations between Spain and the rest of Europe have created even stronger ties.

Survey data collected annually since 1991 by ASEP demonstrate that Spaniards' sentiments towards the European Union and Latin America are similar and higher than those towards any other group of countries,[7] although there is a small but stable difference in favour of the European Union (see Table 1). When the question of Spanish sentiment refers to nationals instead of countries, however, Latin Americans (as represented here by Argentineans) are consistently better evaluated than nationals from any European country (as represented by Italians, Portuguese, Germans, French and British) (see Table 2).

All European nationals are consistently better evaluated than North Americans and Moroccans (with the exception of the British, less valued than North Americans in three years, and the French, less valued than North Americans in 1998). It may be added that when other Latin American nationals have been included, as the Mexicans were in 1991, they were given a better grade than all European nationals, and when all European Union nationals have been included (as in 1992, 1993, and 1994), they all received lower grades than Argentineans but higher grades than North Americans.

When the question refers to countries, the frame of reference seems to be based on economic and political considerations, but when the question asks about nationals, the frame of reference seems to be based more on affective dimensions that have to do with sharing a common culture. This apparent contradiction or, rather, indecision, manifests itself in many other questions. Thus, in the 12 surveys conducted since 1991, a high majority of respondents agree with the statement that 'The Ibero-American Community of Nations is certainly a great idea, but Spain is in Europe, and her place is essentially in Europe'. A significant percentage also agrees, however, that 'Spain is geographically in Europe, but because of her language, history and tradition, she should be linked more especially to Ibero-America'.

The fact that Spaniards feel culturally, historically, and emotionally close to Latin America does not imply any real intention of integration. The idea of a Spanish Commonwealth equivalent to the British Commonwealth was abandoned long ago, though it is also true that, because of the restoration of the Spanish Crown in 1976, Spain maintains a symbolic pre-eminence in Latin American summits and continues to receive some sort of special recognition. In reciprocity Spain has accepted the role of mediator between Latin America and the European Union, at

TABLE 3

OPINION ON THE MEANING OF BEING EUROPEAN

TOTAL	I-92 (1,200) %	I-93 (1,200) %	I-94 (1,200) %	I-95 (1,200) %	IV-96 (1,200) %	II-97 (1,213) %	IV-98 (1,204) %	IV-99 (1,214) %	IV-00 (1,210) %	IV-01 (1,209) %	III-02 (1,220) %
To consider oneself as European	24	23	25	19	20	22	25	25	28	20	26
To live and work in a European country for more than 5 years	16	17	14	20	22	16	15	17	14	19	20
To be born in in a European country	50	49	49	52	49	50	49	50	48	52	46
To have certain physical and cultural traits	6	4	4	3	4	4	3	3	4	2	2
DK/NA	4	6	7	6	5	7	9	6	7	6	5

Source: ASEP Data Archive. (Data from 1992 to 1996 were collected for CIRES, a project sponsored by the BBV, Caja de Madrid, and BBK Foundations.)

times more symbolically than in practice. It is also true that since the late 1980s Spain has acquired a predominant position as investor in many Latin American countries.

For most Spaniards, to be European is to be born in a European country, although one out of five answer that it is 'to consider oneself as European'. The same proportion also thinks it is 'to live and work in a European country'. Only an insignificant minority believes being European has anything to do with 'certain physical or cultural traits' (see Table 3).

Being among the least xenophobic and racist of all Europeans (Díez-Nicolás and Ramírez Lafita 2001a), it is only natural that Spaniards should pay so little attention to physical or cultural traits when deciding who is or is not European. The proportion mentioning that option, small as it has been since the beginning, has even declined steadily to an almost negligible two per cent. On the contrary, the land where one is born seems to be the most important basis for defining someone as European, to the point that about half of the sample chooses that option every year.

The length of time that Spaniards had to wait in order to be admitted to the European Union probably accounts for the favourable attitude Spaniards show toward the EU. Less than ten per cent of

TABLE 4

RESPONDENTS' ATTITUDES TOWARD THE EUROPEAN UNION

TOTAL	I-95 (1,200) %	IV-96 (1,200) %	II-97 (1,213) %	IV-98 (1,204) %	IV-99 (1,214) %	IV-00 (1,210) %	IV-01 (1,209) %	III-02 (1,220) %
Very much in favour	5	6	5	4	5	5	4	5
Quite in favour	32	31	33	28	32	35	31	40
Somewhat in favour	21	22	26	29	33	30	35	33
Neither in favour nor against	26	24	18	27	20	20	18	16
Somewhat against	7	8	5	4	5	3	6	3
Quite against	3	3	2	2	1	1	1	1
Very much against	1	1	1	1	1	–	*	*
DK/NA	6	6	9	5	3	5	4	2
Index*	147	147	157	155	162	166	162	173

Note: * The index has been constructed on the basis of the difference between the proportion of respondents that show favourable attitudes and the proportion that show unfavourable attitudes, adding 100 to make the index positive and varying between 0 and 200.

Source: ASEP Data Archive. (Data from 1995 to 1996 were collected for CIRES, a project sponsored by the BBV, Caja de Madrid, and BBK Foundations.)

respondents usually answer that they are somewhat against, quite against, or very much against the European Union, a proportion so small that it puts Spain in one of the lowest positions of all European countries in terms of the significance and weight of the so-called 'Eurosceptics' – certainly a great distance from the United Kingdom. As a matter of fact, the pro-European attitude has grown over time, reaching an all-time high in 2002 (probably as a consequence of the Spanish Presidency of the European Council during the first semester of this year).

In fact, the two most important parties, *Partido Popular* (PP) and PSOE, have never shown any significant differences with respect to integration in the EU, as they did with respect to NATO in the past. Even the IU, heir to the former PCE, has been in favour of Spain joining the European Union, though at times it may have expressed some criticisms about specific issues, similarly to regional or nationalist parties. Thus in the 2002 survey, the proportions of respondents who show favourable attitudes toward the EU were 78 per cent among PP voters, 73 per cent among PSOE voters, and 70 per cent among IU voters.[8] Nobody has ever dared to really hold up the flag against the construction of Europe, nor even the extreme left or the extreme right. Consensus among political parties, labour unions, and all kinds of interest groups has always been almost unanimous in supporting the integration of Spain into the EU (Alvarez-Miranda 1996), one of the rare issues where such a consensus has been reached.

Three variables measuring the attitudes of Spaniards toward the European Union were included in the ASEP surveys: sentiments toward the European Union (a five-point scale measuring favourable–unfavourable attitudes towards different groups of countries, as shown in Table 1), attitudes towards the European Union (a seven-point scale measuring favourable–unfavourable attitudes toward the EU only, as indicated in Table 4), and degree of identification with the European Union (an 11-point scale measuring the degree of identification with the European Union as well as with the region where the respondent lives, and with Spain, as shown in Table 5). The correlation coefficients among the three variables range between 0.27 and 0.32, all three being statistically significant at the 0.001 level. A main component analysis showed that attitudes toward the European Union (the seven-point scale) are the best measure of the three.

Two regression models have then been constructed having as dependent variables the attitudes toward the European Union, and as independent variables a group of attitudinal variables and a group of socio-demographic variables respectively. The attitudinal variables included the individual's frequency of reading international news in the press, frequency of travelling abroad, self-appraised degree of information about the European Union, perception of relatives' and friends' attitudes toward the European Union, perception of mass media's attitudes toward the European Union, and knowledge of foreign languages. These variables explained 14 per cent of the total variance in the attitudes of Spaniards toward the European Union, and the independent variable that contributed more to this explanation was the respondent's perception of mass media's attitudes towards the European Union, followed by the perception of relatives' and friends' attitudes and the self-appraised degree of information about the European Union, and by the frequency of travelling abroad. All four relationships are positive.

As for the socio-demographic variables, they included the respondent's age, educational level, self-placement on a seven-point left–right scale, self- placement on a five-point scale of Spanish-nationalist sentiments, monthly household income, social position as defined by Galtung (1976) (to construct a nine-point index measuring centre–periphery placement), socio-economic status (on the basis of the person's education, household income, occupational status, and household equipment), exposure to information (an index constructed on the basis of newspapers read, broadcasted information programmes listened to, and television information programmes watched), and Inglehart's post-materialism index (a six-point scale) (Inglehart 1977b, 1990, 1997). The explanatory power of this model was only three per cent of the total variance on the dependent variable, and the only significant relationship with attitudes towards the European Union was monthly household income. These results confirm the findings of other studies.[9]

The results therefore also confirm the positive relationship of income and voting for conservative parties with attitudes toward the European Union (Gabel 1998). They also support Inglehart's cognitive mobilization hypothesis (Inglehart 1977a) in which individuals with more knowledge about the European Union (especially if the media portray the European Union favourably) will be more positively oriented towards it. Thus, the correlation coefficients between the individual's self-appraised degree of information on the European Union and the individual's perception of mass media orientation towards it are positively and significantly related to attitudes toward the European Union (r =.226 and .265 respectively). However, the Spanish data do not support Wessel's (1995) hypothesis about the relationship between the individual's left–right self-placement and attitudes towards the European Union, probably because of the very favourable attitudes of Spaniards toward the EU regardless of political orientation. Neither do the data support Inglehart's hypothesis about the positive relationship between post-materialism and attitudes towards the European Union (the relationship is not statistically significant). In any case, as Díez-Medrano has remarked, these models usually explain a very small effect on attitudes toward the European Union (Gabel's model explains 16 per cent of the variance at most, and the model used here explains 14 per cent of the variance). Quoting Deflem and Pampel (1996), he concludes that 'a person's country of residence remains by far the best predictor of attitudes towards European integration' (Díez-Medrano 2003).

As expected, Spaniards identify themselves more strongly with Spain and the Autonomous Community where they live than with Europe. Traditionally, Spaniards have identified themselves primarily with the place where they live (the town or city), showing some kind of 'localism', but since 1978, when the Autonomous Communities (Regions) acquired constitutional recognition and more powers than many of their equivalent administrative subdivisions, even in federal states, Spaniards have experienced a reshaping of their identities, to the extent that identification with the Autonomous Community exceeded in many regions (especially the Basque Country, Navarra, Galicia, Catalonia, among others) their identification with Spain. In some cases, like the Basque Country, identification with the Autonomous Community is linked to separatist or independent

TABLE 5

DEGREE OF IDENTIFICATION* WITH SPAIN,
THE AUTONOMOUS COMMUNITY, AND EUROPE

	I-93	I-94	I-95	IV-96	II-97	IV-98	IV-99	IV-00	IV-01	III-02
SPAIN	8.2	8.1	8.2	8.1	8.1	7.9	8.0	7.9	8.0	8.0
Autonomous Community	8.3	8.2	8.0	8.1	7.9	7.8	7.9	7.8	7.9	8.0
EUROPE	6.7	6.7	6.4	6.1	6.2	6.2	6.4	6.1	6.4	6.7

Note: * The scale used varies from 0 (lowest) to 10 (highest).

Source: ASEP Data Archive. (Data from 1993 to 1996 were collected for CIRES, a project sponsored by the BBV, Caja de Madrid and BBK Foundations.)

feelings (about 25 per cent of the Basques feel that way) (Díez-Nicolás 1999), but in most cases it only reflects a newly acquired circle of identification perfectly compatible with Spanish identity (Díez-Medrano and Gutierrez 2001). As the novelty of the Autonomous Community is reduced, the compatibility of the local, regional, and national identities is more and more salient. The European identity, however, no matter how European Spaniards claim they are, is still a long way off (see Table 5).

In a sense, one could argue that Spaniards' aim to be European results more from their will to avoid being left out of Europe, as a question of pride, than because they really wanted to integrate and dissolve themselves into a European identity. It is likely that Spaniards want to be Europeans without renouncing their Spanish and regional identities, something that is coherent with their limited geographical mobility, not only toward Europe, but even towards different regions and localities within Spain. Three out of four Spaniards 18-years and older live in the same province in which they were born and in the same province they lived in when they were young (Díez-Nicolás 1999: 15). Besides, only about 19 per cent of Spaniards 18-years and older say they can speak a foreign language (not including regional vernacular languages), 46 per cent have never travelled abroad (as a matter of fact, less than ten per cent admit travelling 'frequently' or 'very frequently' abroad), and only five per cent answer that it is 'very likely' or 'quite likely' that they will go abroad to work within the next ten years (ASEP's III-02 survey). The geographical position of Spain at one extreme of Europe, the natural barrier of the Pyrenees, the great regional heterogeneity and diversity, not only with respect to the natural or physical environment, but also with respect to language, culture, and traditions, probably explains the 'extreme localism' of the population, even though for two and a half decades (1950–75), internal and external migrations forced many people to travel away from their homeland. Nevertheless, it is also true that most migrants (especially those who went to Europe) returned after a few years, and they returned to their homeland, 'to their own', as they would say.

Spaniards have participated in the elections for the European Parliament in no negligible proportion. In 1987, when the first European elections after admission were held in Spain, participation rate was 69 per cent. It dropped to 55 per cent in the regular elections of 1989, only three percentage points below the European average. Participation rate increased to 59 per cent in 1994 (two percentage points above the European average), however, and to 64 per cent in 1999 (15 percentage points above the European average). The trend seems to reflect an increasing interest of Spaniards in European elections, as shown not only in contrast with the European average (which is clearly declining), but also with respect to turnout in Spanish general elections (69 per cent in 1989, 77 per cent in 1993, 78 per cent in 1996 and 69 per cent in 2000). Thus, participation in the last European elections of 1999 was only five percentage points below participation in the last Spanish legislative elections of 2000, a difference that is certainly very small when compared to the differences between European and national elections in other member states of the European Union. Turnout recall in the last European elections of 1999 is better explained by the regression model based on the socio-demographic variables mentioned before (the model explains six per cent of the total variance of attitudes towards the European Union) than by the model based on the attitudinal variables also mentioned previously (the model explains only three per cent of the total variance). Age and social position and leftist self-placement are the best predictors of turnout recall, all negatively related to it, implying that those in the social periphery and self-placed in the right, as well as the young, are more likely to have voted in the last European elections. Besides, though the attitudinal regression model explains such a small proportion of the variance, the individual's appraised degree of information on the European Union is the best predictor of attitudes toward the European Union.

GOALS, HOPES AND FEARS RELATED TO INTEGRATION INTO THE EU

What are the goals that Spaniards want the European Union to reach? What do they expect from the EU? What do they fear from EU? Survey data accumulated during the past 12 years seem to provide some tentative answers to these questions.

Taking the year 2000 as a referential date (2005 after the 1999 survey), questions have been posed since 1991 to find out whether Spaniards wanted the European government or the Spanish government to take responsibility for certain policies. From 1991 to 1994 a majority of respondents were clearly in favour of the single European currency, the Central European Bank, and a European Armed Forces. Public opinion was also moderately in favour of the European government deciding on a joint foreign policy and on the most

TABLE 6

AGREEMENT–DISAGREEMENT INDEX WITH RESPECT TO WHICH GOVERNMENT,
EUROPEAN OR NATIONAL, SHOULD DECIDE ON CERTAIN
POLICIES BY THE YEAR 2000

	I -91	I -92	I -93	I -94	I -95	IV -96	II -97	IV -98	IV -99	IV -00	IV -01	III -02
Most important political decisions	115	125	119	113	104	99	98	103	93	104	96	109
Tax policies	105	115	112	106	102	93	96	99	80	99	91	95
European Armed Forces	121	125	128	122	119	115	114	116	109	116	110	117
Foreign policy and relations	115	123	123	115	112	106	104	104	102	106	102	109
A single currency	145	149	149	141	131	131	135	–	–	–	–	–
A single Central Bank	–	125	134	121	109	106	107	–	–	–	–	–

Note: * The index has been constructed on the basis of the difference between the proportion of respondents that agree and the proportion that disagree, adding 100 to make the index positive and varying between 0 and 200.

Source: ASEP Data Archive. (Data from 1991 to 1996 were collected for CIRES, a project sponsored by the BBV, Cava de Madrid, and BBK Foundations.)

important political decisions, and it was only moderately in favour of the European government deciding on tax policy (see Table 6).

Since 1995, however, support has decreased slightly until 2001 with respect to all those policies, though it has remained quite high with respect to the common single currency and not so high with respect to the joint European Armed Forces. A general recovery of all indicators seems to have taken place in 2002, probably due to the Spanish presidency during the first semester. Since the EU decided in 1997 to adopt the euro as the common single currency, and given that Spain was among the group of countries that first implemented this decision, from 1998 onward the survey asked a question regarding Spaniards' satisfaction with that decision. Results have shown a consistent 50–55 per cent who consider it a very good or good decision, compared to less than ten per cent who consider it a bad or very bad decision. Opinions have become slightly more favourable, however, toward keeping the most important political decisions and tax policies within the authority of the Spanish government. There

TABLE 7

TRUST* IN INSTITUTIONS

	I-95	IV-96	II-97	IV-98	IV-99	IV-00	IV-01	IV-02
1. The Crown	7.2	7.3	7.1	7.0	6.7	7.1	6.8	6.4
2. European Union	5.2	5.7	5.6	5.4	5.4	5.8	5.4	5.5
3. Autonomous Community Government	4.7	5.5	5.4	5.3	5.3	5.6	5.2	5.0
4. Spanish Government	3.9	5.0	5.0	5.1	5.2	5.6	4.9	4.7
5. Armed Forces	5.3	5.2	5.5	5.3	5.1	5.4	5.2	5.1
6. Public Administration	4.2	4.5	4.8	4.5	4.4	4.9	4.7	4.7
7. Courts of Justice	4.5	4.3	4.9	4.5	4.3	4.6	4.4	4.3

Note: * The scale used varies from 0 (lowest) to 10 (highest).

Source: ASEP Data Archive. (Data from 1995 to 1996 were collected for CIRES, a project sponsored by the BBV, Caja de Madrid, and BBK Foundations.)

also seems to be a great of deal controversy about what government, European or Spanish, should decide on a common foreign policy. It seems that, as Spaniards have gained experience in knowing what it means to be part of the European Union, initial thoughts about transferring rapidly most policies to a central European government have become a little more cautious. This does not mean that there is less trust in the European Union. On the contrary, trust in the EU is only lower than trust in the Crown, but higher than trust in the regional government, the Spanish government, the Armed Forces, the public administration, and the courts (see Table 7).

It seems as if Spaniards' feelings about the European Union were more generalist at first, when expectations predominated but no consequences had yet been experienced. As more and more individuals have had direct or indirect contact with decisions and policies emanating from the European Union, however, opinions have become more discriminative and less generalist. Public opinion accepted the common currency since the beginning, probably because Spaniards thought it would be more secure than the peseta. The general acceptance of the European Armed Forces also solves some historical fears from the near past, when the Spanish Armed Forces were more involved in internal than external security, and is coherent with the general acceptance of their new role in humanitarian international missions outside Spain. Spaniards are more hesitant about transferring to European institutions the power to establish taxes, however, knowing that most European countries have higher taxes than Spain, and therefore fearing that empowering Brussels with tax policies might result in higher personal costs. The more conservative orientation of Spaniards toward decisions that might be taken by the European Union is reflected on the three surveys conducted since 2000, where about two out of every three respondents agree that 'EU decisions should be implemented in Spain only if the Spanish government voted in favour of them', and where more than 40 per cent of respondents prefer the European Parliament and only 20 per cent prefer the Council of Ministers to make the most important decisions.

TABLE 8

WHO SHOULD MAKE MOST DECISIONS AFFECTING THE CITIZENS

Total	IV-00 (1,210) %	IV-01 (1,209) %	III-02 (1,220) %
The Autonomous Community	44	46	48
The Spanish State	46	46	44
The European Union	5	5	5
DK/NA	3	4	4

Source: ASEP Data Archive.

TABLE 9

ATTITUDES ON ECONOMIC PROTECTIONISM

I-91	I-92	I-93	I-94	I-95	IV-96	II-97	IV-98	IV-99	IV-00	IV-01	III-02
Law should protect Spanish products against competition of products from other EU countries											
166	173	176	179	182	179	180	178	176	182	176	172
Law should protect Spanish products against competition of products from other non-EU countries											
174	181	183	185	189	188	186	182	184	186	182	185

Note: * The index has been constructed on the basis of the difference between the proportion of respondents that agree and the proportion that disagree, adding 100 to make the index positive and varying between 0 and 200.

Source: ASEP Data Archive. (Data from 1991 to 1996 were collected for CIRES, a project sponsored by the BBV, Caja de Madrid, and BBK Foundations.)

Given the localism to which reference has been made before, it is no surprise to find out that most Spaniards continue to prefer that most decisions that may affect them as citizens be made either by the national or the regional government, and only a very small minority would rather have the European Union do it (see Table 8).

There seem to be no complaints about the EU having too much power, however, since in the three surveys since 2000 about half of the respondents (58 per cent in 2002) answer that the EU has just the amount of power it should have, whereas similar proportions of less than 20 per cent each think that it has too much or too little power. Again, Spaniards seem to be very pro-European Union when they are talking in very general terms, but they become much more cautious and discriminative when they get down to specific issues.

This is precisely the case with respect to protectionism. Spaniards are very much in favour of protecting Spanish products against the competition of foreign non-European products, but also against the competition of European products. More than three-quarters of Spaniards show, beyond any doubt, protectionist attitudes toward Spanish products (see Table 9).

Similar protectionist attitudes are observed with respect to hiring somebody for a job. There is a clear difference, however, between

TABLE 10

ATTITUDES TOWARDS HIRING SPANIARDS OR OTHER
BETTER-QUALIFIED EUROPEANS

	I-92	I-93	I-94	I-95	IV-96	II-97	IV-98	IV-99	IV-00	IV-01	III-02
TOTAL	(1,200)	(1,200)	(1,200)	(1,200)	(1,200)	(1,213)	(1,204)	(1,214)	(1,210)	(1,209)	(1,220)
	%	%	%	%	%	%	%	%	%	%	%
Better-qualified European	54	54	49	37	39	33	26	26	31	28	35
Spaniard	36	31	40	46	45	49	55	54	54	49	49
It makes no difference	7	9	8	14	12	14	15	16	12	18	14
DK/NA	3	6	3	1	4	5	4	5	4	4	3

Source: ASEP Data Archive. (Data from 1992 to 1996 were collected for CIRES, a project sponsored by the BBV, Caja de Madrid and BBK Foundations.)

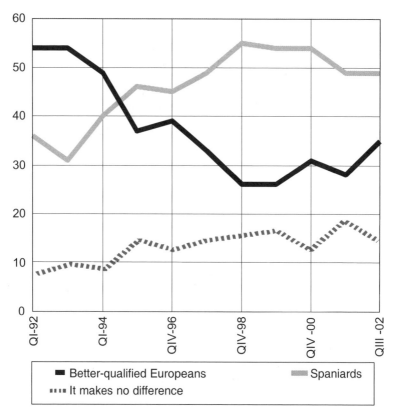

Source: ASEP Data Archive. (Data from 1992 to 1996 were collected for CIRES, a project sponsored by the BBV, Caja de Madrid and BBK Foundations.)

individuals and products. Between 1992 and 1994, when respondents were asked to choose between hiring a Spaniard or a foreigner with higher qualifications, a majority answered they would hire the foreigner with higher qualifications, but since 1995 the choice has increasingly been in favour of the Spaniard (see Table 10 and Figure 1).

It seems that the high rates of unemployment experienced in Spain during the same period of 1992–95 probably had a lessening effect on attitudes toward giving preference to European over Spanish workers, so that, in spite of the fact that unemployment has decreased steadily since 1996, Spaniards have continued to favour their fellow countrymen. The proportion saying that 'it makes no difference', however, has been increasing during the last year, and in 2002 the proportion favouring the Spanish worker is the same as the joint proportion who would rather give the job to the European or who think that 'it makes no difference'. For the time being, however, the fact remains that Spaniards seem not to accept the real consequences (and not the abstract and hypothetical consequences) of the European Union agreement on 'the free movement of products, services and individuals' statement with which a great majority of them would agree.

Thus, when comparing desired and expected goals for the European Union, only one seems to be very desirable and very likely to happen in the eyes of Spaniards: 'the elimination of all barriers to the free circulation of workers throughout the countries of the EU.' The contradiction examined earlier between the expressed importance of this goal and attitudes toward hiring a Spaniard or a better-qualified foreign worker does not need any further comment. Again, the contrast between the general and the particular appears. The high importance attached to 'achieving peace in Europe' (a clear reference to the Balkan conflict), 'reducing economic differences among EU countries', and 'establishing the United States of Europe' is not at all matched by the likelihood that these goals may become realities. Only the importance attached to 'adopting a single currency in the EU' has been matched by a growing likelihood that it would happen, as the date of its adoption became closer and closer (see Table 11).

As a summary measure of Spaniards' most recent attitudes toward the European Union, reference must be made to ASEP's national survey of July 2001, in which three questions were asked about how respondents would vote in three different hypothetical referenda if they were really taken. Results were that 80 per cent of respondents would vote in favour of Spain's permanence in the European Union, two-thirds would vote in favour of Spain's adopting the euro as the common and single currency, and 55 per cent would vote in favour of the enlargement of membership in the EU from the present 15 to the expected 27 member countries – only 17 per cent would vote against it.

The enlargement of the European Union, the regulation of immigration, and the establishment of an European defence system

TABLE 11

INDEX OF IMPORTANCE* ATTACHED TO SEVERAL EUROPEAN GOALS, AND INDEX OF PROBABILITY* THAT GOALS WILL BE REACHED

	I-95	IV-96	II-97	IV-98	IV-99	IV-00	IV-01	III-02
Index of Importance attached to each goal								
Eliminate all barriers to the free circulation of workers among EU countries	163	168	169	166	172	168	173	173
Reduce economic differences among EU countries	186	188	179	172	181	179	179	173
Establish the United States of Europe	134	138	129	116	118	124	127	127
Achieve peace in Europe	193	194	191	–	–	–	–	–
Establish one single currency in the EU	136	139	140	–	–	–	–	–
Index of Probability that the goal will be reached								
Eliminate all barriers to the free circulation of workers among EU countries	125	123	139	137	137	134	136	132
Reduce economic differences among EU countries	66	67	79	74	73	80	63	78
Establish the United States of Europe	82	85	94	89	89	84	77	95
Achieve peace in Europe	90	103	114	–	–	–	–	–
Establish one single currency in the EU	106	123	146	–	–	–	–	–

Note: * The indexes have been constructed on the basis of the difference between the proportion of respondents who consider each goal important or likely to occur, and the proportion who does not consider each goal important or likely to occur, adding 100 to make each index positive and varying between 0 and 200.

Source: ASEP Data Archive. (Data from 1995 to 1996 were collected for CIRES, a project sponsored by the BBV, Caja de Madrid, and BBK Foundations.)

(including the war on terrorism), in addition to the more complex modification of the institutional frame, seem to be the four most important issues facing the European Union at this time. For Spaniards, according to a recent survey (ASEP I-02), the three most important problems (mentioned by more than 50 per cent of respondents) for which the European Union should find a solution are the elimination of ETA's (*Euskadi Ta Askatasuna* – Basque Homeland and Liberty) terrorism, international terrorism, and immigration. Approximately 25 per cent of respondents also mentioned the strengthening of the euro. Again a month later (ASEP II-02), when asked about the most needed actions for the construction of Europe, 54 per cent mentioned European aid to Spain to fight ETA terrorism, 47 per cent mentioned the establishment of the 'euro order' that would permit the arrest of criminals in any European country under a judicial order issued in any other European country, 32 per cent mentioned the establishment of a common European legal system to standardize crimes and punishments, and more than 20 per cent mentioned the establishment of a common European educational system, a common judicial system, and the elaboration of an European Constitution.

With respect to the defence system, it must be underlined that in two consecutive surveys (ASEP II and III-02), Spaniards' opinions are equally divided among those who think the European Union can act independently of the United States and those who think the EU is subordinated to them. There is a high consensus, however, that they wish the European Union could act independently of the United States. For that purpose more than half of the sample in both surveys is in favour of the EU increasing its defence budget in order to be independent from the United States, and less than 20 per cent are in favour of spending less in defence and depending then on the United States.

As regards the enlargement of the European Union, only 15 per cent of respondents (ASEP I-02) admit to being somewhat or very much against admission of new members. A few months later (ASEP IV-02), after a moderate public debate about the consequences of enlargement, 22 per cent were in favour of admitting a greater number of new members as soon as possible, whereas 20 per cent were in favour of the admission of new members, but little by little, and 33 per cent were in favour of waiting until the union of the present 15-member countries was more consolidated. In fact, when respondents were asked to mention the countries that should be admitted immediately, Poland was mentioned by 20 per cent, and Hungary, the

Czech Republic, and Romania were mentioned by more than ten per cent. Once more, the data seem to support the finding that there is a great difference between general and abstract opinions and specific or more concrete opinions.

PERCEIVED CONSEQUENCES OF INTEGRATION INTO THE EU

In contrast to the finding that contradictory attitudes seem to coexist with respect to the degree that Spaniards want their government to renounce important parts of its sovereignty in favour of the European Union, there seems to be a general agreement that joining the EU has been primarily positive for Spain and for Spaniards, with virtually no shadows. Benefits seem to outweigh costs and liabilities by a great margin in Spaniards' perceptions of what have been the consequences of joining the EU, and there seems to be a general trend of increasing positive perceptions when data for the past 11 years are examined (see Table 12 and Figure 2).

It must be underlined that Spaniards have consistently perceived more positive consequences for Spain than for the Autonomous Community, and more for the Autonomous Community than for oneself. This finding is even more interesting as it reverses the findings

TABLE 12

INDEX OF PERCEIVED EFFECTS OF SPAIN'S MEMBERSHIP IN THE EUROPEAN UNION FOR SPAIN, FOR THE AUTONOMOUS COMMUNITY, AND FOR THE RESONDENT

	I-92	I-93	I-94	I-95	IV-96	II-97	IV-98	IV-99	IV-00	IV-01	III-02
SPAIN	167	153	150	142	143	159	158	170	174	166	184
Autonomous Community	156	142	144	134	137	152	150	163	168	160	181
Respondent	140	130	135	127	123	132	145	153	163	156	176

Note: * In April 1998 the question asked for the benefit or cost of membership in the European Union. The index has been constructed on the basis of the difference between the proportion of respondents that perceive positive consequences and the proportion that perceive negative consequences, adding 100 to make the index positive and varying between 0 and 200.

Source: ASEP Data Archive. (Data from 1992 to 1996 were collected for CIRES, a project sponsored by the BBV, Caja de Madrid, and BBK Foundations.)

FIGURE 2

INDEX OF PERCEIVED EFFECTS OF SPAIN'S MEMBERSHIP IN THE
EUROPEAN UNION FOR SPAIN, FOR THE AUTONOMOUS COMMUNITY
AND FOR THE RESPONDENT

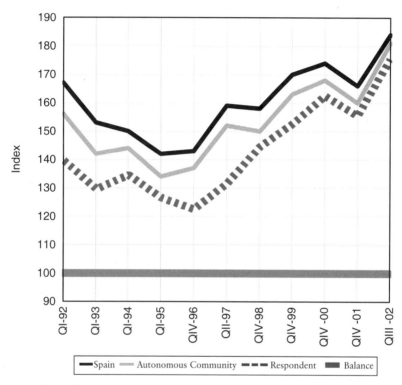

Note: In April 1998 the question asked for the benefit of membership in the European Union. The Index has been constructed on the basis of the difference between the proportion of respondents that perceive positive consequences and the proportion that perceive negative consequences, adding 100 to make the index positive and varying between 0 and 200.

Source: ASEP Data Archive. (Data from 1992 to 1996 were collected for CIRES, a project sponsored by the BBV, Caja de Madrid and BBK Foundations.)

when using Cantril's scale about the comparative evaluation (past, present, and future) that individuals make of the world's, country's, and self's situation. Cantril's findings have been replicated and confirmed in numerous surveys around the world, and also in Spain at very different dates, including ASEP surveys (Cantril 1965; Díez-Nicolás and

Torregrosa 1967; Díez-Nicolás 1997). Similar findings using the Consumer Sentiment Index components (national and personal) consistently show that individuals usually evaluate their past, present, and future economic situations better than they evaluate those of the country. It is true, however, that when comparing the national and personal components of the Consumer Sentiment Index, there are periods when respondents evaluate the national economic situation better than the individual's.

This happened as well in Spain during 1996–2000, when economic recovery after a long period of economic recession (with very high unemployment and inflation rates) was perceived earlier at the national than at the personal level. Such a perception was due to the persuasive influence of mass media and opinion leaders, who apparently convinced the population about the national economic recovery, though individuals could not see the recovery of their personal and household economy. It may also be that, with respect to benefits deriving from integration into the European Union, Spaniards accept the interpretation given by mass media and opinion leaders that benefits outweigh costs for Spain as a whole, and also (but less so) for their Autonomous Community, which they know better because it is closer to them. They do not yet perceive, however, how membership in the EU has benefited them personally (though they accept it because of the external influence of mass media).

Spaniards still consider Spain's economic development below the European level, but opinions seem to acknowledge a reduction of the gap. In 1992, 74 per cent of respondents estimated that Spain was lagging with respect to Europe; that proportion has dropped to 64 per cent in 2002. The proportion that thinks Spain is at the same level of economic development as Europe has increased from 19 per cent to 32 per cent during the same period. Along the same line, when respondents were asked about the degree of social justice in Spain and in the European Union, using a 0 to 10 scale, the ratings were 6.0 for the EU and 5.5 for Spain in 1995, but were 6.0 and 5.8 in 2002. When respondents were asked to express their degree of satisfaction with respect to the level of living in Spain compared to that in the rest of Europe, the proportion that said they were satisfied or very satisfied increased from 52 per cent in 1995 to 74 per cent in 2002. The proportion that felt very or somewhat deceived declined from 40 per cent to 23 per cent during the same period.

Spaniards, therefore, tend to perceive that the gap between Spain and other European Union countries is reducing rapidly, particularly during recent years (the comparisons reported above refer to an eight-year period). It is not only their perceptions and evaluations that have changed; however, they also perceive changes in the Europeans' perceptions and evaluations of Spain.

Thus, only 34 per cent of respondents in 1996 thought Europeans had a positive or very positive opinion about Spain's level of economic development, but that proportion increased to 58 per cent in 2002. Perceptions of negative or very negative opinions have decreased from 27 per cent to nine per cent in the same period. Very much in the same direction, 36 per cent of respondents in 1996 felt that Europeans had a positive or very positive opinion about Spaniards. That proportion increased to 60 per cent in 2002, and 22 per cent thought Europeans had a negative or very negative opinion of Spaniards in 1996, but the latter proportion was reduced to only eight per cent in 2002.

CONCLUSION

The evidence presented and analyzed above seems to support the general hypothesis that Spaniards have been and still are highly in favour of integration into Europe, with virtually no 'euro-sceptics'. This almost unanimous consensus in favour of integration into Europe, even after 16 years of membership, seems to be the consequence of Spain's need to overcome its historical isolation from the rest of Europe since the nineteenth century until the end of the Franco regime in 1975.

In fact, the data support the idea that Spaniards are convinced of the great benefits and low costs that membership in the EU has produced for Spain, for their region, and for themselves. Spaniards perceive that the gap between Spain and other European Union countries has been reduced rapidly with respect to economic development and modernization, social justice, and level of living. They also perceive that the Europeans' perceptions and evaluations of Spain and Spaniards are now much better than in the past, as the data presented above demonstrate. In addition, Spaniards perceive a higher international respect for Spain now than during the Franco regime,[10] and in 2002 they consider almost unanimously the changes that have taken place in Spain during the last 30 years as very positive or positive, to the point that only 19 per cent would admit feeling very or somewhat satisfied with respect to the Franco regime period, against 83 per cent who feel very or somewhat satisfied with the democratic transition period (a great change with respect to 1995, when the same figures were 33 per cent and 73 per cent respectively). On the contrary, those dissatisfied with the Franco regime period were 51 per cent in 1995 and 63 per cent in 2002, whereas those dissatisfied with the democratic transition period have decreased from 23 per cent to nine per cent during the same nine-year period.

To summarize, Spaniards aimed to be Europeans to break with isolation. Their hopes about the benefits they would obtain from joining Europe seem to have been accomplished to a large extent, as opinion data for the past twelve years support with great consistency. Apparently, Spaniards have not yet found any arguments to complain about having joined Europe, though they certainly exhibit protectionist attitudes toward both Spain's products and workers.

NOTES

1. The most conspicuous leaders of the opposition during that period, Ruiz Giménez, Tierno Galván, Satrústegui, and many others, did not miss any opportunity, when they visited other countries or when foreign dignitaries visited Spain, to express their best arguments to achieve the full incorporation of Spain to those three international 'clubs', with the clear goal, of course, of achieving through them the full democratization of Spanish political structures. Certainly, some other opposition leaders, such as Santiago Carrillo, agreed to the desire of Spain being admitted to the Council of Europe and to the Common Market, but absolutely disagreed with respect to the possible incorporation of Spain to NATO. That is another subject that will not be followed up here, however.
2. The *Instituto de la Opinión Pública* (Public Opinion Institute) was founded in 1963 as a governmental department within the Ministry of Information and Tourism, and was part of the reforms toward some liberalization of information during that decade (Díez-Nicolás 1976). The results of all its surveys were published in *Revista Española de la Opinión Pública* [Spanish Journal of Public Opinion], Madrid, and were widely used by Spanish social scientists at that time, though questions that touched very closely the political regime were not included.
3. The *Centro de Investigaciones Sociológicas* (Center for Sociological Research – CIS) substituted the IOP in 1977, after the first democratic elections, as a department of the Ministry of the Presidence, and played an important role in providing information for many of the decisions made by the Government during the political transition to democracy. Its results are published in *the Revista Española de Investigaciones Sociológicas* [Spanish Journal of Sociological Research], Madrid.
4. All data cited here from IOP and CIS may be consulted in CIS Data Archive or in the two mentioned journals, REOP and REIS.
5. ASEP (*Análisis Sociológicos, Económicos y Políticos* – Political, Economic and Sociological Analysis) is a private survey research institute that has conducted a national sample survey of 1,200 every month since 1986. Its Data Archive, accessible by request, includes monthly, quarterly, or annual time series for more than 160 months, more than 45 quarters, and about 16 years.

6. It must be emphasized that, even when Latin Americans are referred to as immigrants into Spain, Spaniards evaluate them better than any other group of migrants, and they perceive them as having more facilities for integration into Spanish society and as being more integrated than any other group of immigrants (Díez-Nicolás and Ramírez-Lafita 2001a), and they themselves feel better integrated into Spanish society than any other group of immigrants (Díez-Nicolás and Ramírez-Lafita 2001b).

7. All references to the 12 surveys conducted by ASEP between 1991 and 2002 on Spaniards' Supranational Identity will be referred to in the text only by the year they were conducted. When data belong to another ASEP survey, the text will make reference to the month it was conducted. Juan Díez-Medrano contributed extensively to the elaboration of the questionnaire that, for the most part, has been replicated for 12 years.

8. PP is the centre-right *Partido Popular* (Popular Party); PSOE stands for the left-left *Partido Socialista Obrero Español* (Spanish Socialist Worker Party); and the IU stands for the leftist *Izquierda Unida* (United Left). These are the three most important national parties, and their share of the total vote in the last general elections of 2000 was, respectively, 44.5 per cent, 34.1 per cent, and 4.2 per cent.

9. For a comprehensive analysis of explanatory models of Spaniards' attitudes toward the European Union and the degree of identification of Spaniards with Europe, see Díez-Medrano (1995: 73–89).

10. In 1995, 30 per cent of respondents believed that international respect for Spain during the Franco regime was high or moderate, whereas 63 per cent believed the same about international respect for Spain at that date. These proportions changed to 15 per cent and 83 per cent respectively in 2002, showing a great increase in the perception of the gap between the two types of regimes in only seven years.

REFERENCES

Alvarez-Miranda, B. (1996): *El Sur de Europa y la adhesión a la Comunidad: Los debates políticos* [Southern Europe and the Access to the Community: The Political Debates], Madrid: CIS.

Cantril, H. (1965): *The Pattern of Human Concerns*, New Brunswick, NJ: Rutgers University Press.

Deflem, M. and F.C. Pampel (1996): 'The Myth of Postnational Identity: Popular Support for European Unification', *Social Forces* 75/1, pp.119–43.

Díez-Medrano, J. (1995): *La Opinión Pública y la Integración Europea* [Public Opinion and European Integration], Madrid: CIS.

Díez-Medrano, J. (2003): *Framing Europe: Attitudes toward European Integration in Germany, Spain, and the United Kingdom*, Princeton, NJ: Princeton University Press.

Díez-Medrano, J. and P. Gutiérrez (2001): 'Nested Identities and European Identity in Spain', *Ethnic and Racial Studies* 24/5, pp.753–78.

Díez-Nicolás, J. (1976): *Los Españoles y la Opinión Pública* [The Spanish and Public Opinion], Madrid: Editora Nacional.

Díez-Nicolás, J. (1997): *La realidad social en España, 1995–1996* [Social Reality in Spain, 1995–1996], Centro de Investigaciones sobre la Realidad Social (CIRES) [Research Center on Social Reality], Bilbao: Fundación BBV, Caja de Madrid, Bilbao-Bizkaia-Kutxa.

Díez-Nicolás, J. (1999): *Identidad nacional y cultura de defensa* [National Identity and the Cultural of Defense], Madrid: Ed. Síntesis.

Díez-Nicolás, J. and M.J. Ramírez-Lafita (2001a): *La Inmigración en España: Una década de investigaciones* [Immigration in Spain: A Decade of Research], Madrid: IMSERSO.

Díez-Nicolás, J. and M.J. Ramírez-Lafita (2001b): *La voz de los inmigrantes* [The Voice of the Immigrants], Madrid: IMSERSO.

Díez-Nicolás, J. and J.R. Torregrosa (1967): 'Aplicación de la Escala de Cantril en España: Resultados de un Estudio Preliminar' [Application of the Scale of Cantril in Spain: Results of a Preliminary Study], *Revista Española de la Opinión Pública* [Spanish Journal of Public Opinion] 10.

Gabel, M. (1998): *Interests and Integration: Market Liberalization, Public Opinión, and European Union*, Ann Arbor, MI: University of Michigan Press.

Galtung, J. (1976): 'Social Position and the Image of the Future', in H. Ournauer *et al.* (eds.), *Images of the World in the Year 2000*, Paris: Mouton.

Inglehart, R. (1977a): 'Long-Term Trends in Mass Support for European Unification', *Government and Opposition* 12, pp.150–77.

Inglehart, R. (1977b): *The Silent Revolution*, Princeton, NJ: Princeton University Press.

Inglehart, R. (1990): *Culture Shift in Advanced Industrial Society*, Princeton, NJ: Princeton University Press.

Inglehart, R. (1997): *Modernization and Post Modernization*, Princeton, NJ: Princeton University Press.

Wessels, B. (1995): 'Development of Support: Diffusion or Demographic Replacement?' in O. Neiedermayer and R. Sinnott (eds.), *Public Opinion and Internationalized Governance*, Oxford: Oxford University Press.

Spanish Membership of the European Union Revisited

CHARLES POWELL

INTRODUCTION

For obvious historical and political reasons, until very recently much of the academic literature on Spain and the EC/EU had centred on issues such as the struggle for accession and the domestic consequences of membership. In recent years, however, the focus of analysis has begun to shift toward considerations of Spain as an actor within the EC/EU, and hence its contribution to the overall process of European integration.[1] In keeping with this trend, this essay will attempt to explore Spain's evolving position and concerns within the EC/EU since accession in 1986, with a view to identifying continuities and innovations in both policy substance and style. More specifically, it will seek to identify both the domestic and external variables that explain the evolution of Spain's European policy over time. In order to do so, it is probably useful to divide this period into three distinct phases: (1) the period running from Spain's accession in 1986 to the Maastricht European Council of 1991, during which its European policy was first defined; (2) a period of crisis and (partial) redefinition of priorities, which began at Maastricht and ended with the departure of Felipe González in 1996 after 13 years in office; and (3) the years since 1996, under the premiership of José María Aznar.[2]

Before seeking to identify the changes that have taken place in Spain's European policy since 1986, it is perhaps pertinent to attempt to identify the more permanent, 'structural' constraints within which it has evolved. First, in geostrategic terms, Spain may be considered a middle-ranking Western European regional power, with security interests in the Eastern Atlantic (because of the Canary Islands) and the Western Mediterranean (at least in part due to Ceuta and Melilla, two North African enclaves that are constitutionally on a par with the autonomous communities of the Spanish mainland, and therefore an integral part of the Spanish state). In economic terms Spain experienced a remarkable transformation during

1959–74, a decade-long crisis during 1974–84, a period of very high growth in the late 1980s, followed by a severe recession in 1992–94, and a second bout of rapid growth in the late 1990s.

By 2000, with a gross domestic product (GDP) per capita of $19,180, its economy was the eleventh largest in the world, and the eighth among OECD (Organization for Economic Co-operation and Developement) countries. Nevertheless, at the turn of the new century, its GDP per capita was still 16 per cent below the EU-15 average. Though increasingly prosperous, during the period under consideration, Spain remained a major beneficiary of the EU's structural and cohesion funds, and its citizens continued to think of their country as being significantly poorer than the wealthier member states.[3] Finally, in institutional and political terms, Spain tended to see itself as one of the EU's 'big five', due to both the presence of two Spaniards in the Commission (on a par with Germany, France, Britain, and Italy) and its eight votes in the Council of Ministers (only two less than the 'big four'). Admittedly, it is not easy to determine the impact of these institutional arrangements on Spain's ability to build (or block) alliances with other member states. As one author has noted, however, the task of Spanish policy-makers may have been complicated by the fact that Spain was the only member of the EU that did not fit into any of the three categories into which all the others may be grouped: (1) the very prosperous and large; (2) the very prosperous and small; (3) the less prosperous and small.[4]

FROM ACCESSION TO MAASTRICHT (1986–91): THE GOLDEN YEARS OF SPANISH MEMBERSHIP

This first period may be seen in terms of the Spanish government's efforts to define a European policy aimed at maximizing both the internal and external benefits resulting from membership. At the domestic level this phase reflects the authority and popularity of a government that had won an unprecedented absolute majority in 1982, only gradually eroded in the 1986 and 1989 elections, a situation largely attributable to the leadership of a highly charismatic prime minister, Felipe González, who was closely identified with the accession negotiations and the 'European project' as a whole. It is also important to note in this context that, unlike Portugal and Greece, in Spain the goal of EC membership had always enjoyed the enthusiastic support of all major social and political actors, without exception. Among other reasons, this was due to the fact that the extent of Spain's exclusion from the international community on account of the authoritarian nature of Franco's regime had been far greater; Portugal under Salazar, for example, had belonged to the European Free Trade Agreement (EFTA) as well as the North Alantic Treaty Organization (NATO).[5]

At the EC level the early stages of Spanish membership were marked by the process leading to the adoption of the Single European Act (SEA) in 1987 and the subsequent implementation of the '1992 programme', culminating in the establishment of the single market. Partly so as to overcome the fears expressed by some member states about the Iberian enlargement, Spain's first priority was to prove that it was a constructive, responsible partner, capable of developing a 'Europeanist' approach that transcended narrow national interest. To put it very bluntly, Madrid had to allay fears that it would be another Greece. In practice this meant supporting initiatives that would further the 'deepening' of the EC, and in particular the single market programme, without seeming to demand too much in return.

In a sense, the SEA complicated matters for Spain because its implementation would coincide with the seven-year transition period during which its industrial products (and many of its agricultural goods) would gradually be exposed to European competition. However, the Commission had effectively acknowledged that fresh regional, structural, and development funds would have to be made available to enable less developed members to adapt to the single market, Spain being one of the largest potential beneficiaries. Rather than attempt to limit its impact, the government thus set out to use the single market programme as a catalyst for domestic economic reform, while at the same time stressing that it was in the EC's interest to reduce the regional differences and structural shortcomings of the poorer states. Consequently, the view that a 'deepening' of the EC was fully compatible with the promotion of national interest rapidly gained currency in Madrid, as did the notion that the latter could best be furthered by presenting it as being in harmony with the interests of the EC as a whole.

It was also during these early years that Spain identified its major allies in Europe. Traditionally, European policy-makers in Madrid have generally been of the opinion that it is in Spain's best interest to have a Commission that is both effective and influential. This was undoubtedly the case in the late 1980s, and González soon established a good working relationship with Commission president Jacques Delors (1985–94), whose approach to European integration he largely shared. More importantly, perhaps, accession negotiations had also taught Madrid that its chances of attaining influence within the EC would largely depend on its bilateral relations with Germany and France. More specifically, González had succeeded in winning over Helmut Kohl to the Spanish cause as early as 1983, when he openly endorsed the Chancellor's decision to deploy Pershing missiles on German soil in the face of stiff opposition from the German Social Democrat Party (SPD), and it was partly in return for this support that Kohl had linked the Iberian enlargement to the budgetary reforms so vehemently sought by France. The link between EC accession and defence issues was also made explicit in connection with Spain's membership of NATO.[6]

Kohl soon understood that, by encouraging Paris to lift its opposition to the Iberian enlargement, he would be assisting González in winning the March 1986 referendum on NATO, thereby enabling Madrid to remain in the Alliance. Ironically, it could thus be argued that the lack of popular support for continued membership of NATO was the Spanish government's strongest card in its EC accession negotiations. Bilateral relations with Paris also improved rapidly in the wake of accession, and thereafter the Spanish authorities did their best to operate under the protection of the Franco-German axis. It is interesting to note in this context that, although popular perceptions of Germany and the Germans remained uniformly favourable during these years, attitudes toward France and the French, which had soured considerably in the late 1970s and early 1980s, improved significantly in the aftermath of accession.[7]

Fully in keeping with the above strategy, Spain was a staunch supporter of Economic and Monetary Union from the outset. The government regarded monetary union as the logical outcome of the single market programme, and rushed to join the exchange rate mechanism of the European Monetary System (EMS) in June 1989. This was coherent with the perceived need to prove to other member states that, in spite of its relative economic inferiority, Spain would not stand in the way of closer integration. The finance minister at the time, Carlos Solchaga, had grave doubts as to the wisdom of this move, and there is some evidence to suggest that Kohl hurried González into this decision as a way of bringing greater pressure to bear on the British government, which was bitterly divided over the EMS.[8] In return, Madrid obtained Bonn's support for the adoption of the Social Charter, one of the major goals of the first Spanish presidency, which nevertheless fell victim to British objections, which were partially overcome later at the Strasbourg Council in December 1989. This episode aptly illustrates González's willingness to sacrifice short-term economic considerations to longer-term political goals, a strategy that was not entirely risk-free.

The Spanish authorities were similarly in favour of Political Union. Following the fall of the Berlin wall in November 1989, González was one of the first European leaders to support the goal of German reunification, an attitude that was in marked contrast to that of France and Britain. From a Spanish perspective, given that unification was inevitable, the challenge was to make it compatible with European integration and, if possible, to turn it into a catalyst for further progress. More specifically, Madrid was determined that the future Union should play a larger role in international affairs, not least because this would help it to overcome its own legacy of isolation and irrelevance. This partly explains the importance the government attributed to joining the Western European Union, first as an observer in 1988 and later as a full member in March 1990, and its subsequent support for efforts to develop a European defence identity. It is important to remember, in this context, that Spanish public opinion believed that the greatest benefit derived from EU membership was in the external arena (measured in terms of Spain's increased role in world affairs), rather than in the domestic one (measured in terms of its contribution to political democratization, social modernization, or economic development). At a more technical level, in the late 1980s European political co-operation gave diplomats access to a degree of knowledge about the world that was unavailable domestically, and Spain's foreign service experienced a significant renewal.[9] Spanish diplomats adapted rapidly and effectively to EC institutions and procedures, and were soon able to make a distinctive contribution of their own.[10]

The above-mentioned concerns largely explain the activism of Spanish representatives in the negotiations leading to the Maastricht Treaty, during which they proved remarkably prolific in putting forward proposals in a wide range of issues. This barely disguised attempt to compete with the 'big four' appeared to bear some fruit, as the high-level meetings held by France, Germany, and Spain in October 1991 (without the participation of the Dutch presidency) would suggest. Grateful for its support over reunification, Germany was happy to allow Spain to emerge as the major southern actor in the EU, a task made easier by Italy's domestic political difficulties.

During the debates leading to Maastricht, Madrid concentrated on advancing three major ideas: the notion of social and economic cohesion, the concept of a European citizenship, and the development of a

Common Foreign and Security Policy (CFSP). If in the late 1980s Spain had argued convincingly that the effort required of poorer states in adapting to the single market would demand some form of redistributive assistance from wealthier partners, in the early 1990s it was similarly successful in institutionalizing the principle of social and economic cohesion, thereby enshrining the notion of supranational solidarity. More specifically, in return for committing itself to meeting the Maastricht criteria for membership of the single currency, Madrid, which had feared that it might soon become a net contributor to the EU's coffers – a development domestic opinion would have found difficult to stomach – obtained the promise of a future Cohesion Fund.[11]

Partly as a way of counterbalancing the Maastricht Treaty's somewhat technocratic style and content, as early as May 1990 González had defended the need to further the notion of a European citizenship, which was to become his most important personal contribution to the debates. The freedom of movement and residence of EU citizens it envisaged was, of course, fully compatible with national interest, given that some 600,000 Spaniards lived and worked in the other 11 member states, while only 150,000 EU citizens had settled (legally) in Spain. Back home talk of citizenship tended to obscure the fact that, like other lower-income countries, the Spanish government resolutely opposed an ambitious social policy it could ill afford, and only agreed not to imitate Britain's opt-out of the social protocol when Delors promised additional structural funding.[12] In addition, the government also welcomed the progress achieved in the field of co-operation in Justice and Home affairs, not least because it hoped it would strengthen its hand in the on-going battle against ETA (*Euskadi Ta Askatasuna* – Basque Homeland and Liberty) terrorism.

Finally, Madrid was also strongly in favour of the development of the CFSP, contrary to the wishes of some member states that advocated maintaining a strictly intergovernmental consensus. Nevertheless, it should be stressed that Spain's attitude toward the CFSP has always been prudent. Indeed at Maastricht González joined others in rejecting Dutch plans to integrate the CFSP within the Community, favouring its 'pillarization' instead. This prudence was also evident with regard to decision-making mechanisms: Spain only supported the use of qualified majority voting for the implementation of policies (joint actions) previously adopted by unanimity, on the grounds that it might otherwise be unable to defend its interests in key regions such as Latin America. In addition, the Spanish government sought a commitment to an eventual

Western EU role as the EC's defence arm, and strongly supported the idea that multinational forces should be able to operate alternatively under Western EU and NATO umbrellas. Overall, Spain's approach to the CFSP has been described as Europeanist in its objectives (because of its strong belief in the need for a common European policy, and its support for a Commission role); intergovernmentalist in its methods (due to its preference for a leading role for the European Council and the Council of Ministers); and gradualist in terms of the processes adopted (on account of its support for the gradual incorporation of the Western EU in the EU). Indeed, the same author has claimed that 'Spanish Europeanism can be distilled into two basic ideas: first, that CFSP is fundamental in order to further the process of broader European integration; and second, that it is necessary to establish the instruments capable of giving Europeans greater initiative in international affairs.'[13]

Spain's achievements within the EU in the run up to Maastricht may be attributed to a combination of domestic and external factors. On the domestic front the government continued to enjoy widespread support, largely thanks to the spectacular performance of the Spanish economy in 1986–91, during which GDP growth rates averaged 3.7 per cent per annum. The fact that this took place in the wake of accession meant that support for EU membership rose steadily, as did the proportion of Spaniards who believed it was beneficial for their country, a view held by a record 62 per cent of those polled in 1991.

Just as importantly, Spain's credibility as an EU actor was enhanced by its determination to break with a long tradition of isolationism. Most significantly, in 1990 Madrid contributed several warships to the naval blockade of Iraq in the context of a Western EU operation, its first non-colonial military operation abroad in centuries. Significantly, the government presented its participation in the conflict as a consequence of Spain's European obligations, a strategy that undoubtedly helped to increase public support for an otherwise unpopular military operation. As we saw before with regard to NATO membership, European integration again provided the government with the instrument with which to present controversial policy options to a public with a distinctively isolationist viewpoint that nevertheless supported González's efforts to use European integration as a catalyst for modernization. Spanish troops also became involved in a number of UN peacekeeping missions in Africa, Central America, and the former Yugoslavia, which had a favourable impact on domestic opinion. At the strictly diplomatic level, initiatives such as the launching of the

Iberoamerican Community of Nations, which held its first summit meeting in Mexico in 1991, and the Middle East Peace Conference held in Madrid later in the year, further enhanced Spain's role as a significant international actor. Paradoxically, proving that Spain's ambitions were not limited to the European arena played a very significant part in a strategy aimed at winning the respect and attention of other EU member states.

FROM MAASTRICHT TO GONZÁLEZ'S DEPARTURE (1991–96): THE STRUGGLE AGAINST GROWING ODDS

This second phase in the development of Spain's European policy was marked by major upheavals at both the domestic and European levels, which fed into each other. At the domestic level, in 1992–94 the government faced the most severe economic downturn experienced in Spain since the 1974 international oil crisis. Initially, the authorities seemed confident of being able to avoid a major recession, but in September 1992 the peseta came under heavy fire in financial markets, forcing the government to undertake three successive devaluations, resulting in a 22 per cent drop in the value of the Spanish currency in barely six months. Determined to prevent the peseta from dropping out of the EMS altogether, a fate already suffered by the pound and the lira, the government requested and obtained a 15 per cent fluctuation rate, in spite of which a fourth devaluation became necessary in early 1995.

On the face of it, the economic crisis barely affected the domestic debate on the Maastricht Treaty, which was on the whole poor and ill informed. Unlike many other European parliaments, the Spanish Congress of Deputies endorsed the Treaty with a handsome majority: 314 votes in favour, three against, and nine abstentions (mostly representatives of *Izquierda Unida*, a Communist-led coalition). Since economic policy was largely dictated by the need to meet the Maastricht criteria, however, criticism of the government's handling of the recession inevitably led to a questioning of its European policy overall. Thus, popular opposition to the treaty, or rather, to the perceived social and economic costs of meeting the criteria, was far greater than this vote would suggest. Indeed, according to an opinion poll conducted in the spring of 1993, only 37 per cent of respondents said they would have voted in favour of the Maastricht Treaty had a referendum been held in Spain, the lowest level of support registered anywhere in Europe except Britain. By 1994 only 43 per cent of Spaniards admitted to being in favour of membership of the EU (as opposed to an EU average of 56 per cent), and as many as 60 per cent believed that Spain did not benefit from membership. In other words, Spain's love affair with 'Europe' had not survived its first major recession since accession.[14] In spite of this, throughout the severe 1992–94 crisis, during which unemployment rates reached 23 per cent, the highest in contemporary Spanish economic history, the government remained steadfast in its commitment to monetary union. From the latter's viewpoint, to have behaved otherwise would have been tantamount to sacrificing Spain's long-standing ambition to be considered a significant European player.

González's determination to remain within the EMS and to meet the Maastricht criteria in spite of the magnitude of the recession meant that he had no alternative but to fight hard for a generous Cohesion Fund at the Edinburgh Council held in December 1992. Although the final outcome was highly favourable to Spain in quantitative terms, José María Aznar, who had become the new leader of the opposition in 1990, was able to dismiss the prime minister's achievements as evidence of the fact that only massive EU transfers could compensate for the shortcomings of what could now plausibly be construed as a deeply flawed economic policy.[15] In spite of the highly favourable impact the Cohesion Fund was to have on the economy, by the early 1990s Spaniards were less inclined to see 'Europe' as the answer to all their troubles than they had been in the past. Paradoxically, Gonzalez's most successful European negotiation ever failed to win him the domestic acclaim he had come to expect for his efforts.

Domestic considerations alone do not fully account for certain changes that became apparent in Spain's European policy in the early 1990s, which are perhaps best understood as evidence of Madrid's reaction to shifting priorities within the EU itself. In the run up to Maastricht, Spain had embraced a highly orthodox view of European integration. This changed somewhat after the Danish referendum and the opening of negotiations with the EFTA candidates, who were keen to retain their traditional neutrality and refused to join the western EU. Initially, Madrid firmly opposed proposals based on notions of 'variable geometry' or a 'multi-speed Europe', largely out of a growing fear of peripheralization, which had existed in government circles since 1989. A bargain was gradually struck in the course of 1992, however, most notably at the Edinburgh Council itself: the Delors II package and the Cohesion Fund were thus partly the consequence of Spain's acceptance of an opt-out clause for Denmark in the area of defence policy, and of its agreement to lift its veto on the EFTA enlargement on account of the neutrality issue. Given that the very existence of a bloc of neutral countries within the EU ran contrary to the Spanish interpretation of the Maastricht settlement, in practice acceptance of these changes implied the adoption of a more flexible approach to European integration as a whole.[16]

The Edinburgh Council marked a new phase in Spain's role in the EU, and a change in member states' perception of its European policy. Although Madrid had fought hard in defence of national interest in the past, not least during the accession negotiations themselves, it had managed to do so without causing undue alarm or disturbance. What took member states and EU institutions by surprise was the determination with which González fought for the Cohesion Fund promised at Maastricht and against any form of asymmetry that might undermine its hopes of playing a leading role in the EU. Later, Spain took full advantage of the negotiations with the EFTA candidates in order to partially renegotiate its own terms of accession, threatening to delay ratification until its demands were met with regard to gaining access to member states' fishing waters sooner than originally stipulated.[17] Curiously, in so doing González was following the advice of none other than Margaret Thatcher, who had told him in 1985 that rather than fight for favourable accession terms, it made better sense to join the European club at the earliest possible opportunity, with a view to renegotiating those terms at a later date, from inside.[18]

From a Spanish perspective, the EFTA enlargement was seen as a threat not only to a continued 'deepening' of the EU, and in particular its cohesion policies, but also to Madrid's ambitions as a major player. It is useful to remember, in this respect, that in May 1992 Gonzalez had proposed that the 'big five' should form a *directoire*, which would assume responsibility for providing leadership in both the Community and the CFSP.[19] The imminent accession of Austria, Finland, Sweden, and Norway (which later decided not to join after all) not only meant that the EU's 'centre of gravity' would shift in a north-easterly direction, but also threatened to diminish Spain's institutional weight, particularly if the threshold for constituting a qualified majority or a 'blocking minority' in the Council of Ministers, which stood at 23 votes in the EU-12, was raised. In short, from Madrid's viewpoint what was at stake was the North–South equilibrium reached within the EU after the accession of Greece, Portugal, and Spain in the 1980s. This resulted in a spirited defence of the institutional status quo, eventually leading to the 'Ioannina compromise' reached in March 1994, whereby Spain and Britain, in the face of stiff opposition from Germany, Italy, and France, temporarily succeeded in retaining the existing blocking minority. For our purposes, what is most significant is that, for the first time since accession, national interest was openly invoked by Spanish representatives who were no longer paralyzed by fear of seeming 'reluctant Europeans', and who increasingly found themselves in the company of their British counterparts. In other words, the mid-1990s saw 'the beginnings of a more careful consideration of exactly what degree and kind of co-operation were required to maximise perceived national interest'.[20]

Largely so as to compensate for the growing fear of peripheralization resulting from German reunification, the EFTA enlargement, and the future Eastern enlargement, during this second phase Spanish policy-makers tried to inject specific Spanish interests into the common definition of an evolving European interest. More specifically, they stepped up their efforts to make the EU look South (to the Mediterranean) and West (to Latin America). In the former case the aim was to link North African and Middle Eastern countries to the EU more closely than had been the case, and to make the latter contribute to the stabilization and development of the southern Mediterranean basin. Already in 1990, and partly in response to Spanish interest, Brussels had adopted a New Mediterranean Policy, the Spaniard Abel Matutes being the commissioner responsible for its implementation.

Spanish efforts in this area, strongly supported by the Commission and some other member states, notably France and Italy, resulted in a policy that looked forward to the progressive establishment of a free trade area in goods by 2010 and for the gradual opening up of trade in services within the framework of a new Euro-Mediterranean Partnership, formally launched at the Barcelona conference held in November 1995 during Spain's second EU presidency. In principle at least, Spain thereby succeeded in convincing the EU to assume the responsibility of increasing resources destined for Mediterranean co-operation, essentially through the MEDA programme. On the whole, Spanish efforts to achieve something comparable in Latin America met more limited success, with the result that fundamental objectives had to be pursued through largely national policies. Nevertheless, it is probably the case that Spanish pressure secured a more generous share of Commission-managed development funds for the region than would otherwise have been made available.[21]

From the moment of accession, one of Spain's overriding concerns was to convince fellow member states that it fully understood that membership entailed certain obligations as well as privileges, particularly in controversial areas such as defence. This largely explains its whole-hearted support for European-led solutions to the problems of European security, undoubtedly one of the hallmarks of Spanish European policy since 1986. The most ambitious sphere that Madrid became involved in was probably the Eurocorps, which Spain joined in 1993 with France, Germany, and Britain, later taking part in the establishment of a Joint Naval Force with Italy and France as well. In 1995 Spain agreed to contribute a mechanized infantry brigade to the Eurocorps, and three years later it increased its commitment by offering the Brunete Armoured Division, the best equipped in the Spanish Army. Internal divisions within the EU over the military dimension of the CFSP left the Eurocorps in an institutional limbo, however, forcing Spain to invest greater resources in the development of the Western EU. The creation of Eurofor and Euromarfor in 1995 with the participation of Spain, France, Italy, and later Portugal appeared to lend credence to the emergence of the Western EU as a viable force available to the EU for operations in the Mediterranean basin, thereby complementing Madrid's own security provisions in this area.

Spain is undoubtedly amongst the member states for which holding the EU presidency has had the greatest domestic political value, and the 1995 edition probably had an even higher internal component than that of 1989, which was already considerable. Having lost his parliamentary majority in the 1993 elections, González was forced to rely on the support of the Catalan nationalists led by Jordi Pujol to remain in office. Very tellingly, Pujol largely justified his support in terms of the need to guarantee the stability necessary to meet the Maastricht criteria, a goal most foreign observers believed to be beyond Spain's reach by this stage. What is more, by 1995 González was under mounting media and opposition pressure to resign over a succession of financial and political scandals that had greatly undermined his credibility and popularity. Fully aware that the 1995 presidency would be his last chance to make an impact on the European scene, González pulled out all the stops, but in vain. In spite of staging highly successful events such as the Barcelona Euro-Mediterranean Conference, the signing of a new Transatlantic Agenda with Bill Clinton, and the naming of the European single currency (euro), to name but a few, Spanish public opinion was unmoved. With the presidency over, Pujol withdrew his support, forcing Gonzalez to call early elections in March 1996, which he narrowly lost to the Popular Party under the leadership of Aznar. Nevertheless, the appointment of Carlos Westendorp as president of the Reflection Group entrusted with the preparation of the Inter-Governmental Conference (IGC) which would pave the way for the Amsterdam Treaty meant that his views on Spain's European policy would continue to exercise a degree of influence beyond his political demise.[22]

AZNAR'S EUROPEAN POLICY (1996 TO THE PRESENT): SIGNIFICANT CHANGE WITHIN FUNDAMENTAL CONTINUITY

Very little was known about the type of European policy Aznar would favour before he was sworn in as prime minister in the spring of 1996.[23] In opposition, the conservative leader had been highly critical of what he portrayed as González's failure to defend Spanish national interest in Europe, but without clarifying how he would tackle this task himself. Similarly, the socialist prime minister had come under attack for accepting Franco-German initiatives unquestioningly, but alternative alliances were not made explicit. At a more ideological level, neoliberals within the Popular Party argued that under *Partido Socialista Obrero Español* (PSOE) rule Spaniards had become accustomed to a bewildering range of public subsidies – many of them the product of González's European policy – that would ultimately prove counterproductive and incompatible with genuine socio-economic modernization. Aznar himself was unusually anglophile for a Spanish politician, and some sectors of his party, strongly under the influence of their Tory friends in Britain, had openly embraced a Spanish variety of Euroscepticism.[24] Since González's answer to Spain's ills had traditionally been 'more Europe', even those who did not share such a radical stance felt that their own recipe would have to be somewhat different, perhaps something along the lines of 'more Europe and more Spain'. This attitude towards European integration would appear to be fully in keeping with the evolution of Spanish public opinion, which had become increasingly intergovernmentalist (and consequently less supranationalist) since accession in the mid-1980s. Thus, the proportion of those advocating the creation of 'a European government which would take important decisions' had dropped from 28 per cent in 1988 to a mere 18 per cent in 1993 (probably due to the severity of the recession), and still stood at only 20 per cent in 1996. Similarly, the view that 'national governments should have the last say in important decisions', which was shared by 48 per cent of those polled in 1988, was held by as many as 61 per cent of respondents in 1996.[25]

While admitting that Aznar's European policy represented a departure from that of his predecessor, some authors have argued that it is best explained in generational, rather than strictly ideological, terms. Whereas González belonged to the 'generation of 1968', which had experienced the isolation endured by Spain under Franco and later played a leading role in the transition to democracy, Aznar and his ministers were members of the 'generation of 1989', which had come of age politically in a fully democratic, European context.[26] By comparison with his predecessor, therefore, Aznar favoured a far less traumatic view of recent Spanish history, one that explained the country's evolving role in Europe in less 'heroic' terms, and that tended to see integration in Europe largely as a consequence of the remarkable socio-economic changes experienced in Spain as of the late 1950s to early 1960s. Hence, whereas the former regarded Spain's presence in Europe as something exceptional, the latter could begin to take it for granted.[27]

Overall, Aznar's European policy since 1996 introduced a number of interesting novelties without questioning the fundamentals of González's legacy, and may therefore be seen as a combination of change and continuity, with the emphasis on the latter.[28] Some of these changes had already became apparent in the debates and negotiations leading to the Amsterdam Treaty, in the course of which Spain advocated institutional reforms that would pave the way for enlargement while strongly resisting attempts by certain member states to undermine the *status quo*.[29] More specifically, Madrid rejected the notion of a 'two-speed Europe' advanced by Paris, out of fear of being pushed to the margins of EU affairs on account of its economic vulnerability. The Aznar government was also sceptical about the slightly different notion of 'enhanced co-operation', seeing in it the danger that some states might be excluded from deeper co-operation against their will. At the institutional level Spain struggled to retain what it had won at Ioannina, namely its right to be considered one of the 'big five'. This required Aznar to put up a lonely fight well into the last night of the Amsterdam Council of June 1997, forcing the Dutch presidency to acknowledge the existence of a 'Spanish problem' that could only be solved by compensating Madrid with more votes in the Council of Ministers in return for the future loss of one of the two Spanish commissioners.

In spite of these continuities, a comparison between the Maastricht and Amsterdam IGCs reveals certain changes in emphasis. At Amsterdam the Aznar government devoted considerable attention to third pillar issues, most notably by rejecting the very notion of political asylum for EU nationals in other members states, a concern largely dictated by its determination to develop EU procedures and institutions (such as Europol and Eurojust) capable of proving effective in the on-going struggle against ETA. Some of these concerns were later given even greater salience at the Tampere Council in October 1999, at which Spain advocated the development of the EU as a space for freedom, security and justice.

With regard to CFSP, Madrid's position remained prudent, advocating the establishment of a permanent organ for planning and analysis, its centralization in the figure of the secretary general of the Council, and the maintenance of unanimity for decision-making while allowing for the introduction of constructive abstention. Overall, during the 1996–97 IGC, the government clearly attached less importance to second pillar reforms than to issues relating to the first (such as the weighting of voting in the Council) or third (terrorism and political asylum) pillars, and CFSP was far less prominent on the Spanish agenda than it had been in the 1990 IGC.[30] It should be noted, however, that this trend was already evident during the final months of the González administration: when the latter listed Spain's future priorities during his farewell speech at the Turin European Council in March 1996, he had discussed the Economic and Monetary Union (EMU) and the challenges of enlargement, forgetting to mention CFSP altogether. All of this suggests that as far as Madrid was concerned the debate on CFSP was by then a question of instruments rather than essence, and that Spain was largely content with the *status quo*.

During his first few years in office, Aznar was driven by an almost obsessive determination to ensure that Spain would be in a position to join the singly currency and take full advantage of Economic and Monetary Union. By 1996 the Spanish economy was beginning to show signs of recovery, and the Maastricht criteria no longer seemed as unattainable as they had during the recent recession. Nevertheless, Aznar could have succumbed to the temptation of seeking a political solution to the nation's economic shortcomings. In September 1996, however, the prime minister turned down Romano Prodi's suggestion to the effect that Spain and Italy should reach an agreement that would make it difficult, if not impossible, for Germany and France to introduce the single currency without them, making it clear that he intended to meet the Maastricht criteria whatever the cost. This exchange had two immediate consequences: on the one hand, it forced Prodi to abandon his plans to delay the structural reforms necessary to enable Italy to meet the criteria; more importantly, it won Aznar the respect of other European leaders, allowing Spain to shed its *Club Med* image almost overnight.[31]

Greatly assisted by a world-wide economic recovery and growth levels reminiscent of the late 1980s, the Spanish government was able to cut public spending, curb inflation, and bring down interest rates in time for the May 1998 Brussels Council, which admitted the peseta into the single currency and the third phase of EMU. The fact that all the other member states that had wanted to join the single currency (except Greece) were finally able to do so did not diminish the significance of this achievement in the eyes of the Spanish government, which reminded public opinion time and again that, for the first time in its history, Spain would be taking part in a key aspect of European integration from its inception. In his determination to neutralize traditional Spanish fears of exclusion from the EU's 'hard core', Aznar was thus treading firmly in González's footsteps.

This fundamental continuity was also evident in the government's efforts to defend the principle of socio-economic cohesion. Spain had always held the view that cohesion was an integral part of the *acquis communautaire*; indeed, from a Spanish perspective, cohesion was more than just the name of an important fund, it was a principle that should inform all EU policies to take into account the chasm that continued to exist between wealthier and poorer member states. Ironically, the impressive performance of the Spanish economy in the late 1990s made it increasingly difficult to defend this principle in the face of growing opposition from net contributors, most notably Germany. In addition, González's closest European ally, Kohl, had left the scene in September 1998 to be replaced by Gerhard Schröder of the German Social Democrat Party (SPD), whereas Delors had been succeeded as Commission president by Jacques Santer (1994–99). Having met the Maastricht criteria, with average annual growth rates of four per cent and GDP levels at 78 per cent of the EU-15 average, it was not easy to justify special treatment for Spain. Additionally, having criticized González in 1992 for the supposedly undignified manner in which he had secured the Cohesion Fund, Aznar was under considerable domestic pressure to outdo his predecessor. This no doubt explains his tough, somewhat abrasive attitude at the Berlin Council held in March 1999, at which Spain was promised 10 billion pesetas for the years 2000–6 from the structural and cohesion funds.[32] Thus, if Edinburgh was the price member states paid to keep Spain sweet on the EFTA enlargement, Berlin could be seen as the concession necessary to ensure that Madrid would not obstruct the forthcoming Eastern enlargement.

It is probably with regard to the defence-related aspects of Spanish European policy that Aznar ventured furthest from the well-trodden path frequented by González. Admittedly, this was largely due to the fact that in the post-cold war era, the Atlanticist–Europeanist fracture that had long divided member states over relations with the United States and questions of security and defence lost much of its salience. More specifically, this had paved the way for Spain's full incorporation into NATO's military structure at the Atlantic Council held in Madrid in July 1997, which effectively put an end to the constraints imposed by the terms of the 1986 referendum. By the late 1990s Spain had joined the 'hard core' of the EU in matters of defence and security thanks to its new role in NATO and its by now traditional support for the Western EU. Unexpectedly, however, this did not lead to greater Spanish presence in defence-related initiatives.

In 1998 the 'big four' embarked on a political dialogue that led to the decision to establish military forces for the prevention of conflict and crisis management adopted at the Helsinki Council in December 1999. Although Spain subsequently supported the birth of a European Security and Defence Policy (ESDP), it was not one of the main promoters of the project. This represented a departure from what had occurred during the negotiations leading to the Maastricht Treaty, in which, as we saw, Spain had been a major player with regard to the birth of CFSP. Paradoxically, this role has been attributed to the replacement of the traditional Franco-German axis by a British 'motor', which in theory should have benefited Madrid given Aznar's 'special relationship' with Tony Blair. Be this as it may, as one author has argued, the implications are fairly clear: 'Spain has joined the hard core (armed forces participation) but without having performed the function of political motor, the traditional function of major players.'[33]

Aznar's attitude toward European defence may have been coloured by his Atlanticist bias. Although González's early relations with the United States were difficult, by the time he left office, they could hardly have been improved. The novelty, however, lies in the fact that Aznar not only accepted and welcomed US leadership, as his predecessor had done, but often appeared to be closer to Washington than Brussels. Since 1996, at times of Europeanist-Atlanticist friction, Spain has tended to side with the United States and Britain, a good example of this being Aznar's reaction to the Anglo-American bombing of Iraq in 1998. This alignment with the United States and Britain represents a departure from the behaviour of PSOE governments, which almost invariably sided with the Franco-German axis in times of crisis.

This latter point leads us to the question of the importance of alliances between member states in the promotion of national interests. As leader of the opposition, Aznar had been highly critical of González's subservience to the Franco-German axis, and was therefore unlikely to follow his lead in this respect. More importantly, however, the Franco-German axis was far less relevant in the late 1990s than it had been a decade earlier. Similarly, Aznar could no longer benefit from the existence of a strong Commission, though he did his best to support Jacques Santer in the face of European Parliament criticism, including that of its president, the Spaniard José María Gil Robles. As we have seen, during the final years of the González administration, Spanish representatives had increasingly found themselves in the same camp as the British, a trend that became even more apparent under Aznar.

In an ideologically hostile European Council (by 1999 Aznar was the only conservative prime minister in Europe, together with that of Luxembourg), it not surprising that the Spanish premier should have found solace in Blair, who has been described (only half-jokingly) as the first Christian democrat to occupy 10 Downing Street. However, talk of a Madrid–London axis should not be taken too literally. As Spain's decision to veto Britain's accession to the Schengen group in 1999 suggests, Gibraltar remains a significant obstacle. More importantly, perhaps, as the Lisbon and Stockholm European Councils revealed, when it came to major economic issues, both Britain and Spain found it difficult to promote their special interests: the former because of its attitude toward EMU, the latter because of its consistently high unemployment levels and its poor performance in areas such as R&D. In these circumstances it was no easy task for them to lead by example.

Many of the continuities outlined above were again in evidence in the negotiations leading up to the Nice Council of December 2000. Broadly speaking, Spain favoured a minimalist IGC, in other words, one that would allow the EU to strike the institutional bargains necessary for enlargement.[34] Madrid was also anxious to prevent the adoption of qualified majority voting as a general rule, essentially so as to retain veto powers over the cohesion and structural funds, but was happy to see it extended to the second pillar, as long as this did not include military operations as such. After lengthy discussions Spain succeeded in retaining its ability to veto decisions on these funds during 2007–13, which was hailed as a major political triumph. More generally, Spanish representatives argued that enhanced co-operation should not apply to the 'heart' of European integration, namely the single market and the principle of social and economic cohesion, one of several battles they would lose.

Overall, however, the government's top priority was to fight attempts to use enlargement as an excuse to alter the institutional settlement reached during accession negotiations. The official view was that in 1985 Spain had been given 'big power' status in the Commission and 'medium sized' status in the Council of Ministers; consequently, if Spain was to lose 'big power' status in the Commission as a result of enlargement, it was entitled to 'big power' status in the Council by way of compensation. This goal was largely achieved when Spain (actively supported by France, which no doubt felt it could do with a large southern ally in an enlarged EU) was allocated 27 votes in the future Council, only two short of the 29 awarded to the 'big four', even though this meant losing more Members of the European Parliament (14) than any other member state.

BY WAY OF CONCLUSION:
THE DANGERS OF PUNCHING ABOVE ONE'S WEIGHT

Since its accession in 1986, Spain has sought to establish itself as one of the 'hard core' members of the EU while recognizing the constraints imposed by its population size, its comparatively low level of economic development, its consistently high levels of unemployment, and its status as a 'cohesion country'. As we have seen, over the past decade-and-a-half, it has attempted to do this in a number of different ways. In the first place, it has taken full advantage of EU policies in order to advance along the road to real – as opposed to merely nominal – convergence with the more economically developed member states. Second, and fully in keeping with the principle that EU membership is about sharing rather than losing sovereignty, and hence about sharing rather than losing influence, Spain has been a consistent advocate of a 'deepening' of the EU, as its attitude toward EMU, among many other major projects, reveals. Third, it has also consistently favoured the EU's ability to play a leading role in world affairs, largely so as to overcome its own shortcomings in this sphere prior to accession. Finally, in order to guarantee all of the above, Madrid has fought hard to retain its institutional status within the EU and reach fruitful alliances with other member states.

The forthcoming enlargement of the EU offers Spain opportunities as well as challenges, but it is by no means certain it will be able to take full advantage of them unless it carries out certain far-reaching reforms. Some of these will require substantial changes in the Spanish economy – most importantly with regard to the labour market – and cannot be expected to take place overnight. Other reforms, admittedly less significant ones, could be tackled with relative ease. The proportion of the budget devoted to the Foreign Ministry – 0.46 per cent of the total in 2001, even less than the 0.48 per cent ear-marked in 1991 – will have to be increased significantly in the future given that the system will be even more over-stretched than it is as present. The Spanish state currently employs some 2,400 civil servants abroad, only a fraction of whom – 455 – are career diplomats, with a further 230 diplomats based in Madrid.[35] Similarly, it is very telling that four candidate countries, namely, Estonia, Latvia, Lithuania and Malta, do not yet have a Spanish embassy. Finally, for many years now defence expenditure has remained one of the lowest in Europe, a trend that has slowed down the transition from a conscript to a professional army currently under way, thereby undermining the credibility of Spain's commitment to the Rapid Reaction Force, among other ventures.

In a sense, it could be argued that Spain is in danger of becoming a victim of its own success, for it has been punching above its weight for many years now. Inevitably, perhaps, this has led to a certain complacency, which may soon become counterproductive. Many of Spain's friends and allies would like to see it move beyond its generally reactive, somewhat defensive stance in the EU and adopt a more ambitious, proactive attitude. If the Madrid government wishes to rise to the challenge, it would probably be well advised to devote greater material and intellectual resources to its European policy in future.

NOTES

1. For a recent example, see Gillespie and Youngs (2000).
2. I have borrowed this periodization – and much else besides – from Barbé (1999: 153–77).
3. In 1995, 27 per cent of those polled believed there was a great deal of economic disparity between Spain and its more developed neighbours, and a further 45 per cent thought it was still considerable, while only 13 per cent claimed there was little difference (Szmolka 1999: 25).
4. See Areilza Carvajal (1999: 34–5).
5. Powell (2000: 156).
6. Felipe González has admitted that 'there has never existed any formal link between the two (NATO and EC membership), but it was clear even before we entered the Community that if we wished to be members of the European family in the creation of an economic space it was very difficult not to be similarly engaged in the defence of Europe, which at the time basically centred around NATO'. Quoted in Kennedy (2000: 111).
7. With the sole exception of Italy, Germany was consistently the most highly regarded country in the EC by Spaniards in the 1980s (Moral 1989: 28).
8. Marks (1997: 114).
9. Barbé (2000: 47).
10. For a comparison with Greece, see Kavakas (2001: 98–101).
11. Moravcsik (1999: 446).

12. Ibid., p.453.
13. Barbé (2000: 48).
14. Barreiro and Sánchez-Cuenca (2001: 29–37).
15. González's efforts enabled Spain to obtain 27 per cent of the EU's structural and cohesion funds during 1994–99, as opposed to the 11.7 per cent that went to each of Greece and Portugal, and the five per cent allocated to Ireland.
16. Barbé (2000: 44).
17. The impact on Spanish public opinion of the fishing dispute with Canada resulting from the capture of a Spanish fishing boat in March 1995 probably strengthened the government's hand in this field of policy.
18. Prego (2000: 235–6).
19. Barbé (1996: 271).
20. Gillespie and Youngs (2000: 5).
21. Youngs (2000: 123).
22. In spite of his acute domestic difficulties, in January 1996, only months before losing office, 13 per cent of those polled believed that González enjoyed a great deal of influence and prestige in the EU and a further 44 per cent thought this was still considerable, whereas 25 per cent thought it was negligible, and six per cent, non-existent (Szmolka 1999: 89).
23. For a first attempt, see Powell (1996).
24. The best expression of this is Guillermo Gortázar's *Visiones de Europa*, published in 1994 as a slightly abridged Spanish version of Stephen Hill's controversial *Visions of Europe* (1993).
25. Predictably, perhaps, Popular Party voters tend to be slightly more intergovernmentalist in their preferences than those of the PSOE (Szmolka 1999: 120–26).
26. Ortega and Mangas (1996: 63).
27. Torreblanca (2001: 507).
28. Grasa (1997: 36).
29. Elorza (1998: 37–45).
30. Barbé (2000: 50).
31. Rodrigo (1998: 30).
32. One of Aznar's most compelling arguments was that, although the Spanish economy only accounted for 6.6 per cent of the EU-15's GDP, Madrid contributed 7.1 per cent of the EU budget. Although the money allotted to the Cohesion Fund dropped from 21,000 to 18,000 million euros, Spain's slice of the cake grew from 55 per cent to 62 per cent.
33. Barbé (2000: 58).
34. Elorza (2001: 24).
35. Sánchez Mateos (2001: 13).

REFERENCES

Areilza Carvajal, J.M. de (1999): 'Las transformaciones del poder europeo: reforma institucional, principio de subsidiariedad y cooperaciones reforzadas' [The transformations of European power: institutional reform, subsidiarity principle, and reinforced Co-operation], in J.M. de Areilza Carvajal (ed.), *España y las transformaciones de la Unión Europea* [Spain and the Transformations of the European Union], FAES, 45, Madrid.

Barbé, E. (1996): 'Spain: Realist Integrationism', in F. Algieri and E. Regelsberger (eds.), *Synergy at Work: Spain and Portugal in European Foreign Policy*, Bonn: Europa Union Verlag.

Barbé, E. (1999): *La política europea de España* [The European Policy of Spain], Barcelona: Ariel.

Barbé, E. (2000): 'Spain and CFSP: The Emergence of a "Major Player"?' in Gillespie and Youngs (eds.) (2000).

Barreiro, B. and I. Sánchez-Cuenca (2001), 'La europeización de la opinión pública española' [The Europeanization of Spanish Public Opinion], in Closa (2001).

Closa, C. (ed.) (2001): *La europeización del sistema politico español* [The Europeanization of Spain's Political System], Madrid: Istmo.

Elorza, J. (1998): 'El Tratado de Amsterdam: una evaluación española' [The Amsterdam Treaty: A Spanish Evaluation], in *España y la negociación del Tratado de Amsterdam* [Spain and the Negotiation of the Amsterdam Treaty], Madrid: McGraw-Hill.

Elorza, J. (2001): 'La UE después de Niza' [The EU after Nice], *Política Exterior* [Foreign Policy] 79, Jan.

Gillespie, R. and R. Youngs (2000): 'Spain's International Challenges at the Turn of the Century', in Gillespie and Youngs (eds.) (2000).

Gillespie, R. and R. Youngs (eds.) (2000): *Spain: The European and International Challenges*, London and Portland, OR: Frank Cass.

Gortázar, G. (ed.) (1994): *Visiones de Europa* [Visions of Europe], Madrid: Alianza.

Grasa, R. (1998): *Política exterior y de seguridad en un año de tránsito* [Foreign and Security Policy in a Transition Year], in *Anuario CIDOB 1996* [CIDOB Yearbook 1996], Barcelona: CIDOB.

Hill, S. (1993): *Visions of Europe*, London: Duckworth.

Kavakas, D. (2001): *Greece and Spain in European Foreign Policy: The Influence of Southern Member States in Common Foreign and Security Policy*, Aldershot: Avebury.

Kennedy, P. (2000): 'Spain', in Ian Manners and Richard G. Whitman (eds.), *The Foreign Policies of European Union Member States*, Manchester: Manchester University Press.

Marks, M.P. (1997): *The Formation of European Policy in Post-Franco Spain*, Aldershot: Avebury.

Moral, F. Moral (1989): 'La opinión pública española ante Europa y los europeos' [The Spanish public opinion toward Europe and the Europeans], *Estudios y Encuestas*, [Reserach and Polls] 17, Madrid: Centro de Investigaciones Sociológicas.

Moravcsik, A. (1999): *The Choice for Europe*, Ithaca, NY: Cornell University Press.

Ortega, A. and P. Mangas (1996): 'Renovación generacional y cambio político' [Generational Renewal and Political Change], *Claves de razón práctica* [Keys of the Practical Reason] 66, Oct.

Powell, C. (1996): 'Aznar y el reto europeo' [Aznar and the European Challenge], in *Retratos íntimos de José María Aznar* [Intimate Portraits of José María Aznar], Barcelona: Ariel.

Powell, C. (2000): 'Cambio de régimen y política exterior: España, 1975–1989' [Regime Change and Foreign Policy: Spain 1975–1989], in J. Tusell, J. Avilés and R. Pardo (eds.), *La política exterior de España en el siglo XX* [The Foreign Policy of Spain in the XXth Century], Madrid: Biblioteca Nueva.

Prego, V. (2000): *Presidentes* [Presidents], Barcelona: Plaza & Janés.

Rodrigo, F. (1998): 'La política exterior española en 1997' [The Foreign Policy of Spain in 1997], in *Anuario CIDOB 1998* [CIDOB Yearbook 1998], Barcelona: CIDOB.

Sánchez Mateos, E. (2001): 'Camino viejo y sendero nuevo: ¿España, hacia una política exterior global?' [Old Road and New Path: Spain, Toward a Global Foreign Policy?], in *Anuario CIDOB 2001* [CIDOB Yearbook 2001], Barcelona: CIDOB.

Szmolka, I. (1999): 'Opiniones y actitudes de los españoles ante el proceso de integración europeo' [Opinions and Attitudes of the Spaniards Toward the European Integration Process], in *Opiniones y actitudes* [Opinons and Attitudes] 21, Madrid: Centro de Investigaciones Sociológicas.

Torreblanca, J.I. (2001): 'La europeización de la política exterior española' [The Europeanization of Spanish Foreign Policy], in Closa (2001).

Youngs, R. (2000): 'Spain, Latin America and Europe: The Complex Interaction of Regionalism and Cultural Identification', in Gillespie and Youngs (eds.) (2000).

Portugal's European Integration: The Good Student with a Bad Fiscal Constitution

JORGE BRAGA DE MACEDO

INTRODUCTION

Portugal's experience with international economic interdependence, begun under a corporatist regime keen on fostering economic and political integration with African and Asian colonies. This regime constrained private initiative, and the absence of multi-party democracy inhibited political freedom. Due to the lack mutual political responsiveness with major members of the North Atlantic Treaty Organization (NATO), let alone with the Organization for European Economic Co-operation (OECD), the experience was largely ignored. The same is true of membership in the European Free Trade Association (EFTA) in 1960, although it paved the way for a free trade agreement with the European Community (now EU) in 1972.

With the 1974 Revolution, mutual political responsiveness emerged, but there was a strong reversal in economic interdependence. In addition to the 1973 oil crisis, civil strife followed the attempt to introduce soviet-style economic planning in the 1976 constitution. The rigidity inherited from the corporatist regime was compounded by the widespread nationalization of heavy industry and banking, together with agriculture in the southern part of the country, and by successive balance of payments crises. As a consequence the democratic regime accommodated substantial macroeconomic instability, a combination not observed since the aftermath of the 1910 Revolution.

This is a companion piece to 'Portugal's European Integration: The Limits of External Pressure', in M. de Fátima Monteiro de Brito and J. Tavares (eds.), *Portugal Strategic Options in a European Context*, Cambridge: Lexington Books, 2002. Comments from José Braz and Sebastián Royo on an earlier version are gratefully acknowledged, but the author alone is responsible for the text.

The prevailing idea was that European integration would serve as 'insurance' against dictatorship rather than against the voracity of vested interests inherited from both the corporatist and the soviet-style regimes. Pressure towards greater reliance on market mechanisms and better governance in a public sector frozen by a constitutional ban on privatization was largely external, especially from the interventions of the International Monetary Fund (IMF) in 1977 and 1979. Although the success of EU accession in 1986 and especially of the first Presidency of the EU in early 1992 brought to the fore the view of Portugal as a good student of European integration, prior experience with OECD and EFTA should not be neglected. The government elected in late 1995 made it a political imperative to join the eurosystem in 1998, while distancing itself from the good student view, seen as excessively deferential toward Community institutions. Whatever the meaning of a 'good student' of European integration, membership in the euro system signalled the 'limits of external pressure'.

Over the span of five decades, international economic interdependence helped bring about macroeconomic stabilization and liberalization – except in what concerns neighbouring Spain, whose free trade agreement with EFTA in 1979 implied incipient trade relations with Portugal. A particular outcome of the simultaneous negotiations for EU membership of Portugal and Spain between 1977 and 1985 has been resistance to increased bilateral integration. On the eve of the 1999 general elections, the government jeopardized the good student reputation by threatening to veto a merger between a Spanish and a Portuguese bank. It lifted the veto after winning the election, albeit with a minority government. The good student appeared to return for a second EU presidency in early 2000, but only to face new elections and a budget crisis in 2002.

The importance of geographical limits to external pressure notwithstanding, those rooted in fiscal history present a greater threat to the good student reputation. To be sure, constitutional aspects are not usually looked at in connection with the euro but they are certainly determinant in Portugal, where the constitution included a ban on privatization from 1976 until 1989 and fiscal institutions have been impervious to reform over an even longer period. This suggests bad relations between the state and the population involving both taxes and transfers: the good student has a bad fiscal constitution.

After this introduction the discussion contains three sections. The second section describes the role of monetary and fiscal policies in the regime change, which culminated in the entry of the escudo into the Exchange Rate Mechanism of the European Monetary System (ERM). The ERM code of conduct – an informal convergence instrument – is shown to have made Portugal a good student of macroeconomic stability. The ERM also helped deal with neighbouring Spain in a multilateral framework. On the contrary, the experience of the eurosystem has been one of divergence.

The third section defines a fiscal constitution where government expenditures only stop growing under threat of a balance-of-payments crisis and focuses on how such a bad fiscal constitution favoured financial repression during the EFTA years. The ability of banks to protect their role as implicit tax collectors remained until after the restoration of full currency convertibility and the creation of a single market in financial services. Consequently, as argued in the next section, the good student fell victim to the euro hold-up.

The conclusion suggests that credibility in the eurosystem is not likely to be restored without overcoming the current budgetary crisis. Different policy areas need specific reform efforts; otherwise they stall. Overcoming the budgetary crisis will thus imply changing the fiscal constitution by improving budgetary control and completing the tax reform initiated in 1989. A more hopeful implication is that flexible integration – of which the ERM is an example – may help Portugal become a good student again.

THE GOOD STUDENT OF MACROECONOMIC STABILITY

When primary government expenditure is too high in relation to the taxpayers' ability to pay, as happened in planned economies and in many emerging markets, macroeconomic instability inevitably follows. Taking the form of excessive deficits on the balance of payments and on the government budget, macroeconomic instability calls for both a multiannual fiscal adjustment strategy (MAFAS) and a pre-pegging exchange rate regime (PPERR). Stabilization helps real and financial liberalization, along with other structural reforms.

As described in Branson *et al.* (2001; also Branson's contribution to my 2001 work with Daniel Cohen and Helmut Reisen), the PPERR avoids the 'inconsistent trio' of fixed exchange rate, free capital movements, and independent monetary policy by freeing monetary policy to be targeted on external balance, represented by a suitable reserve position. The MAFAS then sets fiscal policy to maintain internal balance, as represented by a low rate of inflation.

The durable achievement of nominal convergence requires wage and financial moderation, and the government has a leadership role in negotiating both wage settlements and benchmark operations in international financial markets. In turn, macroeconomic stability is required for sustained economic growth and real convergence.

The convergence record determines policy credibility because it suggests whether policy reversals are likely or not. Under divergence it is difficult to muster the electoral support for structural reforms, although they are most needed to resume convergence. This applies to Portugal, who achieved a remarkable degree of convergence, both nominal and real, in the decade following EU accession then diverged after qualifying for the euro.

Portugal's experience also shows that nominal convergence does not guarantee real convergence. In fact, the reticent liberalization of exchange controls by the Central Bank maintained interest rates too high during the 1991/92 global recession. This made Portugal's recession in 1993 much more severe than it need have been, with resultant real divergence in 1993 and 1994, the end of structural reforms and the election of a new Prime Minister in 1995.

Nevertheless, when compared with other experiences, namely those of the Nordic countries, Portugal's financial liberalization was remarkably problem-free. No banks failed and there was no sudden surge in careless lending although the Central Bank had no experience with supervising competitive banking activity. As detailed in the next section, banks, whether private or nationalized after 1974, had hitherto always been closely regulated, with nominal credit limits and effective barriers to entry.

The major difference between Portugal's liberalization and that of the Nordic countries was that Portugal's took effect in an economic downturn, when banks were in a cautious mood, concentrating on recovering outstanding debt rather than exploring new lending opportunities. By contrast, the Nordic countries liberalized their banking regulations in an economic boom and banks rapidly stretched their limits of prudent lending. The lesson is that the authorities should not wait for a 'favourable' economic climate to liberalize – if anything, it is better to do so in an economic downturn when decision-makers are more cautious.[1]

The remainder of this section describes the process of moving the escudo into the euro as the outcome of the gradual change in Portugal's economic regime toward price stability and currency convertibility that took place from 1989 to 1992, leading the authorities to accept the ERM code of conduct in conditions of high volatility – only to neglect fiscal discipline when enjoying an interest-free ride in the run-up to the euro.

Earning Credibility and the ERM Code of Conduct

Two years after the July 1987 general elections secured a majority government for Prime Minister Cavaco Silva, in power since mid-1985, the two main parties agreed to amend the constitution and allow state-owned enterprises to be privatized. This signalled the beginning of a process of gradual domestic liberalization that still continues. In September 1989 the escudo entered the ECU (European Currency unit) basket at a rate of 172.

With hindsight, this marks the beginning of the change in the economic regime, which eventually would move the escudo into the euro. Two kinds of measures define the change. Some, like a constitutional amendment reversing the 1976 freeze on privatization, were public but their relation to financial liberalization was not immediate. Other measures, like the MAFAS presented to the Commission services, were relevant but not public. In spite of these measures, neither the government nor social partners saw ERM membership as imminent. The cabinet was reshuffled shortly after the 1989 local elections, further delaying public awareness of the ongoing regime change. A Foreign Exchange Law in which criminal charges were replaced by fines had been approved in the fall of 1989 and was heralded by the Minister of Finance as a major reform.

The crawling peg policy (in existence since the IMF intervention of 1977) was replaced sometime in the spring of 1990 by a shadowing of the deutschmark, known – but not officially acknowledged – as the hard escudo policy. Since, like the shadow MAFAS of 1989, the new exchange-rate regime was not announced publicly, it could not be interpreted as a PPERR. But a very low level of unemployment coupled with a strong upward pressure on public sector wages led to strong inflationary pressures and to the appreciation of the real exchange rate. Moreover, the fear that financial freedom would threaten monetary control and the soundness of the banking system was ingrained at the Central Bank. Decree Law 13/90 of 8 January allowed the Central Bank to reinstate several controls, which remained under Decree Law 176/91 of 14 May, in spite of the principle of freedom stated in the article.

The Foreign Exchange Law gave the Central Bank competence to issue *avisos* (regulation notices signed by the Minister of Finance) through which capital controls could be introduced or relaxed. On 21

May the first *aviso* was used to introduce an interest free deposit of 40 per cent of loans contracted abroad (except when the operation related to financing of current transactions) and a prohibition of forward purchases of escudos between resident and non-resident banks (forward sales were still not allowed). The controls were reinforced before the general election (*aviso* 7 of 5 July 1991) with an explicit reference to the threat to monetary and exchange-rate policy that was posed by excessive capital inflows. The tightening of controls was supposed to help prevent inflation from accelerating, whereas the associated increase in the cost of servicing the public debt was looked at with benign neglect.

While shadowing the deutschmark, so as to fight inflation, the Central Bank was accumulating dollar deposits earning five per cent, while paying 20 per cent on the escudo debt being issued to mop up the resultant 'excess' liquidity. Under credible shadowing no exchange rate changes are expected so that this translates into a 20 per cent rate in dollars. Foreign exchange reserves more than doubled from 1989 to 1991, with disastrous consequences for the Central Bank's operating results. The existence of exchange controls allowed banks to delay adjusting to a single market in financial services and the combination of a shadow MAFAS with a shadow PPERR remained until July 1990, when a National Adjustment Framework for the Transition to Economic and Monetary Union, known as QUANTUM, was proposed.

After the 1991 elections confirmed the parliamentary majority, a convergence programme combining MAFAS and PPERR with capital account liberalization (called Q2 to stress the continuity of the gradual regime change) was submitted to the Economic and Financial Committee (ECOFIN) Council and discussed in the Portuguese Parliament. In spite of Q2, the decision to request entry of the escudo in the ERM was a genuine surprise. On the weekend following the approval in parliament of the 1992 State Budget, the government applied to join the ERM at a rate of 180 escudos agreed upon at a special cabinet meeting on Friday afternoon.

The EU response came from the Monetary (now Economic and Financial) Committee whose members were acting as personal representatives of the then 12 minister/governor pairs who meet with the Commission in the so-called informal ECOFIN. Although there was a precedent with sterling, the prior declaration of parity generated great resistance among several members. Under the alleged fear that, on the eve of the British general election, the announced parity of 180 might induce a speculative attack against sterling, parity closer to the market rate was sought. Finally, the notional central rate of 178,735 – that is, the one prevailing since the entry of sterling in October 1990 – gathered consensus.

After the cabinet meeting the Minister of Finance briefed the social partners and the following week ERM entry was debated in parliament. Nevertheless, the rule-based exchange-rate regime, which culminated the gradual change in economic regime, was neglected at home. The ERM code of conduct required full convertibility, and the Central Bank – who managed the derogation to the fourth Brussels directive negotiated by Greece and Portugal until 1995 – hesitated to accept that such derogation should expire in 1993 or 1994 (which is when Greece finished its liberalization), especially because currency convertibility would lessen monetary control.

The ERM crises were felt by the lira and sterling, which left the grid on 17 September 1992 when the peseta also realigned but the escudo did not. The opinion in financial circles was to stick to deutschmark shadowing and deny 'geographic fundamentals'. Exporters, on the other hand, were sensitive to the bilateral rate with the peseta and had been pressing for a devaluation of the escudo relative to the peseta. In the event, the realignment of 23 November was matched and those on 14 May 1993 and 6 March 1995 were followed in part, without ever facing the loss in financial reputation associated with initiating realignment.

The acquisition of financial reputation during ERM turbulence is reflected in weekly measures of exchange rate volatility between the deutschmark and the escudo. Using a technique of analysing changes in the variance of the exchange rate first applied to the US stock market, probabilities of the volatility of the weekly exchange rate from 7 January 1987 until 30 December 1998 are reported in Tables 1 and 2 for a specification with five volatility states.[2] During the period preceding the widening of the bands in August of 1993, the results remain essentially the same, although a rise from the 'very low' to the 'low' volatility state is observed in the last weeks before the creation of the euro.

The period begins with the last accession to the ERM before the crisis and includes some of the realignments involving the peseta and the escudo. The restoration of full convertibility was announced on 13 August 1992 and the Central Bank agreed to have controls renewed for shorter and shorter periods: in Table 1, the probability of the 'very high' volatility rises to 94 per cent the following week but returns to the previous level of 79 per cent until end of September. The few instances of 'very low' volatility in Table 1 show instead massive intervention by the Central Bank shortly before the November 1992 realignment.

TABLE 1

CHRONOLOGY OF THE ERM CRISES REGIME
(from the entry to the first realignment)

Date		Smoothed probabilities			
		Very low	Medium	High	Very high
04/08/92	(10+)	0%	4%	72%	24%
04/15/92	(10+)	0%	3%	71%	27%
04/22/92	(8)	0%	0%	63%	37%
04/29/92	(7)	0%	0%	64%	36%
05/06/92		0%	0%	78%	22%
05/13/92		0%	0%	85%	15%
05/20/92		0%	1%	91%	8%
05/27/92		0%	1%	93%	6%
06/03/92		0%	2%	93%	5%
06/11/92		0%	1%	91%	7%
06/17/92		0%	1%	87%	11%
06/24/92		0%	1%	81%	17%
07/01/92		0%	0%	65%	35%
07/08/92		0%	0%	48%	52%
07/15/92		0%	0%	30%	70%
07/22/92		0%	0%	34%	66%
07/29/92		0%	0%	30%	70%
08/05/92		0%	0%	26%	74%
08/12/92		0%	0%	21%	79%
08/19/92		0%	0%	6%	94%
08/26/92		0%	0%	21%	79%
09/02/92		0%	0%	27%	73%
09/09/92		0%	0%	26%	74%
09/16/92		0%	0%	16%	84%
09/23/92		0%	0%	13%	86%
09/30/92		0%	0%	5%	95%
10/07/92		87%	0%	6%	6%
10/14/92		93%	0%	6%	1%
10/21/92		93%	0%	7%	0%
10/28/92		92%	0%	8%	0%
11/04/92		83%	0%	16%	0%
11/11/92		0%	0%	99%	0%
11/18/92		0%	0%	98%	1%
11/25/92		0%	0%	96%	4%

Note: Numbers in parenthesis after date refer to difference with original when larger than or equal to five per cent.

Source: Macedo *et al.* (1999), updated.

TABLE 2

CHRONOLOGY OF THE ERM CRISES REGIME

(from the first realignment to the widening of the bands)

Date		Smoothed probabilities		
		Medium	High	Very high
12/02/92		0%	96%	4%
12/09/92		0%	93%	7%
12/16/92		0%	90%	10%
12/23/92		0%	84%	16%
12/30/92		0%	88%	12%
01/06/93		0%	87%	13%
01/13/93		0%	92%	8%
01/20/93		0%	93%	7%
01/27/93		0%	95%	5%
02/03/93		1%	95%	4%
02/10/93		1%	94%	6%
02/17/93		0%	89%	11%
02/24/93		0%	92%	8%
03/03/93		0%	93%	6%
03/10/93		1%	94%	5%
03/17/93		3%	95%	3%
03/24/93		3%	94%	2%
03/31/93		5%	93%	2%
04/07/93	(5)	6%	91%	3%
04/14/93	(6)	7%	89%	4%
04/21/93	(6)	7%	84%	9%
04/28/93	(6)	7%	75%	18%
05/05/93	(5)	6%	56%	38%
05/12/93		0%	10%	90%
05/19/93		0%	0%	100%
05/26/93		0%	1%	100%
06/02/93		0%	0%	100%
06/09/93		0%	0%	100%
06/16/93		0%	2%	98%
06/23/93		0%	4%	96%
06/30/93		0%	4%	96%
07/07/93		0%	4%	96%
07/14/93		0%	0%	100%
07/21/93		0%	0%	100%
07/28/93		0%	0%	100%
08/04/93		0%	44%	56%

Source: Macedo et al. (1999), updated.

Full convertibility was restored on 16 December 1992. There is no effect in Table 2, and no instance of 'artificial stability' either. Given that the financial reputation of the country was not fully established, this serves as an illustration of the power of the ERM code of conduct as a convergence instrument. The implications of convertibility were twofold. First, it allowed for greater banking competition. Given the soundness of the banking system (at least in relation to what happened in the Nordic countries), this implied a tighter supervision than the regulators could muster. Second, convertibility would lower money market rates even if it meant letting the escudo slide towards the middle of the six per cent ERM band. Better banking supervision, namely in enforcing greater transparency in effective rates being charged on credits, would lead to a decline in the cost of credit without the need to change the stance of monetary policy. Flexibility within the top of the band would reflect the benefit of the ERM code of conduct relative to deutschmark shadowing.

In the turbulence that followed ERM entry, the lack of credit familiarity with Portugal had to be overcome. International borrowing, however, was still associated with situations of looming payments' crises rather than with the promotion of the nation's credit abroad. Moreover, exceptionally high foreign exchange reserves were not used to boost the Treasury's credit rating: Portugal's external debt issues had been assigned a rating of A1 by Moody's Investors Services in late 1986 and A by Standard and Poor's two years later. The divergence between the two agencies remained until late 1991, when Standard and Poor's upgraded to A+.

As soon as the currency was fully convertible, therefore, a strategy of making the Treasury known in international markets was designed, involving a planned return to international borrowing, successively in yen, marks and dollars. Standard and Poor's upgraded Portugal's foreign debt to AA- in May 1993, although the previous upgrade had been decided less than 18 months earlier. International investors were ready to believe then that economic policy in Portugal would retain a medium-term orientation also; this was the first such rating move since Ireland had been upgraded in 1989. Once again, the strategy was ignored domestically. Shortly after the global dollar issue of September 1993, the deterioration in tax revenue collections, while keeping non-interest expenditure at the nominal amount included in Q2, increased the deficit and had a much greater impact domestically than the credibility earned abroad.

The central rate the escudo kept after the realignment of the peseta in March 1995, around 196, reached without increasing short- and long-term interest rates, showed a greater benefit of ERM membership for Portugal than for Spain. Although the accumulated real appreciation of the escudo may have been perceived as excessive by export-oriented firms and the government may have been sensitive to their pressure, it was certainly less than that of the peseta – who had joined the ERM as far back as 1989. In any event, testing the ERM parity of both currencies made sense when there was accumulating evidence that the recession was hitting their domestic economies.

Quarterly data on capital flows confirm that external credibility was achieved in late 1992 and remained almost as unperturbed by subsequent peseta realignments as it had been by the domestic turbulence of March 1993.[3] In sum, had the decision to join the ERM been delayed, the escudo would have been unable to join the ERM in time to meet the EMU criterion of two years' membership. It would have trailed with the Greek drachma outside the parity grid, rather than accompanying the peseta inside. Foregoing the ERM code of conduct would certainly not have helped the government sell stability at home.

Selling Stability at Home and the Euro Hold-up

The MAFAS retained in the Revised Convergence Programme (PCR) approved with the 1994 State Budget kept the nominal ceiling on non-interest expenditures from Q2 but adjusted the deficit for the revenue shortfall. This was well accepted by international investors who heavily oversubscribed a global bond issue of 1 billion dollars in September 1993 and by the Monetary Committee who approved the PCR in November. A cabinet reshuffle was announced shortly before the December local elections, but economic policy remained consistent with the PCR. In early 1994 a global bond issue in ECU was received with the same success as the previous one. The government's call for lower interest rates, however, although directed at a domestic business audience, had foreign repercussions. In this context an Austrian news agency reported rumours of a military coup in Portugal. Although entirely groundless, the story led to a renewed attack on the escudo – but without any lasting increase in volatility. Differences in banking supervision led to the replacement of most of the Central Bank board in June 1994. This drastic move was well accepted, because – just like in March 1993 – it was understood that the tension did not originate in monetary policy.

As the ERM code of conduct moved the escudo into the euro, the Treaty on European Union and the Banking Law (Decree Law 298/92 of 31 December), which introduced the single market in financial services and called for greater supervision and competition, appeared to consolidate macroeconomic stability under convertibility, to which the Central Bank fully adjusted. Further changes were introduced to the statutes of the Central Bank to make it more independent from the government, to introduce some accountability in parliament, and to improve the regulation and supervision procedures.

Another reflection of the continuity of the MAFAS was that the PCR proposed in 1993 extended the expenditure ceilings into 1997. The PCR remained the basis for the excessive deficit procedures until a Convergence, Stability and Growth Programme from 1998 to 2000 was approved by the ECOFIN in May 1997. A Stability and Growth Programme for 1999–2001 followed shortly after the escudo joined the euro at a rate of 200,482. The MAFAS continued listing structural reforms, especially in the public administration, but unfortunately dropped nominal ceiling on non-interest expenditures.

Portugal's regime change remained misunderstood by public opinion until after the general elections in October 1995. Aside from domestically generated disturbances that obscured the significance of the change, the combination of recession and system turbulence must be recognized. The lack of credit familiarity with Portugal would have been bad enough for firms and citizens in tranquil periods. In the turbulence that followed ERM entry, it was of course much worse and may have contributed to slowing down the learning process.

This lesson reinforces the need for balance in the rising economic interdependence and mutual political responsiveness, which Portugal lacked over the last five decades with respect to OECD, EFTA, and even EU – except as a good student of macroeconomic stability. Moreover, the role of domestic and international media in spreading news about financial reputation to citizens should not be underestimated. It has certainly been far more striking in the reversal of mid-1999 due to the pre-election refusal of a merger between a Portuguese and Spanish bank than it was in 1990–91 when television was still a state-owned monopoly.

Whereas some oscillations in the integration path are explained by political and social variables, macroeconomic indicators like productivity and relative prices of goods and factors tell the same story, once account is taken of the succession of exchange rate arrangements. Thus, wage increases and long-term interest rates converged and diverged before they converged again to the EU average. Wage and financial immoderation certainly contributed to obscuring the significance of the PPERR for firms, trade unions, and the general public before joining the

FIGURE 1

RELATIVE UNIT LABOUR COSTS
(SPRING 2002 vs 01 EC FORECASTS)

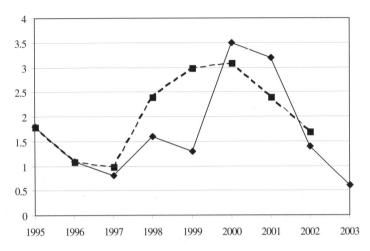

ERM and after 1995. In 1997 the expectation of euro entry ensured financial moderation, although wage moderation was reversed and reached the 1996 level of about three per cent in 2000–1.

The rise in unit labour costs in relation to the eurozone average is reported in Figure 1, which also depicts the substantial changes the spring 2002 forecasts by the European Commission introduced with respect to the ones presented in Winter 2001. Relative unit labour costs deteriorated after the last ERM realignment, from a rate of about one per cent per annum in 1996/97 to a rate of over 2.5 per cent in 1998/2001. To compare, the rate of deterioration in 1993/95, at the time of ERM turbulence, was about two per cent per annum. The trend was so dramatic that there was a warning from the Central Bank governor in early 2001.

Meanwhile, successive revisions of the budget deficit for 2001 culminated in a recommendation by the European Commission, issued on 30 January 2002 'with a view to giving early warning to Portugal in order to prevent the occurrence of an excessive deficit'. The ECOFIN decided against making the recommendation because of the commitments of the outgoing government, but a new Stability and Growth Programme is to follow the new government's revision of the 2002 State Budget.

Meanwhile, the surge in non-interest expenditure diverged from the EU average, as illustrated in Figure 2.[4] In addition to explaining how divergence followed convergence, this state of affairs hurts corporate governance and the fight against corruption. The next section shows how the bad fiscal constitution reversed the monetary and fiscal policies of the good student.

FIGURE 2

PRIMARY EXPENDITURE (NIG), % GDP; PORTUGAL AND EU AVERAGE

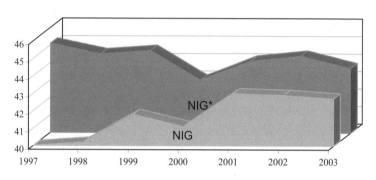

FIGURE 3

SOVEREIGN SPREADS PORTUGAL vs GERMANY BASED ON
DAILY-QUOTED MSCI INDEXES

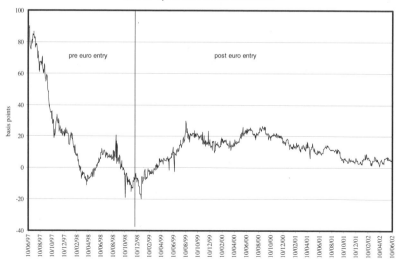

The financial moderation desired by the government when joining the ERM in 1992 turned out to be more difficult to achieve than anticipated. One indicator of such moderation is the spread of long-term interest rates relative to Germany, and its decline after qualifying for the euro is evident from Figure 3.[5]

The decline of some ten percentage points in inflation rates – and interest rates – in the early 1990s gave government expenditures an interest-free ride equivalent to about five percentage points of gross domestic product (GDP) in the late 1990s. In this sense nominal convergence brings with it the risk of giving a temporary illusion of fiscal discipline. The credibility of the MAFAS/PPERR was not fed by additional measures of a microeconomic and structural nature, designed to enhance the competitiveness of production and therefore sustain the catching-up process. Indeed, the greater volatility observed in Figure 3 after the December 2001 local elections suggests that investors remain quite aware of the threat that political instability poses to public sector reform.

Public administration has remained incapable of reforming itself in areas such as justice, home affairs, social welfare, and education. The absence of structural reforms is especially grave in what pertains to the enlarged public sector and the discretionary regulation of private enterprise. The MAFAS/PPERR was a decisive signal of the change in economic regime even though, in the last ten years, the (general and local) election cycles have hindered the implementation of public sector reform.

The national economy is still more open on the trade than on the capital account, but this changed fast due to both large foreign direct investment (FDI) into Brazil in the late 1990s and large outflows after entering the eurosystem. It is unclear whether government policy mattered, since the instruments were available since 1992. Nevertheless, among cohesion countries Portugal was set to gain the most from the single market from 1995 to 2010.[6] The opportunity for structural change afforded by the euro was lost and with it the improvements in fiscal discipline and structural reforms. The macro situation became unsustainable shortly after qualifying for the euro, with a current account deficit reaching ten per cent of GDP. Private credit also rose to 140 per cent of GDP, with limited effects on capital accumulation. Worse yet, structural reforms went into reverse gear, with a punitive tax reform and indulgent public-sector wage negotiations.

The neglect of the ERM code of conduct after qualifying for the euro made for an unfavourable business environment, which led to an acceleration of outward direct investment. Because the business internationalization drive was not accompanied by reform in tax administration, justice, and decentralization toward municipalities, let alone social security and public health, it eroded the legitimacy of integration. Portugal was perhaps in a unique position in that it was able to meet the euro criteria without any fiscal adjustment. Since the opportunity for sustained structural change afforded by the euro and the associated interest-free ride has heretofore been lost, Portugal has become a victim of the euro hold-up.

FISCAL CONSTITUTION AND FINANCIAL REPRESSION

If national governments avoid taking unpopular measures because they fear losing the next election, then populism and nationalism interact in a perverse way. The common good is dissipated. If joining the euro stalls structural reforms, the national economy would become less competitive as a production location in the global economy. An interest-free ride, together with EU structural funds, is harmful when it makes social groups more voracious. This is what Portugal's fiscal constitution brought about.

The fiscal constitution includes the institutions enforcing the social contract and thus incorporates various exchange-rate regimes, monetary standards, and state revenues. The concept of fiscal constitution shows the deep causes of unsustainable fiscal policies, which prevent the benefits of a stable and common currency from materializing. Deficient tax administration has undermined the social legitimacy of taxes as a means to provide for the common good.

It also prevented the reform of the public administration from being initiated, let alone carried out, until the government was elected in early 2002 and the Central Bank discovered a grossly excessive budget deficit for 2001. Since the previous crises had involved the balance of payments, there are still those who doubt an excessive government budget deficit qualifies as financial crisis and would rather call it a legal nuisance. Nevertheless, the interruption of convergence with EU standards of living may last long enough to discredit such a view.

Tax Earmarking by Social Groups

In Portugal, domain revenues associated with the overseas trade monopolies and collected mostly in Lisbon were more significant than those associated with income taxes, levied since 1641. Centralized revenues were easier to administer and they helped maintain monetary stability in the face of recurrent military expenditures. Growing domain revenues gradually narrowed the domestic tax base, however, and divorced taxpayers from transfer recipients. Both of these features came to characterize the fiscal constitution of the 1700s; unfortunately, they remained even after the apparent economic prosperity of these times disappeared. In the late 1700s the combination of foreign and then civil wars, monetary instability, and collapsing revenues stunted Portugal's economic development.

The 1820 liberal revolution was associated with the loss of social confidence and financial reputation, making the taxation of capital and the redistribution among social groups difficult. Civil rights were seen as inimical to monetary stability, so that political and financial freedom clashed until the gold standard brought nominal and real convergence with what is now the EU average from 1854 until the 1891 financial crisis. Exit from gold standard initiated a period of maximum divergence, which lasted until the post-war European integration boom. The preference for hidden taxation included the one achieved through inflation and excess borrowing by the state (Macedo, da Silva and de Sousa, 2001).

Through exports and through migrant remittances, European growth was crucial for the national economic growth. The effects of rising economic interdependence on society, let alone on the polity, were not as simple. Even when expectations of improved standards of living were realized, the isolation of the political regime made the absence of mutual political responsiveness as conspicuous as the consumption of the middle class. Moreover, export- and remittance-led growth reinforced the discrimination between taxable capital on the one hand and informal capital and labour on the other.

It turns out that neither the redistributive revolutions of 1910 and 1974 nor the ensuing political instability changed the fiscal constitution much. EFTA allowed Portugal to develop an export base in manufacturing but without any significant product differentiation. This is why Portugal was sometimes called a 'pyjama republic'. The preference for hidden taxation was exacerbated by the revolutions, however, and macroeconomic instability prevailed in their aftermath. In the early 1980s, for example, the inflation rate reached over 20 per cent of the EU average.

This rigid fiscal constitution discriminated against 'informal capital' and also against labour. In other words, banking, monetary, and exchange-rate policies supported the discrimination against labour evident in the drop in real wages from 1977 to 1985.

Although the state is supposed to promote the common good of the population, taxes are viewed as a common resource, whereas expenditures on goods, services, and transfers benefit particular social groups. Each one of these groups therefore tries to earmark tax revenues to expenditures or transfers from which it can benefit. The fiscal constitution defines the earmarking process. Social groups are then like a kind of capital that is taxable by the state and can be redistributed through the budget to the benefit of other social groups. Very different tax and transfer mechanisms, including implicit or explicit earmarking procedures, are then associated with a certain level of net taxes, or primary budget deficit. This ultimately reflects the constitution, electoral rules, and other related (even informal) practices of the polity. Together with a number of contextual and informal elements, the high level rules that make up the fiscal constitution determine the actual workings of the policy-making system (that is, whether the Judiciary is independent, whether the bureaucracy is professional, whether legislators are policy-oriented, and so on) and include the overall functioning of the political system.[7]

The rigidity of the fiscal constitution prevented European integration from balancing mutual political responsiveness with economic interdependence. Public and private interest groups seeking transfers from the state and thereby holding on to the tax base took advantage of European structural funds. The whole process reinforced some of the interests vested in state intervention. Excessive regulation was pervasive both during the corporatist regime (Royo 2002) and after the 1974 Revolution. In fact, the effectiveness of the resistance of public and private interest groups to broadening the tax base or to tightening the link between taxpayers and transfer recipients has been so remarkable that the fiscal constitution could be described as 'get out of my tax!'

Because it describes relations between the state and the population involving both taxes and transfers, the fiscal constitution includes the institutions enforcing the social contract and thus incorporates exchange-rate regimes, monetary standards, and state revenues. Policies can be seen as lower lever rules that regulate the behaviour of economic agents; for instance, a policy that defines tax bases and tax rates. The rules that determine who has the power, and under what procedures, to legislate on tax bases and tax rate are intermediate-level rules, while high-level rules are those that establish how intermediate-level rules are determined.

Reforms in lower-lever rules (like tax reforms) and intermediate-level rules (like privatization, or granting independence to the central bank) leave high-level rules unaffected, although they heavily condition not only the choice of lower rules but also the details of implementation and effectiveness of those lower-level rules. For example, the capacity that the political system has to enforce certain rules, to make intertemporal commitments, is perhaps more important than the 'title' of the policy in intermediate-level rules (such as 'public enterprises' versus 'regulated private utilities'). Tommasi (2002) applies this view to Argentina, arguing that the inability or unwillingness of powerful social groups to co-operate has raised enormously the political transaction costs of intertemporal co-operation in Argentina. The same insight comes from Portugal's fiscal constitution, which has remained unchanged through the years of the good student, the decades of international economic interdependence, and the centuries of earmarking taxation.

From Excessive Financial Regulation to Delayed Tax Reform

Whereas control of corporate behaviour through mergers or takeovers is restricted (and banks are more regulated), firms tend to be committed to their group's commercial bank, which in turn adopts a more flexible approach and a longer-term view than would be possible in highly competitive and unregulated financial markets. A consequence of the fast economic growth and the excessive financial regulation of the 1960s was therefore that industrial groups needed more finance for their activities than the commercial banks were able to provide. Tight regulation of credit – with ceilings established on an individual bank basis – made it essential for an emerging industrial and financial group to avail itself of a commercial bank.

Most of the seven 'family' groups were indeed called by the name of their respective commercial bank. Because of the close links of these groups with the government, the competitive fringe of new conglomerates did not manage to bring about industrial and financial restructuring. Had this fringe been successful, thriving firms might have been able to shop around for more attractive sources of funding, but the financing of the export enclave of small manufacturing firms did not operate in this competitive way. Most firms outside the groups were also deprived of the option of borrowing abroad and had to finance their long-term investment through their own resources or revolving short-term loans. The oligopoly situation of the seven groups, together with the comfortable external position, explains why non-monetary financial intermediaries failed to develop.

Because of their diversified earnings, large industrial and financial groups do not require a financial market for investment. In the 1960s the managers of the commercial banks at the core of these conglomerates were nurtured in a type of financial intermediation where most of the operations were internal to the group. As the groups could do without a financial market, after the nationalization of 1975, they probably took the same view of the nationalized sector as a whole. The closing down of the stock market, shortly after the revolution, reinforced this perception. At the same time the abnormally high levels of gold and foreign exchange reserves changed the nature of financial intermediation. Urged by revolutionary politicians to put banks 'at the service of the people', the managers saw those reserves as collateral against which the nationalized enterprises were borrowing. When there is imperfect monitoring of projects by banks, however, a rise in collateral makes borrowers more likely to default. To compensate for this decline in the expected return of a loan, the bank selects riskier borrowers and projects, which cause expected bank returns to fall. To avoid a fall in profitability, the bank will prefer to ration credit, even if there are no macroeconomic disturbances.

When credit ceilings on private firms are binding, rationing is exacerbated. In an inflationary environment, where every borrower, especially the government, faces negative real interest rates, the constraint on private credit may be very strong. Financial repression made private firms more dependent on bank credit at a time when retained earnings were low and there was no substitute in the stock or bond markets. The heavy dependence of firms on bank credit made the financial system more fragile because banks did not expect some of the debts would be repaid. This reinforced the lack of incentives for creditors to monitor borrowers. It is thus no surprise that after the stock market was revived in 1987, it attracted mostly firms with insufficient retained earnings and with low collateral.

During the expansion of 1981–82, with high wage inflation and controlled prices, profits and retained earnings fell. When interest rates were raised in 1982, the adverse selection effect toward riskier borrowers (who are less reluctant to pay higher rates) was probably offset by a less binding constraint on credit ceilings. This allowed banks a better mix of borrowers and projects, but in so far as deposit rates were administratively fixed, higher lending rates only increased the intermediation margin. Arrears and bad debts accumulated, peaking at 15 per cent of credit to non-financial enterprises and individuals in 1986. At the time non-performing loans were three times as large as the equity of commercial banks. Bad debts fell to about 11 per cent of credit in early 1989, but the figures would be much higher for the nationalized banks, which were also saddled with the need to provide for their staff's pensions.

Paradoxically, the role of nationalized banks in collecting hidden taxes through excessively wide intermediation margins may have helped stabilize the system. The hidden taxes were passed on through their forced purchases of public debt. In addition, since nationalized banks were acting as tax collectors, depositors were confident the state would bail them out. The implicit tax imposed on borrowers and depositors in the banking system widened the normal intermediation margin to bring a 'revenue' peaking at almost ten per cent of GDP in 1982, falling to close to four per cent in 1987.

Ten years after the great nationalization, the government finally authorized new entrants, both domestic and foreign, into the banking sector, although some of them were direct competitors of the nationalized commercial banks. The new banks avoided holding public debt instruments other than Treasury bills, which had just been introduced, and were reluctant to lend to the troubled state-owned enterprises. This meant that they were less exposed to bad debts. The contrast between 'clean' and 'tainted' banks might have prompted depositors to run on the riskier banks but, once privatization was allowed, the state bought the bad debts of nationalized banks. To the extent that depositors believed the state would ultimately bail out the nationalized banks, this was indeed the appropriate measure. The consequent increase in public debt was offset in part by the proceeds from the privatization of most of the state-owned enterprises that were nationalized in 1975. Also, 'bad' debts turned out not to be so bad, as assets appreciated during the boom that followed. At the same time the growth of private commercial banks had a stronger effect on banking competition than the mere increase in the number of players would imply. Nevertheless, banks continued to serve as implicit tax collectors until after financial liberalization was achieved.

The resistance to the cross border merger was also a reflection of interests vested in the fiscal constitution, exacerbated in this case by the traditional fear of Spanish domination. The Prime Minister went as far as to say on television 'we are not a banana republic!' and vetoed the deal, only to accept it a few months later after winning the elections. As mentioned at the outset, trade between Portugal and Spain began as a by-product of Spain's free trade agreement with EFTA and its growth was the effect of EU membership. Because of the geographical proximity, Spanish imports and investment continue to be resisted, especially in agriculture and banking.

To pursue a defensive strategy with respect to one partner and remain co-operative with respect to others is consistent with the ambiguous responses to external liberalization that prevailed before the good student phase. It is also equivalent to preferring implicit taxation, a habit that stems from financial repression. The habit of implicit taxation is also visible in the resistance to a broader domestic tax base and to budgetary procedures stemming the growth of primary expenditures. The time it took to introduce personal income taxation is yet another example of the resilience of a fiscal constitution favouring certain social groups.

The first attempts at income taxation were made before the 1974 Revolution, and several governments attempted to implement the call to that effect included in the 1976 constitution. Nevertheless, the new taxes on individuals and corporations were not introduced until 1989 – the year the economic constitution was amended to allow for privatization. Since 1989 several attempts at pursuing tax reform, especially in what pertains to administration, have failed. The most visible reversal occurred in 2001, with respect to an attempt at taxing capital gains, as it led to the replacement of the Minister of Finance, who at the time also held the Economy portfolio. It might even be said that the merger after the 1999 elections of the Ministries of Economy and Finance, two agencies with opposite views of the budget process, only helped solve the reversal in EU policy associated with the veto of the cross-border bank merger.

The issue of tax reform was also debated, and the Prime Minister from 1985 to 1995 suggested a 'tax shock' involving a reduction in direct taxes matched by an increase in the value added tax and expenditure reduction. The consequences of such packages vary with the specific measures involved, but Pereira and Rodrigues (2002) find no scenario where the tax shock comes close to being self-financed. Moreover, in spite of steady state gains in GDP levels, private welfare falls in the cases that do not involve lower government expenditure. A compensatory increase in indirect taxation would have to be substantial and permanent.[8]

Quite aside from the resistance to tax reform, the fiscal constitution exacerbates the deficit bias and threatens the role of the Minister of Finance in dampening the 'common pool' problem, at least in a democratic government. Budgetary procedures have scores comparable to Spain, much better than Greece but substantially below Austria (Branson *et al.* 2001). The strategic dominance of the Minister of Finance is associated with strong majority governments between 1985 and 1995. The clear preference for credibility until the qualification for the euro in 1998 was accompanied by increases in primary expenditure.

One reason for the trend illustrated in Figure 2 is that, in the minority governments between 1995 and 2002, removing the responsibility for public administration from the Ministry of Finance to the office of the Prime Minister weakened the strategic dominance of the Ministry of Finance, so that the deficit bias was not resisted and the semi-presidential regime became more unstable than with the reform-minded majority governments of 1987/95, although the President of the Republic and the Prime Minister belong to the same party.

The experience of combining the Ministry of Finance with a spending ministry was short lived and culminated in the approval of emergency measures for expenditure reduction in Spring 2001. This allowed the promised tax reform to be postponed while expenditure control became even harder to apply in the deteriorating external environment following the September 11 attacks on the United States. While the pressure of increased transfers coming from redistribution objectives interacted with the falling tax revenue, public opinion became alarmed at the deteriorating fiscal situation, and fears of EU sanctions for breaching the Stability Pact began to be voiced.

In the 17 December 2001 local elections, the opposition won the major cities and the Prime Minister resigned. General elections were called for 17 March 2002, and in the electoral campaign, economists on both sides of the political spectrum made successive calls for fiscal consolidation. The changes in the 2002 State Budget brought about by the new coalition government and the public sector reform it initiated have met with fierce resistance on the part of trade unions and opposition parties. Nevertheless, the strategic dominance of the Minister of Finance is ensured by the fact that she is also Minister of State, that the Ministry recovered the responsibility for public administration, and that it seems to be in a better position to control local and regional administrations.

CONCLUSION

Portugal's European integration has revealed both convergence and divergence, nominal and real. Since 1997 inflation in Portugal has exceeded the EU average every year, whereas real convergence has been slowing down each year since 1998, actually turning negative in 2000 and with both real and nominal divergence expected to increase until 2003. One of the major gains of financial liberalization, the significant decline in real interest rates, permitted Portugal to be the only euro-zone country to meet the convergence criteria without enacting any major curtailment of government expenditures.

After adopting the PPERR/MAFAS and earning credibility abroad, Portugal was in a unique position: it could join the euro without fiscal adjustment. In other words the fiscal convergence criteria were not binding for Portugal. The risk of this interest-free ride is that nominal convergence can give the illusion of fiscal discipline via the fall in real interest rates. Instead of using the interest-free ride to finance the transition costs of needed structural reforms, the government defeated in the March 2002 general elections used that margin to fund populist measures such as a price freeze on gasoline, increased transfer payments, and large increases in the number of civil servants. On the other side, procrastination relative to unpopular reforms was so pronounced in Portugal that it led to a stagnating economy and higher inflation. By not taking care of the needed structural reforms when they had the opportunity, the Portuguese authorities laid the ground for having both nominal and real divergence.

Original membership in the eurosystem may have suggested to the government that the experience of Portugal was an unqualified success, relative to Greece. Inflation may not have been fully eradicated in Portugal, however, where it is currently higher than in Greece. Put another way, the credibility of Portugal's MAFAS/PPERR must be fed by additional measures of a microeconomic and structural nature, designed to enhance the competitiveness of production and therefore sustain the catching-up process. Structural measures need to be taken at all levels of government, so that cities and regions also benefit from the newly acquired financial reputation of the sovereign.

Belonging to the eurosystem only prevents a currency and public debt crisis. Instead, bank credit remains largely domestic and the current boom could be suddenly reversed. If that happened, there may not be a spectacular crisis, but the current belated attempt at limiting public expenditure growth is likely to have to be pursued over the long haul. Just when the international environment would require more security, Portugal may find itself exposed to a lasting divergence with the EU and with Spain. Policy credibility turns out to be more important than proximity to EU markets in attracting 'right' FDI, because corruption discourages FDI and favours bank loans (Wei 2000).

The benefits of a stable and common currency do not materialize when fiscal policies are unsustainable. Moreover, deficient tax administration undermines the social legitimacy of taxes as a means of providing for the common good. There is no substitute for domestic reform, and in Portugal the first priority is to change the fiscal constitution that has proved resilient to the political, social, and economic changes brought about by 15 years of European integration. The negative effects of the euro hold-up are all the more lamentable since the ERM is an example of flexible integration. Given the complexity of the EU institutional architecture, successful flexible integration schemes such as the euro have a 'snowball' effect that applies both to the other three current EU members and to prospective ones. The issue of building effective governance at the EU level hinges not only on the existence of the European common good but also on the specifics of the public good to be provided and on the transactions costs involved. When the benefits of the public good are exclusively for the members who finance it, then the free ride problem is not as serious as it is with respect to common resources like the tax base. This is behind the success of the ERM or the Schengen agreement, which are based on a mutually accepted code of conduct and also behind the failure of tax harmonization (Kolliker 2000).

By itself, the euro cannot change the fiscal constitution. Different policy areas need specific reform efforts; otherwise they stall and affect each other in a negative way. The good student of macroeconomic stability fell victim of the euro hold-up because of its bad fiscal constitution. The good student must now change its fiscal constitution and reconstruct its financial reputation. Since flexible integration was made easier in the Nice Treaty (Baldwin *et al.* 2001), Portugal may have a chance to become a good student again.

NOTES

1. The argument is developed in my 2002 work with Braz.
2. When he was at the OECD Development Centre, Thomas Chalaux computed the data presented in Tables 1 and 2 updating Tables 4a and 4b in my 1999 work with Nunes and Covas. I want to thank him for that. When the difference between the original results in Tables 1 and 2 (going until 15 October 1998) and is greater than or equal to five per cent, this is reported after the date.
3. EC (1997) for the capital flows and Macedo *et al.* (1999) for the smoothed probabilities corresponding to the data in Tables 1 and 2, where brief jumps to very high volatility are observed in early 1994 and early 1995 but not in early March 1993. The difference may be due to Central Bank intervention. My ongoing research with Nunes seeks to extend our 1999 results reported in Tables 1 and 2 by using daily intervention data subsequently released to us by the Bank of Portugal.
4. Figure 2 uses the Spring 2002 European Commission forecasts, whereas my 2002 with Braz incorporates the IMF forecasts from late 2000.
5. Martin Grandes, of DELTA, Paris collected the data shown in Fiqure 3. I want to thank him for that.
6. According to European Commission simulations, Portugal would experience a 0.7 per

cent growth gain every year, whereas there would be no net effect in Spain and a small negative effect in Greece.

7. Tornell and Lane (1998, 1999) propose the voracity of social groups as the reason why terms of trade gains may lower growth, whereas Tommasi (2002) suggests their inability to commit to intertemporal cooperation. Both routes provide useful insights into the effects of a bad fiscal constitution.

8. It would also penalize consumption, and in a system where the taxation is based on capital and labour income rather than on consumption, this is shown by Correia (2001) to lead to inefficiency as well as to undesirable distributional consequences. These might exacerbate the discrimination against labour present in the fiscal constitution.

REFERENCES

Baldwin, R., E. Berglof, F. Giavazzi and M. Widgren (2001): 'Nice Try: Should the Treaty of Nice be Ratified?' *Monitoring European Integration* 11, London: CEPR.

Branson, W., J.B. de Macedo and J. von Hagen (2001): 'Macroeconomic Policy and Institutions in the Transition towards EU Membership', in R. MacDonald and R. Cross (eds.), *Central Europe towards Monetary Union: Macroeconomic Underpinnings and Financial Reputation*, Boston, MA: Kluwer Academic.

Correia, I. (2001): 'Consumption Taxes and Redistribution', Banco de Portugal mimeo, Dec.

European Commission (1997): 'The Economic and Financial Situation in Portugal in the Transition to EMU', 'European Economy' special reports 1997.

Kolliker, A. (2001): 'Bringing Together or Driving Apart the Union? Towards a Theory of Differentiated Integration', preprints aus der Max Planck Projektgruppe Recht der gemeinschaftsguter, Bonn, 2001/5.

Macedo, J.B. de, I.C. Nunes and F. Covas (1999): 'Moving the Escudo into the Euro', CEPR Discussion Paper, Oct.

Macedo, J.B. de, Á.F. da Silva and R.M. de Sousa (2001): 'War, Taxes and Gold: The Inheritance of the Real', in M. Bordo and R. Cortes-Conde (eds.), *Transferring Wealth and Power from the Old to the New World*, Cambridge: Cambridge University Press.

Macedo, J.B. de, C. Cohen and H. Reisen (eds.) (2001): *Don't Fix Don't Float*, Paris: OECD Development Centre Study, Sept.

Macedo, J.B. de and J. Braz (2002): 'Portugal's Euro Holdup', presented at a seminar at the Polish National Bank, 21 March.

Pereira, A.M. and P. Rodrigues (2002): 'On the Impact of a Tax Shock in Portugal', College of William and Mary, mimeo, March.

Royo, S. (2002): *A New Century of Corporatism? Corporatism in Southern Europe*, Westport, CT: Greenwood/Praeger.

Tommasi, M. (2002): 'Crisis, Political Institutions, and Policy Reform: It Is Not the Policy, It Is the Polity, Stupid', Annual World Bank Conference on Development Economics – Europe, June.

Tornell, A. and P. Lane (1998): 'Are Windfalls a Curse? A Non-representative Model of the Current Account', *Journal of International Economics*, Feb., pp.83–112.

Tornell, A. and P. Lane (1999): 'The Voracity Effect', *The American Economic Review*, March, pp.22–46.

Wei, S.-J. (2000): 'Negative Alchemy? Corruption and Composition of Capital Flows', OECD Development Centre Technical Paper No.165, Oct.

Spain in the EU:
Fifteen Years May Not Be Enough

MANUEL BALMASEDA and MIGUEL SEBASTIÁN

INTRODUCTION

Europe has been the driving force of economic policy in Spain over the last four decades and the key factor behind the modernization and globalization of the Spanish Economy. The accession to the EEC in 1986 was a crucial step in the process of economic and political integration. The process, however, began much earlier, with the implementation of measures (increased competition, privatization of public enterprises, industrial restructuring, deregulation) aimed at modernizing and improving the efficiency of the Spanish economy. These changes, which made possible the accession of Spain to the EU, initially, and made it possible for Spain to become a founding member of the European Monetary Union (EMU), later, were not without cost. Spain's real convergence with Europe ceased for a decade while the reforms were implemented.

The 15 years since can be considered, overall, a success story. Spain has achieved greater economic stability and is now an integral part of Europe, economically and politically. It is difficult, however, to disentangle the progress derived from greater economic liberalization from the progress derived from European integration and greater exchange rate stability (the entry of the peseta into the European Monetary System (EMS), initially, and, finally, the launch of the single currency).

In spite of this, the process is far from over. Spain's income per capita still stands at 84 per cent of the European average. The slow pace of reform, in particular in the labour market, with high labour costs leading to persistent unemployment, and an inappropriate policy mix in the late 1980s prevented Spain from reaping the full benefits of integration. In this sense 15 years may not be enough.

WHAT HAS EUROPE MEANT FOR THE SPANISH ECONOMY?

The process of European integration has conditioned the progress the Spanish economy has made over the last 25 years. Two phases can be distinguished in this period: a transformation phase, between 1975 and 1986, and a converging phase, post-1986. During the first period Spain had to implement an important programme of reforms that had a high cost in the short term. Gross domestic product (GDP) per capita with respect to Europe fell eight points, from 81 per cent in 1975 to 73 per cent in 1986, and unemployment climbed to 21 per cent at the end of the period from 4.6 per cent. This transformation period laid the foundations for the subsequent expansion. The processes of industrial restructuring and land reform were carried out. Subsidies were lowered and the labour market was reformed. Simultaneously, Spanish markets went through an important process of liberalization and foreign exposure, beginning with the privatization of state enterprises and the deregulation of the overly regulated Spanish economy. During this hard process Europe, besides remaining the objective of economic policy, served as a credible excuse for the implementation of policies that, although necessary for long-term growth, induced high short-term costs and, hence, did not have domestic backing.

Once the economic structure was modernized, Europe continued to guide economic policy. The integration of the European economies called for fiscal harmonization and consolidation, increased exposure to foreign markets, the liberalization of capital flows, nominal convergence, and the independence of the Central Banks. In this process Europe continued to serve as an excuse for the implementation of unpopular policies, such as labour reform, privatization, deregulation, foreign direct investment in Spain, and the reduction of subsidies.

European integration was, overall, quite beneficial for the Spanish economy. This is not to say, however, that it did not also induce some costs that will perpetuate. Europe is responsible for the not-so-efficient agricultural policy or fishing policy and has pervaded Spanish external relations, in particular with Latin America. Additionally, the rigidities in the EU in both the labour market and the product markets, and the inherent protectionism of the EU represent a dead weight for the perspectives of Spanish potential growth.

As a whole, the impact of European integration on the Spanish economy can be summarized as efficiency improving and competition fostering. To this end the process of nominal convergence and the external opening of the Spanish economy were crucial.

THE EXTERNAL SECTOR AND FOREIGN DIRECT INVESTMENT

External Sector

The lowering of trade barriers, the suppression of import tariffs, the adoption of economic policy rules (quality standards, harmonization of indirect taxes), and the increasing mobility of goods and factors of production that comes with greater economic integration, together with the lower cost of transactions and greater exchange rate stability associated with the single currency, have boosted trade and enhanced the openness of the Spanish economy. To the extent that, in an open economy, a country's external trade is one of the most important and fastest vehicles for the transmission of shocks, it is interesting to review how Spain's trade links have evolved in recent years. This aspect is particularly relevant in today's context in which neither the exchange rate nor monetary policy can be used as mechanisms to correct the impact of asymmetrical shocks on EMU economies.

Exports, imports, and the degree of openness. Although the opening-up of the Spanish economy has been gradual,[1] one of the key dates was undoubtedly Spain's entry into the EEC because of its implications for the performance of the external sector. The large-scale tariff dismantling required by economic integration and the introduction of value added tax as of 1986 clearly had an impact on the performance of Spain's external trade,[2] and, specifically, on exports and imports, the responses of which to the new situation differed markedly. From Figure 1 it is evident that, whereas imports of goods and services in real terms as a proportion of GDP rose sharply (to 13.6 per cent in 1987 from 9.6 per cent in 1984), the share of exports shrank slightly (to 15.8 per cent of GDP from 16.6 per cent in 1984). As a result, the degree of openness of the Spanish economy increased sharply, although entirely because of the expansion in imports (there was therefore a simultaneous deterioration in the trade deficit).

Among the factors that account for the divergent performance of exports and imports are the following:

(1) Large-scale tariff dismantling;[3]
(2) A shift in consumer spending toward imported durable goods, as consumers showed their preference for goods which prior to 1986 were subject to a high level of protection, and which, therefore, only accounted until then for a small portion of total imports (on customs data, imports of consumer goods represented 9.6 per cent of the total in 1981, compared with 20.4 per cent in 1988);

FIGURE 1
SPAIN'S EXPORTS AND IMPORTS (as % of GDP)

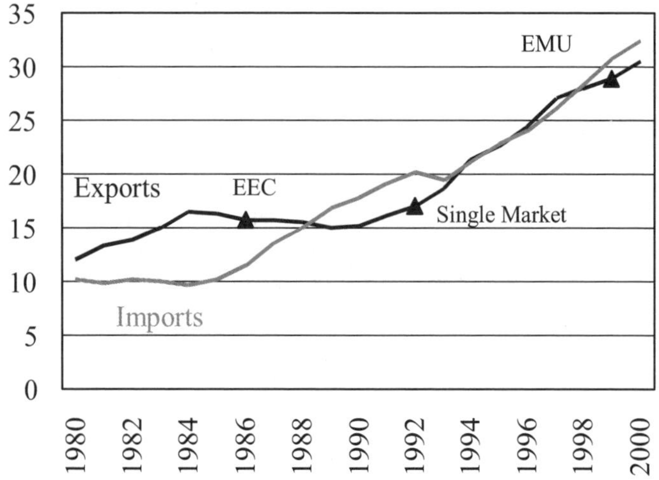

Source: Ministerio de Economía.

(3) An overvalued currency (between 1985 and 1992, the nominal effective exchange rate of the peseta against the Organization for Economic Co-operation and Development (OECD) countries appreciated by 5.4 per cent, while the real effective exchange rate rose by 18.6 per cent);

(4) The scrapping of most state export subsidies;

(5) A production structure that specialized in labour-intensive goods; and

(6) A much faster pace of economic expansion than in the rest of Europe (Spanish GDP registered a 16.7 per cent advance during 1982–87, as compared to 13 per cent in the EU), which pushed up the rate of expansion in imports even further.

The opening-up process and the growing competition of the newly industrialized economies of Asia and Latin America, specializing in the production and marketing of the same kind of goods as Spain, prompted a wholesale restructuring of Spanish exports. As a result of this adjustment, the impact on the external sector of the launch of the single market on 31 December was much smaller. The Spanish economy therefore continued to open up but, in contrast to the previous period, exports were now playing a decisive role. The successive devaluations of the peseta (1992, 1993, and 1995) and the associated gains in competitiveness provided a positive stimulus to sales of Spanish goods overseas (from 17.1 per cent of real GDP in 1992 to 27 per cent in 1997), whereas imports slackened off at the beginning of the 1990s (they contracted by 5.3 per cent in 1993), reflecting the deep recession gripping the Spanish economy. In 1999 trade represented 56.4 per cent of GDP.

As in 1986 and 1992, the structural change that took place in the European Union in 1999 will bolster the opening of the Spanish economy. The lower cost of transactions associated with the single currency (Spain's trade with the euro zone represents around 60 per cent of total Spanish trade) and the reduction (elimination) in exchange rate volatility will encourage trade between the member countries of EMU. Rising trade flows have resulted in a greater cyclical alignment of the EMU economies since 1992 and will therefore help dampen Spain's economic cycle and developments in the external sector.

Whereas the changes to the production structure, and hence in the structure of exports,[4] will clearly work to stave off the large deterioration witnessed in Spain's external balance when the economy opened sharply in the past (1986 and 1992), indicators of the degree of competitiveness of the Spanish economy (human capital skills, stock of capital, technological capital) show that significant differences remain in comparison to the developed economies. This confirms the need to press ahead with the structural reforms required to enhance economic efficiency.

Exchange rate volatility and openness. Like the single currency, the elimination of exchange rate volatility promotes trade by reducing costs. Doménech and Taguas (1999) analyse how the increased stability of the euro against the dollar, in comparison to the stability shown by the peseta against the dollar in the past, can affect trade flows and hence the degree of openness of the Spanish economy. They confirm that the impact on exports and imports, and therefore on the openness of the economy, of a fall in exchange rate volatility is likely to be far more muted than the effects of tariff dismantling prior to Spain's entry into the EEC in 1986. On their estimates, in the long run the growth rate of both exports and imports is likely to rise by only a little over one per cent. The impact on the trade balance would therefore be virtually zero, although the openness of the Spanish economy would experience a permanent increase of just over one per cent.

Foreign Direct Investment (FDI). The evolution of net FDI in Spain can be split into two clearly defined periods. In the first, which runs to the mid-1990s, the Spanish economy is a net recipient of foreign capital while, in the second, Spain is a net investor overseas. That is, it shifts from being a debtor economy to being a creditor economy.

What are the variables behind this shift? When Spain applied to join the EEC at the end of the 1970s, the perception of foreign investors with regard to the economy's growth prospects changed. As a result, FDI in Spain began to rise, slowly at first, in line with the progress being made in the negotiations, and then quickly, after EEC entry in 1986. The process of opening to international trade, improved potential for growth, falling production costs (lower wages), and lower risk premia in response to the brighter macroeconomic outlook (economic reforms) account for the increase in FDI in Spain. FDI has very positive implications for the economy. Being permanent in nature, it facilitates the transmission of technology and paves the way for advances in productivity and, hence, increases the economy's potential GDP growth. In addition, the higher the level of FDI, the greater will be the availability of capital for funding investment.

Figure 2 shows the evolution of FDI both into and out of Spain in terms of GDP. The expansion in FDI in Spain in the 1980s was due to the

FIGURE 2

FOREIGN DIRECT INVESTMENT (as % of GDP)

Source: Bank of Spain.

country's imminent entry into the EEC and a general increase in FDI flows world-wide during those years. Subsequently, after reaching a peak in 1990 (2.7 per cent of GDP), inflows of capital from the rest of the world began to decline because of the recession in Europe (Spain's biggest investor) and the greater appeal of other developing economies with stronger growth prospects (Asia and Latin America). This decline in FDI in terms of GDP, together with the expansion already showing up in Spanish FDI abroad, resulted in Spain becoming a net investor of capital (rather than a recipient country as hitherto). Indeed, in recent years, Spain has become one of the biggest international investors. It ranked sixth in the world in the year 2000 according to UNO (United Nations Organization) data on foreign investment. According to Bank of Spain data, Spanish FDI abroad amounted to 9.6 per cent of GDP in 2000. Specifically, Spain is now one of the main investors in Latin America, not only in relation to its GDP but also in absolute terms. The increase in Spanish FDI abroad is a reflection, on the one hand, of how markets have become more international and, on the other hand, the degree of maturity reached by the Spanish economy and the need to seek out new markets with potentially higher returns.

The increase in FDI in Spain in the year 2000 does not represent a change in trend. Rather, it was the result of one-off operations by large companies (telecommunications operators) within the European Union. Moreover, the degree of maturity reached by the Spanish market, and the potential siphoning-off effect on European capital flows of EU enlargement into Central and Eastern Europe, suggest that FDI in Spain will fall back in the coming years. Spain is likely, therefore, to continue to be a net investor country.

This investment process will produce a future flow of funds toward Spain in the form of earnings by Spanish companies abroad. Although not reflected in GDP, this will translate into an increase in gross national product (GNP) and hence in the incomes of Spanish people. GDP estimates the sum of added values generated domestically in an economy over a specified time period. GNP, meanwhile, corresponds to the value added by factors of production owned by domestic residents over the same period. GNP therefore equals GDP plus net payments to factors affected by the rest of the world. Currently, because Spain has traditionally been a net recipient of FDI, income accruing to foreigners abroad exceeds that accruing to domestic residents, so that GDP is around 1–1.5 per cent higher than GNP. As a result of the Spanish economy's big overseas investment drive in recent years, however, inflows of income will grow at a faster pace than outflows, leading to a net positive flow some time in the future. In the last five years, the Spanish economy has gone from being a net recipient of investment (0.2 per cent of GDP in 1996) to being a net exporter of capital (3.1 per cent of GDP in 2000). If net investment sustains the growth rate witnessed in the last few years, it is reasonable to assume that income from abroad will exceed that paid to the rest of the world in less than a decade. The major overseas investment undertaken by the United States up to 1950, for example, prompted net income from investments abroad to rise from 0.47 per cent of GDP at the end of the Second World War to 1.3 per cent of GDP at the end of 1970s.

Consequently, when assessing future gains in individuals' living standards derived from economic growth, it is necessary to bear in mind that, thanks to the large investment effort by Spanish firms abroad, the increase in incomes in the economy will be higher than that reflected by GDP growth. The faster the growth rate of GNP, the larger this extra cushion will be. In addition, the diversification of the sources of income in line with the rise in overseas earnings will result in a decline in the volatility of individuals' incomes, as the cyclical component associated with the evolution of GDP is dampened.

NOMINAL CONVERGENCE

While accepting the beneficial effects on long-term growth of greater economic stability, the short-term costs associated with lower inflation and the deficit-reduction process delayed, in the case of Spain, the adoption of the economic policy measures needed to correct these imbalances until the admission criteria for EMU were established. Given the rigidities exhibited by the European economies, the surrender of monetary policy and exchange rate control as instruments for dealing with asymmetrical shocks to the European Central Bank calls for a degree of nominal homogeneity among EMU countries.

Nominal convergence has been the paramount objective of Spanish economic policy since 1993. As the achievement of the Maastricht criteria became possible, the financial markets rewarded Spain with a higher probability of accession to EMU. It also allowed for the reduction of inflation expectations and the enhanced the credibility of fiscal policy, giving rise to a virtuous cycle that, at the end, made it possible for Spain to meet the criteria and become a founding member of the EMU.

FIGURE 3
PROBABILITY OF SPAIN JOINING THE EMU

Source: J.P. Morgan.

INFLATION

Inflation first began to fall at the end of the 1970s as a result of the new
monetary policy framework adopted by the Bank of Spain. It began to
announce a targeted growth rate for the monetary aggregate M3, and the
signing of the 'Pactos de la Moncloa'. These developments led to
inflation being reined in from rates in excess of 20 per cent at the end of
the 1970s to around five per cent in 1987. After Spain joined the EEC in
1986, the exchange rate became a key variable in the design of monetary
policy. Monetary policy had to play a dual role: maintain exchange rate
stability with other EEC currencies and bring down inflation. The need
to converge toward the inflation rate of the major EEC countries saw
interest rates rise to quite high levels, generating upward pressure on the
peseta. Achieving compatibility between the external goal of averting
sharp exchange rate fluctuations and the internal goal of controlling
inflation was therefore difficult. With the Spanish economy overheating,
and the consequent worsening of imbalances (external deficit and
inflation), inflation rose again, to stand at around 6.5 per cent in the
summer of 1989. After the peseta entered the EMS,[5] with fluctuation

margins of +/-six per cent, pressure on the exchange rate eased. The Bank of Spain held interest rates high so that inflation again began to trend downward. The need for a stable peseta within the EMS placed restrictions on monetary policy, however, meaning that it alone could not bring inflation down to the rates prevailing in other countries. In addition, also hindering the correction of inflation (at a time of economic recession), were the increase in the public deficit, from three per cent of GDP in 1988 to a peak of 6.7 per cent in 1993, and the wage policy of the early 1990s, in which employee compensation rose by 10.4 per cent on average in 1990–92.

The nominal divergence among the member countries of the EMS stood in the way of monetary policy coordination. Following the drawing up of the Maastricht criteria, economic policies in Spain were aimed at securing compliance with the reference values. Wage moderation and the granting of independence to the Bank of Spain (1994),[6] which brought the introduction of annual inflation targets, allowed expectations of inflation to diminish, as the likelihood that Spain would form part of EMU increased. After 1996 the Spanish economy experienced a sharp disinflationary process. The growth rate of prices fell from 4.3 per cent in December 1995 to two per cent at the end of 1997, paving the way for Spain to meet the Maastricht requirement. Although the inflation differential with EMU continued to decline in 1998 (from 0.6 to 0.2

FIGURE 4

INFLATION (%)

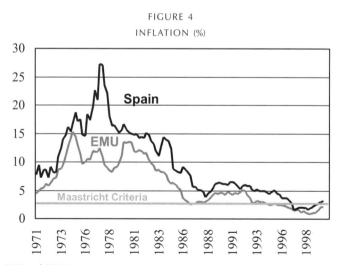

Source: INE and BBVA

percentage points), the rigidities of the Spanish economy prevented further progress. This became apparent in 1999 and 2000, as a result of the reversal of the conditions that had permitted a favourable evolution of the more erratic price components (commodity and food price developments in 1998) and the expansionary character of the policy-mix.[7] The inflation differential with EMU widened to 1.1 and 1.3 percentage points in 1999 and 2000, respectively. The reduction in inflation until 1998 was underpinned by the favourable evolution of the more erratic components of the price index, rather than by economic policies aimed at generating greater market efficiency and flexibility (the inflation differential with EMU in the services sector – which in 1997 was one percentage point, as against 0.3 points for inflation overall – widened in 2000 to 1.8 percentage points).

This inflation performance is a cause for concern, since it represents a loss of competitiveness *vis-à-vis* the EMU, which accounts for around 60 per cent of Spanish trade, and because of the impact in the formation of inflation expectations and their pass-through to wage demands. It must be remembered that wage moderation is one of the keys of the recent cyclical expansion of the Spanish economy. The inflation differential is not the result of a faster rate of productivity growth and is not, therefore, the natural consequence of the convergence process of an economy with a lower per capita income (the Balassa-Samuelson hypothesis). The risk of the inflation differential becoming permanent arises because of the 'double' inflation problem of the Spanish economy; that is, an inflation differential with EMU in both the non-tradable and the tradable sectors. Spain has thus gone from being a country with dual inflation (systematically faster growth in the prices of services than in those of goods) to one with 'double' inflation. Furthermore, the impossibility of resorting to competitive devaluations, as in the past, magnifies the costs associated with the inflation differential due to surplus demand and market inefficiency, as it could lead to a permanent and cumulative loss of competitiveness of the Spanish economy.

In view of the costs that the empirical evidence and theory attribute to inflation, the disinflation process has positive implications for the economy in the long run. First, inflation increases the opportunity cost of holding money, reduces the demand for labour, and introduces inefficiencies in the economy through its interaction with the tax system (inflation reduces real after-tax earnings). In addition to this, the uncertainty generated by inflation with respect to the evolution of the structure of relative prices in an economy leads to inefficient resource

FIGURE 5

INFLATION DIFFERENTIAL: SPAIN VERSUS EMU

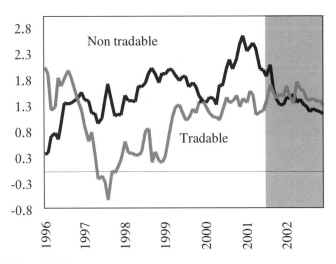

Source: INE and BBVA.

allocation. Many studies have found a negative relationship between inflation and growth in the medium term. For Spain, papers by Andrés and Hernando (1996 and 1997)[8] and Andrés, Hernando and Krüger (1996) conclude that inflation reduces real per capita income growth over an extended period of time, there being a permanent impact on the level but not on the growth rate.

Although empirical evidence indicates that the reduction of inflation improves the long-term growth outlook, a fall in inflation has short-term costs in terms of unemployment. And the lower the flexibility of the labour market, the greater the costs. The decline in inflation in Spain since the end of the 1970s coincided with the rise in unemployment. Thus, whereas the annual rate of inflation fell from 24.5 per cent in 1977 to 8.8 per cent in 1985, the unemployment rate jumped from 5.3 per cent of the labour force to 21.6 per cent. Surging unemployment was not simply due to the adoption of policies targeted at reining in inflation, however, but also reflected the dismantling of the protectionist barriers that had shaped Spain's production structure during the dictatorship. Despite the short-term cost of the disinflation process, in the medium and long term, a more efficient allocation of resources and lower inflation expectations, which allow greater price stability, should raise the growth rate of output and hence reduce unemployment. In the second half of the 1990s, there was a simultaneous decline in both inflation and unemployment rates, from an annual rate of 4.9 per cent in 1995 to 2.5 per cent in 2000 in the former, and from 22.9 per cent to 13.2 per cent in the latter. Although this decline has been linked to the impact of the labour market reforms approved since 1994 (1994, 1997, 1998, and 2000),[9] the continuation of a high structural rate of unemployment (above 15 per cent since 1998), following a sharp fall in the early 1990s (from 27.2 per cent in 1990 to 15.6 per cent in 1995), seems to suggest that the simultaneous decline of inflation and the unemployment rate, rather than the result of labour market reform, was prompted by the wage moderation arising from the shift in trade union attitudes, and the fall in inflation expectations associated with Spain's participation in EMU.

PUBLIC FINANCES

With regard to fiscal policy, the persistence of generalized and continuing public deficits in the prospective EMU participants, and the credibility problems this could generate for the monetary policy of the future European Central Bank (ECB), made it necessary to include two convergence criteria in the Maastricht Treaty, limiting budget deficits to three per cent of GDP and debt to 60 per cent of GDP. After the long period of autocratic rule, the decade before Spain entered the EEC (1975–85) was characterized by the gradual adaptation of the country's institutions to the new environment and a sharp increase in the budget deficit resulting from rapid growth in spending. The development of public services and the creation of a welfare state, similar to that of more developed economies, together with the increase in public support for crisis-hit sectors, are some of the factors behind the rise in public spending (from 20.7 per cent of GDP in 1970 to 40.4 per cent in 1985). In spite of the increase in revenue from 22 per cent to 34.2 per cent of GDP, the result was a sharp deterioration in public sector finances, from a surplus of 0.6 per cent of GDP in 1970 to a deficit of 6.2 per cent in 1985. Reflecting this, public debt surged to 45 per cent of GDP by 1985, up from 17 per cent in 1980. The surge in public spending was partly responsible for the emergence of significant imbalances in inflation and the external sector after Spain joined the EEC.

After the peseta entered the EMS, the pursuit of restrictive monetary policies to offset the expansionary stance of fiscal policy only served to exacerbate the imbalances that had accumulated during the phase of expansion. Public spending rocketed over these years. The introduction of universal healthcare, wider unemployment benefit cover, the increase in public employment and investment policy took public spending up to 47.6 per cent of GDP in 1993, compared with 39.6 per cent in 1988. Following the economic crisis in the first half of the 1990s and the changes in the EMS, Spain's budget deficit rose once more, confirming that the slight correction seen in the public accounts during the expansion was simply due to the favourable economic context. Thus, in 1993 the budget deficit reached a peak of 6.7 per cent of GDP, as compared to three per cent in 1988, remaining at similar levels until 1995 (6.6 per cent of GDP). The inertia shown by spending led to an increase in the structural component of the deficit, which reached 5.3 per cent of GDP in 1993 (3.7 per cent in 1988). In this period, structural public spending rose steadily, confirming the expansionary nature of fiscal policy.

In order to strip out the impact of the economic cycle on the public accounts and assess to what extent fiscal policy was restrictive, we have constructed a fiscal indicator, corrected for the cycle, referred to as the

FIGURE 6

FISCAL IMPULSE (as % of GDP)

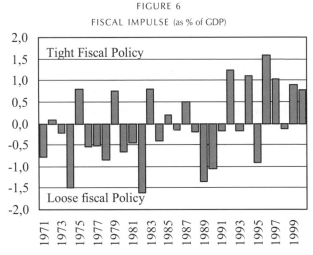

Source: Ministerio de Hacienda and BBVA.

fiscal impulse, which measures the difference between the structural deficits in two consecutive years. A positive fiscal impulse, therefore, indicates that fiscal policy was relatively more restrictive, and a negative value indicates it was more expansionary.

The expansionary nature of fiscal policy at the end of the 1980s and in the early 1990s is apparent in Figure 6. Thereafter, given the pressing need to lower the deficit to the three per cent ceiling by 1997, as stipulated by the Maastricht Treaty, the budget deficit was 2.8 per cent of GDP by 1997. As a result, the structural deficit came down by 2.6 percentage points, to stand at 2.5 per cent of GDP in 1997. Figure 6 confirms the markedly restrictive fiscal policy stance pursued in 1996 and 1997. Although the end of the process of expansion in spending, following the overshoot observed in previous years, is a positive development, an in-depth analysis of its composition shows that expenditure containment was based primarily on two headings that are unlikely to contribute to the same extent to the reduction of the budget deficit in the future. The first of these, interest payments, fell as a proportion of GDP by 0.5 percentage points, reflecting the positive impact of lower interest rates, whereas the second, public investment, declined as a percentage of GDP by 1.2 points. An end to the process of convergence in interest rates with Europe (interest rates on the Spanish Treasury's ten-year bonds fell by 490 basis points over a two-year period), and to the refinancing of debt issued at higher rates, suggests that this expenditure heading will make only a modest contribution to the reduction of the budget deficit in the periods ahead. Likewise, if further progress is to be made in real convergence with the more developed countries, the correction of the budget deficit should not be borne by public investment, in view of the beneficial impact it has on productivity and competitiveness.

In order to prevent deficits from rising as occurred in the past, and thus hampering the design of a single monetary policy, EU countries signed the Stability and Growth Pact, the aim of which was to establish a deficit ceiling (three per cent of GDP) and set the attainment of a balanced budget as a medium-term goal. During the latter part of the 1990s, Spain's budget deficit continued to fall (to -0.3 per cent of GDP in 2000) in response to growing fiscal pressure[10] (despite the 1999 IRPF reform), reflecting favourable economic conditions and lower interest payments (-1.4 percentage points). Although the structural deficit continued to shrink (it stood at around one per cent of GDP in 2000), the rate of decline was much slower than in the mid-1980s. Although this

FIGURE 7
SPAIN: STRUCTURAL DEFICIT (as % of GDP)

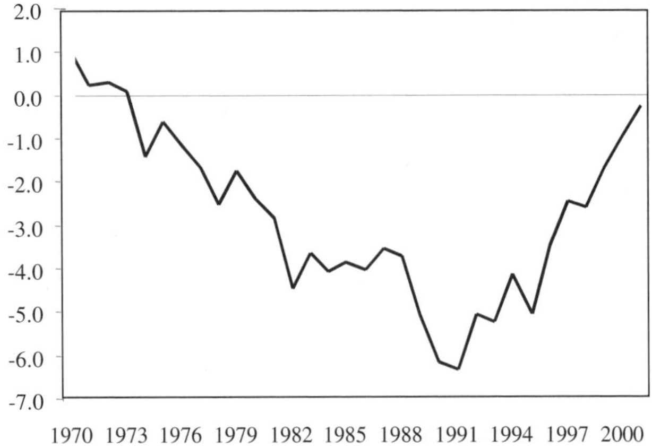

Source: BBVA.

would be sufficient to guarantee a budget deficit of below three per cent in a recession, it does not guarantee a balanced budget in the medium and long term.[11]

In contrast to the experience of Ireland, falling deficits and the favourable domestic economic scene in the second half of the 1990s did not bring about any significant decline in the level of public debt. Bearing in mind that privatization receipts since 1995 amounted to over 5.5 trillion pesetas, this development is particularly worrisome. Public debt in 2000 was still running above the 60 per cent of GDP limit set by the Maastricht Treaty, at 60.6 per cent of GDP. Given the stock of public debt at the end of 1995, and considering both the evolution of the budget deficit and privatization receipts, public debt should have fallen to below 55 per cent of GDP by 2000. Revenue from the sale of financial assets has been used to purchase new financial assets (allocations of loans and guarantees, share acquisitions, and so on). This confirms that, despite the shrinking corporate public sector, cash injections to public entities and loans extended have remained high.

INTEREST RATES

The correction of some of the key disequilibria in the Spanish economy (inflation and the budget deficit) has been accompanied by a decline in

FIGURE 8

PUBLIC DEBT (as % of GDP)

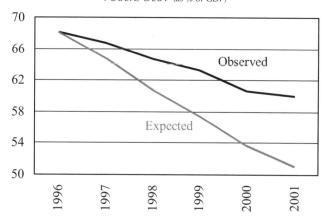

Note: Expected debt refers to the debt level if all privatization receipts had been dedicated to debt reduction.

Source: Ministerio de Hacienda and BBVA.

both nominal interest rates and their volatility. Ten-year rates fell from an average of 16.4 per cent in 1983 to a low point of 4.8 per cent in 1999. This reduction in rates, which is a reflection of the greater macroeconomic stability and the progress in convergence with the leading European countries, translated into a decline in the long-term interest rate differential between Spain and Germany. The narrowing of spreads sped up as markets priced in the growing probability that Spain would be among the first wave of entrants to the EMU. The probability of this occurring, which in mid-1996 was only around ten per cent, had risen to above 50 per cent by early 1997 and to over 75 per cent by the summer of that year. As a result, the interest rate differential shrank from 390 basis points in December 1995 to 100 basis points in January 1997, and to 30 basis points in January 1998, only marginally above an average level of 27 basis points since the launch of the EMU. Lower real interest rates reduce the cost of capital and hence bolster investment and the stock of capital.

However, economic growth is affected not only by the level of interest rates, but also by their volatility. In keeping with the Fisher equation, the

FIGURE 9

LONG-TERM (TEN-YEAR) NOMNAL INTEREST RATES (%)

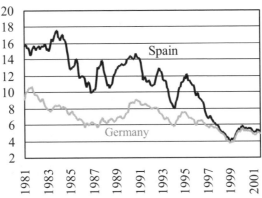

Source: Bank of Spain.

main component of the volatility of nominal interest rates is the volatility of inflation expectations. In so far as the EMU provides a more stable environment, uncertainty seems set to fall. Sebastián and Taguas (1998) find that a permanent reduction in the volatility of Spanish interest rates to close to the historical volatility of German rates raises the growth rate of per capita GDP in the Spanish economy by 0.5 percentage points.

The process of nominal convergence has prompted a reduction in real interest rates. At the end of the 1970s, real interest rates began to rise, reaching an average level that was much higher than in the previous decade and much higher than in the EMU (7.7 per cent and 6.7 per cent, respectively). From 1999 onward both the level of interest rates and the differential started to come down, with the exception of 1995, to stand at around three per cent in both Spain and the EMU at the end of the period. Lower inflation expectations and the correction of the budget deficit lie behind the decline in real interest rates, as these simply reflect the lower risk premium charged on Spanish assets. The decline in Spain's budget deficit has positive implications for national saving and hence for interest rates.[12] There is an estimated statistically significant negative relationship between fiscal surpluses and real interest rates in Spain (the estimated coefficient is -0.65, similar to the one estimated for the EMU: -0.62). This implies that a two per cent increase in the budget deficit corresponds to a rise of approximately one point in real interest rates.[13]

REDISTRIBUTION POLICIES IN THE EU BUDGET:
THE ROLE OF STRUCTURAL AND COHESION FUNDS

The structural funds (reformed in 1988) and cohesion funds (1992)[14] are the instruments designed by the European Commission to develop social and cohesion policy within the European Union (Table 1 summarizes the importance of EU funds in the four cohesion countries). These funds, which amount to just over one-third of the EU budget, have contributed significantly to reducing regional disparities and fostering convergence within the EU. They have played a prominent role in developing the factors that improve the competitiveness and determine the potential growth of the least developed regions.

During 1994–99 EU aid accounted for 1.5 per cent of GDP in Spain (3.3 per cent in Portugal). This is set to fall slightly in 2000–6, to 1.3 per cent of GDP. The decline reflects, on the one hand, a reduction in structural funds over the new programming horizon (structural funds will represent around 0.3 per cent of European Union GDP in 2006, compared with 0.45 per cent in 1999) and, on the other hand, the impact of enlargement (accession aid). This fall-off in funding will clearly affect the long-term growth of the Spanish economy.

The volume of funding has been so large that these funds cannot be omitted from any analysis of the impact of EMU on potential growth in the economies of the cohesion countries. In fact, these funds have made it possible to lessen the negative impact in the short run of compliance with the nominal convergence requirements. Specifically, the negative impact on public investment and hence on the stock of capital of

TABLE 1
STRUCTURAL AND COHESION FUNDS

	Greece	Ireland	Spain	Portugal
GDP %				
1989–93	2.6	2.5	0.7	3.0
1994–99	3.0	1.9	1.5	3.3
2000–6	2.8	0.6	1.3	2.9
% on Gross Fixed Capital Formation				
1989–93	11.8	15.0	2.9	12.4
1994–99	14.6	9.6	6.7	14.2
2000–6	12.3	2.6	5.5	11.4

Source: European Commission. Estimates based on Eurostat data and forecast for 2000–6.

the fiscal adjustment undertaken in Spain to bring the deficit below three per cent of GDP was less pronounced because of the take-up of EU funds.

Figure 10 displays the impact on public investment of EU funding in a number of EMU countries. It is interesting to note that the percentage of public investment financed by EU funds has been rising since 1985, to reach average values of 42 per cent for Greece, 42 per cent for Portugal, 40 per cent for Ireland, and 15 per cent for Spain from 1993 onward (the year the cohesion funds were ratified).

Given the importance of the structural and cohesion funds, the data series for public investment that exclude goods financed from EU funding give some idea of their impact on the stock of public capital and their contribution to the reduction of per capita income differences with the European Union. Figure 11 plots the effect of EU funds on the stock of public capital. Evidently, the cumulative impact of these funds at the end of the period under consideration is highly significant: 23.5 per cent in Portugal in 1977, 17.5 per cent in Greece, 13.2 per cent in Ireland, and six per cent in Spain. EU funding has allowed rates of public investment to remain relatively stable since the mid-1980s, despite the fact that part of the fiscal consolidation process has been achieved at the expense of funding for public infrastructure. These effects stand in marked contrast to the modest impact in net contributor countries. For instance, the impact in Germany and the Netherlands is estimated at -0.7 per cent and -1.1 per cent, respectively, at the end of 1997. EU funds have, therefore, contributed heavily to convergence in per capita stocks of public capital. In the absence of transfers, these differentials would have been 47.5 per cent for Greece, 44.5 per cent for Portugal, 22.4 per cent for Ireland, and 25.3 per cent for Spain, as against the observed differentials of 33.4 per cent, 35.2 per cent, 13.4 per cent, and 22.9 per cent, respectively.[15]

In a recent paper, departing from Solow's neo-classical model (1956), Doménech and Taguas (1999) estimate that the ratio of public investment in the Spanish economy in the past few years has been 0.5 per cent higher as a consequence of EU funding. This increase has in turn had a positive effect on private investment and per capita income in the long run. In the case of Spain, the cumulative long-term impact of EU funding is estimated to have produced a rise of 0.9 per cent in the rate of private investment and an increase in per capita income of 1.7 per cent.[16]

In its latest Cohesion Report (2001), the European Commission estimates the impact on GDP growth and employment in the cohesion countries of EU structural aid (Objective 1 funding, representing around

FIGURE 10

PERCENTAGE OF PUBLIC INVESTMENT FINANCED VIA STRUCTURAL FUNDS

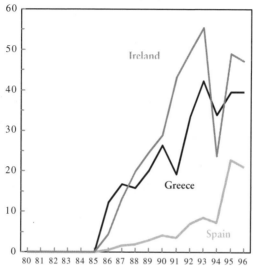

Source: Doménech and Taguas (1999).

FIGURE 11

PERCENTAGE OF PUBLIC CAPITAL STOCK FINANCED WITH EUROPEAN FUNDS

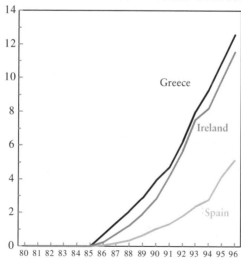

Source: Doménech and Taguas (1999).

70 per cent of the structural funds) approved in the last two EU budget-programming periods (1994–99 and 2000–6). Like Doménech and Taguas (1999), they find that the main beneficiaries are Greece and Portugal, where GDP rose by 9.9 per cent and 8.5 per cent, respectively, in 1999, relative to that forecast in the absence of aid. The increase in Spain and Ireland is smaller – 3.1 per cent and 3.7 per cent – although still significant.

As noted earlier, EU funding (structural and cohesion funds) is set to decline over the new EU budget-programming period, 2000–6 (see Table 2). Using the same methodology as in the previous case, the European Commission has estimated the impact on GDP of the structural funds at the end of the programme horizon. As might be expected, the impact weakens, but in relative terms much less in Spain than in the other countries. The estimated effect in 2006 is an increase in real GDP of over seven per cent for Greece and Portugal, 3.4 per cent for Spain, and 2.8 per cent for Ireland, relative to a scenario with no EU funding.

ESTIMATED IMPACT OF EMU ON GDP AND PER CAPITA INCOME

Doménech and Taguas (1999) analyse the effects on GDP growth of lower inflation, a shrinking public deficit and a more open Spanish economy resulting from economic and monetary integration in the EMU. They conclude that the long-term impact of EMU can be estimated to lead to a 3.3 percentage-point increase in the rate of private investment and a 10.4 per cent rise in per capita income.[17] With regard to the latter variable, the largest effect is generated by the fall in inflation (some 4.5 per cent), followed by the correction of the public deficit (3.8 per cent), EU funding (1.7 per cent), and finally the degree of openness (0.4 per cent).

The above estimates take no account of the short-term cost of the policies applied to secure compliance with the nominal convergence

TABLE 2

	Greece	Ireland	Spain	Portugal
1993	4.1	3.2	1.5	7.4
1996	9.9	3.2	1.5	7.4
2006	7.3	2.8	3.4	7.8
2010	2.4	2.0	1.3	3.1

Note: Deviation wrt a scenario without European Funds.

Source: European Commission, estimations based on HERMIN model (2000).

criteria laid down by Maastricht. Some studies undertaken for Spain reckon that this cost amounts to around one-third of the long-term benefits.[18] Applying this result to the estimates obtained by Doménech and Taguas (1999), the conclusion is that the net effect of economic and monetary integration is likely to translate into approximately a 5.1 per cent increase in per capita income.

REAL CONVERGENCE: FIFTEEN YEARS MAY NOT BE ENOUGH

Nominal convergence (interest rates, inflation, and public deficit) has been the primary objective of economic policy for the past five years. The success of nominal convergence is reflected in Spain's qualification as a founding member of the Economic and Monetary Union, and it is a necessary condition (but insufficient on its own) for real convergence to take place.

Nominal convergence is a necessary condition for two reasons. First, because an ECB monetary policy that inherits the credibility of the more stable countries of the European Union will translate into lower rates of inflation and dampen the volatility of inflation, which is just as important for uncertainty as the level of inflation itself. Second, a sustainable fiscal policy, as enshrined in the Stability and Growth Pact, will contribute to fiscal consolidation in the EMU as a whole. In addition, as noted above, this means that in the long run risk premiums will come down. Nominal convergence and its implications in terms of nominal stability and diminishing uncertainty, however, cannot by themselves produce real convergence.

In spite of the short-term costs of compliance with the nominal convergence criteria, the existence of irrevocably fixed exchange rates (lower volatility), the obligation to secure price stability (ECB target: to keep inflation below the two per cent ceiling in the medium term) and to hold the budget deficit below three per cent of GDP (the Stability and Growth Pact), and the continuing inflow of structural and cohesion funds have helped accelerate the process of real convergence with the major European economies.

In the past 40 years, Spain's per capita income has grown at a rate of 3.4 per cent annually. After correcting for purchasing power parity (PPP), per capita income has risen by 30 per cent more than the average of the European economies. That said, in 2000 Spain's per capita income was still only around 84 per cent of the EU average.

After advancing rapidly up to 1974, the convergence process slowed during 1975–84 as a result of the uncertainty associated with the political

FIGURE 12

SPAIN'S GDP PER CAPITA RELATIVE TO THE EU

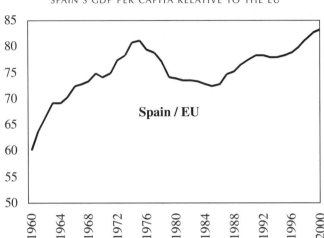

Source: European Commission and BBVA.

transition, a wages shock, and the two oil crises. From 1986 onward, however, the rate of convergence sped up again, continuing further in the 1990s. However, if economic growth were to outpace the European average by one point (as has occurred on average for the past 40 years), it would still take more than 15 years for Spain to converge with Europe.

What are the factors accounting for the real convergence of the Spanish economy? In order to illustrate them, per capita income is decomposed into a set of factors that reflect both the cyclical situation of the economy (productivity and the unemployment rate) and sociological (the participation rate) and demographic (working age population) aspects specific to each country. This gives:

$$\frac{Y}{POP} = \frac{Y}{L} * \frac{L}{L_S} * \frac{L_S}{WP} * \frac{WP}{POP}$$

where Y/POP is per capita income; Y/L labour productivity; L/L_S is: (1-unemployment rate); L_S/WP the participation rate and WP/POP is the working age population as a proportion of the total population.

An analysis of the above four factors shows that convergence has been greater in productivity than in per capita income, so that by 1996 productivity in Spain had virtually caught up with that of the EU as a whole. As regards unemployment, however, the process has been in the reverse direction, so that instead of convergence there has been divergence. After standing at below one point up to 1978, the unemployment rate differential between Spain and the EU had widened to 12 points by 1985, oscillating thereafter in line with the economic cycle, to stand at around six points in the year 2000. The participation rate, meanwhile, has remained stable in the EU, but fell in Spain during 1975–84, making a negative contribution to convergence. This comes as a surprise given the speed at which women entered the Spanish labour force over those years. This did not compensate, however, for the marked reduction in male participation rates. Finally, with regard to the demographic factor, the baby boom and a falling death rate have both helped raise growth in the working-age population and hence aided convergence. Looking forward, however, the demographic factors are expected to make a negative contribution both in Spain and the EU, although more intensely in Spain.

What contribution have these factors made to developments in per capita income? Table 3 and Table 4 report the average growth rate of each of these four explanatory factors, as well as per capita income in different sub-periods for both the Spanish economy and the EU as a whole.

Labour productivity has been the decisive factor behind Spanish per capita income growth, having risen in the past 40 years by 0.3 points more than per capita income, although its contribution is lower than in the 1990s (see Table 3). The most negative contribution has come from unemployment, which subtracted approximately 0.5 points from the average growth of per capita income. Its negative contribution was particularly pronounced in the years 1976–85, when it subtracted over two percentage points. The evolution of the participation rate has had virtually no effect, although the effect of women joining the labour force has been positive in the last ten years. Finally, the demographic factor has provided a slight positive contribution of close to 0.2 percentage points, but will gradually weaken as population ageing makes itself felt.

With respect to the European Union, in the past 40 years per capita income has grown by 2.4 per cent annually, a percentage point slower than in Spain. Productivity has risen by 2.6 percentage points, more than one point less than in the Spanish economy. The unemployment rate has also contributed negatively, but to a lesser extent than in Spain. Finally, the contributions of the participation rate and the demographic factor have on average been of the same sign, although in the latter case around half that of Spain.

TABLE 3

SPAIN: GROWTH RATE OVER THE PERIOD

	Y/POP	Y/Ls	L/L$_s$	L$_s$/WP	WP/POP
1960–75	5.43	6.28	-0.62	-0.06	-0.17
1976–85	0.70	3.06	-2.08	-0.80	0.53
1986–2000	3.02	1.54	0.55	0.64	0.29
1960–2000	3.38	3.71	-0.51	-0.01	0.19

Source: BBVA.

TABLE 4

EU: GROWTH RATE OVER THE PERIOD

	Y/POP	Y/L	L/L$_s$	L$_s$/WP	WP/POP
1960–75	3.37	3.81	-0.11	-0.14	-0.19
1976–85	1.73	1.94	-0.65	-0.15	0.59
1986–2000	1.78	1.53	0.06	0.15	0.59
1960–2000	2.44	2.56	-0.18	-0.03	0.09

Source: BBVA.

The growth differential of Spain *vis-à-vis* the European Union, practically one point for the past 40 years, may therefore be said to be almost entirely attributable to advances in productivity. Indeed, the increase in productivity observed in Spain would have resulted in a quicker pace of convergence had it not been for the larger negative contribution from unemployment.

In addition to economic policies designed to clear the way for gains in productivity, the sources of growth and real convergence in the Spanish economy should be based on: (1) the demographic factor – given the projections based on fertility rates, any significant change to this variable will depend on an appropriate immigration policy; (2) increasing participation (higher activity rates) – this calls for increasing numbers of women in the labour market and a raising of the retirement age (implying a reversal of recent trends in the Spanish economy); and (3) lower unemployment – this requires carrying out major structural reforms in the labour market and a larger stock of physical capital to boost demand for labour.

As already mentioned, the goal of economic and monetary integration in Europe, from an economic standpoint, is, first, to stimulate growth in EU countries as a whole and, second, to nurture the process of convergence between member countries. Spain's participation in the

EMU constitutes the culmination of the process of integration of the Spanish economy with the international environment. In this sense, compliance with the accession criteria for the Economic and Monetary Union, as laid down by the Maastricht Treaty, enabled the Spanish economy to converge nominally with the countries of the European Union. The momentum provided by this process has allowed per capita income to reach 84 per cent of the EU average in 2000, up from 73 per cent in 1986. Nonetheless, despite the great strides made, as mentioned above, even if the Spanish economy were to grow at a one-point faster rate than Europe in the years ahead, real convergence would still take more than 15 years to achieve.

In order to assess the convergence process of the Spanish economy, it is important to look at the course of convergence over time. Up to the mid-1970s, the Spanish economy experienced a high degree of convergence. From then on, the process stalled. As a result of the changes that took place in Spain's economy and society, the ensuing decade was one of divergence rather than convergence. The process was not resumed until 1986, partly because of the impetus provided by membership of the European Union. After 1975, Spain's economic and institutional structure had to be modernized and internationalized, shifting from a highly rigid and controlled economy to a more flexible and open one. These years witnessed the industrial restructuring process, and the privatization of state enterprises got under way, clearing the way for considerable gains in efficiency. The Spanish experience in this decade should serve as a reference for the eastern European countries that are now caught up in the process of modernizing their economic structures and preparing their accession to the European Union. This suggests that, before the process of convergence with the rest of Europe begins, the Eastern European economies may experience a period of diminishing per capita income in relative terms. The duration of this transitory period will depend on the magnitude and depth of the reforms that are undertaken.

From 1986 on, the Spanish economy has been converging continuously with Europe in real terms, though with the United States this process stalled in the 1990s, owing to the strength of US economic growth over this period. Figure 13 shows Spanish per capita income vis-à-vis that of EMU and the United States. A look at the graph reveals how the process of convergence with the United States continued up to the mid-1980s, when real convergence ground to a halt. As a result, despite the considerable progress made, per capita income in the Spanish

FIGURE 13

CONVERGENCE OF SPAIN'S GDP PER CAPITA

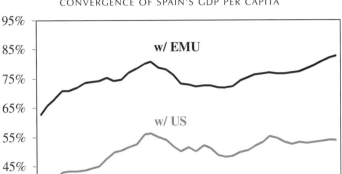

Source: European Commission.

economy is still less than 85 per cent of that of the European Union and under 55 per cent of that of the United States.

Nonetheless, the long-term behaviour of per capita income is determined by developments in productivity. In this case the Spanish and European experiences have been more positive in relation to the United States than those of per capita income. In Spain the apparent productivity of labour has reached 75 per cent of that of the United States and 80 per cent in the European Union (although the trend in the past five years has been in the opposite direction). The advance in US productivity in the 1990s, as a result of the impact of the technological shock connected with the 'New Economy', has led to a widening in the productivity gap between the United States and Europe.

For its part, the Spanish economy has registered even more spectacular gains in productivity than in per capita income, so that the productivity gap with Europe was almost closed by the mid-1980s. In 1960 the productivity of the Spanish economy was only 65 per cent of that of Europe and 33 per cent of that of the United States. By 1985 the apparent productivity of labour had converged with that of the European Union (97 per cent) and had risen to above 70 per cent of that of the United States. Since then Spanish productivity has deteriorated *vis-à-vis* Europe, whereas the gap with the United States has remained unchanged.

FIGURE 14

CONVERGENCE OF SPAIN'S LABOUR PRODUCTIVITY

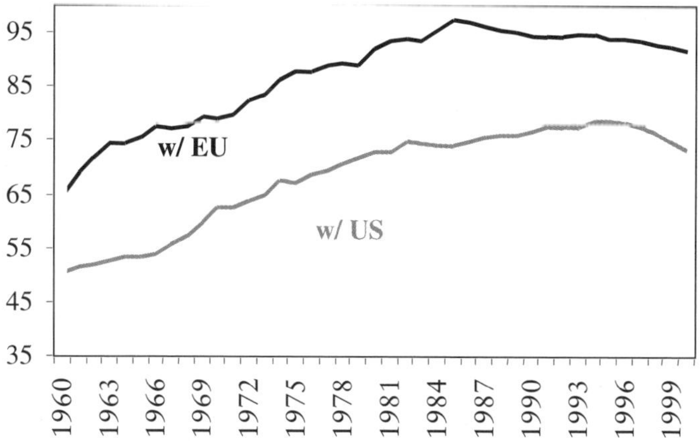

Source: European Commission.

In the past few years, however, Spanish productivity has grown at very moderate rates, widening the gap with the United States and the European Union which, in turn, has stopped converging with the United States.

Nonetheless, the convergence in productivity that took place during the 1980s was accompanied by a substantial rise in unemployment, which at one point climbed to above 20 per cent. Likewise, the fall in the unemployment rate since 1995 has coincided with productivity gains of less than one per cent annually. Estimates for the Spanish economy (De la Fuente and Doménech 2000) suggest that a decline in the unemployment rate relative to the European average would push up the productivity gap by some 13 points, there being only a small impact on per capita income.

In Table 5 it is evident that the productivity growth differential with the United States of both Spain and the EMU, having been positive up to 1990, has now turned clearly negative. As noted earlier, not only has the European economy stopped converging in terms of productivity with the US economy, but the gap is in fact getting wider. This development is particularly troublesome in Spain's case since, with lower productivity growth rates than in EMU, the process of real per capita convergence with the euro area is also likely to slow down. If these trends continue in the period ahead, it would seriously jeopardize the convergence process of the Spanish economy.

For a more comprehensive analysis of the behaviour of Spanish productivity, we must examine the factors governing its growth. For a global view of the situation, the evolution of other factors of production (capital), the degree of substitution between them and total factor productivity (TFP), which reflects technical progress in the economy, must all be taken into account. We use a neo-classical growth model to assess the apparent productivity of labour, allowing us to disentangle the contributions of physical capital per worker from the quality of human capital and TFP, measured as the portion of productivity growth that cannot be accounted for by the other factors.

The evolution of TFP is similar to that of the apparent productivity of labour. In Spain, as in the EMU, TFP slowed down continuously from 1970 onward. This slowdown was much more intense in Spain in the second half of the 1990s, however. From 1995 to 2000 TFP grew at an average rate of 0.2 per cent, lower than the 0.5 per cent rate observed in the EMU. The slower growth rate of TFP in the second half of the 1990s (of the major EMU countries only France recorded a clear recovery in

TABLE 5

LABOUR PRODUCTIVITY

	Spain	EMU	US
1961–70	6.5	4.9*	2.3
1971–80	4.1	2.9	0.9
1981–90	2.3	1.9	1.3
1991–2000	1.5	1.6	2.0
1995–2000	0.7	1.2	2.4

Note: *1964–70.

Source: BBVA.

TABLE 6

TOTAL FACTOR PRODUCTIVITY

	Spain	EMU	US
1961–70	3.2	2.4*	1.7
1971–80	1.0	1.0	0.5
1981–90	0.8	0.9	0.9
1991–2000	0.1	0.5	1.3
1995–2000	0.2	0.5	1.7

Note: *1964–70.

Source: BBVA.

TFP in this period), combined with the advance in TFP in the United States, has widened the differential existing between the economic regions under consideration. These differences reflect the technological gap of the Spanish economy overall relative to EMU and, particularly, to the United States. In fact, Spain is far behind other countries in the promotion of Research and Development (R&D). Investment in R&D, as a percentage of Spain's GDP, has hardly grown in recent years, and has remained below one per cent (compared with 2.6 per cent in the United States or 2.2 per cent in Germany). It remains at rates similar to Italy's spending on this heading in 1980 (see graph for R&D spending by country in 2000). For this reason it is impossible to state, at an aggregate level, that the Spanish economy, or to a lesser extent that of the EMU, is benefiting from the supply momentum created by the 'New Economy'.

The differences in the evolution of the apparent productivity of labour and total factor productivity between the United States and Spain are shown in Figure 15. It is evident that, whereas in the United States both TFP and apparent productivity have steadily increased their growth rate during the last ten years, in Spain (with the exception of the crisis at the beginning of the 1990s) they have slowed continuously.

Given the different behaviour of TFP in the United States, the EMU, and Spain, the convergence in productivity between these economies

FIGURE 15

LABOUR PRODUCTIVITY AND TFP GROWTH

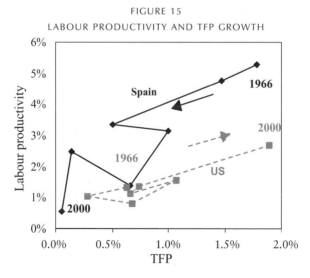

Source: BBVA.

must reflect developments in the other factors of production: physical capital per employee and human capital.

Tables 7 and 8 report the contributions of the stocks of physical and human capital to apparent productivity. The sharp increase in investment in the United States (investment in equipment and software has grown on average by 13.1 per cent annually during 1995–2000) has translated into a substantial contribution of the stock of capital per worker to apparent productivity growth since the second half of the 1980s, overtaking in the 1990s the high points reached in the 1960s. In the EMU and Spain, the situation is very different. Not only have the rates of the 1970s, much higher in both cases than those of the United States, not been equalled, but also the contribution of the physical capital stock has continued to fall, and in the second half of the 1990s was clearly lower than in the United States. The situation is worse still in Spain, where the contribution of the physical capital stock to the apparent productivity of labour, as a reflection of the process of substitution of labour by capital that took place in Spain before 1985 and between 1989 and 1993, has slowed

TABLE 7

CAPITAL PER EMPLOYEE'S CONTRIBUTION TO LABOUR PRODUCTIVITY

	Spain	EMU	US
1961–70	3.1	2.4*	0.4
1971–80	2.7	1.7	0.3
1981–90	0.9	0.8	0.4
1991–2000	0.9	0.8	0.6
1995–2000	0.0	0.4	0.6

Note: *1964–70.

Source: BBVA.

TABLE 8

HUMAN CAPITAL CONTRIBUTION TO LABOUR PRODUCTIVITY

	Spain	EMU	US
1961–70	0.1	0.3*	0.2
1971–80	0.3	0.3	0.2
1981–90	0.5	0.3	0.1
1991–2000	0.5	0.3	0.1
1995–2000	0.5	0.3	0.1

Note: *1964–70.

Source: BBVA.

down during the last phase of expansion. This may be a reflection, on the one hand, of the wage containment of the second half of the 1990s and, on the other hand, of the moderate increase in investment in relation to other economic expansions (an average of 8.4 per cent annually in 1995–2000, compared with 13.9 per cent in the second half of 1980s).

The stock of physical capital in Spain has increased twelvefold in the last 40 years, while in the same period it has only increased eightfold in the EU and threefold in the OECD. This represents an important impulse to convergence in this factor of production. The most important thrust took place in the second half of the 1980s, owing to the structural change that took place with Spain's entry into the European Community. Another factor (noted earlier) is the impact that the structural funds have had on the accumulation of capital in the Spanish economy (six per cent of Spanish public capital has been financed with European funds). The strong impulse toward convergence in the capital stock that took place in the second part of the 1980s had slowed considerably by the mid-1990s, with the result that convergence was not realized. The Spanish economy's physical capital stock is still around 70 per cent of the EU average, and is only higher than that of Portugal, Ireland, and Greece. As for public capital, the accumulated stock is a little higher than that of private capital (in EU terms), that is to say, 83 per cent of the EU average.

All in all, technical progress and the stock of physical capital have contributed only moderately to growth in the apparent productivity of labour in Spain, especially in the last decade. Its meagre relative advance is attributable, fundamentally, to the improvement registered in the quality of human capital. Unlike in the EMU and the United States, human capital in Spain accounts entirely for the slight increase in apparent productivity. This fact is compatible with the increase in the percentage of the working population with advanced studies (in 1977 21 per cent of the labour force had pursued their studies to a secondary or tertiary level; in 2000 this had increased to 71 per cent). This permits certain optimism concerning the future evolution of productivity, as human capital will permit a more efficient use of the new technologies.

Despite this, Spain's accumulated human capital is still significantly lower than that of neighbouring countries (around 75 per cent of that of the EMU). The challenge is to continue the process of convergence in human capital while increasing the participation rate to the European level.

A breakdown of the apparent productivity of labour using a production function also allows us to estimate the potential GDP growth of the economy. Thus, the GDP of the Spanish economy is estimated at between 2.6 per cent and 2.8 per cent, whereas those of the United States and the EMU, estimated using the same method, are around 3.5 per cent and 2.2 per cent, respectively. This implies that the income per capita in Spain will not converge in the medium term with that of the United States, and that, owing to the small growth differential with the EMU (approximately 0.5 per cent), it will take several decades for Spain to achieve convergence in real terms with the EMU.

Moreover, although important advances have already been made in restructuring the production system, more far-reaching reforms are still necessary to guarantee a sustained future growth. As mentioned earlier, the reforms carried out in the decade 1975–85 caused a slowdown in the convergence of the Spanish economy, but made room for the subsequent acceleration and allowed Spain, first, to enter the European Community and, later, to join the EMU. In spite of this, Spain still has one of the highest levels of regulation among OECD economies in both the labour market (collective bargaining, high firing costs, and so on) and in the goods and services market (regulation of trading hours, obstacles to the creation of companies, the slow judicial process). Thus a further impulse is necessary in order to place the Spanish economy among the most competitive in the world.

CONCLUSIONS

The Spanish experience within the EU has allowed its economy to become integrated internationally and to modernize, thus securing convergence in nominal terms with Europe. However, it still finds itself far from achieving one of its main objectives. In spite of the progress made, the Spanish economy has still to achieve convergence in real terms, reconciling convergence in productivity with that of other factors of production and with the creation of employment. In terms of convergence and growth in the long run, 15 years will not be long enough. Moreover, Spain must aspire not to convergence with the European average, but with the most developed countries, and in this process, we still have a long way to go.

NOTES

1. The Preferential Agreement signed in 1979 between Spain and the countries of the EEC boosted Spanish exports.
2. Although important strides had already been made in tariff dismantling, as of then: (i) the quantitative restrictions still in place for a number of products (consumer goods) were eliminated; (ii) the IGTE and luxury taxes were replaced by value added tax; (iii) final adjustments at the point of entry were scrapped; and (iv) the common external tariff was gradually adopted.

3. De la Dehesa, Ruiz and Torres (1991), Buisán and Gordo (1997), and Doménech and Taguas (1997) review the role of taxation in Spain's external sector.
4. In 2000 the technology-intensive sectors represented 22.4 per cent of total trade in manufactured goods, compared with 19.1 per cent in 1999.
5. Integration in an exchange rate mechanism like the EMS generates a credibility and discipline effect that contributes to a reduction in inflation expectations.
6. Fearing a reduction in firing costs as a consequence of the 1994 labour reform, the trade unions scaled back their wage demands.
7. The official ECB interest rate in 2000 was on average 4.0 per cent, whereas a Taylor-style monetary rule was recommending rates of over six per cent for Spain. The Spanish economy is at a more advanced stage of the cycle than the EMU as a whole and higher interest rates were needed. Fiscal policy has not been restrictive enough to offset the expansionary monetary policy stance, so that the policy-mix is expansionary for the cyclical position of the Spanish economy.
8. An average increase in inflation of one percentage point is found to raise the level of steady-state income by between 0.5 per cent to 0.75 per cent. This effect doubles if inflation is below five per cent.
9. A new labour market reform was approved in 2001 as an extension of the 1997 reform. The key issues such as collective wage bargaining, a generalized cut in firing costs, or changes to unemployment benefit were not addressed.
10. Tax revenue (including social security contributions) increased as a proportion of GDP by 1.4 percentage points.
11. In the case of the Spanish economy, estimates show that, in the event of a recession, the economic cycle is likely to swell the budget deficit by 1.5 percentage points of GDP, so that the maximum structural deficit compatible with the Stability and Growth Pact is of the order of 1.5 per cent of GDP.
12. Doménech, Taguas and Varela (1997) find that a four-point increase in the national saving rate raises the rate of GDP growth by 0.3 percentage points.
13. This result holds when the structural deficit is used, since the coefficient for the Spanish economy is estimated to be -0.66.
14. The creation of the cohesion funds was approved at the Maastricht summit in order to compensate for the efforts that countries with the lowest per capita income relative to the EU (Ireland, Greece, Portugal, and Spain) would need to make in the short term to comply with the nominal convergence criteria.
15. Spain is the biggest recipient of EU funds in absolute terms and, although when they are expressed in per capita terms the amount of funding decreases considerably, the differential with the EU is approximately ten per cent smaller than it would have been without such funds.
16. In the case of per capita income, the impact is measured in terms of deviations from the steady state that would have been reached in the absence of EU funding.
17. Inflation is assumed to fall from five per cent to two per cent, and the structural deficit from 6.6 per cent to two per cent; the degree of openness is assumed to rise at a constant four per cent rate, and EU funds are assumed to increase public investment by 0.5 per cent.
18. See Dolado, González-Páramo and Viñals (1997) and Andrés, Hernando and López-Salido (1998).

REFERENCES

Andrés, J. and I. Hernando (1996): '¿Cómo afecta la inflación al crecimiento económico? Evidencia para los países de la OCDE' [How does inflation affect economic growth? Evidence for the OECD countries], Documento de trabajo [Working paper], No.9602, Madrid: Banco de España.

Andrés, J. and I. Hernando (1997): 'Does Inflation Harm Economic Growth? Evidence for the OECD', Working paper, No.9706. Research Department, Bank of Spain.

Andrés, J., I. Hernando and M. Krüger (1996): 'Growth, Inflation and the Exchange Rate Regime', *Economic Letters* 53, pp.61–5.

Andrés, J., I. Hernando and D. López-Salido (1998): 'The Long Run Effect of Permanent Disinflation', Working paper, No.9825. Research Department, Bank of Spain.

Bachetta P. and M. Sebastián (1998): 'Farewell to the Peseta: Macroeconomic Aspects', *Situacion Spain*, Research Deparment, Banco Bilbao Vizcaya, July, pp.89–105.

Baldwin, R., J.F. Francois and R. Portes (1997): 'The Costs and Benefits of Eastern Enlargement: The Impact on the EU and Central Europe', *Economic Policy*, April, No.24, pp.97–105.

Balmaseda, M. *et al.* (2000): 'The Spanish Economic "Miracle": A Macro Perspective', *Situation Spain*, Research Deparment, Banco Bilbao Vizcaya Argentaria, June, pp.19–24.

Bosca, J.E., R. Doménech and D. Taguas (1999): 'La Política fiscal en la Unión Económica y Monetaria' [Fiscal Policy in the European Monetary Union], *Moneda y Crédito* 2008 [Currency and Credit 2008], pp.267–324.

Buisan, A. and E. Gordo (1997): 'El sector exterior en España', Banco de España – Servicio de Estudios, *Estudios Económicos*, p.60.

De la Dehesa, G., J.J. Ruiz and A. Torres (1991): 'Spain', *Liberalizing Foreign Trade*, Vol.6, pp.140–262.

De la fuente, A. and R. Doménech (2000): 'Human Capital in Growth Regressions: How Much Difference Does Data Quality Make?', CEPR, Discussion Paper, No.2466, Centre for Economic Policy Research.

Dolado, J.J., J.M. Gonzalez-Páramo and J. Viñals (1997): 'A Cost-Benefit Analysis of Going from Low Inflation to Price Stability in Spain', Working paper, No.9728, Bank of Spain.

Dómenech, R., D. Taguas and J. Varela (1997): 'The Effects of Budget Deficits on National Saving in the OECD', paper presented at European Economic Association 1997 (Toulouse), mimeo, Ministry of Finance.

Dómenech, R. and D. Taguas (1999): 'El impacto a largo plazo de la Unión Económica y Monetaria sobre la economía española' [The Long-Term Impact of EMU over the Spanish Economy], in *El euro y sus repercusiones sobre la economía española* [The Euro and Its repercussions Over the Spanish Economy], Fundación BBV, pp.92–138.

European Commission (1999): 'Report on Progress Towards Convergence and Recommendation with a View to the Transition to the Third Stage of Economic and Monetary Union, COM (1998).

European Commission (2000): *Public Finances in EMU*, Reports and Studies, No.3.

European Commission (2001): 'The Economic Impact of Enlargement', *Enlargement papers*, Directorate General for Economic and Financial Affairs.

Hernansanz, C. *et al.* (2001): 'El enigma de la productividad' [The Enigma of Productivity], *Situacion España* [Situation Spain], Research Deparment, Banco Bilbao Vizcaya Argentaria, June, pp.25–31.

Research Department, Banco Bilbao Vizcaya (1998): 'EU Structural Deficits', *Situacion Spain*, March, pp.28–9.

Research Department, Banco Bilbao Vizcaya (1998): 'The Competitiveness of the Spanish Economy', *Situacion Spain*, Nov., pp.47–8.

Research Department, Banco Bilbao Vizcaya (1998): 'Déficit públicos y tipos de interés reales' [Public Deficits and Real Interest Rates], *Informe anual* [Annual report].

Research Department, Banco Bilbao Vizcaya (1999): '¿Se cumple la hipótesis Balassa-Samuelson para la economía española?' [Does the Balassa-Samuelson Hypothesis Apply to the Spanish Economy?], *Situación España* [Situation Spain], Dec., pp.51–2.

Research Department, Banco Bilbao Vizcaya (1999): 'Los retos de la economía española' [The Challenges of the Spanish Economy], *Informe anual* [Yearly report] pp.171–7.

Sebastián, M. and D. Taguas (1998): 'Will EMU Affect Long-term Growth in Spain's Economy?' Working paper, Research Department, Banco Bilbao Vizcaya.

Solow, R.M. (1956): 'A Contribution to the Theory of Economic Growth', *Quarterly Journal of Economics*, Vol.70, pp.65–94.

Redesigning the Spanish and Portuguese Welfare States: The Impact of Accession into the European Union

ANA GUILLÉN, SANTIAGO ÁLVAREZ
and PEDRO ADÃO E SILVA

INTRODUCTION

The expression 'Iberian style' is sometimes found in the sociological and politological literature. However, whether the reaction of any Spanish or Portuguese citizen to such an expression ranges from shifting an eyebrow sceptically or showing sheer puzzlement, depending on personality and circumstance, it always elicits surprise and the absence of a clue as to what it may mean. Spain and Portugal do share several common historical developments and cultural traditions. Both countries were imperial powers during long periods of time, were ruled by monarchies, industrialized later than other EU members, went through protracted periods of authoritarian rule, share a strong Catholic religious tradition (resulting in a deep process of laicization during the last 30 years), and indeed are situated in a peripheral European region: the Iberian peninsula. Nonetheless, the list of differences bears at least equal importance. Apart from numerous historical (armed) conflicts that confronted the two Iberian countries, Portugal and Spain differ in many aspects nowadays. Spain is a monarchy and a deeply decentralized political system, whereas Portugal is a centralized republic. Their labour markets function very differently, and cultural attitudes and ways of life vary significantly. Last but not least, their social protection systems show distinct characteristics and evolutionary trends, as we will see below.

When dictatorships came to an end in both countries in the mid-1970s and a period of transition to democracy started, the Spanish and Portuguese economies were capitalist ones, and an intense industrialization process had already occurred. Their social protection systems showed most of the characteristics of an underdeveloped Bismarckian welfare state, segmented by occupational categories and suffering from broad gaps in the protection net. Expenditure on social protection was 18.1 per cent of gross domestic product (GDP) in Spain and 12.8 per cent of GDP in Portugal in 1980, which were much lower levels than the EU average at that time (24.3 per cent) and only higher than that of Greece (9.7 per cent). Both macroeconomic and social protection contexts have changed significantly since the countries' accession to the EU in 1986. This study endeavours to analyse the evolution of social protection between 1980 and the present. Has EU membership affected the development of the Portuguese and Spanish welfare states? Have their social protection systems 'Europeanized'? Before beginning the analysis, however, we need to know precisely what we mean by 'Europeanization'.

That the economic aspects of the European Union bear much more weight than the social and political ones is hardly news and has been profusely documented. Thus it is not necessary to insist on it here. However, integration into such a supranational entity is likely to have had some effect at the national (and sub-national) level not only as regards financing and expenditure trends in social protection but also on cultural and social attitudes and on the character of the policy process. It is our contention that even if direct impact (via compulsory normative) of the EU on social policy formation at the national level is reduced, there exists a 'European social model' that has evolved over time and to which Spain and Portugal have been attracted.

Studies on Europeanization of political frameworks and public policies are still scant. This is indeed a young field of research. Studies on Europeanization of social policies are even less common. Thus, we are confronting here a complicated task. Conceptual frameworks are crucial for any kind of study but they are even more so when addressing novel fields of research. Radaelli (2000), among others, has produced helpful progress in this respect and the empirical effort undertaken in this essay is based mostly in his unpacking and clarification of the concept of Europeanization. Radaelli (2000: 4) understands Europeanization as 'a set of processes through which the EU political, social and economic dynamics become part of the logic of domestic discourse, identities, political structures and public policies'. Further, Europeanization may be sharply distinguished from other processes such as convergence, harmonization, and political integration.

This essay aims to assess whether Europeanization of social policies has occurred in Spain and Portugal during the past two decades and, if so, to what extent. The first part of the discussion is devoted to the analysis of expenditure and financing trends and to finding out whether approximation or distancing to the EU standards has taken place. The second part focuses on the character of the reforms of the respective social protection systems to see if such systems have been Europeanized from a qualitative point of view. The third and final section contains a discussion of the factors that have influenced the distinct national trajectories observed in Portugal and Spain. Social protection is a very broad term that can be stretched to include almost any public action. This study is centered on a narrower, still precise, view of social protection, including income maintenance, healthcare, social services, and unemployment protection.

FINANCING AND EXPENDITURE TRENDS: APPROXIMATION OR DISTANCING?

This section consists of a quantitative analysis of the evolution of the social protection effort in Portugal and Spain for the period 1980–97 and its financing mechanisms.[1] Thus, it assesses the behaviour of the social protection systems of both countries from the years preceding entrance into the EU to the present in order to evaluate whether approximation to the average EU levels has occurred or a widening of the differential with other EU welfare states has been produced.

Evolution of Expenditure on Social Protection

The analysis of the evolution of social expenditure is organized into three sections. The first one evaluates the evolution of absolute levels of protection (as a percentage of GDP). The second one focuses on variations on intensity of social protection (per capita expenditure at purchasing power parities). The third one deals with the composition of social expenditure by function.

Absolute levels of social protection. The evolution of expenditure over GDP is considered a measure of absolute levels of social protection. As Figure 1 shows, the Spanish case is characterized by the persistence of a significant negative differential with respect to the EU average. Despite an increase of 3.4 per cent of the resources dedicated to social protection during the period considered, the differential with the EU average has not been reduced but has rather increased slightly from 6.2 points in 1980 to 6.8 points in 1997. On the contrary, Portugal, departing from much lower levels of protection, has ameliorated its position in comparison to Spain so that the differential with the EU average has been reduced by 50 per cent.

In the Spanish case the most intense approximation to the EU average took place between 1990–93, whereas social expenditure over GDP has decreased considerably since 1993 (2.6 points). Such a decrease is related to the effort of budgetary discipline undertaken by Spain in order to comply with the criteria for convergence for access to the European Monetary Union (EMU), affecting both the reduction of public deficit and public debt. Such budgetary discipline has not borne a similar effect in the Portuguese case, however, where social expenditure over GDP has continued to grow from 1993 onward. The behaviour of social expenditure presents a similar profile to that of public expenditure in Spain, although yearly increases in the former have tended to be much more moderate than the latter (see Figure 2).

In the Portuguese case (see Figure 3), the pattern of evolution differs significantly from the Spanish one. Public total expenditure, departing from higher levels than those of Spain, has decreased in the second half of the 1980s without affecting social expenditure. The main growth of social expenditure has occurred in the first third of the 1990s together with an important growth of total public expenditure. Both total public and social expenditure have tended to grow more moderately from then on, so that again social protection expenditure has not been affected.

The evolution may be appreciated more neatly in relative terms, that is, expressed as a percentage of the average of the EU in social protection expenditure. As Figure 4 shows, the amelioration of the relative situation of Spain between 1989 and 1993 was followed by a continued deterioration of its position up to 1997, related to budgetary restraints applied since 1994. In contrast, Portugal shows continued growth throughout the 1990s.

Evolution of the intensity of social protection. In order to check whether we are in the presence of a process of approximation of the Spanish and Portuguese social protection systems to those of their EU counterparts in terms of intensity of social protection, we use per capita expenditure in purchasing power parities as an indicator, a measure that allows to obviate differences in costs existing in each country.

Figure 5 (including differentials over the EU average) confirms that Spain showed an intensity of protection lower than the EU in 1980 and that such differential has not been significantly reduced. Conversely, Portugal, departing from a very low level, has upgraded its relative position although it has failed to reach the Spanish level of intensity in 1997.

FIGURE 1

EVOLUTION OF SOCIAL PROTECTION EXPENDITURE, % OF GDP, 1980–97

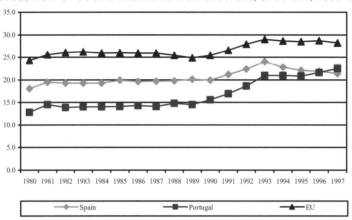

Source: Eudor-Stat 1997 and Eurostat 2000.

FIGURE 2

EVOLUTION OF PUBLIC EXPENDITURE, % OF GDP: SPAIN 1980–97

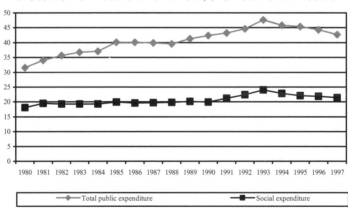

Note: Up to 1989, EU-12; from 1990, EU-15.

Source: Eudor-Stat 1997 and Eurostat 2000.

FIGURE 3

EVOLUTION OF PUBLIC EXPENDITURE, % OF GDP: PORTUGAL 1980–97

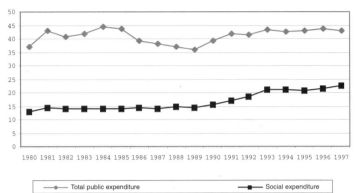

Note: *Up to 1989, EU-12; from 1990, EU-15.

Source: Eudor-Stat 1997 and Eurostat 2000.

FIGURE 4

EVOLUTION OF SOCIAL PROTECTION EXPENDITURE, % OF GDP (EU = 100)

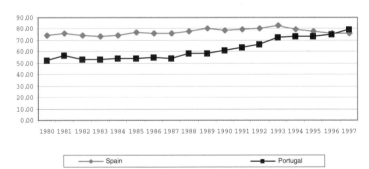

Note: *Up to 1989, EU-12; from 1990, EU-15.

Source: Own elaboration based on Eudor-Stat 1997 and Eurostat 2000.

Thus, comparisons of the evolution of per capita social expenditure leads us to reach conclusions different from those attained by analysing expenditure over GDP. In fact, no deterioration of the position of Spain may be ascertained *vis-à-vis* that of Portugal, despite the significant advances that were produced in the latter country. In the Portuguese case growth of per capita expenditure should be highlighted for it was multiplied by 5.4. Such increase was only surpassed by Greece (multiplied by 6.67), and it shows a much larger entity than that of Spain (3.6 times) or that of the EU average (3.17 times). Nonetheless, per capita social expenditure remained lower in Portugal than in Spain (53.77 and 61.81 of the EU average respectively).

In Table 1 the evolution of per capita social expenditure and per capita GDP is compared to the EU average. This comparison helps us observe stagnation in Spain in the second half of the 1990s as compared to growth in Portugal.

Composition of social expenditure. Let us turn to consider how the general evolution of social expenditure has affected the different areas of social protection. As may be observed in Figure 6, in the Spanish case in 1997, expenditures for illness, disability, and old age show percentages of total social expenditure similar to those of the EU average. Unemployment protection almost doubles the EU average, which is not

FIGURE 5

EVOLUTION OF SOCIAL PROTECTION EXPENDITURE, PER CAPITA, PPP (EU = 100)

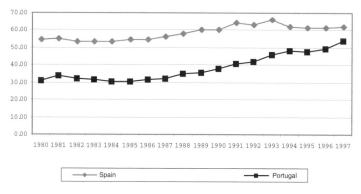

Note: Up to 1989, EU-12; from 1990, EU-15. PPP = purchasing pwer parity.

Source: Own elaboration based on Eudor-Stat 1997 and Eurostat 2000.

SPAIN AND PORTUGAL IN THE EUROPEAN UNION

TABLE 1

EVOLUTION OF GDP PER CAPITA AND SOCIAL EXPENDITURE PER CAPITA,
PPP (EU 15 = 100)

Year	Spain		Portugal	
	Expenditure on social protection, per capita, PPP (EU = 100)	GDP per capita, PPP (EU = 100)	Expenditure on social protection, per capita, PPP (EU = 100)	GDP per capita, PPP (EU = 100)
1980	54.52	70.4	31.23	55.2
1981	55.03	70.0	33.82	55.8
1982	53.53	70.2	31.93	56.2
1983	53.41	70.3	31.34	55.0
1984	53.22	69.6	30.32	52.7
1985	54.57	69.5	30.37	52.8
1986	54.35	69.7	31.41	54.1
1987	56.03	71.6	32.14	56.1
1988	57.12	74.6	34.85	58.1
1989	60.50	75.6	35.58	59.3
1990	60.00	76.5	37.99	60.7
1991	64.48	79.2	40.94	64.3
1992	63.31	79.1	41.94	65.4
1993	66.21	79.8	45.92	68.0
1994	61.74	77.9	48.00	69.8
1995	61.45	78.5	47.56	70.6
1996	61.35	79.3	49.20	70.2
1997	61.81	79.9	53.77	70.9

Source: Eudor-Stat 1997, Eurostat 2000 and European Economy, No.68, 1999.

surprising if we take into account that Spain bears the highest unemployment rate in the Union. At the other extreme, however, family protection is very low (one-quarter that of the EU average). Figure 8 shows such differences clearly.

Portugal, in turn, presents a share of expenditure dedicated to illness and disability ranking higher than the EU mean but showing lower levels than the average in the remaining social protection areas. In comparison with Spain, unemployment protection is lower in Portugal but family protection is significantly higher. When the volume of resources dedicated to each social policy area is analysed in terms of their proportion of GDP, Figure 7 reinforces the conclusions attained above.

Finally, Figures 8 and 9 show the evolution of social expenditure by function for the Spanish and Portuguese cases respectively.

FIGURE 6

SOCIAL EXPENDITURE BY FUNCTION
(% OF TOTAL SOCIAL EXPENDITURE), 1997

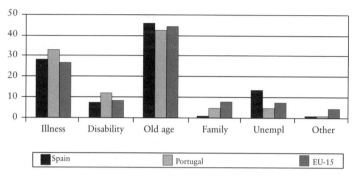

Source: Eudor-Stat 1997 and Eurostat 2000.

FIGURE 7

EXPENDITURE ON SOCIAL PROTECTION BY FUNCTION
(% of GDP), 1997

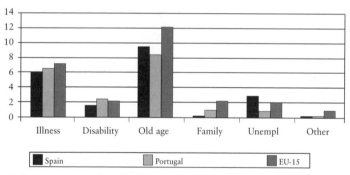

Source: Eudor-Stat 1997 and Eurostat 2000.

In the Spanish case it may be observed that:

- Expenditure on old age and survivors increased between 1990 (8.3 per cent) and 1993 (9.3 per cent) to stagnate in the following years at around 9.6 per cent of GDP.
- Expenditure on healthcare increased by one point, namely from 5.6 per cent in 1990 to 6.6 per cent in 1993, to decrease from then on to 6.0 per cent of GDP in 1997.

- Expenditure on disability stagnates at around 1.6 per cent for the whole period.
- The downward trend of social expenditure is concentrated mainly on the reduction of unemployment protection, from 5.1 per cent in 1993 to 2.9 per cent in 1997. Such a reduction was favoured by the fall in the unemployment rate from 20.3 per cent of the active population to 22.8 per cent between the same years.[2]
- Family protection and the rest of social protection programmes have remained at low levels, in particular, 0.4 per cent and 0.3 per cent of GDP respectively.

In the Portuguese case, the following trends are to be noted:

- A continued growth – if only decelerated in the central years of the decade – in old age and survivors' protection.
- Stagnation of unemployment protection (around 1.1 per cent of GDP), family protection (one per cent of GDP), and the rest of the social protection areas (0.2 per cent of GDP) throughout the 1990s.
- The significant weight of expenditure on healthcare, which conditions social expenditure in general. Expenditure on healthcare grew from 4.1 per cent to 6.5 per cent in 1990–94; it fell half a point in 1995 and then recovered again.
- Expenditure on disability also shows significant proportions throughout the whole period: around 2.5 per cent of GDP.

Financing of social protection. Figure 10 summarizes the different sources of financing of social protection systems, as a percentage of total expenditure on social protection. What the data in Figure 10 show is that the financing of social protection in Spain has relied and still relies fundamentally on employers' contributions, in a proportion that is the highest of the EU-15, whereas workers' contributions and public revenues are around five points below the EU average, and 'other sources' of financing show a very moderate proportion.

The Portuguese case is totally different from the Spanish one. Employers' contributions are ten points below the EU average – almost half of the weight of the contribution of employers in the Spanish context – with a significant reduction in the 1990s. Workers' contributions are also below the EU average and show a level similar to the Spanish one. The Portuguese social protection system relies mainly on public contributions. Finally, 'other sources' of financing (such as rents on properties, diverse transfers) double the EU level and triple the Spanish one.

FIGURE 8

SOCIAL EXPENDITURE BY FUNCTION (% OF GDP): SPAIN 1990–97

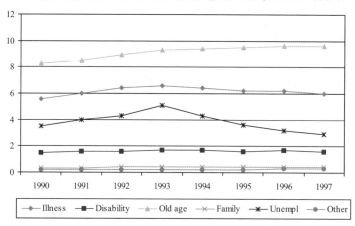

Source: Eudor-Stat 1997 and Eurostat 2000.

FIGURE 9

SOCIAL EXPENDITURE BY FUNCTION (% OF GDP): PORTUGAL 1990–97

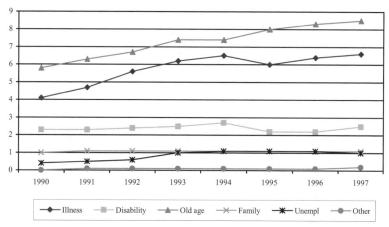

Source: Eudor-Stat 1997 and Eurostat 2000.

FIGURE 10

SOURCES OF FINANCING OF SOCIAL PROTECTION, 1997

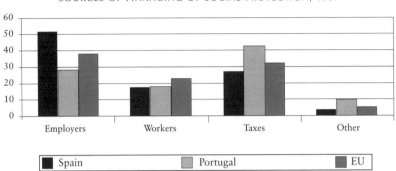

Source: Eurostat 2000.

To sum up, while Portugal has showed more success in the approximation of social protection expenditure to EU standards as a percentage of GDP, Spain continues to show a higher intensity of protection (per capita expenditure on social protection) than that of Portugal, although no significant effort in approximation to EU standards may be ascertained. From the financing point of view, the Spanish welfare state still relies heavily on employers' contributions, whereas the Portuguese one has come to use a large proportion of public revenues for the financing of social policy.

REDESIGNING SOCIAL PROTECTION: UNIVERSALISM VS. SELECTIVISM

The question to be answered in this section is whether the EU social policy dynamics are becoming part of the logic of domestic discourse, identities, political structures, and public policies in Spain and Portugal. Departing from underdeveloped Bismarckian (occupational) social protection systems in the mid-1970s, both the Spanish and Portuguese welfare states have undergone deep processes of change during the last decades, meaning a clear overcome of path dependency in many cases. To what extent is Europeanization responsible for such changes?

EU social policy has undergone a salient process of change since the creation of the European Community by the Treaty of Rome in 1958. The evolution of EU social policy has been illustrated in many studies that highlight its comparative backwardness when compared with the economic aspects of European integration (Leibfried and Pierson 1995;

Rhodes and Mény 1998). Two distinctive features characterize EU social policy. In the first place, EU social policy is directed at workers rather than at citizens. This is consistent with the salience of the economic aspect of European integration, because EU policy is aimed at securing free mobility of workers within the EU market. In the second place, 'hard' EU social policy based on compulsory normative has tended to incorporate developments already achieved long ago in national settings, including those of Southern European countries. All the Council Directives issued in the fields of labour and working conditions, equality of treatment for women and men, free movement of workers and health, and safety at work have been transposed into the legislation of Portugal and Spain (European Commission 2000: 251–65). In most cases national legislation already contemplated the provisions of Directives. Thus, the *acquis communautaire* and its transposition into domestic legislation can hardly be held responsible for full redesign of the Portuguese and Spanish welfare states.

Furthermore, it has been argued that the poorer economies of the EU have been able to profit from the Structural and Cohesion Funds (having an origin in the better off EU economies) since their accession to the EEC. Whether such funds have been used in Southern European countries to ameliorate their social protection networks or, conversely, used to follow a social-dumping/social-devaluation strategy has already been a matter of research that has rejected the social-dumping/ devaluation hypothesis (Guillén and Matsaganis 2000; Guillén and Álvarez 2001). Precisely for this reason the impact of EU social funds on the development of the Spanish and Portuguese welfare states should be taken into account as a direct effect of accession into the EU on the advancement of their social protection systems. The economic fluxes from the Funds may have contributed the generation of growth, wealth, and employment. They may also have helped in triggering initiatives at the national/regional/local level and enhancing the visibility of the problems of certain social groups.

Nonetheless, even if direct influence of EU social policy is moderate but still significant, other indirect impacts could be considered. Influences of the EU dynamics on domestic contexts include 'soft' EU social policy, namely, the realm of recommendations, EU social discourse, and demonstration effects. We would like to label this aspect of Europeanization as 'cognitive Europeanization', bearing an impact on national political discourses, identities, elite ideologies, the attitudes of policy-makers, and public preferences. It is our contention that whereas 'hard' EU policy has had a moderate influence on the evolution of the Portuguese and Spanish welfare states, 'soft' EU social policy, EU discourses, and demonstration effects have constituted crucial factors inducing change, together with domestic developments. For example, the insistence on the part of the EU of the need to fight poverty, promote social inclusion, close the gaps of social protection networks, and pursue equity between women and men has been most important in the reorientation of Southern welfare states toward social citizenship. On the other extreme, EU statements on the need to rationalize social protection systems and improve efficiency during the 1990s have also been influential and have provided national governments with the necessary support to legitimize cost-control measures.

Demonstration effects bear even more crucial importance. Political democratization of the regimes of Southern Europe was always linked in the minds of the elites and of the public in general to social democratization. That is, 'becoming Europeans' has not only meant a shift from authoritarian to democratic political institutions and ameliorating capitalist production, but also the achievement of a fully-fledged welfare state 'European style'. It is true that political democratization by itself has reinforced civil societies, enhanced the possibility of exerting pressure on the part of interest groups, and fostered the opportunities for redistribution in Southern Europe (Maravall 1995). We are talking here, however, about actions based on broadly shared attitudes and preferences among the citizenry and governmental will (especially among the political parties in the left interval of the spectrum when in office). Such aspirations of southern countries for the construction of strong welfare states have been already documented in detail (Silva 2003; Guillén 1992; Guillén and Álvarez 2001) but it is important to state it here once again. Joining the European Union has reinforced the already existing attitudes during the transition to democracy period.

Finally, provided different welfare traditions and social policy models coexist in Europe, which of them has been followed by Spain and Portugal? In terms of models, aspirations in Spain and Portugal have been framed in a peculiar way. The model for welfare services as declared in the political discourse of the left-wing parties and in public preferences has consisted of that of the Scandinavian social citizenship tradition, whereas the model for income maintenance policies has remained that of conservative/occupational Central Europe (Guillén 1992). This is consistent with the fact that the redesign of southern welfare states has framed them so that at present their most salient characteristic is the mix of welfare principles à la Esping-Andersen, that is, conservative in income maintenance policies and social-democratic in healthcare and educational issues.[3]

Let us now turn to analyse the evolution of the Spanish and Portuguese welfare states in detail in order to ascertain whether qualitative Europeanization has taken place.

Spain

Three distinct periods may be differentiated in the evolution of the Spanish welfare state, namely, a period of expansion without departure from the historical path (1975–82), a period of universalization (1982–93), and a period of rationalization (1993–2001).

The first period ranging from the fall of the authoritarian regime in 1975 to the victory of the Socialist party in the 1982 general elections is characterized by intense expansion of social policy programmes in quantitative terms without departure from the inherited macro-institutional design of the social protection system (Guillén 1992). Some administrative rearrangements took place, for example, the creation of four National Institutes devoted respectively to the management of pensions, healthcare, unemployment, and social services, and the establishment of a Ministry of Health as independent from the Ministry of Labour. This latter development is very relevant for it eased the departure from the occupational principle to be experienced by healthcare policies from the mid-1980s on. Also in this period, a deep reform of fiscal policies (both direct and indirect taxation) took place in order to adapt the Spanish fiscal system to the prevailing model in the European Community. This was also relevant in order to facilitate the introduction of universalizing measures in the 1980s, for it allowed the state to tap the necessary resources to finance them in the future.

The only relevant qualitative modifications of the period ranging from the mid-1970s to 1982 consisted, first, of the approval of the Law on Social Integration of the Disabled in 1981, implemented from the mid-1980s on and including protection in economic terms and services for disabled people. Second, divorce was legalized and female activity rates began to grow significantly. Third, the devolution process to autonomous regions foreseen in the 1978 Constitution was initiated in the social policy domain by the transfer of powers in healthcare to Catalonia. Most prominently, however, the Spanish welfare state grew significantly in size during this period so that expenditure on social protection over GDP was increased by 50 per cent. Equally important, the policy-making process was democratized. Several social pacts were signed, starting in 1977 with the Moncloa Pacts (among parliamentary forces). The ANE (National Agreement on Employment) was reached in 1981 and the AES (Social and Economic Agreement) four years later.

Several factors hindered more radical departures from the inherited Bismarckian model during the transition to democracy (Guillén 1992). In the first place, the period of transition coincided with the oil shocks, and privileged attention had to be paid to the restructuring of the economy. In the second place, the priority was placed on the redesign of political institutions and on the stabilization of the new democratic regime. In the third place, the Spanish transition to democracy bore a 'reformist' character based on the attainment of consensus, a process that slowed down decisions. This is different from the Portuguese case, where transition to democracy showed a more 'rupturist' character allowing for breakthrough decisions, such as the creation of a national health service (NHS) as early as 1979. Nonetheless, the Spanish welfare state grew both in financial effort (especially as regards the use of general revenues) and in population coverage terms pushed by the emerging social needs – accentuated by the economic crises – and the need to legitimize the new democratic regime. Finally, in this period, the intentions of the left-wing parties, the unions, and the population preferences in relation to the social aspects of democratization were already clear and pointed to the attainment of an intensification of social protection and the extension of tax-funded non-contributory benefits. Such a move was closely linked to what was labelled at the time the 'European Project'.

The second period of evolution of the Spanish welfare state comprises the years 1982 to 1993 and produced a major departure from past social policies. The Socialist party gained office with an absolute majority in 1982, a circumstance repeated in the general elections of 1986 and 1989. Socialist rule lasted for 14 consecutive years (the last period ranging from 1993 to 1996 with a reduced majority), which allowed the government to exercise a decisive and protracted action in the field of social policy. The economy was far from having attained the right balance to overcome the economic crises in 1982, however, so the Socialist cabinet had to devote a lot of effort to curbing inflation and the staggering unemployment rates. As noted above, several social pacts had been attained starting in 1977 that allowed for the moderation of salary increases, but economic adjustment was still seen as the main objective in order to confront adhesion to the EEC in 1986. This possibly explains why expansionary reforms were initiated only in the mid-1980s.

Expansionary reforms are the hallmark of this period and clearly outmoded restrictive ones. In fact, the only major restrictive reform affected retirement pensions. The first half of the 1980s was a hard time for the Socialist government. The need to restructure the productive apparatus and fight unemployment and inflation resulted in the adoption of a strict monetary policy. Further, the pension reform of 1974 (that is, still under authoritarian rule) had impinged an expansionary thrust into the income maintenance system. This, together with the rise of new social needs stemming from the economic crises and intense use of early retirement and disability pensions to protect redundant workers, posed a challenge to the financing of the social security system. All these pressures resulted in the adoption of a restrictive reform of contributory pensions in 1985. The reform enlarged the minimum contributory period from ten to 15 years and reduced the replacement rate by introducing more salaried years (eight instead of two) into the formula to calculate the initial amount of the pension (Cruz Roche 1994; Guillén 1999a). In 1983–84 the first wave of labour market flexibilization measures was passed, allowing for broad use of new temporary contracts. Such reforms resulted in the end of the era neo-corporatist agreements and the termination of the 'historical brotherhood' between the Socialist party and the Socialist Union (UGT), which was desperately against the restrictive pension reform and the introduction of temporary contracts.

Expansionary reforms affected the welfare services above all, but also affected income maintenance. These reforms produced quick growth of social expenditure and the most intense narrowing of the negative differential with the EU average in 1993 (as shown in the previous section). In the realm of healthcare, the reform of primary care was passed in 1984, followed by the creation of a national health system in 1986 and the inclusion of former beneficiaries of poor relief in 1989. Thus the healthcare system came to cover 99.9 per cent of the Spanish population for a broad set of healthcare services (comparable to those of other EU countries), although access has not been turned into a citizenship right yet. Healthcare powers were transferred to five other autonomous regions (namely Andalusia, the Basque Country, Valencia, Galicia, and Navarre), and these regions, together with Catalonia, quickly started to make their own innovations. For example, the introduction of an individual health card in the Basque Country to substitute the old family card had a quick spill over effect on other regions and ended up having an impact on the entire healthcare system. Moreover, healthcare came to be financed mainly out of state revenues at the end of the 1990s (Guillén 1999b).

As regards personal social services and social assistance for the elderly, children, and the young, Spain also witnessed considerable expansion in this period in terms of the number of beneficiaries and expenditure (Barea Teijeiro 2000). In the late 1980s and early 1990s, powers in the domain of social services were devolved to all 17 Spanish autonomous regions and municipalities. Social services were universalized and made dependant on income levels for access. The creation of the Ministry of Social Affairs in 1988 fostered expansion, as did the activities and innovative undertakings of the autonomous regions (Casado 1994; Muñoz Machado *et al.* 1997: 529–99). Nonetheless, the provision of social services remained low in comparison to that of other EU members at the end of the period because it departed from almost negligible levels.

Reforms were intensified in the late 1980s, when the unions decided they had restrained their demands long enough and went on general strike in December 1988. Furthermore, the positive cycle of the economy allowed the devotion of more resources to social policy. Structural and Cohesion Funds amounted to 0.7 per cent of the Spanish GDP on average for the period of 1989–93, helping the expansionary trend on social policy and, especially, on the construction of infrastructures (*Second Report on Economic and Social Cohesion*). Income maintenance policies also underwent expansion. Pensions were indexed to past inflation in 1988, and non-contributory retirement and disability pensions were introduced in 1991 in order to universalize the coverage of the pension system. Also, supplements to minimum pensions grew in number in order to secure the level of the minimum pension for those workers having failed to contribute enough to reach it. This, together with the establishment of non-contributory pensions, meant the intensification of a sort of internal redistribution within the pension system (Herce San Miguel 1998; Guillén 1999a).

Furthermore, coverage and intensity of protection in the field of unemployment went through its golden period, so that the highest coverage rate was reached in 1992, when 82 per cent of the unemployed received cash benefits. This is also the period in which the effort on activation policies grew most during the last 25 years (Toharia 1997; Gutiérrez and Guillén 2000). Family allowances were also reformed in 1990 with the aim of making them universal in scope and targeted to low-income families. Finally, between 1989 and 1993 regions decided unilaterally and in opposition to the opinion of the central administration to introduce minimum income schemes for people of working age. Spain thus became the first Southern European country to establish minimum income programmes (Laparra and Aguilar 1997; Moreno and Arriba 1999).

All these expansionary reforms stemmed from domestic preferences, attitudes, and aspirations, but were also in line with the European Community's social discourse of the time, which was focused on the fight against poverty and social exclusion and insisted on the reduction of gaps in access to social protection. Despite the fact that EU social policy started intensifying precisely in the late 1980s, other more determinant developments in the EU sphere soon arrived in the economic domain, thereby conditioning the development of social policy. We refer obviously to the conditions for convergence the EMU agreed on in the Maastricht Treaty.[4]

The third and final period of evolution of the Spanish welfare state (1993–2001) witnessed a clear redesign of existing policies. Rationalization, increased efficiency, and cost-control are the processes characterizing reform in this period. This does not mean that indiscriminate retrenchment took place. In fact, some expansionary moves were undertaken. Among them one could highlight the reform of maternity benefits that increased the replacement rate to 100 per cent of previous salary and the more generous regulation of parental leaves, both produced in 1995 while still under Socialist rule. Under the rule of the Conservative party, in office since 1996, some expansionary measures were undertaken, such as the increase of tax exemptions for families, the approval of a law on conciliation of family and working life, and an equalization of social security rights for part-time and fixed-term contracts to those of full-time contracts. A Family Aid Plan was approved in November 2001, consisting mainly of subsidizing social housing for young people and low-income families and fiscal exemptions proportional to family size. Structural and Cohesion Funds were increased in the period ranging from 1994 to 2000, so that they came to reach 1.5 per cent of the Spanish GDP. They were important in order to overcome the economic crisis of the early 1990s and for the promotion of employment and social protection.

Still, rationalizing measures bore more weight. The most salient of them was the restrictive reform of unemployment subsidies of 1992, which reduced both the time-span of the benefit and its amount and the minimum contributory period needed to have access to the benefit (Toharia 1997). The consequences of this reform in terms of the reduction in expenditure can be clearly observed in Figure 8, which shows that it is the main reason for the substantial reduction of expenditure on social policy as a percentage of GDP that took place from 1993 on. Also, private non-profit employment agencies were allowed to operate in the same year. These moves were related to internal unbalances of the unemployment protection system, exhausted by the continuous entrances to and exits from the labour market due to the growth of temporary jobs. They were also related, however, to the prescriptions of the *White Paper on Growth, Competitiveness and Employment* regarding the need to reduce passive unemployment protection and ameliorate activation policies, or at least the government tried to legitimize the reform by referring to the mentioned document. In 1993–94 a second wave of labour market de-regularization took place.

Adjustment in the field of healthcare was initiated already in 1991, when a parliamentary commission (the so-called 'Abril Committee') was set up in order to propose cost-control measures. Expenditure growth in healthcare in Spain had been the highest in the EU during the second half of the 1980s, due to the introduction of the universalizing and decentralizing reforms. Hence worries about the rapid increase of expenditure were already present among the top administration in the late 1980s. The rationalizing measures proposed by the Abril Committee, however, met strong opposition from the unions who managed to block the whole reform (Guillén 1999b).

Other efficiency-seeking measures were more successful. Prospective funding of hospital services, negative lists of publicly financed pharmaceuticals, and measures aimed at improving the management of public healthcare institutions were introduced. Also, a positive and negative list of healthcare services to be financed publicly was passed in 1995, but the positive list was not restrictive and included instead new health services. Last, no cost-sharing measures were set up for healthcare due to frontal opposition on the part of the population, users' associations, and the unions. In sum, efficiency was sought for in the domain of healthcare but no challenge of already attained levels of equity may be ascertained. The reason for this lies in the electoral arena and also in the arena of interest mediation. The electorate and possibly the unions would not have accepted restrictive reforms in health just because the expansionary reforms had taken place far too close in time (Guillén 1999b). Decentralization of healthcare came to a halt after the transfer of powers to the Canary Islands in 1994, and was not pursued until 2000, when the government announced that negotiations for devolution to the remaining ten regions were to be completed by 2002.

Income maintenance policies underwent more restrictive thrusts. The first measure to be introduced was the indexing of pensions to the next year's expected inflation rather than to past inflation in 1994. In 1995 another parliamentary commission reached a crucial agreement on the future reform of the pension system, which came to be called the Toledo Pact, and to which interest groups and even the private banking sector adhered. One of the provisions of this pact was that financing sources of economic transfers and healthcare services should be separated, the first to be based on social contributions and the second on state revenues. Such a reform proposal was implemented incrementally so that healthcare services came to be financed totally out of taxes in 1999. This means that Spain and Italy are the only two EU members for whom healthcare services are financed 100 per cent out of taxes (Guillén 1999b).

A social pact on the reform of the pension system was reached in October 1996, soon after the Conservative party won the general elections. Such a pact put in practice several of the reform proposals agreed on by the Toledo Pact. A new law on pensions was passed in 1997 and is still being implemented. The number of salaried years to calculate the initial pension was enlarged from eight to 15, thus reducing replacement rates for new pensions. What the unions got in exchange was an amelioration of the lowest widows' and orphans' pensions and a more generous treatment of short contribution careers (Herce San Miguel 1998). Another reform of the pension system has taken place only recently, namely in April 2001. This latter reform was based on a pact reached between the government, the employer's association, and only one of the main unions. It has entailed an increase of minimum widows' and survivors' pensions, the softening of the conditions for pre-retirement, increasing incentives for partial retirement, and a reinforcement of the reserves of the system.

Furthermore, a pact on the reform of labour market was also reached in 1997, this time reducing redundancy payments for the first time in the entire period of analysis. Since then, achieving another pact has proved impossible. In April 2001 negotiations broke off and the government ended up decreeing a reform of the labour market in the next month. Redundancy compensations were further lowered and social security contributions were decreased for employers signing contracts with women and/or workers over 55 years old. All in all, it could be defended that both the reform of the pension system and that of the labour market has not only followed general reform trends across the EU, but has also been tailored in agreement with the prescriptions of the Union in order to gain efficiency and sustainability of social protection programmes.

Finally, social services continued to expand during the 1990s at the regional level, where innovative policies continued to be introduced (Barea Teijeiro 2000). The Ministry of Social Affairs was merged with that of Labour by the Conservative government in 1996, however, thus rendering such policies less visible and possibly less significant at the national level.

To sum up, the Spanish welfare state has undergone a deep process of change in qualitative terms, entailing the introduction of several universal polices and a broad extension of tax-funded non-contributory benefits and services. Many gaps have been either closed or narrowed, so that protection for insiders and outsiders of the labour market has reached a better balance. Moreover, better quality levels have accompanied coverage expansion. The low protection of families and the comparative backwardness of social services remain challenges for the future.

Portugal

The process of Europeanization is a crucial explanatory variable to understanding the nature of societal transformations in Portugal in the last two decades. Integration into the EU is a background in which transformations are embedded. Therefore, one cannot fully understand the impact of Europeanization on Portugal's social policies without taking into account its overall impact on Portuguese social and political structures.

Actually, the impact of the process of European integration on Portuguese society goes well beyond 1986, the actual year of adhesion. The idea of Europe was at the core of the political dispute during the period of political transition, in which the nature of the regime that came out from the 1974 revolution was defined in the public sphere. In a time of deep political mobilization and rapid transformation, as the years of 1974–75 were, Europe was always proposed as a political alternative to the idea of a 'socialist regime the Portuguese way'. At the same time, it was suggested as being a new place of belonging, a replacement to the independence of the former African colonies – in the same way it happened more than one century before when these were seen as replacements to the 'loss' of Brazil. But if the adhesion to the then-EEC was an aspiration for the political forces that came out victorious from the political arena in 1974–76, it was also a project with roots that went far beyond the democratization process. As suggested by António Barreto (2000: 73), Europe had long been a political and cultural reference for the Portuguese, starting with the human integration that resulted from the migratory fluxes, particularly intensive after the Second World War, passing through the trade and economic integration with the European Free Trade Agreement (EFTA), during the 1960s, and culminating in full membership with the political, economic, and social integration in the EEC.

From 1976 onwards, with the approval of the Constitution, and with the first general elections, in which the pro-European Socialist party, led by Mário Soares, came out victorious, European integration became the endeavour of democratic consolidation, and an external constraint to reforms that became widely seen both as legitimate and necessary. The need to accomplish the adhesion criteria, both by establishing a regulatory framework like the ones of the European counterparts and by normalizing the functioning of the economy, after the period of economic experimentation of 1974–76, was, to a great extent, responsible for making Portugal move away from its specific route to socialism – as explicitly defined in the constitution – and establishing a political and economic framework similar to that of the other Western European countries. This process implied a political pact between the two major Portuguese political parties, the Socialists (PS – centre left) and the Social Democrats (PSD – centre right), in order to push forward reforms required to enter the EEC, even if often some of these were extremely unpopular. This political pact culminated in the decision of ruling together, instead of alternating in power, in the years prior to the adhesion (from 1982 to 1985) in a 'strange bedfellows' coalition that became known as 'bloco central'. This coalition made financial austere policies possible, with controlled political conflict. The years of the bloco central government were years of financial austerity, with a second International Monetary Fund (IMF) loan and the launching of a 'stabilizing programme' that brought unemployment to an uncommon maximum, by Portuguese standards, of 12 per cent in 1984–85. By this time it was the expectations of adhesion in 1986, as well as the popular reaction to the economic collapse of 1974–75, that, even before effective integration, generated a wide political consensus that enabled structural reforms that until then had been frozen (Medeiros 1992).

Summing up, one can say that after a brief spell during the transition to democracy, the idea of Europe became a driving force that moved reforms forward and a fundamental factor for bringing together political stabilization, economic recovery, and democratic consolidation. After the adhesion, this process was even deepened. The entrance to the EEC coincides with the decrease of political passions and with the first cabinets with absolute majorities (centre right), counterbalanced by the election of the Socialist party's (centre left) leading figure, Mário Soures, to President. This election played a crucial role in pushing Portugal into entering the EEC. After 1986 Portugal enters a period of overall expansion of the economy, following a counter-cycle period that preceded the entrance. Society suffers important transformations, primarily as a result of the new experience of openness that resulted from being part of the single European market, and that contradicted the history of the country during most of the twentieth century. The adhesion to the EEC was, in the words of Fernando Medeiros (1992: 921), an exit door from the social and institutional crisis the country had been facing since the 1960s and an efficient antidote to the traditional international isolation of the country. It was also a structuring element of a social formation that until then had few democratic traditions and that had been economically depressed since the Revolution.

It is against this background, herein briefly presented, that one should understand the role of Europe in the development of social policies in Portugal, as the latter is part of a broader trend that characterizes the impact of Europeanization on Portuguese society.

Nonetheless, to understand the impact of the process of Europeanization on the field of social policies, it is important to understand the developments that policy field had suffered until then. Considering the period that goes from the transition to democracy to the EEC adhesion, one can distinguish three periods in the development of social policies. A first one of 'expansion' that characterizes the democratization period; a second one of 'design of the system' that characterizes the consolidation of democracy; and a third one of 'growth without differentiation' that characterizes the first years of EEC membership. This third period created the endeavour for the 'redesign of the system' that has been followed in the last years, namely since the Socialist party came to power in 1995 under the leadership of António Guterres.

As with the other Southern European countries, Portugal was ruled by a right-wing authoritarian system, although in the Portuguese case it not only lasted longer (almost 50 years), but it also differed from those of the other Southern countries, namely, the Spanish one. *Estado Novo's* particular blend of mild corporatism, political enforcement, Catholicism, and a strong anti-modernization ideology can work as a feasible explanation for the difficult catch-up of the Portuguese welfare system.

Nevertheless, the abrupt end of the *Estado Novo* with the Carnation Revolution of 1974 represented a radical path shifting in all fields of Portuguese society. With the transition to democracy social policies suffered important transformations. Not only were symbolic and political compromises established, but social expenditures also grew enormously, effective rights were guaranteed, and benefits and wages were raised. While pre-existent low levels of benefits explain this trend, it is also explained by the growing social and political mobilization of the period, namely, as a function of ascendancy of the left and of a labour-dominated political constellation. On the other hand, as stated by Juan Mozzicafreddo, in a period of profound disarticulation of the economic system, as that of the transition, social policies worked as a main element of social integration. The balanced resolution of the revolutionary process was due in part to the shaping of the democratic state as a welfare state (1992: 71–6). This process culminated in the approval of the 1976 Constitution, which explicitly indicated a welfare state model as a transition to a Socialist state and society, and that is in European terms the one that gives more importance to social policies (Hoffman cited in Esping-Andersen 1993: 598).

With particular intensity during the first two years after the Revolution, governments embarked on a strategy of income redistribution and of guaranteeing social and labour rights. In the weeks that followed the *coup d'état*, wages rose in an unprecedented way, a statutory minimum wage was established, a social pension was created, the statutory minimum pension was doubled, and the highest salaries and pensions were subject to a plafond. One week after the Revolution, 1 May was already a bank holiday, and soon after an important set of non-existent labour rights was guaranteed. Social partners' organizations began to be created in order to replace the corporatist ones. This global strategy was achieved through an abrupt increase in public spending and by a high degree of political voluntarism. The result was the definition of an ambitious programme of social rights that never had a complete practical correspondence. If this was a short and turbulent period, however, it was when the actual nature of the welfare system started to be established, even if with low effectiveness. In the framework of no more than one year, social rights in Portugal grew enormously. Nevertheless, this growth was not sustainable and consequently jeopardized the complete development and establishment of a welfare state.

After a brief, though intense, spell during which the legitimization of the political system relied on popular or revolutionary mechanisms, and not on liberal and parliamentary ones, Portugal started a process of consolidation and institutionalization of its democracy that culminated in the adhesion to the EEC. This process was paralleled by the consolidation and definition of its welfare state, and corresponds to the second period mentioned above – 'design of the system'. In what is a common feature with Spain, the design of the welfare structures coincided with the severe economic crisis that began in the mid-1970s, which were particularly intense in Portugal, leading to two IMF loans.

This context posed serious political problems. If democracy were to be born in a context of economic and financial austerity, government's capacity to deal with the growing and unfrozen amount of demands, together with the necessity to reform both the institutions and the economy in order to accede the EEC, was diminished. This led to the deterioration of the living conditions of the population, just after a period when they increased abruptly. Moreover, economic difficulties eroded state's capacities (that is, resources) and undermined both public order and the reform process itself. The only feasible option left was for parties and social partners to accept inter-temporal trade-offs and hence moderate their demands. Paradoxically, as the political crisis deepened, the capacity to launch policies of macroeconomic austerity and cost containment in the field of social policies increased. After the consequences of the revolutionary period and its economic experimentation, a process of collective learning from previous experiences made it easier to make decisions, even hard ones (Maravall 1997: 29–33). In this context one can also apply Esping-Andersen's well-known metaphor of a 'frozen welfare state landscape' (1996: 24), though to an altogether different degree. In Portugal the freezing occurred when social rights were not fully accomplished.

However, this image has to be nuanced. The period from 1976 to 1986 can be described as one of 'permanent austerity', namely, in financial terms, and was combined with an extension of social rights, although not with the same intensity as the previous period. It is as if the previous period corresponded to a short 'golden age' of no more than two years, followed by a retrenchment period that, nonetheless, can only be considered as such when compared with the expansionary phase that preceded it.

In fact, the ten years of democratic consolidation, which had as an important reformist driving force the will to become member of the EEC, correspond to an effort to design the overall architecture of the welfare system. They are also characterized, however, by the creation of new rights – for example, the institutionalization of an NHS in 1979 – and the widening of existing ones, namely, income replacement schemes. No less important, it was during this period that the institutional and organizational features of the system were defined. The transfer of the medical-social services to the Ministry of Health – with the aim of creating the NHS – the approval of the organic law of social security, the subsequent creation of central and regionalized (district and sub-district) structures of social security, the creation of the Institute for Employment and Vocational Training (IEFP), as well as that of the Institute for the Financial Management of Social Security (IGFSS) are a few examples of this trend. The process of design of the system culminated in 1984 with the approval of the social security base law that only recently was changed – in 2000.

Fundamental to understanding the political context of this period, and the way it produced feedback effects on the side of social policies, is the evolution of social dialogue structures. In fact, one of the decisive questions in the political arena during the transition period was that of the trade union unity. Given that the labour movement, namely, the confederation National Portugese labour union (CGTP-in), was clearly dominated by the Communist party (PCP), and some minor extreme left parties, the two main parties of the parliamentary spectrum (the Socialists and the Social Democrats) created a second trade union confederation, based on the main trade unions that were close to the socialists (for example, that of the bank sector workers). This process dates back to the year of 1976 and culminates in 1978 with the institutionalization of the UGT; however, it produced effects on the nature of social dialogue in Portugal that are relevant still. When in 1984 a genuine tripartite social dialogue structure was created – the Permanent Council for Social Dialogue (CPCS), which replaced the existent National Council for Income and Prices – all social partners were given permanent seats, Initially, however, the CGTP-in refused to occupy its place, and when it finally did in 1987, it refused to sign any of the social pacts.[5] This meant that during a period when there was a strong need for establishing inter-temporal trade-offs, and when this was being widely accomplished in the political arena – with the coalition of the Socialists with the Social Democrats – the same cannot be said of the field of industrial relations, where the main trade union confederation was self-marginalized from any attempt to negotiate and establish pacts.

In 1986 the adhesion to the EEC changed the face of Portugal's financial situation, and therefore its welfare arrangements. The first six years after adhesion were a period of economic growth, even one of the more prosperous of the last decades. This resulted from a particular combination of a favourable internal and external conjuncture. The stabilization programme of the pre-adhesion period (1983–85), the oil counter-crisis of 1986, the strong repercussion of the expansion of the international economy in Portugal, and the impact of the massive transfer of structural funds that brought together an important capital flux were all responsible for an important economic dynamic (Medeiros 1992: 919). This economic expansion was responsible for unemployment's re-absorption, which previously had reached uncommonly high levels for Portuguese standards, for a slight decrease in the poverty rate, as well as for the solving of the wage arrears phenomenon.[6] It was also after adhesion that Portugal ended a period of political instability for the first time, leading to the landslide absolute majority of the PSD (centre-right) in 1987, which was repeated in 1991.

Contrary to the previous period, this was one of political stability, associated with an overall strengthening of the State's financial and budgetary capacity, and with a significant increase in social expenditures. If the overall architecture of the system maintained its basic features, however, there was a substantive growth of the amount of benefits, with a consequent upgrade of social standards, as well as a movement toward the institutionalization of social dialogue, with the signature of the first social pacts in 1986. At the same time, the need to transpose EEC's regulatory framework, the *acquis communautaire*, and the role played by the structural funds contributed widely to this upgrade movement, namely, the European Social Fund (ESF), responsible for a vast amount of resources for social policies.

As mentioned earlier, an important indirect influence of EU dynamics on domestic social policies has to do with 'soft' EU social policy. The impact of 'cognitive Europeanization' seems to be particularly relevant in Portugal. The fields of employment active measures, anti-poverty programmes, and social services suffered especially profound changes. A new culture of policy implementation was spread among policy-makers and policy implementers. Territorialized policies, local partnerships, promotion of equity between women and men, conciliation of family and working life, and binding of employment active measures with social security are a few examples of a new social policy culture that started to pave its way. The impact of the First European Framework of Support, through the actions financed by the European Social Fund, was particularly impressive. It not only worked as an important tool for the generalization of vocational training in order to face the extremely low levels of qualifications of the Portuguese working population, but it was also an important support for the expansion of the educational system.

One can say that after a period of austerity, from 1986 on Portugal started maximizing the opportunities created by full European membership. This was a period characterized by an overriding modernization trend, but also one in which the role assigned to social policies was not primary. There was not a redesign of the overall system – excepting the field of health services, with a move toward privatization (for example, co-payments for health services, opting-out of public insurance allowed) – but rather an increase in previously defined paths. Therefore, this period can be labelled as one of 'growth without differentiation'. The core domains of the welfare system maintained its basic structure unaltered, although there was a significant increase in spending and on the amount of benefits (maximum pensions, namely through the creation of the fourteenth month). We can stress, however, that the Europeanization process, by opening new possibilities in unexplored domains, paved the way to a modernization of the architecture of the welfare system, particularly visible after the government change of 1995.

In the general elections of 1995, after ten years of centre-right government, a new cabinet led by the Socialist party came to power. Even before the electoral campaign, the Socialist party held social policies as a distinctive feature when compared with Cavaco Silva's government. Given that in the management of macroeconomic policies, in order to accomplish the Maastricht criteria, there were no substantial lines of disagreement, social policies were chosen as an important demarcating zone. This ideological redefinition of the political elite gave a new role to employment, social security, and solidarity policies (Nunes 2000).

During the previous period social policies had been shadowed by an overriding modernization process, visible for instance in the massive building of infrastructures. With the elections a new set of social measures was in the limelight. A combination of investment toward the protection against classic social risks (pensions, unemployment benefits) was complemented by a modernization process that led to the launch of new measures and a profound reorientation of the functioning of the overall system, both in terms of benefits and institutions.[7]

If it is too early to assess the overall impact and success of this 'path shifting' strategy, it is, however, possible to identify some dimensions where the modernizing intentions were already accomplished. Considering the institutional and organic dimension of reforms, one can identify two levels of transformation – one that has to do with the internal organization and functioning of public services, and a second related to the widening of social dialogue.

Considering the first dimension, apart from activation, both in financial and physical terms, of all the services under the Ministry of Labour and Solidarity, there was a set of important organic reforms aimed at responding to one of the typical pathological features of the Southern European system – institutional fragmentation.

The recent creation of the Institute for Solidarity and Social Security (ISSS) is a clear example of this. This structure binds together social security and solidarity policies that were previously under the responsibility of different bodies. At the same time, it reduces the substantial autonomy the regional structures of social security enjoyed. The creation of this national body allowed for the standardizing of procedures and aimed at overcoming the risks that resulted from the appropriation of the system by local/regional interests.

A second dimension has to do with the widening of social dialogue. First, there was a strong political investment in the signature of social pacts – an overarching first one in 1996, dealing with almost all governmental fields, aiming at a risk avoidance strategy to accomplish the Maastricht criteria, and recently two other ones, although of a 'middle range' nature. Second, there was a commitment to new forms of social dialogue. This was the case of the signature of a 'social pact for solidarity', signed by the government and the associations of municipalities, charities, and mutual aids, which aimed at civil society's involvement in the implementation of the new solidarity policies, namely, through local partnerships. The creation of regional networks for employment, in the framework of the Portuguese NAP, is another example of a willingness to mobilize new modes of social dialogue.

Recently, the parliamentary approval of a new base law for social security, by an unusually wide left-wing coalition, at the same time defined a framework for the organic architecture of the system. It also paved the way for new forms of financing the social security scheme, through a mix of public-funded and public-capitalized system, together with important changes in calculating the amount of the pensions (Cabral 2000).

If the new institutional features are important elements in considering the real extent of the reform process, however, the ways benefits are developed are essential for evaluating the real impact of the system in dealing with social problems. Again, one can distinguish two lines along which the reform process advanced.

A first one deals with investment in response to classic social risks. There was a systematic increase in the lower social pensions (pensioners are one of the groups more affected by poverty in Portugal), the lengthening of parental leave, the definition of an early retirement scheme, and the reduction of the work-week to 40 hours. There was also a reformulation of unemployment benefits by lengthening them according to age groups, or by allowing for the accumulation of partial benefits with part-time jobs. No less important, because it served as a clear sign of the legitimizing of the system, was the definition of stricter rules and improved control over sickness pay – an area known to be permeable to fraud and manipulation.

There was a second dimension that had to do with the development of a new generation of social policies, showing awareness of new social risks and dealing with classic ones in a different way. The rationalization of family allowances in one single benefit that became means tested, as well as the expansion of family care in a revalorized policy mix with the third sector, are examples of the latter. The development of the Social Market for Employment, an umbrella under which a new set of employment policies, targeted to different groups, was developed (for example, insertion enterprises and local initiatives for employment), and primarily the introduction of a guaranteed minimum income (GMI) are examples of the former.[8]

The extent to which this reform mix will be successful is yet to be unveiled. Nonetheless, there are elements that show that there was a strong political commitment to reform and re-orient the nature of the welfare system, through a systematic intervention in its different realms. It is also clear that the nature of this reform process is deeply embedded in a policy culture that entered the Portuguese social policy arena after 1986. It was the launching of the first EU initiatives, as well as the development of the ESF programmes, that brought to Portugal a set of social policies until then underdeveloped. Initially these new policies started working at the margins of the system, but slowly they permeated the core of social policies. With the cabinet shift of 1995, they clearly became structuring elements in the re-orientation of the overall Portuguese welfare system.

WHAT HAS ALLOWED FOR EUROPEANIZATION?

What may be concluded from the previous sections is, in a nutshell, that significant Europeanization has taken place both in Spain and Portugal. Whereas Spain has been less successful than Portugal in quantitative approximation to the European average in terms of expenditure over GDP, qualitative progress in terms of gains in equity and social citizenship is notorious. Such progress was especially intense from the mid-1980s to the early 1990s. In particular, social citizenship was enhanced in the fields of healthcare, non-contributory benefits, social services for dependent people, and labour insertion policies. In turn, Portugal showed better capacities than Spain in quantitative approximation throughout the whole period of analysis, even if departing from much lower levels. In general, qualitative approximation lags behind that of Spain in terms of chronology and intensity (with the important exception of labour insertion success). Still, advancement has been weighty in Portugal and may well be even weightier provided the recent norm is fully implemented. Thus, protection gaps have been either closed or narrowed in both countries. How does one explain these developments? What were the factors allowing for Europeanization?

Spain departed from higher levels of welfare effort and intensity than Portugal did. Economic adjustment after the oil shocks and the stabilization of the new democratic regime prevented radical movements up to the mid-1980s. This period was followed by intense economic growth and marked expansion of the Spanish welfare state both in quantitative and qualitative terms, however, until the early 1990s. Such expansion meant a clear departure from path dependency in many aspects of social protection toward universalist policies. The last period of evolution was one of austerity imposed by the economic conditions for convergence and previous intense expansionary trends in public spending. This resulted in a clear deceleration of growth of expenditure on social policies (especially regarding passive unemployment protection) during the 1990s. Developments in Portugal were somewhat different. The Portuguese governments underwent severe economic difficulties for expanding social policies after the short expansionary spell following the revolution. As a consequence, some of the most far-reaching reforms – such as the introduction of a national health service in 1979 – suffered from incomplete implementation. Still, Portugal managed to expand coverage and expenditure, and, even more salient, Portugal was able to go through the era of austerity imposed by the Maastricht Treaty without negative impacts on the growth of expenditure on social policy. From 1995 on several outstanding reforms were introduced, among them a national minimum income scheme.

Such approximation to the EU standards was related to several factors. First, the EU has meant an external constraint but also a positive pressure for Spain and Portugal in a period of redesign of their respective welfare systems. In Portugal, the political pressures for constructing a particular kind of socialism after the 1974 revolution found a functional opposition to the role of welfare policies à la EEC countries. In Spain the amelioration and expansion of social protection systems was made synonymous with democratic modernization.

Second, as far as direct impact is concerned, it has to be noted that EU directives on social policy never caught Spain or Portugal unprepared: social policy reforms were either in the making or already attained when EU directives were issued and had been triggered by endogenous (that is, social and political mobilization) rather than exogenous processes. As Mangen notes (1996: 319), however, directives may well have constituted added value to already existing provisions. As regards European Funds, they have clearly helped develop social policies and the construction of infrastructures related to them. They have also enhanced new undertakings in social policy and have endorsed such initiatives with visibility. In many occasions Structural Funds allowed for Brussels to spur (or 'tenderly impose') both the development and character of measures, programmes, and initiatives that were far from being a priority from a national point of view. Such was the case, for instance, of the resources allocated to vocational training and active labour market policies.

Third, it is our contention that the influence of 'soft'/indirect EU recommendations on social policy and demonstration effects has been greater than direct action. Europeanization is a process where the cognitive dimension of political life becomes crucial. Changes in policy core beliefs in the domain of social policy have been enhanced in Spain and Portugal by the political democratization of their regimes, coupled by a strong emphasis on social advancement. Also, spatial proximity to the European Community (leading to quicker and more accurate information of what is going on inside it) and becoming a member of such a supranational institution has had a significant effect on the evolution of identities and attitudes toward social policy and on the perception of social problems. For the Spanish and Portuguese populations, becoming Europeans meant, among other things, attaining 'European levels of social protection'. Inclusion in European standardized data sets on social protection increased comparative knowledge of the standing of new access countries within the Union. In doing so (indirect) Europeanization has facilitated learning and non-incremental change. In other words, the incorporation of the EU discourse on the fight against poverty and social exclusion, gender equality, conciliation of family and working life, and active employment policies into the national (and sub-national in the case of Spain) discourse, references, and aspirations has been of the utmost importance. Such a discourse may well have started to enter the public debate by the back door, in a superficial and/or cosmetic fashion, or as a sort of trade-off between each country and the EU for the economic support gained through European Funds. Still, it has succeeded in permeating social policy actions in many spheres with tangible results.

Fourth, some domestic factors have either enhanced or hindered the process of Europeanization. Such factors also constitute an explanation of the differences in the timing and implementation of the reforms in Spain and Portugal. Authoritarian regimes and processes of transition to democracy presented differences in both countries, thus leading to dissimilarities in the initial redesign of the inherited social protection system. The initial reform thrust in social policy expansion witnessed in Portugal could be linked to the character of the transition, in this case a *coup d'état*. Subsequent deceleration in reform and expansion of the welfare system was tied to the renegotiation of the political model. Conversely, the reformist character of the Spanish transition to democracy – initiated by an elite pact – meant that reforms were to be consensual. Therefore, radical social reforms were postponed until broad agreements had been reached.

From the comparative analysis it may be deduced that social policy expansion seems to have been tightly linked in both countries to the presence of the Socialist parties in office. In Spain the long Socialist rule (1982–96) provided for the presence of an integrated executive leadership and a political elite that was clearly in favour of the expansion of social protection. Center and centre-right parties gained office more frequently in Portugal than in Spain during the last two decades. This may explain differences in qualitative social policy gains between both countries, because continuity of public policy was more difficult to attain in Portugal.

Again, the comparison of the two national cases shows that in the case of Spain, the role the regions played in a decentralized system of government was crucial, whereas such an enhancing factor was absent in Portugal. Provided that Spanish regions maintain offices in Brussels, direct communication flows between the regions and the EU also helped. Spanish regions also count on institutional infrastructures to allow them to develop policies without having to wait for national-level decisions and may tailor their policies to the exigencies of their populations. This means a departure from the Portuguese context, which has undergone significant administrative deconcentration but no political devolution. In many instances Spanish regions have shown (and still show) a high capacity for innovation in the field of social policies, creating a sort of domino effect on the rest of the regions and also forcing the central state to recognize that such modifications were to be incorporated to the national norm. Nonetheless, decentralization has both assets and liabilities. Among the latter are the potential increase of territorial inequalities, the upsurge of comparative grievances, and the incurring of higher administrative costs.

The evolution of the social dialogue and union action (strikes, protests, declarations) has been closely linked to that of social policy in both countries, which is proof that the role of organized labour is relevant even in countries with low affiliation rates. Unions have acted in many occasions as conveyor belts of the European social model.

To sum up, the comparative study of social policy Europeanization has allowed for the singling out of several influential factors. There is much more to be researched, however. One important issue would be to clarify why labour markets show such a difference in behaviour in Portugal and Spain in terms of employment/unemployment rates and structural patterns and which aspects of the difference are tied to the construction of a certain social protection model. Another crucial line of research is related to the analysis of social policies that were *not* Europeanized and the reasons for such a negative result. Last but not least, the Portuguese and Spanish social protection systems may not only have Europeanized, but Portugal and Spain may have also contributed (so far, outstandingly the former, as proved by the last Portuguese Presidency of the Union and the Lisbon summit of March 2000) to the construction of the European Social Model. Such contribution and its impact should also be researched further.

NOTES

1. The main sources used in the quantitative analysis of the evolution of social expenditure are: (i) The Eudor-Stat database, compiled by Eurostat, in its 2/1997 version. We have obtained data from it for the period 1980–90 (cited as Eurostat 1997). (ii) The publication of Eurostat, entitled *Dépenses et recettes de protection*

sociales, Données 1980–1997, Luxembourg, 2000. We have relied on this publication for the data corresponding to 1990, although in some cases we have used it to cover the entire 1980–97 period (cited as Eurostat 2000).

2. See European Communities (1999): *1999 Broad Economic Policy Guidelines*, No.68, p.100.

3. Personal social services policies and social assistance could be labelled as 'liberal' in South Europe. Such policies have come to approximate the liberal model because of historical inheritance. Contrary to pensions or healthcare, public social services were almost undeveloped under dictatorships and have tended to become financed out of state revenues and universal but subject to means-testing during the last 25 years of democratic rule. Means-testing was introduced because the effort to universalize them (cover the whole population) was economically unfeasible, departing from very low levels of provision.

4. According to Mangen (1996: 319), not only did the 1992 Convergence Plan impose stricter criteria on the Spanish economy than those established in the Union Treaty, but Brussels also exerted strong pressures in the following years to ensure budgetary rigor by mentioning the possibility of reducing Cohesion Fund allocations to Spain.

5. It only signed one on vocational training in 1991, and two others more recently, both in 2001, one again on vocational training, and a second on health and safety in the workplace.

6. As Manual Villaverde Cabral stresses, the wage arrears phenomenon was 'a striking feature of the 1980s which illustrates the reluctance of Portuguese society to deal with overt unemployment. Employers, instead of closing factories or laying off the workforce, just stopped paying any wages, while the workers went on laboring and called for State intervention' (1999: 238).

7. For a description of the transformations that occurred in the period from 1995 to 2000, see the volume edited by the Department of Studies, Prospective and Planning of the Ministry of Labour and Solidarity, namely, the introductory chapter (Capucha *et al.* 2002a).

8. The GMI deserves some particular attention, as it is not only the most visible of the new measures that played a strong symbolic role, but also a paradigmatic one that enabled the 'path-shifting' movement, and pushed further reforms forward. It is aimed at guaranteeing a new right, addressing the high poverty levels, and at the same time represents a breach with institutional path dependency. On the path shifting nature of the GMI in the Portuguese case, see Pedroso (1998); Silva (1998, 2000); Pinto (2000); Capucha *et al.* (2002b).

REFERENCES

Barea Teijeiro, J. ed. (2000): *El gasto público en servicios sociales* [Public expenditures in social services], Madrid: Ministerio de Trabajo y Asuntos Sociales.

Barreto, A. (2000): 'Portugal e a Europa: quatro décadas', in Barreto (ed.), *A Situação Social em Portugal 1960–99* Vol.II, Lisbon: ICS, pp.37–75.

Cabral, M.V. (1999): 'Unemployment and the Political Economy of the Portuguese Labour Market', in N.G. Bermeo (ed.), *Unemployment in Southern Europe: Coping with the Consequences*, London and Portland, OR: Frank Cass, pp.222–38.

Cabral, N.C. (2000): 'Lei de bases da segurança social' [Basic Law of Social Security], *Cadernos de Política Social* [Journal of Social Policy], No.2–3, Lisbon: APSS, pp.249–66.

Capucha, L. (2002): 'Introdução', in Capucha *et al.* (eds.), *Portugal 1995–2000: Perspectivas da Evolução Social*, Oeiras: DEPP/MTS, pp.1–12.

Capucha, L., T. Bomba, R. Fernandes and G. Matos (2002b): 'Draft Report on Fighting

Poverty and Exclusion in Southern Europe – The Case of Portugal', Paper presented at the seminar on 'Fighting Poverty and Exclusion in Southern Europe', Milan, 23–24 May.

Casado, D. (1994): 'Acción social y servicios sociales' [Social Action and Social Services], in *V Informe sociológico sobre la situación social en España* [V Sociological Report on the Social Situation of Spain], Madrid: Fundación FOESSA.

Comissão do Livro Branco da Segurança Social (1999): *Livro Branco da Segurança Social* [White Book on Social Security], Lisbon: IGFSS and INA.

Cruz Roche, I. (1994): 'La dinámica y estructura de la universalización de las pensiones' [The Dynamic and Structure of the Universalization of Pensions], in *V Informe sociológico sobre la situación social en España* [V Sociological Report on the Social Situation of Spain], Madrid: Fundación FOESSA.

Esping-Andersen, G. (1993): 'Orçamentos e democracia: o Estado-Providência em Espanha e Portugal, 1960–1986' [Democracy and Benefits: The Welfare State in Spain and Portugal], in *Análise Social* [Social Analysis], No.122, Lisbon: ICS, pp.589–606.

Esping-Andersen, G. (1996): 'After the Golden Age? Welfare Dilemmas in a Global Economy', in G. Esping-Andersen (ed.), *Welfare States in Transition – National Adaptions in Global Economies*, London: Sage, pp.1–31.

European Commission (2000): *Employment and Social Affairs, Current status 15 October 1999*, Luxembourg: Office for Official Publications of the European Communities.

European Communities (1999): *European Economy, No.68, 1999 Broad Economic Policy Guidelines*, Belgium.

Eurostat (1997): Data Base *Eudor-Stat, No. 2/1997* (CD Edition).

Eurostat (2000): *Dépenses et recettes de protection sociale. Données 1980–1997*, [Recommendations and Evaluation of Social Protection in the Years 1980–97], European Communities, Luxembourg.

Guillén, A.M. (1992): 'Social Policy in Spain: From Dictatorship to Democracy', in S. Ferge and J.E. Kolberg (eds.), *Social Policy in a Changing Europe*, Boulder, CO: Campus/Westview.

Guillén, A.M. (1999a): 'Pension Reform in Spain (1975–1997): The Role of Organized Labour', *European University Working Papers*, No.99/6.

Guillén, A.M. (1999b): 'Improving Efficiency and Containing Costs: Health Care Reform in Southern Europe', *European University Working Papers*, No.99/16.

Guillén, A.M. and S. Álvarez (2001): 'Globalization and the Southern Welfare States', in R. Sykes, P. Prior and B. Palier, *Globalization and European Welfare States*, London: Macmillan.

Guillén, A.M. and M. Matsaganis (2000): 'Testing the "Social Dumping" Hypothesis in Southern Europe: Welfare Policies in Greece and Spain during the Last 20 Years', *Journal of European Social Policy* 10/2, pp.120–45.

Gutiérrez, R. and A.M. Guillén (2000): 'Protecting the Long-Term Unemployed: The Impact of Targeting Policies in Spain', *European Societies* 2/2, pp.195–216.

Herce San Miguel, J.A. (1998): 'La reforma de las pensiones en España' [The Reform of Pensions in Spain], in E. Alvarado Pérez (ed.), *Retos del estado del bienestar en España a finales de los noventa* [Challenges to the Welfare State in Spain in the Nineties], Madrid: Tecnos.

Laparra, M. and M. Aguilar (1997): 'Social Exclusion and Minimum Income Programmes in Spain', in M. Rhodes (ed.), *Southern European Welfare States*, London and Portland, OR: Frank Cass.

Leibfried, S. and P. Pierson (eds.) (1995): *European Social Policy: Between Fragmentation and Integration*, Washington, DC: Brookings Institution.

Mangen, S. (1996): 'The "Europeanization" of Spanish Social Policy', *Social Policy & Administration*, 30/4, pp.305–23.

Maravall, J.M. (1995): *Los resultados de la democracia* [The Results of Democracy], Madrid: Alianza.

Maravall, J.M. (1997): *Regimes, Politics and Markets: Democratization and Economic Change in Southern and Eastern Europe*, Oxford: Oxford University Press.

Medeiros, F. (1992): 'A formação do espaço social português: entre a sociedade providência e uma CEE providencial' [The Development of a Portuguese Social Space: Between a Welfare State and a Providing EEC], *Análise Social* [Social Analysis], No.118–19, Lisbon: ICS, pp.919–42.

Medeiros Ferreira, José (1993): 'A evolução da sociedade portuguesa' [The Evolution of Portuguese Society], in *Portugal em Transe (1974–1985)* [Portugal in Transition 1974–1985], Lisbon: Círculo dos Leitores, pp.139–65.

Menezes Ferreira, J. de (1994): 'Os sindicatos. As associações patronais' [Unions and Employers Associations], in A. Reis (ed.), *Portugal: 20 Anos de Democracia* [Portugal 20 years of Democracy], Lisbon: Círculo dos Leitores, pp.160–69.

Moreno, L. and A. Arriba (1999): 'Welfare and Decentralization in Spain', *European University Working Papers*, No.99/8.

Mozzicafreddo, J. (1992): 'O Estado-Providência em Portugal: estratégias contraditórias' [The Welfare State in Portugal: Contradictory Strategies], *Sociologia – Problemas e Práticas* [Sociology – Problems and Practices], No.12, pp.57–89.

Muñoz Machado, S. *et al.* (eds.) (1997): *Las estructuras del bienestar* [The Structure of Welfare], Madrid: Civitas.

Nunes, F. (2000): 'As políticas de solidariedade nos programas eleitorais do Partido Socialista' [The Politics of Solidarity in the Electoral Programmes of the Socialist Party], *Cadernos de Política Social* [Journal of Social Policies] Nos.2–3, Lisbon: APSS, pp.107–42.

Pedroso, P. (1998): 'Direitos e Solidariedade: perspectivas para a promoção da integração para todos' [Rights and Solidarity: Perspectives for the Promotion of Integration for Everyone], *Sociedade e Trabalho* [Society and Work] 3, pp.6–17.

Pinto, J.M. (2000): Paper presented at the conference on 'Europe, Globalization and the Future of Social Policy', Lisbon, May.

Quintin, O., and B. Favarel-Davas (1999): *L'Europe sociale. Enjeux et realité* [The Social Europe: A Challenge and Reality], Paris: La Documentation Française.

Radaelli, C.M. (2000): 'Wither Europeanization? Concept Stretching and Substantive Change', Paper presented at the Political Studies Association Annual Conference, London, 10–13 April.

Rhodes, M. and Y. Mény (eds.) (1998): *The Future of European Welfare: A New Social Contract?* London: Macmillan.

Silva, P.A. e (1998): 'O RMG e a nova questão social' [The RMG and a New Social Question], *Sociedade e Trabalho* [Society and Work] 3, pp.34–49.

Silva, P.A. e (2003), 'Putting the Portuguese Welfare System in Context', in F. Monteiro, J. Tavares, M. Glatzer and Â. Cardoso (eds.), *Portugal: Strategic Options in a European Context*, Boston, MA: Lexington Books.

Toharia, L. (1997): 'El sistema español de prestaciones por desempleo' [The Spanish System of Unemployment Benefits], *Papeles de Economía Española* [Papers of Spanish Economy] 72, pp.192–213.

The Role of the State in the Labour Market: Its Impact on Employment and Wages in Portugal as Compared with Spain

JOSÉ DA SILVA LOPES

INTRODUCTION

Since Portugal became a member of the European Economic Community (EEC) in 1986, the evolution of its labour market has presented significant differences as compared to the average of the European Union and to Spain: its unemployment rates have been lower, its wages have increased faster, and its labour regulations have continued to be tighter.

The contrasts between the Portuguese labour market experience and those of Spain and other European Union countries (EU-15) have puzzled many economists. Several analyses have been undertaken with the objective of trying to find explanations for such contrasts. The conclusions, however, have not always been sufficiently clear-cut.

The present analysis describes the behaviour of Portuguese unemployment and wages in the last two decades, and in particular since accession to the EEC in 1986. It comments on the explanations that have been proposed in several studies on the differences in relation with Spain. It also emphasizes the role of the government and central bank policies, especially regarding the management of domestic demand and the exchange rate.

UNEMPLOYMENT

In the four-year period from 1974 to 1978, Portuguese unemployment rates rose from 1.7 per cent to 7.9 per cent. As in other European countries, this sudden increase was to a large extent explained by the adverse effects of the first oil price shock. Two other causes specific to Portugal, however, had even more weight: the troubles of the revolutionary period of 1974–75, after the change of political regime; and the influx of more than 700,000 refugees from the former colonies of Angola and Mozambique. In such conditions, the Portuguese unemployment rate in 1978 was higher than the average of Western Europe and higher than that of Spain.

Beginning in 1978, however, Portugal's unemployment ceased to increase – in contrast to what happened in most European countries and especially in Spain. As shown in Figure 1, it fluctuated in accordance with economic cycles, but it remained below the European average. During that period, Spain always had the highest unemployment rate in the EU-15 and Portugal one of the lowest. Accession to the EEC in 1986 does not appear to have had a significant impact, either positive or negative, on the Portuguese unemployment rates.

It has sometimes been argued that the Spanish statistics overstate true unemployment and that the Portuguese ones understate it. Careful comparisons and some specific tests, however, suggest that the possible errors in statistical measurement were almost certainly not large enough to invalidate the wide differences in unemployment between the two countries.[1]

The following sections discuss possible causes for such differences that have been investigated by a certain number of authors. They will deal with the labour intensity of economic growth, the flexibility in the volume of

FIGURE 1

UNEMPLOYMENT RATES (%)

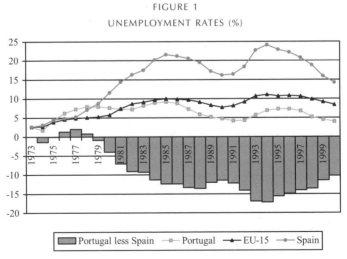

Source: European Commission 2000.

employment, and the behaviour of wages. The concluding section analyses the impact of the constraints imposed by the European Monetary Union (EMU) on Portugal's unemployment outlook for forthcoming years.

The levels of employment have also been influenced by the active labour policies of the government, but these are not examined in the present study.

LABOUR INTENSITY OF ECONOMIC GROWTH

One of the explanations for the contrast in the unemployment experiences of the two Iberian countries is based on the argument that economic growth has been more labour-intensive in Portugal than in Spain.[2]

According to that argument Spain implemented deep structural reforms in its industrial sector in the late 1970s and early 1980s, whereas in Portugal few changes of that type were introduced. The Spanish reforms involved large cuts in the output of several industries and the loss of many jobs. Such reforms resulted in a serious worsening of the employment situation. It is suggested, however, that they created the conditions for significant productivity improvements, for fast real wage increases, and for gains in international competitiveness. In contrast, by the light of this explanation, Portugal maintained its traditional industries (textiles, clothing, shoes, and so on) without significant restructuring, and relied heavily on them to expand gross domestic product (GDP). According to such an interpretation, Portugal opted for a strategy of weak progress in productivity, of a slow increase real wages, and of the maintenance of international competitiveness on the basis of low wages costs.

This explanation is based, however, on statistical data that do not provide an adequate picture. The data covering a larger period, on which Figures 4 and 5 are based, tell a very different story:

- Labour productivity increased in Portugal as much as in Spain from 1975 to 1986, but it rose much more rapidly from 1986 to 2000;
- It is true that average wages in Portugal are substantially lower than in Spain (in correspondence to differences in productivity levels) and that, in real terms, they increased less than in Spain from 1977 to 1985. However, their slow growth in real terms from 1977 to 1985 corresponds mainly to the gradual correction of the unsustainable wage explosion in Portugal that occurred during the revolutionary period of 1974–75. If the entire period from 1974 to 2000 is considered, the increases in real wages appear to be far higher in Portugal than in Spain.

It cannot therefore be said that the comparatively low unemployment levels of Portugal are due to weak improvements in labour productivity and to more stagnant wages, as compared with Spain and with the average of the EU-15 countries.

A more plausible explanation can be found by looking at the statistical data on employment and GDP. Figure 2 suggests that the satisfactory experience of Portugal in the area of unemployment results to a large extent from faster economic growth than in Spain and the EU-15 during most of the years of the last quarter of the twentieth century. It has also been due to slower increases in the labour force than in Spain, except during the second half of the 1970s (Figure 6).

On the basis of the information provided by Figures 3 to 5, it cannot be said that Spain's unemployment record was poor because its economic growth has been based on high productivity increases rather than on job creation or because its labour costs have risen too much. The key explanation seems to be that the Spanish labour force has increased very fast since the beginning of the 1980s and that, with a comparatively low rate of economic growth, it has been difficult for labour demand to adapt quickly to such an increase.

FIGURE 2

VOLUME OF GDP (INDICES, 1985=100)

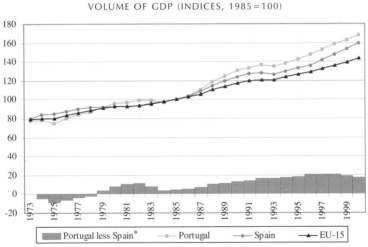

Note: *Difference between Portugal and Spain accumulated since 1974.

Source: European Commission 2000.

FIGURE 3

VOLUME OF EMPLOYMENT (INDICES, 1985 = 100)

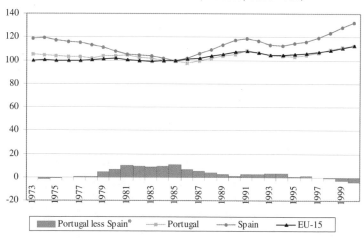

Note: *Difference between Portugal and Spain accumulated since 1974.

Source: European Commission 2000.

FIGURE 4

LABOUR PRODUCTIVITY (INDICES, 1985 = 100)

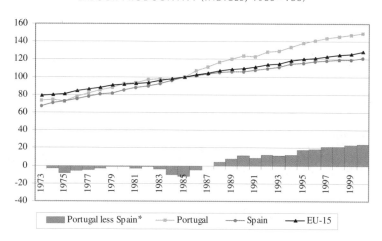

Note: *Difference between Portugal and Spain accumulated since 1974.

Source: European Commission 2000.

FIGURE 5
REAL WAGES (INDICES, 1985=100)

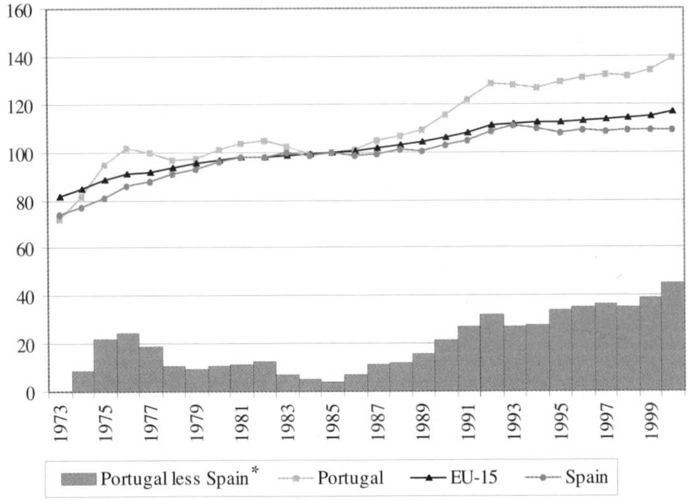

Note: *Difference between Portugal and Spain accumulated since 1974.
Source: European Commission 2000.

FIGURE 6
SIZE OF THE LABOUR FORCE (INDICES, 1985=100)

Source: European Commission 2000.

It should, however, be pointed out that from 1993 to 2000, the unemployment situation in Spain improved considerably and that the differences in its unemployment rates in relation to Portugal became much smaller due to the dynamism in the creation of new jobs (but not in productivity increases).

UNEMPLOYMENT AND THE RIGIDITY OF LABOUR REGULATIONS

Many of the studies on the persistence of high unemployment levels in the European Union conclude that the main explanations lie in the rigidity of labour regulations, especially those that seek to improve employment protection for workers (EPL). On the basis of the argument that tight labour regulations increase the natural rate of unemployment, the flexibilization of such regulations has been one of the key recommendations of the 'Jobs Strategy' of the Organization for Economic Co-operation and Development (OECD).

International comparisons published by OECD show that, among its members, Portugal has been the country with the strictest labour regulations, in particular as regards EPL (see Table 1).[3] This is still the situation at present, despite changes introduced in 1989. These changes made some of the regulations slightly less restrictive (mainly by allowing dismissals on the grounds of lack of economic performance and of economic redundancy). In the 1980s Spain had, on average, almost the same tightness in labour regulations as Portugal, but they were relaxed in the 1990s. Now they seem to be more flexible than in several other European countries.

In the OECD comparisons, the countries involved are ranked on the basis of the ascending order of the strictness of a variety of aspects of labour legislation. One of the more recent of such comparisons produced the results summarized in Table 1.

The explanation of the coexistence in Portugal of rigid labour regulations with low unemployment rates has been a challenging problem to many labour-market analysts. If the tightness of labour regulations is considered a good explanation for high unemployment, it is difficult to understand why it applies to Spain but is not valid for Portugal.

Several interpretations have been proposed for this puzzle. First, recent research suggests that the effects of EPL on unemployment levels are weaker than assumed previously. Empirical studies published by the OECD show that tight EPL regulations tend to affect certain groups of workers (such as the new entrants into the labour market) and tend to

TABLE 1

RANKINGS IN ASCENDING ORDER OF THE INDICATORS
OF THE STRICTNESS OF EPL

Types of regulations	Late 1980s			Late 1990s		
	Number of countries covered	Rank of Portugal	Rank of Spain	Number of countries covered	Rank of Portugal	Rank of Spain
Employment protection for regular employment						
Regular procedural inconveniences	22	19	20.5	27	24.5	12
Notice and severance pay for non-fault individual dismissals	20	20	19	27	27	23
Difficulty of dismissal	20	20	15	27	26.5	16
Overall strictness against dismissals	20	20	19	27	27	18
Regulations of temporary employment						
Fixed-term contracts	19	11	8	27	19	21
Temporary work agencies	24	15	20	26	23	24
Overall strictness of the regulations	19	12	13	26	21	22
Regulations of collective dismissals						
Overall strictness relative to individual dismissals				27	20	13
Overall strictness of Employment Protection Legislation	19	19*	17*	26	26**	22**

Notes: * Average of indicators for regular contracts and temporary contracts.
   ** Weighted average of indicators for regular contracts, temporary contracts, and collective contracts.
   Higher ranks represent higher strictness of the regulations. When two countries have the same rank, the average of that rank and the following integer is attributed to both of them. Thus, for instance, if two countries have the rank of 26, the value 26.5 is attributed to each of them.

Source: OECD (1999: 57, 63, 65).

increase self-employment, but are not significantly correlated with unemployment levels.[4] If these results are valid, the coexistence in Portugal of strict employment protection regulations (EPL) with low unemployment can be more easily understood.

Second, the measures of EPL provided in Table 1 are not entirely adequate. Small differences in the texts of the regulations of two countries may result in widely divergent real effects: the specific institutional structures of each country may have a strong influence on the strictness of the country's regulations when they are actually implemented. This is the reason why surveys based on employers' assessments of the restrictions they face in dismissing workers (Table 2) put Portugal and Spain in better relative situations than the comparisons of Table 1.

Finally, non-compliance with labour regulations is also an important factor for reducing the effects of the rigidity of EPL. In Portugal, that non-compliance is mainly found among small and medium-sized enterprises, and these account for a larger proportion of the total economic activity than in other EU-15 countries, except Greece.

In view of these explanations, it is not difficult to understand why the average labour market flexibility in Portugal appears to be higher than in Spain and other European countries, despite the high rigidity of the regulations shown in Table 1. The fact is that the Portuguese labour market has a dual structure: approximately half of the workers, especially those who have jobs in the public sector and in large enterprises, enjoy levels of employment protection that are among the highest in Europe; the other half (including workers in small and medium-sized enterprises, the self-employed, and irregular workers) receives little protection from labour market regulations, and provides high flexibility to the labour market.

WAGES, INFLATION, AND UNEMPLOYMENT

Real wage flexibility is commonly considered the most important explanation for the comparatively low employment in Portugal. It has been remarked that such flexibility has been much higher in Portugal than in Spain and in other EU countries. Consequently, in periods of economic slowdown and in the face of economic shocks, unemployment has increased less in Portugal than in other economies.

TABLE 2

EMPLOYER ASSESSMENTS OF THE STRICTNESS OF EMPLOYMENT
PROTECTION REGULATIONS
(Ranks in ascending order of restrictiveness)

	International Organization of Employers	EC ad hoc surveys	
	1989	1989	1994
Number of countries compared	14	10	10
Rank of Portugal	7.5	10	4
Rank of Spain	13	3	2

Source: OECD (1999: 67).

As already shown (Figure 5), during the last two decades real average wages per worker have risen more in Portugal than either in Spain or in the whole of the European Union. The trend has, however, been irregular.

A wage explosion immediately followed the change in the Portuguese political regime in April 1974. During the revolutionary period of labour unrest in 1974–76, real wages shot up by around 40 per cent. The excessive labour cost increases that were thus imposed on enterprises rendered the situation unsustainable for nearly all of them, and led to a serious crisis in the external competitiveness of the economy.

In order to restore the equilibrium, the authorities imposed nominal wage ceilings during 1977–79. These were lower than expected inflation at a time when substantial devaluations of the escudo were contributing to rapid increases in the domestic price level. During those three years real wages fell by about four per cent, despite rising labour productivity, and real unit labour costs dropped by about 17 per cent (see Figures 5 and 7). The equilibrium of the balance of payments was thus re-established.

The cuts in real wages that occurred then corresponded to a correction of the excesses of 1974–75, but they were a first sign of flexibility of real wages in Portugal. They were tolerated by workers, without substantial labour unrest, because of the menace of rising unemployment. Similarly, during the 1980s Portuguese real wages increased less than productivity. Unit labour costs fell much more than the EU-15 average (Figure 7).

With the objective of fighting inflation, in 1989 the Portuguese authorities dismantled the crawling peg, and replaced it by a stable exchange rate, anchored to the currencies of the European Monetary System (EMS). As expected, the new exchange regime had an immediate impact on the behaviour of the prices of tradable goods, which began to follow closely those of the EMS countries. The inflationary expectations of workers and producers of nontradable goods adjusted at a much slower speed, however. The consequence was that in 1989–93, nominal wages and the prices of nontradables rose far more than those of tradable goods and the overall inflation. This is the reason for the sharp increases in real wages from 1989 to 1992, which can be seen in Figure 5.

In the subsequent years, those increases were not reversed except temporarily in 1993, mainly as a consequence of the depreciation of the escudo, associated with the troubles of the EMS in 1993. In spite of rising real wages, unemployment after 1995 was not negatively affected: first,

FIGURE 7
REAL UNIT LABOUR COSTS (INDICES, 1985 = 100)

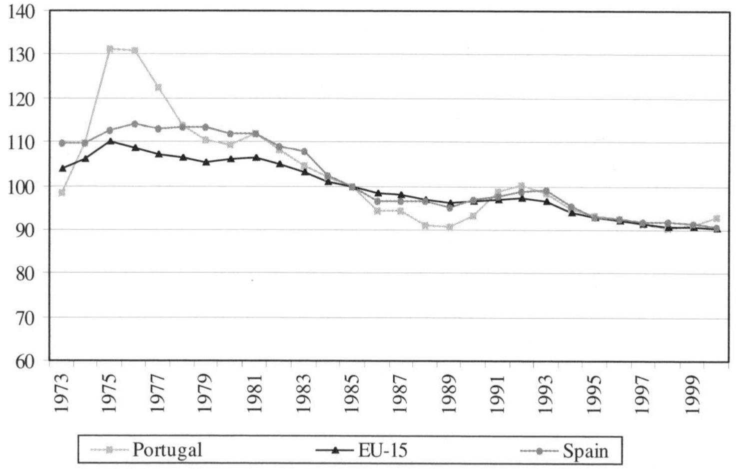

Source: European Commission 2000.

because productivity improvements offset a large proportion of the increases in real wages; and, second, because the rapid fall of interest rates and large increases in foreign borrowing allowed quite a good expansion of domestic demand.

As shown in Figure 8, real wages tended to fall or to increase more slowly in years of big devaluations of the nominal effective exchange rate of the escudo and in years of high and rising unemployment.

These relationships are confirmed by a linear regression covering 1980–2000. That regression shows that changes in real wages were correlated positively with devaluations of the exchange rate and negatively with increases in the unemployment rate. The regression coefficients of the two independent variables have the expected signs and are significantly different from zero, the first at the 95 per cent confidence level and the second at the 90 per cent confidence level.[5]

The escudo depreciated continuously under the crawling peg system from 1977 to 1989. Many economists tend to express the view that the effects of currency depreciation on real unit labour costs are usually temporary, and will disappear after one or two years. This view does not seem to be borne out by the Portuguese experience. It can be seen in Figure 8 that when the depreciation of the nominal effective exchange rate of the

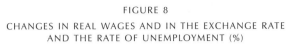

FIGURE 8

CHANGES IN REAL WAGES AND IN THE EXCHANGE RATE
AND THE RATE OF UNEMPLOYMENT (%)

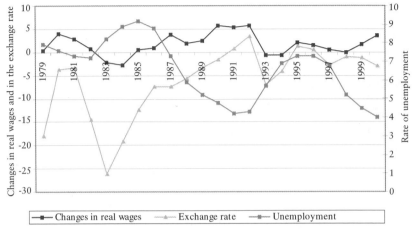

Note: Negative changes in the exchange rate mean depreciation.

Source: European Commission 2000.

escudo accelerated, there were reductions or slower increases in real wages, and that the cuts in unit labour costs that they produced persisted to a large extent in the subsequent years. What happened was that high rates of depreciation accelerated domestic inflation beyond the levels previously expected by economic agents and led in consequence to nonanticipated declines in real wages that were not entirely reversed afterward.

The accumulated depreciations of the exchange rate during the 1980s led thus to falling unit labour costs, which contributed to the creation of jobs and helped prevent large increases in unemployment. Figure 8 and the regression equation confirm that the influence of changes in unemployment rates on the behaviour of real wages was almost as important as that of the exchange rate policy.

For these reasons, there is no doubt that real wage rigidity has been very low in Portugal. The same conclusion has been reached by means of more sophisticated analysis.[6] Due to the higher flexibility of real wages, employment in Portugal was less affected by economic shocks (resulting for instance from shifts in prices, in demand, in the labour force, in productivity, or in external competitiveness) than in Spain or in other European countries.

There have been three main explanations for the low rigidity of real wages in Portugal. First, inflation was high and variable from 1975 to the early 1990s, and in several years it generated large differences between the inflationary expectations of workers and other economic agents and the actual changes in the aggregate price level. Second, actual wages have frequently exceeded the wages agreed upon in collective agreements; in periods of high or increasing unemployment, the excesses can be reduced quite easily, and actual real wages may fall or increase less than contractual wages. Third, there have been big fears among workers of losing their jobs when unemployment is high or increasing.

There are good indicators to justify the last of these reasons – the workers' fears that they may lose their jobs. One of such indicators is the attachment of workers to their workplaces, repeatedly found in enterprises in serious financial situations, even when their wages cease to be paid or begin to be paid with long delays. Often they continue to cling to their jobs, despite the weak prospects of recovering their wages in arrears. Another is the low degree of protection provided in the past by unemployment benefits.[7] Up until 1989 the eligibility criteria for unemployment benefits were so strict that less than 20 per cent of the actual unemployment was covered. In 1989 those criteria were relaxed and the coverage rose to around 40–50 per cent. In Spain the generosity of the unemployment benefits system was much greater than in Portugal during the 1980s, but it was reduced in the 1990s, and the two countries are now in a more similar situation.[8]

The weakness of the Portuguese system of unemployment subsidies as compared with that of Spain has been considered a major explanation for the high real wage flexibility and for the low employment rates since 1978. The contrast in the experiences of both countries became smaller during the 1990s, however. In Spain the reductions of the generosity of unemployment benefits and the relaxation of the strict EPL were apparently important factors in explaining why unemployment has been falling quickly since 1994. In Portugal the more generous system of unemployment subsidies, combined with the maintenance of tight EPL, with lower inflation rates and with the stability of the exchange rate, may have resulted in a reduction of real wage flexibility in recent years. The fact that Portuguese real wages increased from 1994 to 1996, despite unemployment rates of around seven per cent, may be a sign of higher real wage rigidity than in the preceding decade, but so far the statistical data do not allow a robust conclusion (see Figure 8). In any case, even if we accept the hypothesis that real wage flexibility is now lower than in the 1980s, there are no signs yet that unemployment has been negatively affected by that change.

WAGES AND EXTERNAL COMPETITIVENESS

It was shown in the preceding section that in the 1980s the rapid growth of real wages in Portugal was, in comparative terms, offset by high increases in labour productivity and that, in consequence, the behaviour of real unit labour costs expressed in the national currency was not much different from that of Spain or the European average. In the 1990s the experience was different: real unit labour costs in domestic currency did not increase much more in Portugal than in Spain; but when expressed in euros they became much less competitive. This was a consequence of the fast real appreciation of the escudo from 1989 to 1992.

As already explained, the stabilization of the exchange rate after 1989 was reflected only with a long lag in the reduction of the inflation of non-tradables and in the slowing down of nominal wage increases. Consequently, Portuguese nominal wages, denominated in euros, rose abruptly from 1989 to 1992. Since 1994 inflation has continued to exceed the European average, although by smaller margins than before. The increases of nominal wages in euros tended, therefore, to exceed those of Spain and of other EU-15 countries. And since the differences in such increases were larger than differences in productivity improvements, unit labour costs in euros at current prices rose far more in Portugal than in the EU-15 as a whole or in Spain (Figures 9 and 10).

The outcome was a considerable deterioration in the competitiveness of tradable goods produced in Portugal. A regression covering the period of 1977–2000 shows that the growth of the volume of imports was positively correlated with the growth of GDP and with unit labour costs denominated in euros relative to the average of the EU-15.[9] As one would expect, the higher those relative unit labour costs, the faster the increase in imports tended to be. The fast increase of labour costs denominated in euros in Portugal as compared with the EU-15 average explains why, during the 1990s, the volume of imports increased by two percentage points, on an annual basis, for each percentage point of expansion in the volume of total demand.

FIGURE 9

NOMINAL UNIT LABOUR COSTS IN EUROS (INDICES, 1985=100)

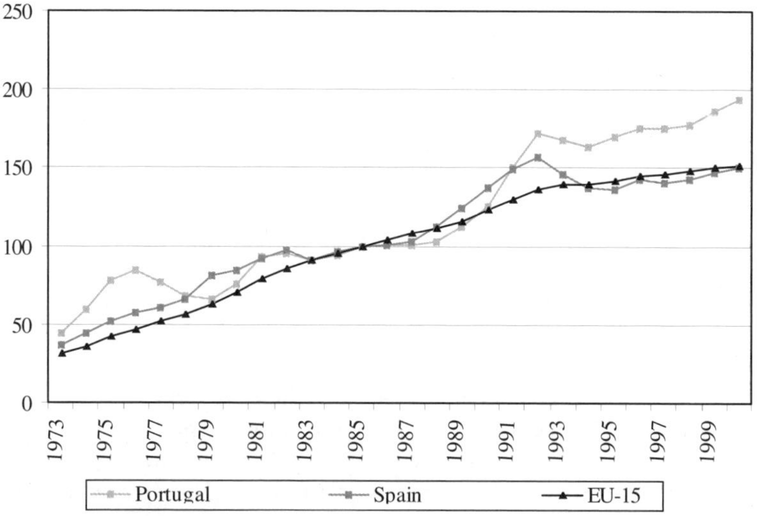

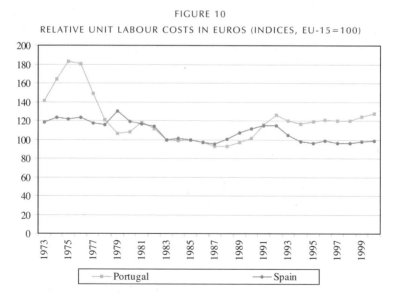

Source: European Commission 2000.

FIGURE 10

RELATIVE UNIT LABOUR COSTS IN EUROS (INDICES, EU-15=100)

Source: European Commission 2000.

A regression aimed at explaining the growth in the volume of Portuguese exports by the increases in the real import demand of the EU-15 and the relative unit labour costs does not produce entirely satisfactory results. It shows that the behaviour of those exports depends closely on import demand in the EU-15, but the influence of relative unit costs seems to be weak. The regression coefficient for the last of these variables is negative, as would be expected, but it is low in absolute terms (-0.17) and is not significantly different from zero.[10]

The main explanation for the weakness of the impact of relative unit costs on the volume of exports is provided by the fact that between 1990–95 Portuguese exports continued to grow very satisfactorily, despite much higher relative unit labour costs. The start of the operations of a few large export-oriented projects (mainly in the automobile industry), financed by foreign direct investments that were negotiated in the late 1980s or early 1990s, continued to boost exports for several years. After 1996, however, there was a return to the pattern of 1976–80: foreign investments in new industrial undertakings fell to very low levels as a result of the strong rise of relative Portuguese unit labour costs; and the country's export performance in 1997–2000 became very disappointing (see Table 3).

The result of the unsatisfactory performance of exports and rapidly increasing imports was that the deficit in the balance of goods and services rose progressively from 6.2 per cent of GDP in 1995, to 12.2 per cent in 2000. This growing gap between imports and exports was partially covered by emigrants' remittances and transfers from the Structural Funds of the EU. Since these have not been sufficient, however, the gap necessitated sharp increases in loans and other forms of capital inflows from abroad. In 2000 almost ten per cent of domestic spending in Portugal was financed by foreign borrowing and by portfolio or direct investments.

TABLE 3

EXPORT PERFORMANCE OF PORTUGUESE MANUFACTURED GOODS
(percentage changes from previous year)

	1995	1996	1997	1998	1999	2000
Export performance	3.3	6.4	-0.9	-5.2	-3.7	-3.9

Note: Export performance is calculated as the percentage change in the ratio of of export volumes to export markets.

Source: OECD Economic Outlook, Nos.58, 61, 63, 65, 67, and 69.

The dramatic intensification of the dependence on foreign financing during 1995–2000, as a remedy for the losses of competitiveness, made it possible to achieve annual increases of GDP above three per cent. It is clear, however, that such a dependence cannot be maintained for many years at present levels. Foreign financing will inevitably diminish, necessitating a decrease in the difference between imports and exports. Reducing dependence on foreign financing will impose strict constraints on the growth of domestic demand, unless there are quick improvements in external competitiveness, achieved by increases in unit labour costs at lower rates than those of the EU-15, which in principle will imply faster increases in labour productivity than in real wages.

Quick improvements in labour productivity would reduce Portuguese unit labour costs in relation to the EU average. The problem is that steady productivity increases require structural changes (in technologies, in human capital, in the environment for enterprises and so on) that can only be achieved in the medium and long term. Apart from cyclical fluctuations, it is not realistic to expect strong productivity improvements over a period of only a few years.

It is also unrealistic to expect that Portuguese wages will fall in nominal terms, or that they may fall easily in real terms if inflation in the EMU is kept at the very low levels the European Central Bank intends to maintain. In the 1980s reductions in real wages were feasible because it was possible to resort to devaluation and to higher than expected inflation, but those instruments are no longer available. The only feasible way to increase competitiveness therefore seems to be to curb inflation over several years and bring it to levels lower than the European average – a situation that is just the opposite of the experience of the last few years. There may even be the danger that Portugal may need deflation in order to recover its lost competitiveness in labour costs. In such a case, the risks of rising unemployment would be very serious. In the last 20 years, Portugal has had an enviable unemployment record. Because of the loss of competitiveness of the country's labour costs in the 1990s, however, the risks of high unemployment cannot be avoided by exchange rate depreciations as in the past, and the prospects for the forthcoming years are far from encouraging.

NOTES

1. Blanchard (1999: 26).
2. Marimón (1996: 24–5, 79–85).
3. OECD (1999).
4. OECD (1999: 75–99).
5. The regression for the period 1980–2000 is
   $$w = 2.75 + 0.20\ e - 0.90\ u_{-1}$$
   (t=5.53) (t=3.74) (t=1.90) R^2 =0.55 F=10.9 d.f.=18
   where
   w = annual increases in real wages
   e = annual depreciation of the nominal effective exchange rate
   u_{-1} = increase in the unemployment rate in the preceding year.
6. Castillo, Dolado and Jimeno (1997).
7. Blanchard and Jimeno (1995).
8. Bover, García-Perea and Portugal (2000).
9. The import regression is: M=-406.1+3.19Y+1.47L
   (t=-12.5) (t=27.7) (t=3.63) R^2=0.977 F=455.1 d.f.=21
   where: M=Index of the volume of imports of goods and services;
   Y=Index of real GDP; L=Index of relative unit labour costs.
10. The export regression is: X=-69.6 + 1.68D -0.17L
    (t=-2.37) (t=3.40) (t=-0.55) R2=0.980 F=521.6 d.f. 21
    where: X=Index of volume of the exports goods and services; D=Index of the volume
    of total imports into EU-15; L=Index of relative unit labour costs.

REFERENCES

Blanchard, O. (1999): *Macroeconomics*, 2nd edition, New York: Prentice Hall.
Blanchard, O. and J.F. Jimeno (1995): *Structural Unemployment, Spain versus Portugal*, *American Economic Review*, 85.
Bover, O., P. Garcia-Perea and P. Portugal (2000): *A Comparative Study of the Portuguese and Spanish Labour Market*, *Economic Policy*, Oct. 2000, pp.381–428.
Castillo, S., J.J. Dolado and J.F. Jimeno (1997): *A Tale of Two Neighbour Economies: Does Wage Flexibility Make the Difference Between Portuguese and Spanish Unemployment?* Paper presented at a Workshop of Banco de Portugal, July 1997.
European Commission (2000): *European Economy*, 71, Bruxelles.
Marimon, R. (1996): *La Economia Española (1996): Una Vision Differente* [The Spanish Economy (1996): A Different Vision], Barcelona: Universitat Pompeu Fabra.
OECD (1999): *Employment Outlook*, June, Paris: OECD.

The 2004 Enlargement: Iberian Lessons for Post-Communist Europe

SEBASTIÁN ROYO

INTRODUCTION

After decades of relative isolation under authoritarian regimes, the success of processes of democratic transition in Portugal and Spain in the second half of the 1970s paved the way for full membership in the European Community (EC).[1] For Spain, Portugal, and their EC partners, this momentous and long-awaited development had profound consequences and set in motion complex processes of adjustment.

There was no dispute that the Iberian countries belonged to Europe. This was not just a geographical fact. Spain and Portugal shared their history, traditions, culture, religion, and their intellectual values with the rest of Europe, and both countries had contributed to the Christian occidental conceptions of mankind and society dominant in Europe. Their entry into the European Community was a reaffirmation of that fact.

At the same time, Spain and Portugal offered a new geo-political dimension to the Union, strengthening it southwards, and ensuring closer ties with other regions that had been peripheral to the EC. Indeed, the Iberian enlargement strengthened Europe's strategic position in the Mediterranean and Latin America. This process was fostered by the Spanish accession to the North Atlantic Treaty Organization (NATO) on June 1982, after a long controversy within the country. Finally, Iberian integration has led to the further development of a European system of cohesion and solidarity.

Entry into the EC has allowed both countries to have influence on European decisions over which they previously had little influence, and in any case, no voting power. Since their accession Portugal and Spain have played important roles in the process of European integration and have again become key actors in the European arena.

The discussion proceeds in three steps. First, based on some of the main conclusions from the preceding essays, I summarize the consequences of the EU integration for the Iberian countries. In the second section, I examine the challenges the ongoing enlargement of the EU presents for Portugal and Spain. The analysis closes with some lessons for eastern European countries. A central argument will be that political considerations were key in Spain and Portugal's decision to join the EC.

CONSEQUENCES OF EU INTEGRATION

Political and Sociological Consequences

The EC played a significant role in the success of Portugal and Spain's democratization processes. It exercised a key demonstrative and symbolic influence based on its association with democracy and freedoms. During the early phases of the democratization processes, the most important lever was, obviously, the democratic precondition for EC entry. Brussels defined explicitly the institutional conditions that would satisfy this requirement, and European leaders made them very specific to the Iberian ones. Indeed, the EC had important indirect levers, particularly during the negotiations for accession, to influence the direction of events and the decisions of policy-makers and economic actors (that is, economic incentives). The decision to proceed with negotiations was the ultimate lever in the hands of the EC to push for democratization in both countries.[2]

EC membership has also contributed to the consolidation of the Iberian democratic regimes. Pridham (2002) has argued that membership has had the following impact: First, it helped link 'enhanced national self-image with possible feelings for democracy'. In addition, financial contributions from the EC budget as well as the economic benefits of membership (that is, foreign direct investment) helped improve economic conditions and mitigated some of the negative effects of liberalization and modernization of the outdated economic structures of both countries. Improved economic conditions and better prospects for social and political stability, in turn, influenced public opinion and helped legitimize the new system and strengthen support for democracy. Membership also forced the Iberian countries to align their institutions to the *acquis communautaire*, which reinforced democratic practices and induced democratic governments to push for administrative reforms and decentralization (for instance, Portugal reformed its Constitution in 1989 to allow for reprivatization of companies that had been nationalized during the revolution). Finally, membership also promoted elite socialization and the development of transnational networks, which proved vital for the strengthening of interest groups and political parties (such as the Spanish and Portuguese Socialist parties, which received substantive support from their European counterparts). The development of economic interests and networks at the European level also strengthened the support of economic actors for democracy.[3]

The EC, however, lacked the direct intervention instruments (such as armed intervention) that could have had a systemic effect on the Iberian democratization processes. Hence, the essays in this volume look at interactions between the international environment and domestic politics. The actors involved in the transition had the powers to influence events and, hence, they were the ones that ultimately determined the final outcomes. Domestic dynamics are thus, critical. The process of European integration interacted with a wide variety of domestic social, political, and economic factors that shaped the new democracies. In Spain a radical and unparalleled process of devolution to the autonomous regions has led to a decentralized state that has culminated with the development of the State of Autonomies.[4] In Portugal, following the collapse of the revolutionary attempt, the state also undertook a systemic process of modernization. The two transitions were substantially different, however. In Portugal the road to democracy started with a clear break, the coup of 25 April 1974. In Spain, on the contrary, the transition was more consensus-oriented. These two paths to democracy (among other factors) have resulted in enduring differences in the two Iberian democracies in terms of institutional developments (that is, in Portugal a decentralization attempt was defeated in a referendum), economic performance (that is, Spain has experienced higher levels of unemployment), and collective life (that is, support for unions and political parties is higher in Portugal than Spain, and differences exist in labour participation rates). Indeed, European integration has not eliminated major differences between the Iberian countries. Also, integration cannot explain the broader patterns of political transformation with its clearly identifiable underpinnings in the two countries. These enduring differences illustrate the limitations of research attempts that have sought to causally link the Iberian democratic transitions to internationally rooted and domestically supported pressures for European integration. In the end, as it has been correctly stated by Fishman (2001: 8):

the political motivations guiding their assessment of Europe during the crucial years leading up to EC membership were strongly shaped by the Iberian-held attitudes toward democracy and regime transition, attitudes formed within the context of the distinctive political experience of each case.

From a sociological standpoint EU membership has also resulted in attitudinal changes that have influenced the political culture of both countries. From the beginning there was strong support from public opinion and elites for the integration of both countries into Europe as a means of consolidating the new democratic regimes. They viewed democratization and European integration as part of the same process. Hence, successive governments in Portugal and Spain associated European integration with the modernization of their countries. This association helped shift public opinion toward their governments and democracy. In addition, other scholars have noted that by allowing for the active involvement of both countries in European institutions, European integration helped change the 'isolationist-fatalist attitude' of the political classes.[5] Public opinion surveys from Eurobarometer and Madrid's *Centro de Investigaciones Sociológicas* (CIS) have shown a sustained increase in positive ratings effects for the functioning of democracy. Furthermore, support for the relationship between the Iberian countries and the EU has been widespread in both countries since 1986 despite fluctuations. This almost unanimous consensus in favour of integration into Europe seems to be the consequence of Portugal and Spain's need to overcome their historical isolation from the rest of Europe since the nineteenth century until the end of the authoritarian regimes in 1970s (Magone 2002: 223–33). This development contributed to the legitimating of the new democratic system (and thus the consolidation of democracy).

The greatest consensus elicited toward the EU is instrumental (particularly in Spain), however, with levels of diffuse affective support for the EU being low, although high in comparative perspective. Approval of Europe therefore seems to coincide with the economic cycles: low during economic recessions and high during periods of economic growth.

Finally, it is important to stress that in terms of political behaviour, EU membership has not transformed activism or political participation in Portugal or Spain. Levels of support for democracy as a legitimate political regime, preferably to any other alternative, have usually remained high (around 80 per cent of the responses in surveys), and Portuguese and Spaniards declare themselves satisfied with the functioning of democracy. Political cynicism continues, however, to be a major component of political attitudes and the political behaviour of Portuguese and Spanish citizens. These countries still have the lowest levels of participation of western Europe, and membership in political and civic associations remains very low. At the same time, citizens do not have a feeling of political influence and express a strong sense of ambivalence toward political parties and the political class, which is translated into a rather low interest in politics.[6]

Economic and Social Consequences

EC integration was a catalyst for the final conversion of the Iberian countries into modern Western-type economies. It led the political and economic actors to adopt economic policies and business strategies consistent with membership and the *acquis communautaire* (which at the time included the custom union, the value added tax, the Common Agriculture and Fisheries Polices, and the external trade agreements). This is not to say that membership was the only reason for this development. The economic liberalization, trade integration, and modernization of these economies started in the 1950s and 1960s, and both countries became increasingly prosperous over the two decades prior to EU accession.

EU membership, however, facilitated the micro- and macroeconomic reforms that successive Iberian governments undertook throughout the 1980s and 1990s. Indeed, in a context of strong support among Iberian citizens for integration, membership became a facilitating mechanism that allowed the Iberian governments to prioritize economic rather than social modernization and hence, to pursue difficult economic and social policies (that is, to reform their labour and financial markets), with short-term painful effects. Moreover, in the 1990s the decision to comply with the European Monetary Union (EMU) Maastricht Treaty criteria led to the implementation of macro- and microeconomic policies that resulted in fiscal consolidation, central bank independence, and wage moderation.[7]

Since 1986 the Portuguese and Spanish economies have undergone profound economic changes. For instance, EU membership has led to policy and institutional reforms in the following economic areas: monetary and exchange rate policies (first independent coordination, followed by accession to the Exchange Rate Mechanism [ERM] of the European Monetary System, and finally EMU membership); reform of the tax system (that is, the introduction of the VAT, and reduction of import duties); and a fiscal consolidation process. These changes have led to deep processes of structural reforms aimed at macroeconomic stability and the strengthening of competitiveness of the productive sector. On the supply side these reforms sought the development of well-functioning capital markets, the promotion of efficiency in public services, and the enhancement of flexibility in the labour market. As a result, markets and prices for a number of goods and services have been deregulated and liberalized; the labour market has been the subject of limited deregulatory reforms; a privatization programme was started in the 1980s to roll back the presence of the government in the economies of both countries and to increase the overall efficiency of the system; and competition policy was adapted to EU regulations.

In terms of *static effects*, EU accession has resulted in trade creation in the manufacturing sector, but also in more competition for Iberian manufacturers. The intensity of the adjustment, however, has been mitigated by the behaviour of exchange rates (prior to EMU) and a dramatic increase in the levels of investment in these two countries. In agriculture the main source of adjustment problems has been trade creation because greater import penetration led to a contraction in domestic production. Indeed, the fears of trade diversion materialized after accession (in favour of other EU members such as Italy or France), which contributed to increasing migration from rural areas to the cities. Finally, for Spain one of the main challenges of accession has been the result of the regional diversity of its agriculture. It has not been easy for farmers affected by the Common Agricultural Policy (CAP) to switch to other products given the differences in the environment, weather, and fertility conditions.[8]

A critical factor to determine the positive outcome of integration was based on *dynamics effects*. Spain and Portugal had a number of attractions as a production base, including good infrastructure, an educated and cheap labour force, and access to markets with a growing potential. In addition, EC entry would add the incentive of further access to the EC countries for non-EC Iberian investors, namely, Japan or the United States. As expected, one of the key outcomes of integration has been a dramatic increase in foreign direct investment (FDI), from less than two per cent to more than six per cent of gross domestic product (GDP) over the last decade. This development has been the result of the following processes: economic integration, larger potential growth, lower exchange rate risk, lower economic uncertainty, and institutional reforms. Another significant dynamic effect has been the strengthening of

Iberian firms' competitive position. Indeed, as a result of changes to the production structure and in the structure of exports, the indicators of the degree of competitiveness of the Portuguese and Spanish economies (that is, in terms of human capital skills, stock of capital, technological capital) shows important improvements, although significant differences remain in comparison to the leading developed economies.

The EU contributed significantly to this development. During 1994–99 EU aid accounted for 1.5 per cent of GDP in Spain and 3.3 per cent in Portugal. EU funding has allowed rates of public investment to remain relatively stable since the mid-1980s. As a result major infrastructural shortcomings have been addressed, and road and telecommunication networks have improved dramatically both in quantity and quality. In addition, increasing spending on education and training have contributed to the upgrading of the labour force. In sum, these funds have played a prominent role in developing the factors that improve the competitiveness and determine the potential growth of the least developed regions of both countries.[9]

Nominal convergence, however, has advanced at a faster pace than real convergence. Indeed, 15 years have not been long enough. Portugal and Spain's European integration has revealed convergence and divergence, nominal and real. Since 1997 inflation in Spain has exceeded the EU average every year. In Portugal real convergence has been slowing down each year since 1998, actually turning negative in 2000, and with both real and nominal divergence expected to increase until 2003. Per capita GDP has experienced a cyclical evolution in the Iberian countries with significant increases during periods of economic expansion and sharp decreases during economic recessions. Since Spain joined the EU in 1986, per capita income has increased 'only' 11.5 per cent and Portugal's has increased 14.2 per cent. Ireland's, in contrast, has increased 38 per cent. Only Greece, with an increase of 6.8 per cent, has had a lower real convergence than Spain and Portugal.

According to observers, a possible explanation for this development has been the fact that whereas Spain has grown an average of 2.1 per cent between 1990 and 1998, Portugal has grown 2.5 per cent, and Ireland 7.3 per cent over the same period. This growth differential explains the divergences in real convergence. Other explanations include: the higher level of unemployment (15.4 per cent in Spain); the low rate of labour participation (that is, active population over total population, which stands at 50 per cent, meaning that expanding the Spanish labour participation rate to the EU average would increase per capita income to

98.2 per cent of the EU average); the inadequate education of the labour force (that is, only 28 per cent of the Spanish potential labour force has at least a high school diploma, in contrast with the EU average of 56 per cent); low investment in Research and Development (R&D) and information technology (the lowest in the EU); and inadequate infrastructures (that is, road mile per 1,000 inhabitants in Spain is 47 per cent of the EU average and railroads 73 per cent). The inadequate structure of the labour market with high dismissal costs, a relatively centralized collective bargaining system, and a system of unemployment benefits (particularly in Spain) that guarantees income instead of fostering job search have also hindered the convergence process.[10]

From a social standpoint, as noted in this volume, this was a decade and a half of political stability, associated with an overall strengthening of the State's financial and budgetary capacity, and with a significant increase in social expenditures. The overall architecture of the system has been maintained, but there was a substantive growth of the amount of benefits, with a consequent upgrade of social standards. There has also been a movement toward the institutionalization of social dialogue, with the signature of social pacts. For instance, in 1980 expenditure on social protection was 18.1 per cent of GDP in Spain and 12.8 per cent of GDP in Portugal, much lower levels than the EU average at that time (24.3 per cent) and only higher than that of Greece (9.7 per cent). Since EU accession, despite an increase of 3.4 per cent of the resources dedicated to social protection in Spain (the Spanish welfare state grew significantly in size during this period and expenditures on social protection over GDP increased by 50 per cent), the differential with the EU average has not been reduced. Instead, it has increased from 6.2 points in 1980 to 6.8 points in 1997. Portugal, starting from lower levels of social protection, has been more successful in reducing the differential with the EU average by 50 per cent. Spain, however, continues to show a higher intensity of protection (per capita expenditure on social protection) than that of Portugal. In the end, the Portuguese and Spanish welfare states have undergone a deep process of change in qualitative terms, entailing both the introduction of several universal polices and a broader extension of tax-funded non-contributory benefits and services. At the same time, the need to transpose the EC's regulatory framework, the *acquis communautaire* (that is, in the fields of labour and working conditions, equality of treatment for women and men, free movement of workers, and health and safety at work), as well as the role played by the structural funds, have contributed to this development.

THE 2004 ENLARGEMENT: CHALLENGES FOR PORTUGAL AND SPAIN

During the European Council that took place in Copenhagen on 13 December 2002, the European Union threw open its doors to the east and concluded years of difficult negotiations with ten candidate countries: Estonia, Latvia, Lithuania, Poland, Czech Republic, Slovakia, Hungary, Slovenia, Malta, and Cyprus. This historical summit marked the last act in the reunification of eastern and western Europe following the end of the cold war. As a result of this round of enlargement, the EU will extend from Portugal to the borders of Russia (growing from 15 to 25 countries in 2004, provided referendums in the candidate countries ratify the accession treaties), and it will have a population of 451 million, a GDP of $8,800 billion, and a GDP per head of $21,410.[11] Not only is this enlargement process historical, but also unique. This is the largest single enlargement of the EU since it was established and, as opposed to the Greek and Iberian enlargements, this one entails former communist and totalitarian states where a civil society, independent institutions, a free press, and entrepreneurial class have been largely absent since the end of the Second World War. Since the collapse of the Soviet Union in 1991, these countries have built, virtually from scratch, new social, political, and economic institutions. This process and the sacrifices involved, as in Iberia, have been supported by the prospect of joining Europe. Enlargement will have a large impact in the Iberian countries and it raises a number of policy and research issues.

As we have seen, in 16 years Portugal and Spain have been able to change the terms of accession and to negotiate compensatory mechanisms to mitigate the negative consequences of unfavourable accession treaties (particularly for Spain). In the end, integration has had a positive outcome, and both countries have benefited greatly from European funds and policies. For instance, in 2001 Spain was allocated nearly 63 per cent of the EU's structural funds budget ($27.8 billion). Since the Iberian countries are major beneficiaries of the EU redistributive funds, the entrance of central and eastern European countries (some, like Poland, with large agricultural sectors) will likely result in a reduction of the resources that Iberian countries currently receive from European funds. Structural and agricultural funds will be available, at least through 2006. After that year, however, a new scenario will open that is characterized by increasing competition for European funds, foreign direct investment, and trade. These developments will force the Spanish and Portuguese governments (as well as the economic actors) to re-evaluate current strategies and policies. In addition, enlargement will bring new demands from the new eastern European members in a context in which the richer countries are committed to keep (or even reduce if possible) the existing budgetary ceilings, which currently stand at 1.27 per cent of the EU GDP. This will likely result in a shift of resources to the east, which means that both Portugal and Spain will receive less funds from the EU budget and that, hence, they will contribute more financially to the EU.

At the same time, since the new member states are significantly poorer, enlargement will reduce the EU's average GDP per capita by between ten and 20 per cent. Hence, the per capita income of Spain and, to a lesser extent, Portugal will be closer to the EU average (this is the so-called 'statistical effect'). This means that many Iberian regions will no longer be eligible for aid, as funds are switched to the new member states. Under existing rules, only the regions with an average per capita income of less than 75 per cent of the EU average (which includes practically all the regions of the new member states) qualify to receive structural funds as regions *Objective 1*. In addition, only the countries with an average income of less than 90 per cent of the European average have access to the Cohesion Fund (which would include all of the new member countries, for example, the average income in Poland is 40 per cent, Lithuania is 36 per cent, and Cyprus is 78 per cent). Regional funds currently represent 34.5 per cent of the EU budget, and CAP funds represent 45 per cent.

As a result of enlargement, there will be three groups of countries. First, there will be a group of poorer countries that includes eight of the ten new members (all except for Cyprus and Slovenia), with an average per capita income of 42 per cent of the EU's and 21 per cent of the population. A second group will consist of five countries (Cyprus, Greece, Portugal, Slovenia, and Spain), with an average per capita income close to 90 per cent of the Union and 13 per cent of the population. The last group will be comprised of the richer countries of the Union, with a per capita income of 66 per cent of the population and an average income of 115 per cent of the EU's. Hence, many Iberian regions will not qualify for structural and cohesion funds. For instance, 11 of Spain's 17 regions (Extremadura, Andalusia, Galicia, Asturias, Castile-León, Castile-La Mancha, Murcia, Valencia, Ceuta, Melilla, and under special conditions Cantabria) currently receive EU structural funds because their per capita incomes are below the 75 per cent threshold and, therefore, are included as *Objective 1* territories. After the 2004 enlargement, however, only four

Spanish regions (Andalusia, 67.4 per cent; Extremadura, 58.4 per cent; Castile-La Mancha, 73.6 per cent; and Galicia, 71.3 per cent) will remain below 75 per cent of the EU average income, which will allow them to qualify for European funds in the same conditions. In addition, the expected entrance of Bulgaria and Romania in 2007 (the two poorest countries of the Union, with per capita incomes of 27 per cent and 26 per cent of the EU's respectively) will increase further the average of the current members, and only two regions (Andalusia and Extremadura) will qualify.[12]

The EU countries and the Commission are discussing mechanisms to allow for a progressive phasing out of these funds to prevent their sudden cancellation as a result of the 'statistical effect'. The affected countries (including Spain and Portugal) are suggesting proposals to raise the ceilings above 75 per cent in order to have access to the funds, or to establish different access criteria for current members and new ones. In the end it is very likely that in the near future both Iberian countries (particularly Spain) will become net contributors to the EU budget. Hence, the political, electoral, and budgetary implications of these developments are taunting and unprecedented. As we have seen, the European Commission has estimated that the impact of EU structural funds on GDP growth and employment has been significant: GDP rose in 1999 by 9.9 per cent in Portugal and 3.1 per cent in Spain relative to that forecasted without this aid. In the absence of these funds, public investment will be greatly affected.

Moreover, Spain and Portugal will have to further speed up the reform of their productive and economic structures to increase the productivity of their labour force, which is still significantly lower that the EU average. As a result of the enlargement process, Portugal and Spain will face increasing competition for their main non-agricultural exports – such as clothing, textiles, and leather. Problems should be anticipated in labour-intensive industries given the relatively low level of wages in central and eastern European states. Central and eastern European countries with lower wages produce all of these goods at cheaper costs. Therefore, these countries will attract foreign investment in sectors where traditionally Portugal and Spain have been favoured. Moreover, since the new ten members have lower labour costs, it is likely that manufacturing plants currently producing in Iberia will be tempted to move production to Eastern Europe (this is already happening; the car manufacturer Seat moved a plant from Pamplona, Spain to Slovakia in 2001). In this context it will be important for the leaders of both Iberian countries to continue pushing for a shift toward more capital-intensive industries that will require greater skills in the labour force, while relying on standard technology (for example, chemicals, vehicles, steel and metal manufacturers).

Enlargement, paradoxically, may help in this process because it will also bring significant opportunities to the Iberian countries (and the other EU members). Indeed, Portuguese and Spanish products will now have access to new markets, which will provide access to cheaper labour, and may help improve competitiveness. This may also allow for the development of more diversified investment patterns to reduce risks. Spanish (and to a lesser extent Portuguese) firms have invested very heavily in Latin America over the last decade. Current political and economic uncertainties in Latin America countries, however, suggest that diversification to eastern and central Europe may be an appropriate strategy for Iberian firms, which are still underrepresented *vis-à-vis* companies from the larger EU countries (that is, Spanish investment in these countries currently stands at amere 200 million euros).

In terms of the agricultural impact of enlargement, Iberian farmers should also expect to face serious adjustments problems, particularly given the fact that membership in the EU will imply full membership into the CAP for the new ten members, and that agricultural prices in the central and eastern European states (particularly in Poland) are in general lower than those in Iberia. First, when barriers for eastern European states' agricultural products are dropped, market prices in Iberia may decline given the new entrants' lower prices and their potential for expansion of production. In addition, in the case of some agricultural products, EU membership is expected to provide incentives to increase production in the new states. Finally, membership is expected to open the new member states' markets to substitutes, thus resulting in surplus disposal that the European budget would have to support. These concerns have been reflected in the final agreements.

In addition, in the next decade CAP funds will be redesigned and most likely reduced. The EU leaders agreed in October 2002 to effectively freeze CAP spending until 2013 (it is supposed to increase merely one per cent after 2006, well below inflation levels). Furthermore, in order to facilitate enlargement (and the World Trade Organization Doha world trade round), the European Commission proposed a plan in January of 2003 to reform EU farming, including: the elimination of subsidies linked to production; the channelling of subsidies into rural development funds; the reduction of payments to large and medium-sized farms to achieve fairer distribution; the cutting of payments to farmers if they fail to follow new criteria on food safety, environment, and animal welfare; and the lowering of prices at which the EU guarantees to buy up grain and dairy products. Spain and Portugal (among other countries, particularly France, Ireland, Italy, Greece, and Austria) remain bitterly opposed to these plans. The reduction of the CAP's funds for many Iberian farmers will most likely result in the cofinancing of agricultural policies (something that the Portuguese and Spanish governments have not been willing to consider so far).

In addition, the EU enlargement will likely result in a shift toward the north, and the so-called Mediterranean block (including Italy and Greece), which shares substantive similarities and interests, will carry less weight. Indeed, enlargement will shift the EU's centre of gravity to the east and the north, which will have economic and political implications on the Iberian countries because it will reduce the voting power of Portugal and Spain (and the Mediterranean bloc in general), while changing the cultural character of the EU. In a Europe of 25 members, the institutional powers and influence of Spain and Portugal will be further diluted. First, Iberian votes will be less decisive in European institutions such as the European Commission, the Council, or the Parliament. Second (and this is currently under consideration by the ongoing European Convention), enlargement is likely to result in the extension of qualified majorities to additional policy areas that until this time had to be decided by unanimity. Finally, the shift in budgetary priorities and the limited resources will also mean that some of the policy priorities that Portugal and Spain have defended within the European Union, such as support for Latin America or Northern Africa – the Magreb – are likely to receive less attention and resources (and there is even the possibility that they may no longer be European policies).[13]

Finally, from an economic convergence standpoint, given the existing income and productivity differentials with the richer countries, regardless of enlargement the Iberian states will have to continue increasing their living standards to bring them closer to the current EU average. For this to happen, it is necessary that their economies grow faster than the other rich European countries. This will require further liberalization of their labour structures (both internal and external), as well as increasing competition within their service markets. It will also require a better utilization of their productive resources. In addition, convergence will demand institutional reforms in R&D policies, in education, improvement of civil infrastructures, as well as further innovation, an increase in business capabilities, more investment in information technology, and better and more efficient training systems. Finally, a successful convergence policy will also demand a debate about the role of public investment and welfare programmes in both countries. In the Iberian countries increases in public expenditures to develop their welfare state have caused unbalances in their national accounts. Both countries, however, still spend significantly less in this area than their European neighbours (for example, Spain spends 6.3 points less in welfare policies than the EMU average). Effective real convergence would demand not only effective strategies and policies, but also a strong commitment on the part of Spanish and Portuguese citizens to this objective.

CHALLENGES FOR THE NEW MEMBER STATES

Political factors lay at the heart of the Portuguese and Spanish decision to join the EU. Both countries wanted to strengthen their new democratic regimes and finish with the relative isolation they had faced during the authoritarian years. Portugal and Spain (as well as Greece) demonstrate how important the democratic pre-requirement for membership has been to bring and consolidate democracy in all three countries. Yet, the differences between 1986 and 2002 are remarkable. Portugal and Spain now have advanced capitalist economies, strong and modern states, social institutions supportive of markets, well-developed civil societies, trade unions and interest groups, and a high degree of integration between the two Iberian economies that has resulted in a cluster of interests.

When we contrast this situation with the status of eastern European countries and compare the challenges the Iberian countries faced in the 1980s with the ones that the new states from central and Europe will face, the latter look far more daunting. In central and eastern Europe, we face barely functional market economies and unstable democracies. In addition, none of the new members has a previous tradition of democracy (except the Czech Republic). Furthermore, in the EU we now have the Single Market and EMU. Finally, the current economic and political climate (particularly after 9/11) will make enlargement even more difficult. Therefore, the current enlargement process is very different and more problematic.

As in Iberia, the new member states are transforming their political and economic systems, and have adapted their regulations to the *acquis communautaire*. The costs of this transformation for the new ten, however, have been so far even higher than in Iberia. Unemployment has increased up to 40 per cent in some regions, and taxes have been increased by up to ten per cent as a result of the introduction of VAT. Economic and institutional transformations have exposed the weaknesses of these governments and, in many cases, have led to the return of former communists to the governments of these countries, which has hindered the reform process.

Joining the EC was much simpler in 1986 than it is today. Since the 1986 Iberian enlargement, the number of EU members has increased to 15, the Single Market and EMU have been introduced, and the Amsterdam and Nice treaties (with the incorporation of new policy areas such as justice and home affairs) have been ratified. Therefore, the complexity of the *acquis communautaire* has increased dramatically and the difficulties new members are likely to experience meeting it are much higher. Moreover, as other authors have noted, the differing cultural and historical experiences of the new entrants will complicate the convergence process toward a common European identity.[14]

In addition, the economic and political environments are substantially different and even more complex. Indeed, the timing of accession was an important contributing factor to the success of Iberian integration (Tovias 2002: 175–6). Not only were the Iberian economies market economies with fully institutionalized market mechanisms in place (with the parenthesis of the failed revolutionary attempt in Portugal in the mid-1970s), but also the Iberian enlargement coincided with the end of the economic recession, the lowering of oil prices, the beginning of a period of economic expansion within the European economies, and a new period of *détente* between the Soviet Union and the United States. Current economic (the world-wide recession) and political uncertainties (the so-called war on terrorism, as well as the conflict in the Middle East, Iraq, and North Korea), combined with the economic difficulties Germany and other EU member states (as well as the United States and Japan) are currently experiencing, will make integration far more difficult for new members.

Furthermore, there are also significant differences in economic performance in Eastern Europe. Given the scope of the new enlargement process and the disparities and geographical distance among the new entrants, harmonization is likely to be even more difficult. Some of these differences can be explained in terms of geographical proximity to the EU countries, but this factor does not explain everything.

Domestically, the integration prospects in Eastern Europe are far more complicated. For the new members economic modernization will be the result of a systemic challenge, not merely a consequence of an adjustment process as in the Iberian countries. Hence, the economic benefits will be lower and will take longer to materialize. Moreover, increasing nationalism in these countries will also hinder the cultural effects of integration. The new member states will face problems similar to those of previous entrants. Cameron (2002) has argued that the new member states will face four major domestic challenges: first, the ability to reform their administrative and institutional settings to develop the capacity to implement the *acquis*; second, the willingness to deepen the necessary reforms to transform their economies into functional market systems; third, the ability to reduce unemployment levels while addressing the structural imbalances of their economies; and finally, the political challenges to finalize the transition to membership in face of increasing opposition within (and outside) their countries about enlargement.

The ten new entrants will have to undergo reform of nationalized industries, tackle corruption, strengthen their judiciary systems (a key problem in these countries is the lack of strong courts) and their administrative capacities to implement the EU rules (for example, on food safety), eliminate conflicting tax rules, end political cronyism and politically-driven appointments to the civil service and public companies (there is widespread politization of public-sector jobs), reform their public finances, strengthen their weak economic management, reduce industry's subsidies, reform and in many cases privatize their large and outmoded public companies (for example, in Poland 2,000 state-owned companies generate one-quarter of employment and GDP), introduce competition in many economic sectors, improve the overall business climate (by promoting privatization, fair taxation, deregulation, investment, and by limiting abuses of market power), strengthen financial regulation, develop transparent procurements procedures, and uphold EU rules. One of the consequences of concerns over the ability of these countries to move ahead in these areas (and also an outcome of Greece's integration experience) has been the inclusion of so-called safeguard clauses into the accession treaties that allow the EU to suspend certain privileges (such as structural funds and farm aid) if the new member states breach the single market rules. Moreover, EU enlargement will increase competition and force the liberalization of economic sectors in these states, and the CAP will bring not just subsidies but also more regulation and competition. Finally, the ability of the new member states to prepare viable projects to qualify for partial EU financing and to raise matching funds will also determine their success in capitalizing from EU accession.

Furthermore, the levels of financial support from European policies (cohesion and structural funds, or the CAP) will also be far more limited for the new member states compared with previous enlargement processes. The new accession treaties provide 40.8 billion euros in EU aid for the ten states for 2004–6 (and an additional 1 billion from regional aid for Poland). This represents just 0.15 per cent of the EU GDP. This figure is gross, however, and the net transfer of funds will be even smaller after taking account of the contributions of the new member states to EU funds (with some analysts estimating that it could be as little as 12 billion euros – or just four per cent of the EU budget, or 0.05 of the EU GDP). Since the average per capita income of the new member states is 44 per cent of the EU average and their GDP is just five per cent of the EU GDP, these funds will be hardly enough to help them close this gap. With this level of support, it has been estimated that it will take more than 20 years to narrow this gap. To put these figures in perspective: Greece has received more than 35 billion euros from the EU since accession and during 1994–99, and EU aid accounted for 1.5 per cent of GDP in Spain and 3.3 per cent in Portugal.

That the new members' farmers must wait until 2013 to receive the same level of support farmers from current members receive (they will start at 25 per cent of current EU levels in 2004) further aggravates the above-mentioned difficulties. This fact is critical for countries in which agriculture still represents a large proportion of their economies (58.9 per cent per cent of the Polish territory is devoted to agricultural operations, and two out of ten Polish are farmers contributing only 3.4 per cent to the country's GDP). All of this is in a hard economic context in which two out of ten Polish are unemployed, Slovenian unemployment is 19.4 per cent, and Lithuanian unemployment is 16.5 per cent. In addition, public deficits are high (5.6 per cent of GDP in Slovakia, or 5.5 per cent in the Czech Republic).

A key additional concern is the increasing growth of disenchantment within the new member states over EU integration. Whereas a few years ago support was widespread and the assumption within the EU was that the biggest obstacles would come inside the existing union (according to Eurobarometer in 2001, only 44 per cent of Europeans supported enlargement and expressed concerns over the costs of admitting the new states, as well as fears about labour migration), disillusionment over the accession conditions and the costs of structural reforms necessary for EU membership as well as fears of being swamped by foreign capital and influence have led to increasing discontent among the citizens of the new members states, growing Euroscepticism, and the rise of anti-EU voices. Sensitive issues such as domestic concerns (for example, high levels of unemployment, or the unpopularity of local governments), farm subsidies, Cyprus, immigration, the Benes decrees, the Sudetenland dispute, or possible demands from former owners of property expropriated by Nazis and Communists in some countries have been further soured by the global economic slowdown and the accession conditions (particularly the decision to limit migration during the first seven years). According to Eurobarometer support for enlargement is running at about 65 per cent (with support ranging from 80 per cent in Hungary and 60 per cent in Poland, to barely 50 per cent in the Czech Republic), but given increasing political resentment, there is a serious risk that one (or more) of the new members may vote 'no' in the forthcoming accession referendums, particularly if voters decide to stay away from the polls. Approval is no longer a certainty.[15]

The uncertainties over the course of the institutional reforms of the EU compound these challenges. The risk of institutional decision-making gridlock is a real possibility. The logistical issues of ruling an institution with 25 members will be daunting, from administrative issues, to languages, to decision-making processes. One of the key questions is what kind of institutional reforms will result from the ongoing European Convention. Some of the outcomes from the convention may include: more qualified majority voting (for example, over issues such as taxation or justice and home affairs), European Parliament co-decision, a new system of EU presidency that will eliminate the current system based on a rotation among member states of the EU presidency every six months, and an increasing role for national parliaments. Whereas some of the larger countries (France and Britain) are pushing for a stronger EU presidency, the smallest states are arguing in favour of a strong European Commission that will act as its biggest ally and protector (but it will also require reform because 25 commissioners may be too many). It will be in the best interests of the new members to uphold the current decision-making system based on consensus with a strong European Commission as opposed to majority vote. In the end the key will be to build a Constitution of Europe that reflects the vision of the peoples of Europe. Unfortunately, for decades most governments across Europe have been treating public opinion as an obstacle to be circumvented or simply ignored. Consequently, voters' scepticism has grown and European citizens are getting tired of political elites telling them what to do in matters concerning the European Union. Politicians can ignore this at their own peril.

IBERIAN LESSONS FOR POST-COMMUNIST EUROPE[16]

The Iberian enlargement process provides useful feedback for the ongoing process, not only for negotiation strategies, but also in terms of the consequences of membership.[17] What are the Iberian lessons for post-Communist Europe?

First, any negotiations (even with the EU) should not be based on an 'us versus them' approach, but instead on a 'them versus them' approach that will allow the new member states to take advantage of divisions among current member countries. Poland has played this strategy quite skilfully so far. In addition, although the new members (like Portugal and Spain before) will find themselves on the same side on many issues (that is, on social questions, on the EU structural funds, and on the concept of cohesion), each new member should develop its own *ad hoc* coalitions with other members based on common interests. The Iberian experience shows that despite similar interests and objectives, after 16 years there has not been a consistent approach to EU negotiations between Portugal and Spain. They have often co-operated, but they have also worked separately and with other EU members. The Portuguese and Spaniards choose alliances depending on the issue at stake.

Second, one of the most important lessons from the Iberian enlargement is that the terms of accession are not always final. Renegotiations after accession are possible and compensatory mechanisms can be developed. Therefore, whatever the accession terms for 2004–6, the focus of the new member states should be on 2006, when the EU will start its next seven-year budget period. The focal point should be on 'accession economics' instead of 'development economics'. The EU will pursue stability and homogenization, but the new member countries will want to grow. In this regard the Iberian experience shows that the central and eastern European states should focus on finding the best ways to maximize the benefits of membership once they are in. A naked, selfish strategy that would look only at their particular needs is also bound to fail. The new members also need to look at their potential contributions to the EU and the model of European integration they want to build. Paraphrasing President Kennedy, they should ponder not only what the EU can do for them but also what they can do for the EU. This should not be a zero-sum game but instead a positive-sum game.

Third, the experience of Portugal and Spain demonstrates the limits of peer pressure and the ability of the *acquis communautaire* to force change. The commission has pointed out in successive enlargement overviews of the new ten the need to combat corruption and economic crime, to strengthen independent judiciaries, and to develop the capacity to implement the *acquis*. Both Spain and Portugal (or Greece), however, have had (and still face) problems in all of these areas.

The Iberian enlargement also illustrates that patterns of migration can be reversed. Both countries were made to wait for accession in the 1980s, partly over immigration fears that never materialized. As in 1986, the new treaty of accession has established a seven-year period for the new member states of central and Eastern Europe. Fears of uncontrolled migration were not substantiated after 1986 (or even after the seven-year transition period). On the contrary, as a consequence of improved economic conditions in Iberia, one of the key results of EU access was that by 1995 there were 100,000 fewer Spaniards and 110,000 Portuguese living in other EU member states than before enlargement. Furthermore, the reverse process took place when thousands of Europeans (particularly from Germany and Britain) migrated to Spain. Such concerns are likely to be unfounded again with the new member states.

The European Commission estimates that 70,000 to 150,000 workers (out of a population of 350 million people) could migrate from Eastern Europe to the current EU states. This is hardly a large number. The continuing existence of language, cultural, and structural barriers will most likely continue to hinder labour mobility in an enlarged Europe. In addition, the rapid economic growth of eastern European countries (particularly compared to some of the sclerotic EU members, like Germany) is likely to have the same effect it had on migration patterns in Spain and Portugal after 1986. Finally, although it is likely that migration will cause difficulties in particular regions (particularly on the eastern borders zones of Austria and Germany) and industries, the problem may not be too much migration from the east but instead too little. Given the aging of EU population and the low levels of fertility rates, it will be important to facilitate the migration of more young people from eastern European countries. In the end, instead of displacing local people from the labour market or lowering wages, immigrants from the new members states will contribute to the host economy by adding value, creating jobs, and pushing up wages because these workers will now be able to work legally (several hundred thousand currently work illegally in the EU).[18]

It is also necessary to note that the support they received from the EU funds largely influenced the success of the Iberian countries. As noted, during 1994–99 EU aid accounted for 1.5 per cent of GDP in Spain and

3.3 per cent in Portugal. EU funding has allowed rates of public investment to remain relatively stable since the mid-1980s. The percentage of public investment EU funds finances has been rising since 1985, to reach average values of 42 per cent for Portugal and 15 per cent for Spain. Moreover, the European Commission has estimated that the impact of EU structural funds on GDP growth and employment has been significant: relative to the GDP forcasted without this aid, GDP rose in 1999 by 9.9 per cent in Portugal and 3.1 per cent in Spain. These funds, which amount to just over one-third of the EU budget, have contributed significantly to reducing regional disparities and fostering convergence within the EU. They have played a prominent role in developing the factors that improve the competitiveness and determine the potential growth of the least developed regions of both countries.[19] We have seen, however, that new member states should not expect the same level of aid. Therefore, adjustments costs will be higher and it will take them longer to catch up.

While acknowledging the critical role EU funds play in the success of Iberian integration, however, it is also important to stress that successful integration is not only a budgetary issue. On the contrary, the Iberian experience demonstrates that the main benefits of integration derive from the opportunities it generates in terms of trade and foreign direct investment. Portugal and Spain show that a critical factor in determining the final outcome of integration will depend upon the pattern of investment, which would bring about important *dynamics effects*. Dynamic effects should be more important than static ones. Indeed, the process of opening to international trade improves potential for growth, lowers production costs, and reduces the risk premium in response to a brighter macroeconomic outlook, which results from economic reforms. These developments help account for the increases in FDI in Portugal and Spain (where it reached a peak of 2.7 per cent of GDP in 1990). FDI, in turn, has had positive implications for the Iberian economies because it has facilitated the transmission of technology, paved the way for advances in productivity, and, therefore, fostered an increase in the potential GDP growth of both economies.

The difficulties the Iberian economies experienced in the early 1990s provide an additional lesson for new members, namely, that 'automatic pilots' do not work. The credibility of monetary and economic authorities cannot be built by attaching them to semi-rigid institutional mechanisms (like Spain and, to a lesser extent, Portugal tried to do in the late 1980s and early 1990s with European Monetary System [EMS] membership). It must be earned through the adequate management of existing discretionary powers. In addition, the Iberian EMU integration shows that the consolidation of integration processes is contingent on an adequate coordination of macroeconomic policies among members prior to the (possible) adoption of a monetary currency. In Portugal and Spain EU integration has required a set of measures including increased competition, privatization of public enterprises, industrial restructuring, and deregulation. These measures have translated into efficiency gains, which have been reinforced by a more stable macroeconomic framework. At the same time, lower inflation and fiscal consolidation have led to lower real (and nominal) interest rates, which, in turn, have resulted in a higher sustainable growth. There have also been short-term costs associated with monetary integration, however. Indeed, the losses of the exchange rate and of monetary sovereignty require a process of nominal convergence and fiscal consolidation, as well as higher cyclical correlation, for euro membership to be successful. This should be taken into account for future Eastern European economies.

The Iberian enlargement also shows that prior to monetary integration, candidates must carry out a process of modernization and nominal convergence without fixing their exchange rate. An additional lesson is that financial institutional reform does not necessarily force institutional changes in other areas (for example, the labour market or fiscal policies). The virtual collapse of the EMS in 1992, caused in part by successive devaluations of the Iberian currencies, showed the limits of financial and monetary instruments to impose institutional reforms in other areas and to balance domestic and external economic objectives. Institutional reforms require governments that are willing to pay the short-term political prices for unpopular actions and policies. The jury is still out regarding the domestic institutional impact of EMU.

One of the important lessons drawn from the Iberian enlargement should be that economic success drives public opinion. As we have seen, in Iberia the greatest consensus elicited toward the EU is largely instrumental. The image of a 'European community' among Iberian people is very weak. Indeed, they perceive the EU as an economic community, not so much as a European community. The Eurobarometer and CIS polling data show that the Iberian citizens' perceptions about the personal and collective benefits derived from EU membership are one of the key factors that help explain their attitudes toward the process of European integration. Hence, approval of Europe seems to coincide with the economic cycles: low during economic recessions and high during periods of economic growth.

Finally, although Portugal and Spain pursued feverishly their integration in the Community, the effects of EU integration have not always been favourable to both countries. As we have seen, both in manufacturing and in agriculture, there has been trade diversion and trade creation. The latter resulted in more adjustment problems, since greater import penetration led to a contraction in domestic production. This was particularly true in the case of the Iberian manufacturing sector. Factors such as the behaviour of the exchange rate or the strategies of multinational companies with subsidiaries in both countries also played a critical role in the final outcome of integration. This analysis proves that the expected static effects, which were not always favourable to Spain and Portugal, should not be the main economic expectation behind the ten's entry to the EU. Based on the Iberian experience, dynamic effects provide an important rationale for the support of integration. Over the long term, they will affect the rate of economic growth of the new member states, which will be largely influenced by investment patterns, by the efficiency with which these resources are used, and finally, by their distributional effects among regions.

CONCLUSIONS

Whereas the short-term outlook can be difficult, the prospects of EU entry have already transformed the economies of the candidate countries. From an economic standpoint, although central and eastern European countries have low GDP per capita, they are growing quickly (certainly more quickly than most of the EU economies). For the new members a key benefit will be additional FDI (currently 78 per cent of the investment in the ten member states comes from the EU). Market-oriented reforms have also taken place over the last decade in all ten countries and they have been compounded by private investment, including FDI. As a result the private sector in many of the ten countries is flourishing and showing resourcefulness in competitive markets. The EU Commission has estimated that membership could help raise the annual economic growth rate of these ten countries by an extra 1.3 to 23.1 per cent. In addition, these countries already compare well in surveys of global competitiveness *vis-à-vis* EU members (for example, the World Economic Forum ranks Hungary and Estonia above Portugal, and Slovenia, the Czech Republic, and Poland above Greece). Long-term prospects for growth are also good because of the region's low-cost labour, its skilled workers, and its proximity to western European export markets. These countries have become flexible because the drive to dismantle the Communist apparatus has led to the development of a more open administrative environment than in many EU member states and more labour flexibility.[20]

Moreover, producers from the new member states will now have access not only to their respective national markets but also to the European one. This will offer incentives for investment and will allow for the development of economies of scale, which in turn will result in more competitive products in the European markets. Furthermore, the entry of these new states to the EU will make their citizens European citizens, thus ending some of the discriminations those emigrants currently suffer. Finally, access to the EU cohesion and structural funds will facilitate the accession of new members. Indeed, the structural and cohesions funds and the CAP (limited as they will be) are powerful support instruments to mitigate the negative impact of accession.

For the Iberian countries and the new central and eastern European member states, the EU symbolizes modernization and democracy. In Iberia the European integration process has facilitated the reincorporation of both countries to the international arena, has contributed to the legitimacy of the new democratic regimes, has acted as a buffer in controversial issues (such as the process of decentralization in Spain, or the implementation of economic reforms), and has facilitated and accelerated the process of convergence and modernization of financial, commercial, and manufacturing structures. The idea of Europe became a driving force that moved reforms forward and was a fundamental factor for bringing together political stabilization, economic recovery, and democratic consolidation.

As we look to future research agendas, it is important to stress that whereas the majority of the research in this project has focused on the policy effects and the influence of EU policies on the Iberian countries, it is also imperative to study the impact of EU membership on domestic institutions.[21]

Despite all the significant progress accomplished over the last one and half decades, the Iberian countries still have considerable ground to cover. At a time in which the European Commission is reporting that the EU is 'losing the battle on competitiveness' in a list of 44 indicators, including economic performance, reform, employment, and research, Portugal and Spain (together with Greece) are among the worst countries in the majority of the areas.[22] Lack of political willingness to reform and sluggish growth will hinder further the convergence process. At the same time, the accession of the central and eastern European states will exacerbate differences in economic performance within the EU. Indeed, with the ten new member states joining in, there is an increased risk of a 'two-tier' Europe in which some countries will do better than others. The EU has limited direct powers to force outcomes. The experiences of Portugal and Spain show that the influence of indirect EU recommendations on policy and demonstration effects has been greater than direct action. Hence, it is not surprising that European states, and particularly the Iberian countries, are failing to live up to the ambitious targets established in the European Council of Lisbon in March of 2000, which aimed at making the EU more competitive.[22] Although EU membership will facilitate (and in many cases ameliorate) adjustment costs and provide impetus for reforms, the experience of the Iberian countries shows this is no substitute for the domestic implementation of reforms, which should proceed further in areas such as labour, product, and capital markets. The success of enlargement and institutional reforms will hinge to a considerable degree on the ability of European leaders to implement reforms in the face of domestic resistance and increasing scepticism about enlargement. The enlargement process and the new convention will largely determine the future of Europe. Lack of progress will bring institutional paralysis and loss of competitiveness. The survival of the European model is at stake.

NOTES

1. References to the European Economic Community (EEC) or the European Union can be misleading if the historical period covered extends past the last two decades. This essay addresses themes in the European Economic Community prior to the introduction of the European Union label in the Maastricht Treaty of 1991. The terms 'the European Community' (EC) or 'the European Union' (EU) are used indistinctly to refer to the European integration process and institutions throughout the essay. Similarly, 'Europe' is here always used to refer to the countries that are members of the European Union, either before or after the Maastricht Treaty. In the second section when I focus on the ongoing enlargement process, I refer to the EU.
2. Pridham (2002: 188–9) and Pridham (1991: 234–5).
3. Pridham (2002: 194–205).
4. Supporters of decentralization and the regionalist parties viewed the process of European integration as a model of decentralization, and saw EC integration as an instrument to ensure the decentralization of the Spanish political system. See Alvarez-Miranda (1996) and Magone (2002: 229).
5. Magone (2002: 225).
6. Pérez-Díaz (2002: 280–84) and Magone (2002: 232).
7. See Tovias 2002. EU pressures have contributed to the implementation of policies and rules for the sound management of the economy. This influence has been explicitly acknowledged by Iberian policy-makers. The Portuguese Prime Minister, José Durao Barroso, reflecting on the impact of the Stability Pact has recognized that 'the Portuguese usually respond best when they face an external challenge. Some of the reforms we have implemented–such as setting limits on local government debt–would not even have been accepted by members of my own party if there had not been this pressure from the outside.' See 'Portugal Learns to Love Stability Pact', *Financial Times*, 29 Jan. 2003, p.4.

8. Hine (1989: 16–18).

9. See Sebastian (2001: 25–6).

10. From 'La Convergencia Real a Paso Lento', *El País*, 14 Feb. 2000.

11. Today the EU is rich and homogeneous with a population of 376 million, a GDP of $8.660 billion, and a GDP per head of $23,550. The richest EU country is Luxembourg with a per capita GDP of $27,470 and its poorest is Greece with $16,860. In contrast, the new member states have a combined population of almost 75 million (Poland accounts for 39 million) and their GDP per head is only an average of $10,550. See Martin Wolf, 'Europe Risks Destruction to Widen Peace and Prosperity', *Financial Times*, 11 Dec. 2002, p.15.

12. See 'Sólo dos comunidades de las 11 actuales podrán recibir fondos europeos en 2007' [Only two of the current 11 communities will be able to receive European funds in 2007], in *El País*, 24 Jan. 2003; 'La ampliación ahonda la brecha económica y social en la UE' [Enlargement widens the economic and social gap within the EU], *El País*, 12 Dec. 2002.

13. For a discussion on the effects of enlargement in Spain, see José Ignacio Torreblanca, 'Por fin, la ampliación: la Unión Europea tras el Consejo de Copenhague' [Finally Enlargement: The EU After the Copenhagen Summit], mimeo, *Real Instituto Elcano de Estudios Internacionales y Estratégicos*, 19 Dec. 2002.

14. Magone (2002).

15. See Stefan Wagstyl, 'EU Accession States Woo the Voters', *Financial Times*, 9 Jan. 2003, p.4.

16. I would like to thank Jeffrey Kopstein, Ramón de Miguel, Kalypso Nicolaidis, George Ross, and Franciso Seixas da Costa for their valuable comments during the last roundtable of the conference 'From Isolation to Europe: 15 Years of Spanish and Portuguese Membership in the European Union'. Their comments inform this analysis.

17. Some observers have noted that these new members may learn even more from Greece than from Portugal and Spain. In Greece, for instance, the government was reluctant to cede control of vital economic sectors, it was behind in consumer protection and in environmental and competition policies, and corruption was a systemic problem. In addition, Greece had weak civil institutions, which slowed the convergence process. For years Greece squandered the opportunities of EU membership through poor fiscal management, corruption, political cronyism, justice mismanagement, and misadministration and mismanagement of domestic and European funds. Although fiscal discipline has been achieved, the change of attitudes and values is still a pending issue. See 'Is Poland the new Greece? Why Warsaw's Entry into the European Union May Be Rough', *Financial Times*, 9 Dec. 2002, p.11. See also Verney (2002).

18. See 'UK Leads Way on Opening Borders to New Workers', *Financial Times*, 13 Dec. 2002, p.2; 'Fears of Big Move West May be Unfounded', *Financial Times*, 2 Dec. 2002, p.4.

19. See Sebastian (2001: 25–6).

20. For instance, according to the World Economic Forum, starting a company in Poland takes three permits compared to an average of five in France and ten in Italy. See 'Into the West', *The Financial Times*, 22 July 2002. Spain, in contrast, is listed by the European Commission as the country in which the cost to create a business is the highest (1,572 euros when the EU average is 250), and the second in which the process is the slowest (24 days – twice that of the EU average; only Italy is behind with 35 days). According to the Commission some of the key difficulties include: administrative barriers, difficult access to financing, bankruptcy provisions, employment protection, discrimination against women, and inadequate education and training.

21. See Morlino (2002).

22. See 'The EU "Is Losing Battle on Competitiveness"', *Financial Times*, 13 Jan. 2003, p.3. Spain has lost three positions (is listed at number 20) in the last Globalization Index

published by *Foreign Policy* (Jan./Feb. 2003, No.134, p.60) and Portugal is listed at 14. In addition, the World Economic Forum has placed Spain and Portugal among the least competitive countries in the European Union (only Greece is behind) in its *Report on Global Competitiveness*. This report examines economic conditions in 80 countries, focusing on two main indexes: MICI (Microeconomic Competitiveness Index), which measures the quality of business development, and the GCI (Growth Competitiveness Index), which examines growth perspectives in five to eight years based on macroeconomic stability.

REFERENCES

Alvarez-Miranda, B. (1996): *El sur de Europa y la adhesion a la comunidad: Los debates politicos*, Madrid: CIS.

Cameron, D.R. (2002): 'The Challenges of EU Accession', Paper presented at the annual meeting of the American Political Science Association, Boston, Sept.

CIS (1999): *Opiniones y actitudes de los españoles ante el proceso de integración europea* [Opinions and attitudes of Spaniards towards the process of European integration], Madrid: Consejo de Investigaciones Sociológicas.

Costa Pinto, A. and N.S. Teixeira (eds.) (2002): *Southern Europe and the Making of the European Union*, New York: Columbia University Press.

Costa Pinto, A. and N.S. Teixeira (2002): 'From Africa to Europe: Portugal and European Integration', in Costa Pinto and Teixeira (eds.) [2002].

Fishman, R. (2001): 'Shaping, Not Making, Democracy: The European Union and Spain's Post-Franco Political Transformation', Paper presented at the conference 'From Isolation to Integration: 15 Years of Portuguese and Spanish Membership in Europe', Minda de Gunzburg Center for European Studies, Harvard University, 2–3 Nov.

Hine, R.C. (1989): 'Customs Union Enlargement and Adjustment: Spain's Accession to the European Community', *Journal of Common Market Studies* XXVIII/1, Sept.

Magone, J. (2002): 'Attitudes of Southern European Citizens Towards European Integration', in Costa Pinto and Teixeira (eds.) [2002].

Morlino, L. (2002): 'The Europeanisation of Southern Europe', in Costa Pinto and Teixeira (eds.) [2002].

Pérez-Díaz, V. (2002): 'From Civil war to Civil Society: Social Capital in Spain from the 1930s to the 1990s', in R.D. Putnam (ed.), *Democracies in Flux: the Evolution of Social Capital in Contemporary Society*, New York: Oxford University Press.

Pridham, G. (1991): 'The Politics of the European Community: transnational networks, and democratic transitions in Southern Europe', in G. Pridham, *Encouraging Democracy: The Institutional Context of Regime Transition in Southern Europe*, Leicester: Leicester University Press.

Pridham, G. (2002): 'European Integration and Democratic Consolidation in Southern Europe', in Costa Pinto and Teixeira (eds.) [2002].

Sebastian, M. (2001): 'Spain in the EU: Fifteen Years May not be Enough', Paper presented at the conference 'From Isolation to Europe: 15 Years of Spanish and Portuguese Membership in the European Union', Minda de Gunzburg Center for European Studies, Harvard University, 2–3 Nov.

Tovias, A. (2002): 'The Southern European Economies and European Integration', in Costa Pinto and Teixeira (eds.) [2002].

Verney, Susannah (2002): 'The Greek Association with the European Community: A Strategy of State', in Costa Pinto and Teixeira (eds.) [2002].

Portugal and Spain: A Fifteen-Year 'Quasi-Experiment' with European Integration in a Pair of 'Most Similar Systems'

PHILIPPE C. SCHMITTER

INTRODUCTION

Normally, social scientists are deprived of the opportunity to experiment with their 'subjects'. Introducing some treatment, holding everything else constant, and measuring what happens is simply not feasible or would not be tolerated in the real world of complex, unpredictable, and costly human relations. Hence, most economists, sociologists, and political scientists must rely heavily upon comparison between 'naturally' occurring events or processes in their attempt to draw generally valid inferences about causality or to put forward compelling arguments about specific historical situations. Needless to say, getting away with this admittedly second-best mode of scientific analysis is even more difficult when those involved come from diverse academic disciplines and national backgrounds – as is the case with the authors in this volume.

A STRATEGY FOR COMPARISON

These essays make use of a frequently advocated, but rarely executed, comparative strategy. First, the collaborators have selected two countries, namely, Portugal and Spain, that seem to share many background conditions; second, they have focused in a concerted and multi-dimensional fashion on the impact of a single, common, and contemporaneous treatment, that is, entry into the (then) European Community (now) European Union (EC/EU); and, third, they have allowed sufficient time to elapse (15 years) so that the similarities and differences in the impact of that treatment should have manifested themselves.

This 'paired' plus 'most-similar-systems' plus 'quasi-experimental' design, when well executed, provides about as good a basis for causal inference and reasoned historical argument as one is likely to find in the real world. It is not, however, flawless. The countries may have less in common than is initially supposed. The treatment may not be quantitatively or qualitatively the same. The time period may be insufficient to capture all of the effects. Other things can also be happening to the countries within the same time frame. Factors not initially taken into consideration, once introduced, may render even the most convincing correlations spurious. Theoretical concepts and empirical indicators may not have been used consistently across the cases or by authors from different academic disciplines.

A COMPELLING SET OF FINDINGS

Even taking these caveats into consideration, I am convinced that the contributors to this volume do come up with inferences and conclusions that will stand up to virtually all challenges. Moreover, one cannot help but be impressed by their extraordinarily high level of agreement on three macro-findings:

(1) European integration has had a significant impact on a wide range of economic, social, and political outcomes in both countries;
(2) This impact has been positive for most of these outcomes and for most of the people affected by them; and,
(3) Specifically with regard to the consolidation of democracy, European integration did contribute to its success in both countries, even if it was not the determining factor.

The contributors all agree that joining the EC/EU has made a real difference and that this difference has, on balance, been good for most people in both countries. Portuguese and Spaniards have attained economic, social and political goods – and, presumably, avoided economic, social, and political 'bads' – that they would otherwise have not attained. These two countries began to change from autocracy to democracy before joining the EC/EU. Indeed, this was a precondition for even entering into serious negotiations. Both the anticipation of membership and its subsequent occurrence, however, made it easier for politicians to compromise on an acceptable set of liberal democratic rules and more likely that mass publics would regard these rules as legitimate. In short, in terms of the perception of elites as well as citizens, Europeanization and democratization became inextricably related to each other.

The authors' inferences and conclusions differ a bit more in terms of the relative magnitude than the direction of change over this 15-year period. Portugal tends to come out a bit ahead; however, everyone declares both countries to be winners. I can recall very few edited volumes, however, in which the contributors managed to reached such a high level of consensus about the causal impact and direction of change embedded in such complex processes of eco-socio-political transformation.

A POLITICAL LOGIC OF TRANSFORMATION

Moreover, everyone seems to agree that the 'logic' of this transformation was essentially political, even if the actual negotiations for entry into EC/EU primarily concerned economic matters. There is no convincing evidence in any of the essays that the decision to join was driven either by rigorous calculations of material cost and benefit or by pressure from organized business or labour. These interests may have been more in agreement and more favourable to membership in the case of Spain than in Portugal where the internal division within both social classes was much greater due to the 'revolutionary' nature of its regime change. In neither case, however, were rational calculations and/or economic interests determinate. Politicians played the key role in both cases and on both sides of the negotiation. They took the risk of enlargement, supported only by a loose consensus of public opinion in the candidate countries and (probably) by mild opposition or indifference in most of the member-states, and they did so before democracy was fully consolidated in either country. Indeed, Spain suffered an attempted *golpe de estado* after it was a member, and Portugal still had major constitutional revisions ahead of it. Political elites in both applicant-states and in the then EC member-states seem to have accepted the notion that what mattered most was to use entry as a sort of 'insurance policy' against potential regression to authoritarian rule. Certainly, the former conducted very little serious research about the eventual economic consequences of their membership and the latter tolerated 'Southern' political practices and uncertainties they would not accept from the countries currently involved in 'Eastern' enlargement. 'Political conditionality' was not yet a buzzword and, even if it had been, it would have been applied sparingly.

This consensus among authors with regard to both substance and process is all the more puzzling in that the 'most-similar-systems' design is usually searching for differences, not similarities, in outcome that can be attributed to those variables that continue to discriminate between the cases being examined. For example, when two countries are alike in culture, level of development, and geo-strategic location, but differ widely in political institutions, most analysts will be looking for variation in government stability, social equity, or economic performance that they can attribute to those institutional variations. In the case of Portugal and Spain, there were certainly some very marked differences between them at the moment both entered into the EC/EU. Portugal was smaller, poorer, less economically diverse and socially developed, just emerging from a set of disastrous colonial wars, and suffering a tumultuous transition from authoritarian rule – but also more integrated into international and regional institutions. Spain had chosen earlier to break with a development pattern of national/colonial autarchy and had a price and production system much closer to the existing members of the EC/EU – but had had virtually no previous experience with the institutions of the EC/EU. Nothing illustrates the difference better than the fact that virtually all political forces in Spain – parties, associations, movements – were strongly in favour of membership. In contrast, the issue generated considerable dissent among similar groups in Portugal.

A MIX OF (ALLEGED) DISADVANTAGES

In short, there were ample reasons to suspect the response to European integration would differ, and that Portugal would find it more difficult to adjust politically, socially, and economically to being 'in Europe'. Spaniards had long since given up the idea of playing an extra-European role, whereas Portuguese were still debating well into the 1970s what region of the world they belonged to. The rest of Europe may have long placed both of these trans-Pyrenean countries together 'in Africa', but they harboured very different illusions about themselves and their prospects.

By an analogous logic, the 'quasi-experimental' design also anticipates differences not similarities. Not only is it expected that the units will behave differently after they have been 'treated' with some policy, but also that the magnitude (if not the direction) of this change should vary with differences in how stringently the treatment was applied. Since there is general agreement that the terms under which Portugal (and Greece) joined the club were more favourable than in the case of Spain, the former should have done significantly better. Whereas there is something of a consensus among the analysts that this was indeed the case (and was not apparently countermanded by Portugal's generally less favourable structural and attitudinal points of departure), none of them evoked a specific item of EC/EU leniency as especially pertinent. My inclination would be to agree with the counter-intuitive evidence of Portugal's having done relatively better, but to attribute this to the sort of intrinsic advantage of playing 'catch-up' to its more developed peninsular neighbour that Alexander Gerschenkron pointed to some time ago. *A contrario*, I would point out that Greece was also given more and longer *dérogations* by the EC/EU negotiators and performed markedly worse over the next 15 years. Moreover, now that Portugal has almost caught up to Spain, its growth rate and public finances are no longer doing so much better.[1]

A METHODOLOGICAL DIFFICULTY

The major methodological conclusion I would therefore draw from this exercise in comparison is that of 'equifinality'. As John Stuart Mill pointed out, one of the most serious obstacles to developing a cumulative science of society is the likelihood that different combinations of factors might produce the same outcome. Spanish public opinion was initially more favourable to the EC/EU than the Portuguese was, but after 15 years they have converged toward a roughly similar position: Spaniards have become less Euro-philic and Portuguese more so, apparently for different reasons having to do with the relative impact of structural/regional funds and patterns of foreign investment. Countries can follow different trajectories and be subjected to different events and still emerge with rather similar characteristics – in this case, they both end up as well-consolidated democracies playing according to the rules of European integration and benefiting more-or-less equally from the experience.

By my (admittedly crude) calculation, the similarities between Portugal and Spain in initial structure, timing in entry, and treatment in policy were insufficient to explain the remarkable similarity in outcome between these neighbouring countries. There are simply too many factors that should have made more of a difference. Most of them have been political. For example, the mode of transition from autocracy, the extent of territorial devolution of power, the relative continuity or discontinuity in politico-administrative elites, the degree of fragmentation of the party system, and the presence or absence of a serious internal security threat should have had some impact on performance. Admittedly, these factors are (at least hypothetically) mixed. Some should have favoured Spain, some Portugal. It is therefore logically possible that they might have cancelled each other out and could dialectically account for the similarity in outcome with regard to European integration.

A (REJECTED) THOUGHT EXPERIMENT

Such logic suggests to me an alternative explanation to the puzzle: what if membership in the EC/EU had no significant impact – positive or negative – on either Portugal or Spain? What if these two countries had not joined 15 years ago? Would they not have converged toward the rest of Europe without the impetus of EC/EU directives and incentives? Would their present political, social, and economic status have been any different? Might not the range of probable outcomes in western European polities at this historical moment be determined by global and/or regional forces that have little to do with the formal integration process itself? Norway and Switzerland decided in a democratic fashion not to join the EU and they do not seem to have suffered a remarkably different fate. Granted that both countries in this pair were much better established in their political institutions and much more privileged in their economic situation when they chose to opt out, but is it so far-fetched to infer that Portugal and Spain would have followed the same pattern? After all, Norway and Switzerland are in reality members of the EC/EU in that its decisions have a major impact on virtually all areas of 'national' public policy and there are very few deviant courses of action they can afford to take. Would not the 'Iberian Pair' have been caught in a similar 'benevolent' trap if they had chosen to stay out?

Only Robert Fishman's contribution comes close to posing this counter-factual and, not surprisingly, his conclusions about the significant and benevolent impact of EC/EU membership are more muted. This sort of 'thought experiment' – especially when coupled with a 'quasi-experiment' in policy – is hardly likely to lead to any firm conclusions. For what it is worth, my impression from reading the essays is that alternative explanations for economic and political success are less plausible. NATO (North Atlantic Treaty Organization) membership probably had a momentary impact on both the radicalized Portuguese military and the reactionary Spanish officer corps during the transition period, but did not contribute that much during the consolidation – especially since NATO had already demonstrated its 'strategic' compatibility with autocracy on several previous occasions. No essay in the volume even mentions the impact of other European organizations – the Council of Europe, the

European Free Trade Area, the Helsinki Process, or the Organization for Security and Co-operation in Europe – as relevant. The role of the United States and individual European neighbours, again, was important (even crucial at a particular moment in the Portuguese *Revolução*) during the early phases of regime change, but faded thereafter.

Among the economic 'suspects', none of the usual factors promoting growth were particularly favourable or, if they were, they depended upon EC/EU membership. Both countries were initially lucky in their timing, since entry coincided during the first five years with a general upturn in the European economy. This was followed by a severe downturn, and yet they continued to do well. Net domestic saving and investment were relatively low (especially in Portugal), although the flow of structural/regional funds and agricultural subsidies compensated for this. Whether that compensation resulted in a significant and permanent increase in productivity seems disputable. The foreign investment that did pour into both countries, as expected, was not likely to have occurred without the market access and politico-legal assurance of full EC/EU membership. Granted that receipts from tourism were high and increased during the period (and that was probably quite independent of membership), but emigrant remittances must have decreased relatively when more Portuguese and Spaniards chose to return home rather than leave and exploit the new opportunities for labour mobility included (with a delay) in the treaties of accession. There is little or no evidence in the essays of a major impact of European integration upon the level of unemployment (especially in the case of Spain, where it remained the highest in Western Europe), labour market policies, human capital provision, or 'the fiscal constitution' (at least, in Portugal).

A (POTENTIALLY MISLEADING) LESSON

Most of the readers of this collection of essays will be primarily interested in the countries involved, or in the process of integration in Western Europe. There may, however, be an intrepid few who will use it as a device for inferring what might happen when Eastern Enlargement takes place – now promised for ten countries by 2004. In my view this exercise in comparative lesson-drawing is likely to prove misleading.

No doubt, the lesson of Portuguese and Spanish accession seems encouraging. If you join the EU, you will be able to consolidate (and legitimate) your liberal democracy, grow (and diversify) your liberal economy, and all the while be admired (and envied) by your non-EU neighbours! Now, that is a deal that few countries can resist – and belief in it goes a long way toward explaining why the queue to get into the EU is so long.

Leaving aside some rather significant differences in point of departure – ten rather than three countries; much higher burdens of economic, administrative, and legal reform in domestic institutions; relatively lower levels of per capita income (with one or two exceptions); more volatile party systems (in most cases); much less productive agriculture; and many more inefficient state enterprises – the Eastern candidates find themselves in a very different negotiating process. Their interlocutors (now 15) are much less likely to be lenient. Backed by very sceptical publics (and a raising tide of xenophobic parties), faced with much greater 'up-front' costs, and knowing the entry of these Eastern countries will put an enormous strain on an already shaky set of EU decision rules, existing member-states have dramatically upped the ante. Conditions are being imposed now that would have been unthinkable back in the 1980s. Rights for ethno-linguistic minorities, resolution of all territorial boundaries and extra-territorial claims on 'nationals' living in other countries, marginalization of nationalist parties and leaders, administrative probity, political decentralization, privatization of public enterprises, removal of state subsidies, iron-clad guarantees for private property, independent judiciaries, proof of the rule of law – none of these, as far as I can tell, were demanded of Portugal and Spain when they were negotiating entry.

The danger is that if the Easterners take the treatment of the Southerners as the norm, they are going to be disillusioned by the time they have negotiated their fee for getting into the club. And if they expect to perform as well during the subsequent 15 years, they are going to be even more disappointed. They may be exploiting the same normative–constructivist–political logic that helped Portugal and Spain overcome their obvious shortcomings from a materialist–realist–economic perspective, but they are not getting the same deal – far from it. This raises a question that does not seem to have been asked during Southern enlargement: How will the new members behave once they have been admitted to the club? Portugal and Spain provide a reassuring precedent.[2] Once admitted, they played according to the pre-existing rules – even if they increasingly sought to bend those rules in order to extract materialist–realist–economic advantages for themselves and (in the case of Spain) to apply them aggressively in order to resist any reduction in payoffs in favour of the new members of the club. In the case of Southern Enlargement, the conditions of entry seem to have been regarded as fair;

the distribution of initial burdens and benefits reasonably equitable; the assignment of voting weights and thresholds relatively proportionate; the side payments and exemptions generous enough; and the EU institutions sufficiently flexible so that elites in neither country seem to have regretted their decision to join and their gamble to do so was amply ratified by public opinion.

Eastern enlargement, however, seems likely to shake that comfortable assumption. The conditions demanded have been more onerous, and they have been much more intrusively political. The willingness of EU members to extend existing subsidies and compensations and to allow exemptions from the *acquis communautaire* for 'sensitive' products and issues has been much less forthcoming. In this context, extending the EU from 15 to 25 may not ensure subsequent conformity to its rules of the game – even as modified by the Treaty of Nice and, eventually, the present Convention for a 'constitutional treaty'. The Easterners will be admitted (the assurances have been sufficiently strong and specific that they cannot be retracted), but once inside I doubt they will behave as obediently as the Southerners. They are likely not only to exploit the rules for maximum material advantage (everyone does that), but also to work hard to change those decision-rules and, hence, the basic institutional arrangements that have, so far, guided European integration. Whether this will weaken or strengthen these institutions remains to be seen. In retrospect, Portuguese and Spanish accession definitely strengthened them and made a significant positive contribution to the integration process as such. In prospect, I doubt the same thing will be said of Czech, Estonian, Hungarian, Latvian, Lithuanian, Polish, Slovak, and Slovenian accession.

NOTES

1. There is one note of dissent with regard to Portugal's relative superiority. Jorge Braga de Macedo argues convincingly that membership in the EC/EU did little to improve its 'fiscal constitution'. Unfortunately, this is one of the few essays without a Spanish content or counterpart so it is impossible to judge whether the latter's entry produced a better outcome. My suspicion is that no well-functioning democracy could possibly support the sort of neo-liberal fiscal constitution that Braga de Macedo outlines and, therefore, what he is effectively demonstrating is that Portugal is democratic and, hence, fiscally sub-optimal. Moreover, this is hardly a fair test of the 'potency' of European integration since fiscal policy remains one of the most zealously guarded of national policy domains. National politicians may try to use the EC/EU as an excuse for imposing 'fiscal sanity', but they each possess a veto on any collective action in this regard.
2. Greece, at least until recently, is another story. It demonstrates how 'exceptional' were the success stories of Portugal and Spain.

ABSTRACTS

Some Lessons from the Fifteenth Anniversary of the Accession of Portugal and Spain to the European Union
SEBASTIÁN ROYO and PAUL CHRISTOPHER MANUEL

This study examines the integration process and how it has affected political, economic and social developments in Portugal and in Spain over the last 15 years. Since the last century, the obsession of Spanish and Portuguese reformists has been to make up the lost ground with modernized Europe. EU membership has been a critical step in this direction. The record of the past 15 years is that this dream is becoming an economic reality. Despite impressive achievements, however, namely, since 1986, Portugal's average per capita income has grown from 56 per cent of the EU average to about 74 per cent, whereas Spain's has grown to 83 per cent – both Iberian countries still have a long way to go to reach the EU average wealth.

Shaping, not Making, Democracy:
The European Union and the Post-Authoritarian Political Transformations of Spain and Portugal
ROBERT M. FISHMAN

This essay argues that the forces and attitudes shaping the politics of transition in the two Iberian cases should be understood as prior to and deeper than those underpinning the ultimate form taken by the politics of European integration (although clearly EC membership had been pursued by some actors prior to democratization). The Spanish and Portuguese democracies have been shaped, but not made, by the successful effort of both countries to achieve full EC membership. The process of European integration has interacted with a wide variety of domestic political and economic factors, thus shaping the new democracies. European integration has not eliminated major differences between the cases, however, and above all it cannot explain the broader pattern of political transformation with its clearly identifiable (yet remarkably dissimilar) underpinnings in the two cases.

European Integration and Civil Society in Spain
KERSTIN HAMANN

This essay argues that, while not a causal determinant for a successful transition to democracy in Spain, the promise of EU membership helped Spain's democratization and consolidation process, partially overcoming its notorious dearth of voluntary associations. In addition, the EU also exerted significant influence on prominent segments of civil society, most notably organized labour, which helped shape the context for state–society relations.

Portugal and Eastern Europe:
After the Revolution, Democratic Europe
LUÍS SALGADO DE MATOS

This essay argues that there exists a crucial triangle for speedy European integration and the institutionalization of representative democracy: a strong state-nation, strong elites and a reasonable level of economic development. In his view, Portugal was able to accomplish a democratic revolution and accession to the EU because it was a strong state-nation, had competitive elites, and was a cohesive society. Eastern European candidates weaker on these variables. The essay suggests that eastern European candidates should rebuild their elites and increase social cohesiveness before becoming full EU state-members. If they come in too quickly, they will be unable to cope with the challenges they will have to deal with later on.

Portuguese Attitudes Towards EU Membership:
Social and Political Perspectives
MARINA COSTA LOBO

Drawing on extensive sets of Eurobarometer data, this contribution presents and analyses Portuguese attitudes towards European integration. The data show that the Portuguese electorate continues to use political parties in order to make sense of complex reality, adopting their chosen party's stance on European integration. This leads to another conclusion relating to the relationship between the EU and the public in general: national parties seem to be the missing link for an improvement in the relationship between the EU as a political institution and the public in general.

Spaniards' Long March Towards Europe
JUAN DÍEZ-NICOLÁS

This essay argues that Spaniards supported the integration of Spain into the European Economic Community because they wanted to lose the feeling of isolation that they had experienced for several decades during the Franco regime, and they were anxious to prove they were fully Europeans. This almost unanimous consensus in favour of integration into Europe, even after 16 years of membership, seems to be the consequence of Spain's need to overcome its historical isolation from the rest of Europe since the nineteenth century until the end of the Franco regime in 1975.

Spanish Membership of the European Union Revisited
CHARLES POWELL

This contribution attempts to describe and account for the major changes undergone by Spain as an EU player since her accession in 1986. Many analysts appear to have espoused the view that most if not all of these can be attributed to the fact that, following the 1996 general election, a decidedly pro-integrationist Felipe González was replaced as prime minister by a vaguely Eurosceptical José María Aznar. Undoubtedly, ideological considerations (and, more importantly perhaps, differences in political culture) must be taken into account when examining the evolution of Spain's European policy over the past 15 years. However, this study will argue that changing policy styles and contents should be understood in terms of both the learning process undergone by all new member states as they mature, and the need to adapt and respond to developments within the EU, most notably the evolution of the European integration process itself.

Portugal's European Integration:
The Good Student with a Bad Fiscal Constitution
JORGE BRAGA DE MACEDO

This study examines the role of monetary and fiscal policies in Portuguese economic regime change, which culminated in the entry of the escudo into the ERM (Exchange Rate Mechanism) of the EMS

(European Monetary System) in 1992. It measures trends in nominal and real convergence and attributes the current divergence to the resilience of the fiscal constitution. In addition, it discusses the structural changes achieved during the period of convergence and those still needed for Portugal to avoid suffering the 'euro hold-up'. It illustrates the limits of external pressure and the constraints imposed by the historical fiscal model. Indeed, the Portuguese experience shows that the euro, by itself, cannot change the fiscal constitution. Different policy areas need specific reform efforts; otherwise they stall and affect each other in a negative way.

Spain in the EU: Fifteen Years May Not Be Enough
MANUEL BALMASEDA and MIGUEL SEBASTIÁN

The accession to the EEC in 1986 was a crucial step in the process of economic and political modernization and a key factor behind the internationalization and globalization of the Spanish economy. Integration has required a set of measures (increased competition, privatization of public enterprises, industrial restructuring, deregulation) that have translated into efficiency gains. In addition, a more stable macroeconomic framework has reinforced these efficiency gains. The process of real integration could have been even more successful, however. The slow pace of reform, in particular in the labour market, with high labour costs leading to persistent unemployment, and an inappropriate policy mix in the late 1980s, prevented Spain from reaping the full benefits of integration. Finally, the role of Structural Funds has also been crucial. These allowed for the construction of public infrastructure vital for private sector productivity and real convergence.

Redesigning the Spanish and Portuguese Welfare States:
The Impact of Accession into the European Union
ANA GUILLÉN, SANTIAGO ÁLVAREZ and PEDRO ADÃO E SILVA

Despite the fact that the normative issued by the European Union regarding the regulation of social protection policies is scant, becoming a member of such a supranational institution can be expected to have influenced the redesign of welfare states. This contribution assesses to what extent the enlargement of the EU toward the South has impacted the reform of social policies. In particular, it focuses on the cases of Spain and Portugal. The discussion includes both a quantitative and a qualitative analysis. From the quantitative point of view, it assesses the evolution of financing and expenditure trends. From the qualitative point of view, it analyses direct and indirect effects of EU membership on social policy, and considers the development of social policy in the domestic sphere in relation to the European Social Model. The concluding section discusses the influence of both external and internal interests and challenges in the redesign of the Spanish and Portuguese welfare states.

The Role of the State in the Labour Market:
Its Impact on Employment and Wages in Portugal
as Compared with Spain
JOSÉ DA SILVA LOPES

During the last two decades, unemployment rates in Portugal were significantly lower than the average of the European Union. The contrast in the evolution of unemployment between Portugal and Spain has been a source of perplexity for many analysts. This study presents some possible explanations for that contrast. It argues that in spite of labour regulations that are among the tightest in Europe, unemployment has been comparatively low in Portugal because there is a very large proportion of workers who are not adequately protected by those regulations, increasing the flexibility of the Portuguese labour market. Lower unemployment rates result also from the combination of faster GDP growth and lower growth of the labour force than in the average of EU countries. High unemployment rates in Spain are due, to a large extent, to slower growth of GDP than in Portugal combined with a much more rapid expansion in the labour force.

The 2004 Enlargement:
Iberian Lessons for Post-Communist Europe
SEBASTIÁN ROYO

The purpose of this study is to outline the main consequences for Portugal and Spain of EU integration. It will use the integration of Portugal and Spain into the European Union as an opportunity to draw some lessons that may be applicable to East European countries as they pursue their own processes of integration into the European Union. It examines challenges and opportunities that new member states from central and Eastern Europe will face when trying to integrate in the EU. Finally, the discussion analyses the impact the 2004 enlargement will have on the Iberian countries.

Portugal and Spain: A Fifteen-Year 'Quasi-Experiment' with European Integration in a Pair of 'Most Similar Systems'
PHILIPPE C. SCHMITTER

This concluding analysis outlines and challenges the main findings of the volume. It summarizes the main consequences of integration on Portugal and Spain, and argues that the logic of transformation was essentially political. The discussion also explores alternative explanations for political and economic outcomes. Finally, it warns against taking the integration experiences of the Iberian countries as a blueprint of what EU candidate countries should expect as a result of the ongoing enlargement process.

NOTES ON CONTRIBUTORS

Sebastián Royo is Assistant Professor in the Government Department at Suffolk University in Boston and affiliate and co-chair of the Iberian Study Group at the Minda de Gunzburg Center for European Studies, Harvard University. His publications include *From Social Democracy to Neoliberalism: The Consequences of Party Hegemony in Spain 1982–1996* and *A New Century of Corporatism? Corporatism in Southern Europe: Spain and Portugal in Comparative Perspective.*

Paul Christopher Manuel is Professor and Chair of the Department of Politics at Saint Anselm College, Research Director of the New Hampshire Institute of Politics, and affiliate and co-chair of the Iberian Study Group at the Minda de Gunzburg Center for European Studies, Harvard University. His publications include *Uncertain Outcome: The Politics of Portugal's Transition to Democracy, The Challenges of Portugal's Consolidation of Democracy, 1976–1991,* and *Checks and Balances* (with A.-M. Cammisa).

Robert M. Fishman is Associate Professor of Sociology and Kellogg Institute Fellow, University of Notre Dame (1992–). Between 1984–91 he held the positions of Instructor; Assistant Professor and Associate Professor of Government and of Social Studies at Harvard University. Visiting teaching positions include Juan March Institute, Madrid and Universitat Pompeu Fabra, Barcelona. He is the author of *Working Class Organization and the Return to Democracy in Spain.*

Kerstin Hamann is Associate Professor of Political Science at the University of Central Florida, Orlando. She has published essays on contemporary Spanish politics, especially the transition to democracy, political parties and interest groups (in particular, labour unions), and federalization. Her research also extends to other countries in western Europe and Central America.

Luís Salgado de Matos is Senior Fellow of Instituto de Ciências Sociais of Universidade de Lisboa and a member of Instituto de Estudos Políticos da Universidade Católica Portuguesa. His latest book is *Armed Services in a Time of Change,* a survey of the Portuguese public opinion. He writes a weekly column in the Lisbon daily newspaper *Público*, and he is a consultant of the President of the Republic of Portugal.

Marina Costa Lobo recently obtained her D.Phil. in Politics from St. Antony's College, Oxford University. She is Assistant Researcher at the Social Sciences Institute of the University of Lisbon. She has published on Portuguese political parties in *Party Politics* and the *Journal of Southern Europe and the Balkans*, as well as in the Portuguese *Análise Social*.

Juan Díez-Nicolás is Professor of Sociology, Universidad Complutense de Madrid and President of ASEP. He held political offices for ten years in Suarez's governments during the transition to democracy, and since 1986 conducts a monthly national survey in Spain through ASEP, in addition to participating in three major international research projects (WVS, ISSP and CSES). He has published 25 books and almost 200 articles in professional journals.

Charles Powell is Senior Analyst at the Real Instituto Elcano (Madrid). He was previously a Junior Research Fellow at St. Antony's College, Oxford and Lecturer in History at Corpus Christi College, Oxford. His publications include *El Piloto del Cambio* (1991), *Juan Carlos of Spain: Self-made Monarch* (1996), and *España en Democracia* (2001), which won the prestigious award '*Premio Asi Fue: La Historia Rescatada 2001*'.

Jorge Braga de Macedo is President of the OECD Development Centre, Paris and Professor at the Faculty of Economics, of Nova University, Lisbon (on leave). He was formerly Minister of Finance (1991–93). His publications include *Bem Comum dos Portugueses* (1999), *Sustaining Social Security* (1996), *Currency Convertibility: The Gold Standard and Beyond* (1996), and *Unity with Diversity in the European Economy: The Community's Southern Frontier* (1990).

Miguel Sebastián is Professor of Economics in the Economics Department at the Universidad Complutense, Madrid. He has served as Chief Economist of Banco Bilbao Vizcaya Argentaria and General Director of Intermoney. He has published books on Spain's macroeconomic analysis and articles both on theoretical and empirical analysis. He has also served as managing editor of the journal *Moneda y Crédito*, and as member of the editorial board of several economic journals, including *Expansión*.

Manuel Balmaseda is Chief Economist for Spain of Banco Bilbao Vizcaya Argentaria (BBVA). He has been professor of Macroeconomics at CEMFI (Centro de Estudios Monetarios y Financieros), Director of the department of Economic Analysis for Capital Markets and Treasury at BBV, editor of the *Revista Española de Economía*, Visiting Researcher at the Federal Reserve Bank of Minneapolis, and has collaborated with the IMF.

Ana M. Guillén is Associate Professor of Sociology at the University of Oviedo. Her publications include *La construcción política del sistema sanitario español: de la postguerra a la democracia* (2000). She has done consulting work for the European Commission and the ILO, and in 1998–99 she was a Jean Monnet Fellow and participant in the European University Institute's European Forum 'Recasting the European Welfare State'.

Santiago Álvarez is Associate Professor of Public Finance at the University of Oviedo. His research interests include taxation theory, public spending on social policy and fiscal federalism. He has authored two monographs and published various articles in specialized journals. He is currently working as Director of Research Studies on Public Budget and Expenditure at the National Institute of Fiscal Studies of the Ministry of Finance.

Pedro Adão e Silva is Researcher at the Social and Political Science department of the European University Institute (Florence) preparing a Ph.D. dissertation on the 'Welfare State in Southern Europe: The Portuguese Case'. He has a degree in Sociology from ISCTE, Lisbon and, from 1997 to 2000, was adviser to the Portuguese Secretary of State for Labour and Training. He has also published articles on the transformations of the welfare state in Portugal.

José da Silva Lopes is President of the Economic and Social Council of Portugal and former Minister of Finance and former Governor of the Bank of Portugal. Has been temporary professor in several Portuguese Universities and a consultant to the World Bank and IMF. His publications include *A Economia Portuguesa desde 1960* (1995), *Portugal and EC Membership Evaluated* (1993), and *Portugal and the Internal Market of the EEC* (1991).

Philippe Schmitter is Professor in the Department of Politics and Social Sciences at European University Institute. Since 1967 he has taught in the Politics Department of the University of Chicago, at the European University Institute (1982–86) and then at Stanford (1986–96). He has been Visiting Professor at the Universities of Paris-I, Geneva, Mannheim and Zürich, and Fellow of the Humboldt Foundation, Guggenheim Foundation and the Palo Alto Centre for Advanced Studies in the Behavioral Sciences. His current work is on the political characteristics of the emerging Euro-polity, on the consolidation of democracy in Southern and Eastern countries, and on the possibility of post-liberal democracy in western Europe and North America.

INDEX

Titles of Relations Interest

The European Union, Mercosul and a New World Order

Helio Jaguaribe, Institute of Political and Social Studies, Rio de Janeiro
and Alvaro de Vasconcelos, Institute of Strategic and international
Studies, Lisbon (Eds)
Foreword by Pierre Hassner

This volume, to which various prominent European and Latin
American scholars have contributed, provides critical insight into the
politics and economics of relations between the EU and Latin America,
particularly Mercosul, and on the significance of such relations for
multilateralism and the international order. The events of 11
September shed new light on the analyses provided, and give even
more credence to the point made in many chapters regarding the
serious obstacles to the creation of an international order firmly based
on universally accepted norms and rules in which regional groupings
would play a greater role. The book provides a timely reminder of just
how important less politically visible but consistent efforts at
multilaterally focused regional integration projects can be to
counteracting the force of unilateral action and zero-sum power
politics.

The book is the result of a joint project promoted by the Institute of
Political and Social Studies (IEPES) in Rio de Janeiro and the Institute
of Strategic and International Studies (IEEI) in Lisbon.

256 pages 2003
0 7146 5405 1 cloth
0 7146 8338 8 paper

FRANK CASS PUBLISHERS
Crown House, 47 Chase Side, Southgate, London N14 5BP
Tel: +44 (0)20 8920 2100 Fax: +44 (0)20 8447 8548 E-mail: info@frankcass.com
NORTH AMERICA
920 NE 58th Avenue Suite 300, Portland, OR 97213-3786 USA
Tel: 800 944 6190 Fax: 503 280 8832 E-mail: cass@isbs.com
Website: www.frankcass.com

Unemployment in Southern Europe Coping with the Consequences

Nancy G Bermeo, Princeton University (Ed)

In southern Europe, the public ranks unemployment as one of its greatest concerns while the politicians devote increasing attention to means of job creation. Policymakers have observed that unemployment rates are no longer coupled with economic growth; wealth creation is no longer synonymous with job creation. The essays in this book investigate the way in which unemployment affects political behaviour and key political institutions in southern Europe. New empirical evidence and original theoretical insights are offered about individual countries, highlighting differences and similarities. The collection offers serious insights and lessons on the profound human consequences of unemployment.

320 pages 2000
0 7146 4935 X cloth
0 7146 4495 1 paper

A special issue of the journal South European Society & Politics

FRANK CASS PUBLISHERS
Crown House, 47 Chase Side, Southgate, London N14 5BP
Tel: +44 (0)20 8920 2100 Fax: +44 (0)20 8447 8548 E-mail: info@frankcass.com
NORTH AMERICA
920 NE 58th Avenue Suite 300, Portland, OR 97213-3786 USA
Tel: 800 944 6190 Fax: 503 280 8832 E-mail: cass@isbs.com
Website: www.frankcass.com